Mercedes-Benz Sprinter
Owners Workshop Manual

Peter T Gill

Models covered

(4902 - 256)

Mercedes-Benz Sprinter:
van, chassis cab and bus derivatives in short-, medium- and long-wheelbase configurations

2.2 litre (2148cc) and 2.9 litre (2874cc) diesel

Does NOT cover petrol models, 2.3 litre or 2.7 litre diesel models, automatic transmissions, 4x4 models or specialist bodywork conversions

Does NOT cover new Sprinter range introduced May 2006

© Haynes Group Limited 2011

ABCDE
FGHIJ
K

A book in the **Haynes Owners Workshop Manual Series**

ISBN **978 0 85733 981 2**

British Library Cataloguing in Publication Data
A catalogue record for this book is available from the British Library.

Printed in India

Haynes Group Limited
Sparkford, Yeovil, Somerset BA22 7JJ, England

Haynes North America, Inc
2801 Townsgate Road, Suite 340, Thousand Oaks, CA 91361

Disclaimer
There are risks associated with automotive repairs. The ability to make repairs depends on the individual's skill, experience and proper tools. Individuals should act with due care and acknowledge and assume the risk of performing automotive repairs.

The purpose of this manual is to provide comprehensive, useful and accessible automotive repair information, to help you get the best value from your vehicle. However, this manual is not a substitute for a professional certified technician or mechanic.

This repair manual is produced by a third party and is not associated with an individual vehicle manufacturer. If there is any doubt or discrepancy between this manual and the owner's manual or the factory service manual, please refer to the factory service manual or seek assistance from a professional certified technician or mechanic.

Even though we have prepared this manual with extreme care and every attempt is made to ensure that the information in this manual is correct, neither the publisher nor the author can accept responsibility for loss, damage or injury caused by any errors in, or omissions from, the information given.

Contents

Contents

REPAIRS AND OVERHAUL

The Mercedes-Benz Benz Sprinter was launched in the UK in May 1995. The Sprinter attracted very favourable reviews, featuring as it does the traditional excellent Mercedes-Benz design and engineering combined with first-class build quality.

All engines are developments of well-proven engines, which have appeared in many Mercedes-Benz vehicles. The engines covered in this manual are of single or double overhead camshaft 4-valves-per-cylinder design, mounted longitudinally ('north-south') with the transmission mounted behind the engine.

Fully-independent suspension is fitted front and rear, with a transverse leaf spring inside the front subframe and dampers bolted under the front wings and a semi-floating rear axle with leaf springs and dampers.

Anti-lock brakes (ABS), power steering, central locking, electric mirrors, and airbags are available for all vehicles. As the range has developed, more equipment has been fitted as standard, with the most recent models featuring passenger and side airbags, electric front windows, traction control and cruise control.

Provided that regular servicing is carried out in accordance with the manufacturer's recommendations, the Sprinter should prove very reliable and durable. The engine compartment is well designed, and most of the items requiring frequent attention are easily accessible.

Your Mercedes-Benz Sprinter manual

The aim of this manual is to help you get the best value from your vehicle. It can do so in several ways. It can help you decide what work must be done (even should you choose to get it done by a garage). It will also provide information on routine maintenance and servicing, and give a logical course of action and diagnosis when random faults occur. However, it is hoped that you will use the manual by tackling the work yourself. On simpler jobs it may even be quicker than booking the vehicle into a garage and going there twice, to leave and collect it. Perhaps most importantly, a lot of money can be saved by avoiding the costs a garage must charge to cover its labour and overheads.

The manual has drawings and descriptions to show the function of the various components so that their layout can be understood. Tasks are described and photographed in a clear step-by-step sequence. The illustrations are numbered by the Section number and paragraph number to which they relate – if there is more than one illustration per paragraph, the sequence is denoted alphabetically.

References to the 'left' or 'right' of the vehicle are in the sense of a person in the driver's seat, facing forwards.

Acknowledgements

Thanks are due to Draper Tools Limited, who provided some of the workshop tools, and to all those people at Sparkford who helped in the production of this manual.

We take great pride in the accuracy of information given in this manual, but vehicle manufacturers make alterations and design changes during the production run of a particular vehicle of which they do not inform us. No liability can be accepted by the authors or publishers for loss, damage or injury caused by any errors in, or omissions from, the information given.

Project vehicle

The main vehicles used in the preparation of this manual, and which appear in many of the photographic sequences, was a 2001 Mercedes-Benz Sprinter 313 CDi fitted with the 2.2 litre turbocharged diesel engine. Also used was a 1998 Mercedes-Benz Sprinter 310D fitted with the 2.9 litre turbocharged diesel engine.

Working on your car can be dangerous. This page shows just some of the potential risks and hazards, with the aim of creating a safety-conscious attitude.

General hazards

Scalding

• Don't remove the radiator or expansion tank cap while the engine is hot.
• Engine oil, transmission fluid or power steering fluid may also be dangerously hot if the engine has recently been running.

Burning

• Beware of burns from the exhaust system and from any part of the engine. Brake discs and drums can also be extremely hot immediately after use.

Crushing

• When working under or near a raised vehicle, always supplement the jack with axle stands, or use drive-on ramps.
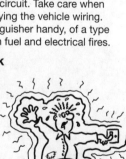
Never venture under a car which is only supported by a jack.
• Take care if loosening or tightening high-torque nuts when the vehicle is on stands. Initial loosening and final tightening should be done with the wheels on the ground.

Fire

• Fuel is highly flammable; fuel vapour is explosive.
• Don't let fuel spill onto a hot engine.
• Do not smoke or allow naked lights (including pilot lights) anywhere near a vehicle being worked on. Also beware of creating sparks (electrically or by use of tools).
• Fuel vapour is heavier than air, so don't work on the fuel system with the vehicle over an inspection pit.
• Another cause of fire is an electrical overload or short-circuit. Take care when repairing or modifying the vehicle wiring.
• Keep a fire extinguisher handy, of a type suitable for use on fuel and electrical fires.

Electric shock

• Ignition HT and Xenon headlight voltages can be dangerous, especially to people with heart problems or a pacemaker. Don't work on or near these systems with the engine running or the ignition switched on.

• Mains voltage is also dangerous. Make sure that any mains-operated equipment is correctly earthed. Mains power points should be protected by a residual current device (RCD) circuit breaker.

Fume or gas intoxication

• Exhaust fumes are poisonous; they can contain carbon monoxide, which is rapidly fatal if inhaled. Never run the engine in a confined space such as a garage with the doors shut.
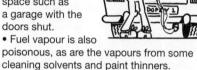

• Fuel vapour is also poisonous, as are the vapours from some cleaning solvents and paint thinners.

Poisonous or irritant substances

• Avoid skin contact with battery acid and with any fuel, fluid or lubricant, especially antifreeze, brake hydraulic fluid and Diesel fuel. Don't syphon them by mouth. If such a substance is swallowed or gets into the eyes, seek medical advice.
• Prolonged contact with used engine oil can cause skin cancer. Wear gloves or use a barrier cream if necessary. Change out of oil-soaked clothes and do not keep oily rags in your pocket.
• Air conditioning refrigerant forms a poisonous gas if exposed to a naked flame (including a cigarette). It can also cause skin burns on contact.

Asbestos

• Asbestos dust can cause cancer if inhaled or swallowed. Asbestos may be found in gaskets and in brake and clutch linings. When dealing with such components it is safest to assume that they contain asbestos.

Special hazards

Hydrofluoric acid

• This extremely corrosive acid is formed when certain types of synthetic rubber, found in some O-rings, oil seals, fuel hoses etc, are exposed to temperatures above 4000C. The rubber changes into a charred or sticky substance containing the acid. *Once formed, the acid remains dangerous for years. If it gets onto the skin, it may be necessary to amputate the limb concerned*.
• When dealing with a vehicle which has suffered a fire, or with components salvaged from such a vehicle, wear protective gloves and discard them after use.

The battery

• Batteries contain sulphuric acid, which attacks clothing, eyes and skin. Take care when topping-up or carrying the battery.
• The hydrogen gas given off by the battery is highly explosive. Never cause a spark or allow a naked light nearby. Be careful when connecting and disconnecting battery chargers or jump leads.

Air bags

• Air bags can cause injury if they go off accidentally. Take care when removing the steering wheel and trim panels. Special storage instructions may apply.

Diesel injection equipment

• Diesel injection pumps supply fuel at very high pressure. Take care when working on the fuel injectors and fuel pipes.

⚠️ *Warning: Never expose the hands, face or any other part of the body to injector spray; the fuel can penetrate the skin with potentially fatal results.*

Remember...

DO

• Do use eye protection when using power tools, and when working under the vehicle.

• Do wear gloves or use barrier cream to protect your hands when necessary.

• Do get someone to check periodically that all is well when working alone on the vehicle.

• Do keep loose clothing and long hair well out of the way of moving mechanical parts.

• Do remove rings, wristwatch etc, before working on the vehicle – especially the electrical system.

• Do ensure that any lifting or jacking equipment has a safe working load rating adequate for the job.

DON'T

• Don't attempt to lift a heavy component which may be beyond your capability – get assistance.

• Don't rush to finish a job, or take unverified short cuts.

• Don't use ill-fitting tools which may slip and cause injury.

• Don't leave tools or parts lying around where someone can trip over them. Mop up oil and fuel spills at once.

• Don't allow children or pets to play in or near a vehicle being worked on.

The following pages are intended to help in dealing with common roadside emergencies and breakdowns. You will find more detailed fault finding information at the back of the manual, and repair information in the main chapters.

If your vehicle won't start and the starter motor doesn't turn

☐ Open the bonnet and make sure that the battery terminals are clean and tight.
☐ Switch on the headlights and try to start the engine. If the headlights go very dim when you're trying to start, the battery is probably flat. Get out of trouble by jump starting (see next page) using a friend's vehicle.

If your vehicle won't start even though the starter motor turns as normal

☐ Is there fuel in the tank?
☐ Is there moisture on electrical components under the bonnet? Switch off the ignition, then wipe off any obvious dampness with a dry cloth. Spray a water-repellent aerosol product (WD-40 or equivalent) on ignition and fuel system electrical connectors like those shown in the photos.

1 Check the airflow meter wiring is connected securely.

2 Check the security and condition of the battery connections.

Check that electrical connections are secure (with the ignition switched off) and spray them with a water-dispersant spray like WD-40 if you suspect a problem due to damp.

3 Check all the multiplugs and wiring connectors for security (2.2 litre model shown).

4 Check that all the fuses are still in good condition and none have blown.

Jump starting will get you out of trouble, but you must correct whatever made the battery go flat in the first place. There are three possibilities:

1 *The battery has been drained by repeated attempts to start, or by leaving the lights on.*

2 *The charging system is not working properly (alternator drivebelt slack or broken, alternator wiring fault or alternator itself faulty).*

3 *The battery itself is at fault (electrolyte low, or battery worn out).*

When jump-starting a car using a booster battery, observe the following precautions:

✔ Before connecting the booster battery, make sure that the ignition is switched off.

Caution: Remove the key in case the central locking engages when the jump leads are connected

✔ Ensure that all electrical equipment (lights, heater, wipers, etc) is switched off.

Jump starting

✔ Take note of any special precautions printed on the battery case.

✔ Make sure that the booster battery is the same voltage as the discharged one in the vehicle.

✔ If the battery is being jump-started from the battery in another vehicle, the two vehicles MUST NOT TOUCH each other.

✔ Make sure that the transmission is in neutral (or PARK, in the case of automatic transmission).

1 Connect one end of the red jump lead to the positive (+) terminal of the flat battery

2 Connect the other end of the red lead to the positive (+) terminal of the booster battery.

3 Connect one end of the black jump lead to the negative (-) terminal of the booster battery

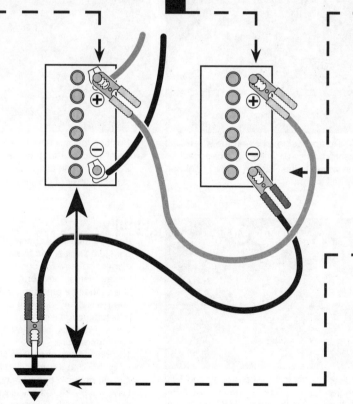

4 Connect the other end of the black jump lead to a bolt or bracket on the engine block, well away from the battery, on the vehicle to be started.

5 Make sure that the jump leads will not come into contact with the fan, drivebelts or other moving parts of the engine.

6 Start the engine using the booster battery and run it at idle speed. Switch on the lights, rear window demister (where fitted) and heater blower motor, then disconnect the jump leads in the reverse order of connection. Then turn off the lights, heater motor, etc.

Wheel changing

 Warning: Do not change a wheel in a situation where you risk being hit by other traffic. On busy roads, try to stop in a lay-by or a gateway. Be wary of passing traffic while changing the wheel – it is easy to become distracted by the job in hand.

Preparation

☐ When a puncture occurs, stop as soon as it is safe to do so.
☐ Park on firm level ground, if possible, and well out of the way of other traffic.
☐ Use hazard warning lights if necessary.

☐ If you have one, use a warning triangle to alert other drivers of your presence.
☐ Apply the handbrake and engage first or reverse gear.
☐ Chock the wheel diagonally opposite the

one being removed – a couple of large stones will do for this.
☐ If the ground is soft, use a flat piece of wood to spread the load under the jack.

Changing the wheel

1 The jack, jack handle and wheel brace are located in a stowage compartment in the front passenger footwell. Remove the trim cover, and then undo the retaining straps to remove them from the footwell.

2 The spare wheel is located under the rear of the vehicle, held in place by two securing hooks, attached to a metal framed carrier.

3 Locate the two bolts in the rear cross-member of the vehicle, and then remove the plastic caps and slacken the two bolts.

4 Turn the two bolts until the spare wheel carrier can be released and the spare wheel removed.

5 Where applicable, prise off the wheel bolt plastic covers or wheel trim for access to the wheel bolts. Slacken each wheel bolt by half a turn.

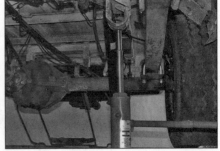

6 Position the jack under the vehicle jacking point nearest the punctured wheel. Turn the jack handle clockwise until the wheel is raised clear of the ground.

7 Undo the wheel bolts and remove the wheel. Fit the spare wheel and screw in the bolts. Lightly tighten the bolts with the wheel brace.

8 Lower the vehicle to the ground and fully tighten the wheel bolts. Tighten the bolts in the sequence shown. Refit the wheel bolt covers or wheel trims as applicable.

Finally . . .

☐ Remove the wheel chocks. Stow the punctured wheel and tools back in the carrier and stowage compartment, and secure them in position.
☐ Check the tyre pressure on the tyre just fitted. If it is low, or if you don't have a pressure gauge with you, drive slowly to the next garage and inflate the tyre to the correct pressure.
☐ The wheel bolts should be slackened and retightened to the specified torque at the earliest possible opportunity.
☐ Have the punctured wheel repaired as soon as possible, or another puncture will leave you stranded.

Identifying leaks

Puddles on the garage floor or drive, or obvious wetness under the bonnet or underneath the car, suggest a leak that needs investigating. It can sometimes be difficult to decide where the leak is coming from, especially if an engine undershield is fitted. Leaking oil or fluid can also be blown rearwards by the passage of air under the car, giving a false impression of where the problem lies.

 Warning: Most automotive oils and fluids are poisonous. Wash them off skin, and change out of contaminated clothing, without delay.

 The smell of a fluid leaking from the car may provide a clue to what's leaking. Some fluids are distinctively coloured. It may help to remove the engine undershield, clean the car carefully and to park it over some clean paper overnight as an aid to locating the source of the leak. Remember that some leaks may only occur while the engine is running.

Sump oil

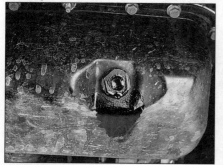

Engine oil may leak from the drain plug...

Oil from filter

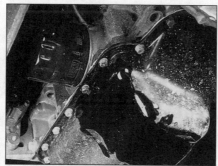

...or from the base of the oil filter.

Gearbox oil

Gearbox oil can leak from the seals at the inboard ends of the driveshafts.

Antifreeze

Leaking antifreeze often leaves a crystalline deposit like this.

Brake fluid

A leak occurring at a wheel is almost certainly brake fluid.

Power steering fluid

Power steering fluid may leak from the pipe connectors on the steering rack.

Towing

When all else fails, you may find yourself having to get a tow home – or of course you may be helping somebody else. Long-distance recovery should only be done by a garage or breakdown service. For shorter distances, DIY towing using another vehicle is easy enough, but observe the following points:

☐ Use a proper tow-rope – they are not expensive. The vehicle being towed must display an ON TOW sign in its rear window.

☐ Always turn the ignition key to the 'On' position when the vehicle is being towed, so that the steering lock is released, and the direction indicator and brake lights work.

☐ Before being towed, release the handbrake and make sure the transmission is in neutral.

☐ Note that greater-than-usual pedal pressure will be required to operate the brakes, since the vacuum servo unit is only operational with the engine running.

☐ The driver of the vehicle being towed must keep the tow-rope taut at all times to avoid snatching.

☐ Make sure that both drivers know the route before setting off.

☐ Only drive at moderate speeds and keep the distance towed to a minimum. Drive smoothly and allow plenty of time for slowing down at junctions.

Introduction

There are some very simple checks which need only take a few minutes to carry out, but which could save you a lot of inconvenience and expense.

These *Weekly checks* require no great skill or special tools, and the small amount of time they take to perform could prove to be very well spent, for example:

☐ Keeping an eye on tyre condition and pressures, will not only help to stop them wearing out prematurely, but could also save your life.

☐ Many breakdowns are caused by electrical problems. Battery-related faults are particularly common, and a quick check on a regular basis will often prevent the majority of these.

☐ If your vehicle develops a brake fluid leak, the first time you might know about it is when your brakes don't work properly. Checking the level regularly will give advance warning of this kind of problem.

☐ If the oil or coolant levels run low, the cost of repairing any engine damage will be far greater than fixing the leak, for example.

Underbonnet check points

◀ **2.2 litre engine**

A *Engine oil filler cap*

B *Engine oil level dipstick*

C *Coolant reservoir*

D *Brake and clutch fluid reservoir*

E *Washer fluid reservoir*

F *Battery*

G *Power steering fluid reservoir*

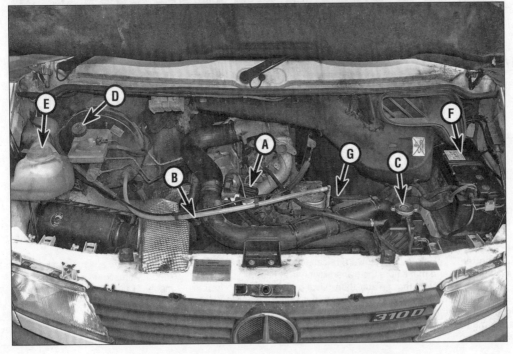

◀ **2.9 litre engine**

A *Engine oil filler cap*

B *Engine oil level dipstick*

C *Coolant reservoir*

D *Brake and clutch fluid reservoir*

E *Washer fluid reservoir*

F *Battery*

G *Power steering fluid reservoir*

Engine oil level

Before you start

✔ Make sure that the vehicle is on level ground.
✔ Check the oil level before the vehicle is driven, or at least 5 minutes after the engine has been switched off.

 HAYNES HINT *If the oil is checked immediately after driving the vehicle, some of the oil will remain in the upper engine components, resulting in an inaccurate reading on the dipstick.*

The correct oil

Modern engines place great demands on their oil. It is very important that the correct oil for your vehicle is used (see *Lubricants and fluids*).

Vehicle care

● If you have to add oil frequently, you should check whether you have any oil leaks. Place some clean paper under the vehicle overnight, and check for stains in the morning. If there are no leaks, then the engine may be burning oil.
● Always maintain the level between the upper and lower dipstick marks (see photo 3). If the level is too low, severe engine damage may occur. Oil seal failure may result if the engine is overfilled by adding too much oil.

1 The dipstick is brightly coloured (red) for easy identification (see *Underbonnet check points*). Withdraw the dipstick.

2 Using a clean rag or paper towel remove all the oil from the dipstick. Insert the clean dipstick into the tube as far as it will go, and then withdraw it again.

3 Note the level on the end of the dipstick, which should be between the upper (MAX) mark and the lower (MIN) mark. Approximately 1.5 litres of oil will raise the level from the lower mark to the upper mark.

4 Unscrew the oil filler cap and place some cloth rags around the filler cap aperture, then top-up the level. Add the oil slowly, checking the level on the dipstick frequently. Avoid overfilling (see *Vehicle care*).

Coolant level

 Warning: Do not attempt to remove the expansion tank pressure cap when the engine is hot, as there is a very great risk of scalding. Do not leave open containers of coolant about, as it is poisonous.

Vehicle care

● With a sealed-type cooling system, adding coolant should not be necessary on a regular basis. If frequent topping-up is required, it is likely there is a leak. Check the radiator, all hoses and joint faces for signs of staining or wetness, and rectify as necessary.

● It is important that antifreeze is used in the cooling system all year round, not just during the winter months. Don't top-up with water alone, as the antifreeze will become diluted.

1 The coolant level varies with the temperature of the engine. When the engine is cold, the coolant level should be up to the level marker (MAX) inside the filler neck of the expansion tank.

2 If topping-up is necessary, wait until the engine is cold. Slowly unscrew the cap to release any pressure present in the cooling system, and then remove the cap.

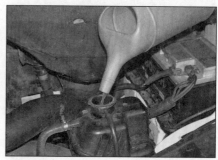

3 Add a mixture of water and the specified antifreeze (see *Lubricants and fluids*) to the expansion tank until the coolant level is up to the (MAX) level marker. Refit the cap and tighten it securely.

Brake and clutch fluid level

⚠️ **Warning:**
- *Brake fluid can harm your eyes and damage painted surfaces, so use extreme caution when handling and pouring it.*
- *Do not use fluid that has been standing open for some time, as* *it absorbs moisture from the air, which can cause a dangerous loss of braking effectiveness.*

Safety first!
● If the reservoir requires repeated topping-up this is an indication of a fluid leak somewhere in the system, which should be investigated immediately.

● If a leak is suspected, the vehicle should not be driven until the braking system has been checked. Never take any risks where brakes are concerned

1 The MIN and MAX marks are indicated on the reservoir. The fluid level must be kept between the marks at all times.

2 If topping-up is necessary, first wipe clean the area around the filler cap to prevent dirt entering the hydraulic system. Unscrew and remove the reservoir's cap.

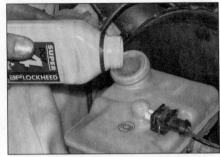

3 Carefully add fluid, taking care not to spill it onto the surrounding components (use a funnel). Use only the specified fluid (see *Lubricants and fluids*); mixing different types of fluid can cause damage to the system. On completion, securely refit the cap and wipe away any spilt fluid.

Power steering fluid level

✔ Park the vehicle on level ground.
✔ Set the steering wheel straight-ahead.
✔ The engine should be turned off.

Safety first!
● The need for frequent topping-up indicates a leak, which should be investigated immediately.

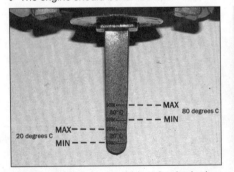

1 The fluid level should be checked when the engine is cold; the level should be up to the MAX mark on the dipstick. Note that there are two sets of markings, one at 20°C and one at 80°C.

2 If topping-up is necessary, first wipe clean the area around the filler cap to prevent dirt entering the hydraulic system. Unscrew and remove the reservoir's cap.

3 Carefully add fluid, taking care not to spill it onto the surrounding components (use a funnel). Use only the specified fluid (see *Lubricants and fluids*). On completion, securely refit the cap and wipe away any spilt fluid.

Tyre condition and pressure

It is very important that tyres are in good condition, and at the correct pressure - having a tyre failure at any speed is highly dangerous. Tyre wear is influenced by driving style - harsh braking and acceleration, or fast cornering, will all produce more rapid tyre wear. As a general rule, the front tyres wear out faster than the rears. Interchanging the tyres from front to rear ("rotating" the tyres) may result in more even wear. However, if this is completely effective, you may have the expense of replacing all four tyres at once! Remove any nails or stones embedded in the tread before they penetrate the tyre to cause deflation. If removal of a nail does reveal that the tyre has been punctured, refit the nail so that its point of penetration is marked. Then immediately change the wheel, and have the tyre repaired by a tyre dealer.

Regularly check the tyres for damage in the form of cuts or bulges, especially in the sidewalls. Periodically remove the wheels, and clean any dirt or mud from the inside and outside surfaces. Examine the wheel rims for signs of rusting, corrosion or other damage. Light alloy wheels are easily damaged by "kerbing" whilst parking; steel wheels may also become dented or buckled. A new wheel is very often the only way to overcome severe damage.

New tyres should be balanced when they are fitted, but it may become necessary to re-balance them as they wear, or if the balance weights fitted to the wheel rim should fall off. Unbalanced tyres will wear more quickly, as will the steering and suspension components. Wheel imbalance is normally signified by vibration, particularly at a certain speed (typically around 50 mph). If this vibration is felt only through the steering, then it is likely that just the front wheels need balancing. If, however, the vibration is felt through the whole car, the rear wheels could be out of balance. Wheel balancing should be carried out by a tyre dealer or garage.

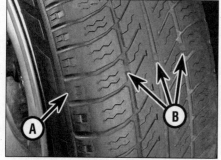

1 Tread Depth - visual check
The original tyres have tread wear safety bands (B), which will appear when the tread depth reaches approximately 1.6 mm. The band positions are indicated by a triangular mark on the tyre sidewall (A).

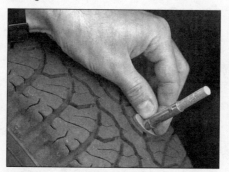

2 Tread Depth - manual check
Alternatively, tread wear can be monitored with a simple, inexpensive device known as a tread depth indicator gauge.

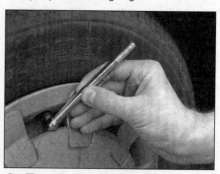

3 Tyre Pressure Check
Check the tyre pressures regularly with the tyres cold. Do not adjust the tyre pressures immediately after the vehicle has been used, or an inaccurate setting will result.

Tyre tread wear patterns

Shoulder Wear

Underinflation (wear on both sides)
Under-inflation will cause overheating of the tyre, because the tyre will flex too much, and the tread will not sit correctly on the road surface. This will cause a loss of grip and excessive wear, not to mention the danger of sudden tyre failure due to heat build-up.
Check and adjust pressures
Incorrect wheel camber (wear on one side)
Repair or renew suspension parts
Hard cornering
Reduce speed!

Centre Wear

Overinflation
Over-inflation will cause rapid wear of the centre part of the tyre tread, coupled with reduced grip, harsher ride, and the danger of shock damage occurring in the tyre casing.
Check and adjust pressures

If you sometimes have to inflate your car's tyres to the higher pressures specified for maximum load or sustained high speed, don't forget to reduce the pressures to normal afterwards.

Uneven Wear

Front tyres may wear unevenly as a result of wheel misalignment. Most tyre dealers and garages can check and adjust the wheel alignment (or "tracking") for a modest charge.
Incorrect camber or castor
Repair or renew suspension parts
Malfunctioning suspension
Repair or renew suspension parts
Unbalanced wheel
Balance tyres
Incorrect toe setting
Adjust front wheel alignment
Note: *The feathered edge of the tread which typifies toe wear is best checked by feel.*

Washer fluid level

• The windscreen washer reservoir also supplies the headlight washers.

• Screen wash additives not only keep the windscreen clean during bad weather, they also prevent the washer system freezing in cold weather – which is when you are likely to need it most. Don't top-up using plain water, as the screen wash will become diluted, and will freeze in cold weather.

Caution: On no account use engine coolant antifreeze in the screen washer system – this may damage the paintwork.

1 The screen wash fluid reservoir is located on the right-hand side (as seen from the driver's seat) of the engine compartment. Pull the filler cap to release it from the reservoir.

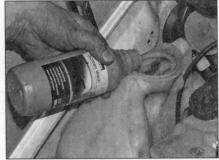

2 When topping-up the reservoir, a screen wash additive should be used in the quantities recommended on the bottle. On completion, securely refit the cap and wipe away any spilt fluid.

Wiper blades

• Only fit good-quality wiper blades.

• When removing an old wiper blade, note how it is fitted. Fitting new blades can be a tricky exercise, and noting how the old blade came off can save time.

• While the wiper blade is removed, take care not to knock the wiper arm from its locked position, or it could strike the glass.

• Offer the new blade into position the same way round as the old one. Ensure that it clicks home securely, otherwise it may come off in use, damaging the glass.

 If smearing is still a problem despite fitting new wiper blades, try cleaning the glass with neat screenwash additive or methylated spirit.

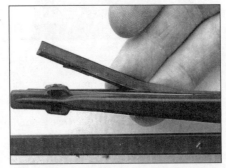

1 Check the condition of the wiper blades; if they are cracked or show any signs of deterioration, or if the glass swept area is smeared, renew them. Wiper blades should be renewed annually, regardless of their apparent condition.

2 To remove a windscreen wiper blade, pull the arm fully away from the glass until it locks. Position the blade at 90° to the arm and lift it from place.

Battery

Caution: Before carrying out any work on the vehicle battery, read the precautions given in 'Safety first!' at the start of this manual.

✔ Make sure that the battery tray is in good condition, and that the clamp is tight. Any 'white' corrosion on the terminals or surrounding area can be removed with a solution of water and baking soda; thoroughly rinse all cleaned areas with water. Any metal parts damaged by corrosion should be covered with a zinc-based primer, then painted.

✔ Periodically check the charge condition of the battery. On some batteries, the state of charge is shown by an indicator 'eye' in the top of the battery, which should be green – if the indicator is clear, or red, the battery may need charging or even renewal (see Chapter 5).

✔ If the battery is flat, and you need to jump start your vehicle, see *Roadside Repairs*.

HAYNES HiNT

Battery corrosion can be kept to a minimum by applying a layer of petroleum jelly to the clamps and terminals after they are reconnected.

1 The battery is located at the front, left-hand side of the engine compartment.

3 If corrosion (white, fluffy deposits) is evident, remove the cables from the battery terminals, clean them with a small wire brush, then refit them. Automotive stores sell a tool for cleaning the battery post . . .

2 Check the tightness of battery clamps to ensure good electrical connections. You should not be able to move them. Also check each cable for cracks and frayed conductors. The exterior of the battery should be inspected periodically for damage such as a cracked casing or cover.

4 . . . as well as the battery cable clamps

Bulbs and fuses

✔ Check all external lights and the horn. Refer to the appropriate Sections of Chapter 12 for details if any of the circuits are found to be inoperative.

✔ Visually check all accessible wiring connectors, harnesses and retaining clips for security, and for signs of chafing or damage.

HAYNES HiNT *If you need to check your brake lights and indicators unaided, back up to a wall or garage door and operate the lights. The reflected light should show if they are working properly.*

1 If a single stop-light, indicator or headlight has failed, it is likely that a bulb has blown and will need to be renewed. Refer to Chapter 12 for details. If both stop-lights have failed, it is possible that the switch has failed (see Chapter 9).

2 If more than one indicator light or headlight has failed, it is likely either that a fuse has been blown or that there is a fault in the circuit (see Chapter 12). To gain access to the fuse/relay box under the driver's seat, release the catches and the front will tilt down. The fuse locations are on the inside of the cover.

3 Additional fuses are located under the steering column. To gain access, release the catch at the top and pull the trim cover down. The fuse locations are on the inside of the cover.

Lubricants and fluids

Engine	Multigrade engine oil with a viscosity suited to the ambient temperature (see illustration) approved in accordance with MB sheets 229.1 or 229.3
Cooling system	MB 325.0 000 989 08 25 or 000 989 21 25 antifreeze
Manual transmission	Gear oil MB 317 or MB 235.10 transmission oil 001 989 2603
Final drive (differential)	Universal hypoid gear oil – SAE 85 W-90 or SAE 75 W-85
Power steering reservoir	MB 345.0 hydraulic fluid A 001 989 2403
Brake fluid reservoir	MB 331.0 hydraulic fluid 000 989 08 07 or DOT 4 plus

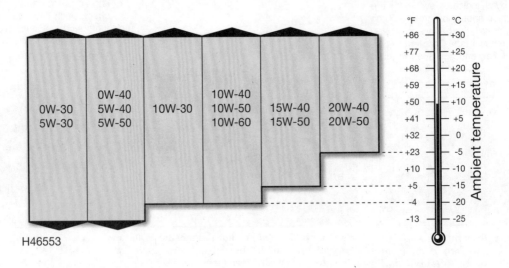

H46553

Tyre pressures (cold)

Note: *The recommended tyre pressures for each vehicle are given on a sticker attached to the fusebox lid on the drivers seat base (see illustration). The pressures given are for the original equipment tyres – the recommended pressures may vary if any other make or type of tyre is fitted; check with the tyre manufacturer or supplier for latest recommendations. Pressures are also given in the vehicle handbook.*

Chapter 1
Routine maintenance and servicing

Contents

Degrees of difficulty

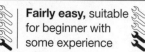 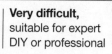

Easy, suitable for novice with little experience	Fairly easy, suitable for beginner with some experience	Fairly difficult, suitable for competent DIY mechanic	Difficult, suitable for experienced DIY mechanic	Very difficult, suitable for expert DIY or professional

Lubricants and fluids............................ Refer to the end of *Weekly checks*

Capacities

Engine oil (including filter):
    2.2 litre engines .... 8.5 litres
    2.9 litre engines .... 9.5 litres
    Difference between dipstick minimum and maximum marks....... 1.5 litres
Cooling system.................................... 9.5 litres
Fuel tank:
    Standard....................................... 75.0 litres
    Optional extra tank .... 100.0 litres
Screen washer system .... 6.0 litres
Rear axle .... 1.8 litres
Transmission...................................... 2.2 litres

Cooling system

Antifreeze mixture:
    50% antifreeze .... Protection down to -37°C
    55% antifreeze .... Protection down to -45°C
Note: *Refer to antifreeze manufacturer for latest recommendations*

Auxiliary belt

Length (new):
    2.2 litre engines:
        With air conditioning.................................. 2271 mm
        Without air conditioning .... 2196 mm
    2.9 litre engines:
        With air conditioning.................................. 2145 mm
        Without air conditioning .... 2080 mm

Braking system

Minimum brake pad lining thickness .... 2.0 mm
Minimum handbrake shoe lining thickness .... 1.0 mm

Torque wrench settings

	Nm	lbf ft
Auxiliary belt 'shock absorber' tensioner to cylinder head (2.9 litre model) .	23	17
Belt tensioner guide pulley bolts	35	26
Engine oil drain plug:		
2.2 litre engines	30	22
2.9 litre engines	25	18
Engine oil filter screw cap	25	18
Fuel filter cartridge retaining bolt (2.9 litre model)	16	12
Handbrake compensator mounting bracket	25	18
Rear axle drain plug	100	74
Rear axle filler/level plug	100	74
Roadwheel bolts..	190	140
Transmission filler/level plug................................	60	44

The maintenance intervals in this manual are provided with the assumption that you, not the dealer, will be carrying out the work. These are the minimum maintenance intervals recommended by us for vehicles driven daily. If you wish to keep your vehicle in peak condition at all times, you may wish to perform some of these procedures more often. We encourage frequent maintenance, because it enhances the efficiency, performance and resale value of your vehicle.

If the vehicle is driven in dusty areas, used to tow a trailer, or driven frequently at slow speeds (idling in traffic) or on short journeys, more frequent maintenance intervals are recommended.

When the vehicle is new, it should be serviced by a dealer service department (or other workshop recognised by the vehicle manufacturer as providing the same standard of service) in order to preserve the warranty. The vehicle manufacturer may reject warranty claims if you are unable to prove that servicing has been carried out as and when specified, using only original equipment parts or parts certified to be of equivalent quality.

Every 250 miles or weekly
☐ Refer to *Weekly checks*

Every 9000 miles or 6 months, whichever occurs first
☐ Renew the engine oil and filter (Section 3)
Note: *The manufacturers recommend that the engine oil and filter are changed every 18 000 miles or 12 months if the vehicle is being operated under normal conditions. However, oil and filter changes are good for the engine and we recommend that the oil and filter are renewed more frequently, especially if the vehicle is driven in dusty areas, used to tow a trailer, or driven frequently at slow speeds (idling in traffic) or on short journeys.*

Every 18 000 miles or 12 months, whichever occurs first
In addition to the item listed in the previous service, carry out the following:
☐ Check the battery and clean the terminals (Section 4)
☐ Check the auxiliary drivebelt (Section 5)
☐ Check the electrical system (Section 6)
☐ Check under the bonnet for fluid leaks and hose condition (Section 7)
☐ Renew the fuel filter (Section 8)
☐ Check the condition of all engine compartment wiring (Section 9)
☐ Check the condition of all air conditioning system components (Section 10)
☐ Check the seat belts (Section 11)
☐ Check the antifreeze concentration (Section 12)
☐ Check the steering, suspension and roadwheels (Section 13)
☐ Check the propeller shaft and centre bearing for wear (Section 14)
☐ Check the exhaust system (Section 15)
☐ Check the underbody, and all fuel/brake lines (Section 16)
☐ Check the brake pad lining thickness (Section 17)
☐ Check the operation and adjustment of the handbrake (Section 18)
☐ Check the doors and bonnet, and lubricate their hinges and locks (Section 19)
☐ Check the security of all roadwheel bolts (Section 20)
☐ Road test (Section 21)

Every 36 000 miles or 2 years, whichever occurs first
In addition to the items listed in the previous services, carry out the following:
☐ Renew the pollen filter element (Section 22)
Note: *If the vehicle is used in dusty conditions, the pollen filter should be renewed more frequently.*
☐ Renew the air filter element (Section 23)
☐ Check the transmission oil level (Section 24)
☐ Check the rear axle oil level (Section 25)
☐ Renew the brake fluid (Section 26)

Every 10 years
☐ Renew the coolant (Section 27)

Underbonnet view

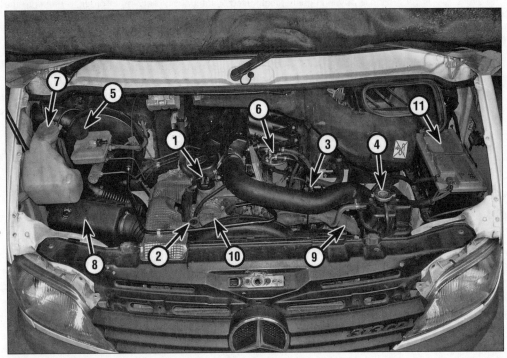

1 Engine oil filler cap
2 Engine oil dipstick
3 Oil filter
4 Coolant expansion tank
5 Brake fluid reservoir
6 Fuel filter
7 Windscreen/headlamp washer fluid reservoir
8 Air filter
9 Radiator top hose
10 Brake vacuum pump
11 Battery

Front underbody view

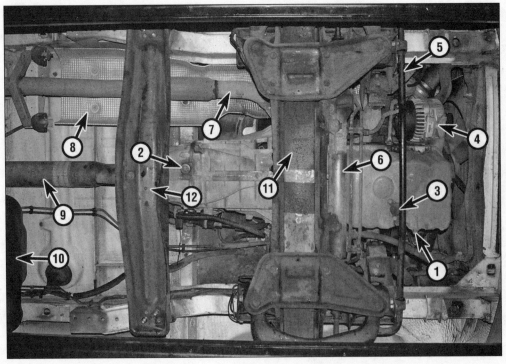

1 Engine oil drain plug
2 Transmission oil drain plug
3 Engine oil level sensor
4 Alternator
5 Anti-roll bar
6 Power-assisted steering rack
7 Exhaust system front pipe
8 Exhaust heat shield
9 Propeller shaft
10 Fuel tank
11 Transverse leaf spring
12 Rear mounting crossmember

Rear underbody view

1 Propeller shaft
2 Final drive unit
3 Anti-roll bar
4 Brake load sensing valve
5 Spare wheel
6 Exhaust tailpipe
7 Handbrake cable
   compensating plate
8 Suspension shock
   absorbers (dampers)
9 Handbrake cables and
   ABS wiring
10 Rear jacking points

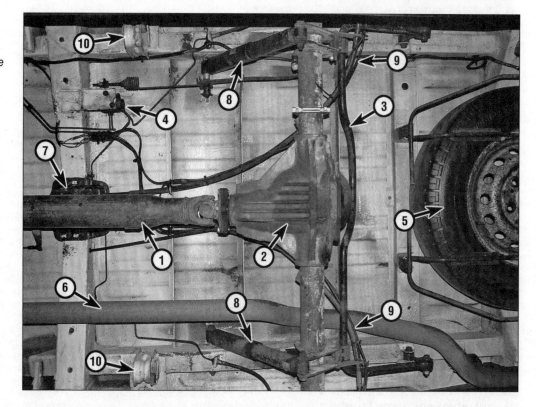

Maintenance procedures

1 General information

1 This Chapter is designed to help the home mechanic maintain his/her vehicle for safety, economy, long life and peak performance.
2 The Chapter contains a master maintenance schedule, followed by Sections dealing specifically with each task in the schedule. Visual checks, adjustments, component renewal and other helpful items are included. Refer to the accompanying illustrations of the engine compartment and the underside of the vehicle for the locations of the various components.
3 Servicing your vehicle in accordance with the mileage/time maintenance schedule and the following Sections will provide a planned maintenance programme, which should result in a long and reliable service life. This is a comprehensive plan, so maintaining some items but not others at the specified service intervals will not produce the same results.
4 As you service your vehicle, you will discover that many of the procedures can – and should – be grouped together, because of the particular procedure being performed,

or because of the proximity of two otherwise unrelated components to one another. For example, if the vehicle is raised for any reason, the exhaust can be inspected at the same time as the suspension and steering components.
5 The first step in this maintenance programme is to prepare yourself before the actual work begins. Read through all the Sections relevant to the work to be carried out, then make a list and gather all the parts and tools required. If a problem is encountered, seek advice from a parts specialist, or a dealer service department.

2 Regular maintenance

1 If, from the time the vehicle is new, the routine maintenance schedule is followed closely, and frequent checks are made of fluid levels and high-wear items, as suggested throughout this manual, the engine will be kept in relatively good running condition, and the need for additional work will be minimised.
2 It is possible that there will be times when the engine is running poorly due to the lack

of regular maintenance. This is even more likely if a used vehicle, which has not received regular and frequent maintenance checks, is purchased. In such cases, additional work may need to be carried out, outside of the regular maintenance intervals.
3 If engine wear is suspected, a compression test or leakdown test (refer to Chapter 2A or 2B) will provide valuable information regarding the overall performance of the main internal components. Such a test can be used as a basis to decide on the extent of the work to be carried out. If, for example, a compression or leakdown test indicates serious internal engine wear, conventional maintenance as described in this Chapter will not greatly improve the performance of the engine, and may prove a waste of time and money, unless extensive overhaul work is carried out first.
4 The following series of operations are those most often required to improve the performance of a generally poor-running engine:

Primary operations

a) Clean, inspect and test the battery (see 'Weekly checks' and Section 4).
b) Check all the engine related fluids (refer to 'Weekly checks').

c) Check the condition and tension of the auxiliary drivebelt (Section 5).
d) Check the condition of all hoses, and check for fluid leaks (Sections 7 and 16).
e) Renew the fuel filter (Section 8).
f) Check the condition of the air filter, and renew if necessary (Section 23).

5 If the above operations do not prove fully effective, carry out the following secondary operations:

Secondary operations

All items listed under *Primary operations*, plus the following:

a) Check the charging system (refer to Chapter 5).
b) Check the pre/post-heating system (refer to Chapter 5).
c) Check the fuel system and emissions control systems (refer to Chapters 4A and 4B).

Every 9000 miles or 6 months

3 Engine oil and filter renewal

1 Before starting this procedure, gather together all the necessary tools and materials. Also, make sure that you have plenty of clean rags and newspapers handy, to mop-up any spills. Ideally, the engine oil should be warm, as it will drain more easily and more built-up sludge will be removed with it. Take care not to touch the exhaust or any other hot parts of the engine when working under the vehicle. To avoid any possibility of scalding and to protect yourself from possible skin irritants and other

harmful contaminants in used engine oils, it is advisable to wear gloves when carrying out this work.
2 Access to the underside of the vehicle will be greatly improved if it can be raised on a lift, driven onto ramps, or jacked up and supported on axle stands (see *Jacking and vehicle support*). Whichever method is chosen, make sure that the vehicle remains level, or if it is at an angle, that the drain plug is at the lowest point **(see illustration)**. Where necessary, remove the undershield from under the engine compartment.
3 Open the bonnet and remove the oil filler cap, and withdraw the dipstick from the guide tube **(see illustrations)**.
4 Working under the vehicle, unscrew the

engine oil drain plug about half a turn. Position the draining container under the drain plug, then remove the plug completely – recover the sealing washer **(see illustrations)**.
5 Allow some time for the oil to drain, noting that it may be necessary to reposition the container as the oil flow slows to a trickle.
6 After all the oil has drained, wipe off the drain plug with a clean rag, and fit a new sealing washer. Clean the area around the drain plug opening, and refit the plug. Tighten the plug to the specified torque.
7 Move the container into position under the oil filter, which is located on the left-hand side of the cylinder block. Place a wad of rag around the filter housing to absorb any spilt oil,

3.2 The sump drain plug is located on the left-hand side of the sump

3.3a Remove the oil filler cap . . .

3.3b . . . and withdraw the dipstick

HAYNES HiNT

As the drain plug releases from the threads, move it away sharply so the stream of oil from the sump runs into the container, not up your sleeve.

3.4a Remove the sump drain plug . . .

3.4b . . . and drain it into a suitable container

3.8a Oil filter location – 2.2 litre engine

3.8b Oil filter location – 2.9 litre engine

8 Unscrew the oil filter cap **(see illustrations)**. **Note:** *By removing the cap, the oil will drain from the filter housing into the sump.* Remove and discard the paper filter element. Renew the O-rings on refitting.

9 Remove the O-ring seal(s) and obtain new ones **(see illustrations)**.' Clean the filter housing and cover and fit the new O-ring seal(s) onto the cover/housing and lubricate it with a little engine oil.

10 Fit the new oil filter element to the housing and tighten the cap to the specified torque **(see illustrations)**.

11 Remove the old oil and all tools from under the vehicle, then lower the vehicle to the ground.

12 If not already done, remove the dipstick, and then unscrew the oil filler cap from the camshaft cover. Fill the engine, using the correct grade and type of oil (see *Lubricants and fluids*). An oil can spout or funnel may help to reduce spillage. Pour in half the specified quantity of oil first, and then wait a few minutes for the oil to fall to the sump. Continue adding oil, a small quantity at a time, until the level is up to the lower mark on the dipstick. Refit the filler cap.

13 Start the engine and run it for a few minutes, then check for leaks. Note that there may be a delay of a few seconds before the oil pressure warning light goes out when the engine is first started, as the oil circulates

through the engine oil galleries and the new oil filter before the pressure builds-up.

14 Switch off the engine, and wait a few minutes for the oil to settle in the sump once more. With the new oil circulated and the filter completely full, recheck the level on the dipstick, and add more oil as necessary.

15 Dispose of the used engine oil and filter safely, with reference to *General repair procedures* in the Reference Chapter of this manual. Do not discard the old filter with domestic household waste. The facility for waste oil disposal provided by many local council refuge tips and/or recycling centres generally has a filter receptacle alongside.

3.8c Remove the screw-on cap complete with filter element

3.9a Fit new seals . . .

3.9b . . . to oil filter screw-on cap . . .

3.9c . . . and lubricate with clean oil

3.10a Fit new oil filter element to cap . . .

3.10b . . . and refit to filter housing

Every 18 000 miles or 12 months

4 Battery maintenance and charging

> ⚠️ *Warning: Certain precautions must be followed when checking and servicing the battery. Hydrogen gas, which is highly flammable, is always present in the battery cells, so keep lighted tobacco and all other open flames and sparks away from the battery. The electrolyte inside the battery is actually dilute sulphuric acid, which will cause injury if splashed on your skin or in your eyes. It will also ruin clothes and painted surfaces.*

General

1 A routine preventive maintenance programme for the battery in your vehicle is the only way to ensure quick and reliable starts. For general maintenance, refer to *Weekly checks* at the start of this manual. Also at the front of the manual is information on jump starting. For details of removing and installing the battery, refer to Chapter 5.

Battery electrolyte level

2 On models not equipped with a sealed or 'maintenance-free' battery, check the electrolyte level of all six battery cells.
3 The level must be approximately 10 mm above the plates; this may be shown by maximum and minimum level lines marked on the battery's casing.
4 If the level is low, use a coin or screwdriver to release the filler/vent cap, and add distilled water.
5 Install and securely retighten the cap, then wipe up any spillage.
Caution: Overfilling the cells may cause electrolyte to spill over during periods of heavy charging, causing corrosion or damage.

Charging

> ⚠️ *Warning: When batteries are being charged, hydrogen gas, which is very explosive and flammable, is produced. Do not smoke, or allow open flames, near a charging or a recently charged*

battery. Wear eye protection when near the battery during charging. Also, make sure the charger is unplugged before connecting or disconnecting the battery from the charger.
6 Slow-rate charging is the best way to restore a battery that's discharged to the point where it will not start the engine. It's also a good way to maintain the battery charge in a vehicle that's only driven a few miles between starts. Maintaining the battery charge is particularly important in winter, when the battery must work harder to start the engine, and electrical accessories that drain the battery are in greater use.
7 Check the battery case for any instructions regarding charging the battery. Some maintenance-free batteries may require a particularly low charge rate or other special conditions, if they are not to be damaged.
8 It's best to use a one- or two-amp battery charger (sometimes called a 'trickle' charger). They are the safest, and put the least strain on the battery. They are also the least expensive. For a faster charge, you can use a higher amperage charger, but don't use one rated more than 1/10th the amp/hour rating of the battery (ie, no more than 5 amps, typically). Rapid boost charges that claim to restore the power of the battery in one to two hours are hardest on the battery, and can damage batteries not in good condition. This type of charging should only be used in emergency situations.
9 The average time necessary to charge a battery should be listed in the instructions that come with the charger. As a general rule, a trickle charger will charge a battery in 12 to 16 hours.

5 Auxiliary drivebelt check and renewal

General

1 Due to their function and construction, the belts are prone to failure after a period of time, and should be inspected periodically to prevent problems.
2 The number and type of belt used on a particular vehicle depends on the accessories

fitted. Drivebelts are used to drive the coolant pump, alternator, power steering pump and air conditioning compressor.
3 The good condition and proper tension of the auxiliary drivebelts are critical to the operation of the engine. They must, therefore, be regularly inspected.

Check

4 With the engine switched off, open and support the bonnet.
5 To improve access for belt inspection, if desired, remove the viscous cooling fan and cowl as described in Chapter 3.
6 With the engine stopped, using your fingers (and an electric torch if necessary), move along the belts, checking for cracks and separation of the belt plies. Also check for fraying and glazing, which gives the belt a shiny appearance.
7 Both sides of the belts should be inspected, which means the belt will have to be twisted to check the underside. If necessary turn the engine using a spanner or socket on the crankshaft pulley bolt so that the whole of the belt can be inspected.
8 Use your fingers to feel the drivebelt where you can't see it. If you are in any doubt as to the condition of the drivebelt, renew it as described later in this Section.

Drivebelt tension

9 The auxiliary drivebelts are tensioned by an automatic tensioner; regular checks are not required, and manual 'adjustment' is not possible.
10 If you suspect that a drivebelt is slipping and/or running slack, or that the tensioner is otherwise faulty, it must be renewed.

Drivebelt renewal

11 Where applicable, remove the engine covers from the top of the engine and the cooling fan/cowling to improve access, with reference to Chapter 3.

2.2 litre engines

12 Engage a socket or Torx T60 bit/socket with the tensioner body below the pulley, and then lever the tensioner anti-clockwise to relieve the tension in the belt **(see illustrations)**.

5.12a Use a Torx socket . . .

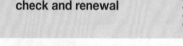

5.12b . . . and turn anti-clockwise to remove the belt

5.13 Insert metal pin to lock tensioner in position

5.14a Auxilliary drivebelt configuration without air conditioning (2.2 litre)

5.14a Auxilliary drivebelt configuration with air conditioning (2.2 litre)

13 Hold the tensioner in position with the spanner/socket, and slide the belt from the pulleys. If necessary, the tensioner can be retained in its released position by inserting a suitable bolt or metal dowel through the holes provided **(see illustration)**.

14 Fit the new belt around the pulleys, starting with the crankshaft pulley. Check that the belt is correctly seated on all the pulleys **(see illustrations)**. Where applicable, remove the metal dowel/bolt from the tensioner.

15 Release the spanner/socket, and allow the tensioner to move into position against the belt.

16 Where removed, refit the cooling fan and cowl as described in Chapter 3.

2.9 litre engines

17 Unscrew the nut from the end of the tensioner lever bolt **(see illustration)**.

18 Insert a suitable lever (approximately 12.0 mm diameter and 300 mm long) into the hole in the tensioner lever, and press the lever anti-clockwise until the lever bolt can be slid back towards the inlet manifold.

19 Release the tensioner spring by pivoting the lever clockwise.

20 Push the idler pulley back, and withdraw the belt from the pulleys.

21 Fit the new belt as follows.

22 Raise the idler pulley slightly, and hold in position during the following procedure.

23 Form a loop in the belt, with the drive ribs on the outside, then slide the belt between the coolant pump and crankshaft pulleys **(see illustration)**.

24 Slide the belt over the tensioner pulley and the crankshaft pulley, then open out the remainder of the belt, and fit it around the remaining pulleys in the order shown **(see illustration)**.

25 Release the idler pulley.

26 Press the tensioner lever as necessary to enable the lever bolt to be pushed into position.

27 Push the bolt back through the lever,

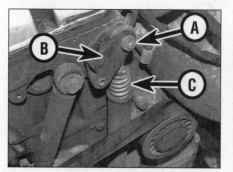

5.17 Auxilliary drivebelt tensioner components

A Tensioner lever nut	B Tensioner lever
	C Tensioner spring

5.23 Tensioner pulley (A) and idler pulley (B)

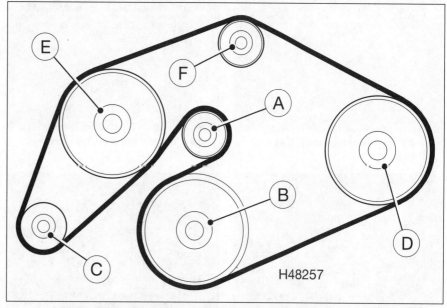

5.24 Auxilliary drivebelt configuration without air conditioning (2.9 litre)

A Tensioner pulley	D Power steering pump pulley
B Crankshaft pulley	E Coolant pump pulley
C Alternator	F Idler (guide) pulley

H48257

A leak in the cooling system will usually show up as white- or antifreeze-coloured deposits on the area adjoining the leak.

checking that the tensioner spring locates correctly.

28 Refit the nut to the tensioner lever bolt, and tighten to the specified torque whilst counterholding the bolt.

29 Where removed, refit the cooling fan and cowl as described in Chapter 3.

6 Electrical system check

1 Check the operation of all external lights and indicators (front and rear).

2 Check for satisfactory operation of the instrument panel, its illumination and warning lights, the switches and their function lights.

8.1 Fuel filter location (2.2 litre)

8.3 Disconnect the wiring connector from the sensor

3 Check the horn(s) for satisfactory operation.

4 Check all other electrical equipment for satisfactory operation.

7 Underbonnet check for fluid leaks and hose condition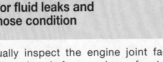

1 Visually inspect the engine joint faces, gaskets and seals for any signs of water or oil leaks. Pay particular attention to the areas around the camshaft cover, cylinder head, oil filter and sump joint faces. Bear in mind that, over a period of time, some very slight seepage from these areas is to be expected – what you are really looking for is any indication of a serious leak. Should a leak be found, renew the offending gasket or oil seal by referring to the appropriate Chapters in this manual.

2 Also check the security and condition of all engine related pipes and hoses, and all braking system pipes and hoses and fuel lines. Ensure that all cable-ties or securing clips are in place, and in good condition. Clips that are broken or missing can lead to chafing of the hoses, pipes or wiring, which could cause more serious problems in the future.

3 Carefully check the radiator hoses and heater hoses along their entire length. Renew any hose, which is cracked, swollen or deteriorated. Cracks will show up better if the hose is squeezed. Pay close attention to the hose clips that secure the hoses to the cooling system components. Hose clips can

8.2 Unscrew the drain tap – arrowed

8.4a Release the clip to disconnect the hose . . .

pinch and puncture hoses, resulting in cooling system leaks. If the crimped type hose clips are used, it may be a good idea to update them with standard worm-drive clips.

4 Inspect all the cooling system components (hoses, joint faces, etc) for leaks (see Haynes Hint).

5 Where any problems are found on system components, renew the component or gasket with reference to Chapter 3.

8 Fuel filter renewal

Caution: Before starting any work on the fuel filter, wipe clean the filter assembly and the surrounding area as it is essential that no dirt or other foreign matter is allowed into the system. Place rags or similar material under the filter assembly to catch any spillages. Do not allow diesel fuel to contaminate components such as the alternator and starter motor, the coolant hoses and engine mountings, and any wiring.

Note: *Before carrying out the following procedure, read carefully the precautions given in the Section 1 of Chapter 4A.*

2.2 litre models

1 The fuel filter is located to the left-hand side front of the cylinder head (see illustration). To minimise fuel spillage, pad the surrounding area with absorbent rags.

2 Where applicable, unscrew the drain tap at the bottom to remove it from the fuel filter (see illustration). Place a container below the filter to catch the fuel draining from the filter.

3 Where applicable, disconnect the wiring plug from the sensor at the bottom of the fuel filter (see illustration).

4 Release the securing clips and disconnect the fuel hoses from the top of the fuel filter. Note the fitted positions for refitting, and the different types of fittings. Plug the ends of the fuel hoses to prevent dirt ingress (see illustrations).

5 Undo the two retaining screws and twist the fuel connection to release it from the top of the fuel filter (see illustrations).

8.4b . . . then release the securing clip . . .

8.4c . . . to disconnect the centre pipe

8.5a Undo the two retaining screws . . .

8.5b . . . and twist, to release fuel pipe connector

8.6a Slacken the retaining bolt . . .

8.6b . . . and withdraw the filter from the mounting bracket

8.8a Fit sensor . . .

6 Slacken the retaining bolt from down the side of the filter, and then withdraw the filter from its mounting bracket **(see illustrations)**. On completion, dispose of the old filter safely.

7 Remove the filter canister from the engine bay, keeping the openings facing upwards to minimise fuel spillage.

8 Take the new fuel filter canister and fit it into the mounting bracket and tighten the retaining bolt. If required, remove the sensor and fuel drain tap from the old filter and fit them to the new filter **(see illustrations)**.

9 Refit the fuel hoses to the top of the fuel filter in their correct positions (as noted on removal), making sure they are secure. Note the direction arrows on the top of the fuel filter **(see illustration)**.

10 Start and run the engine at idle and check around the fuel filter for fuel leaks. **Note:** *The fuel pump is self-priming, but it may take a few seconds of cranking before the engine starts.*

11 If required, slacken the bleed screw on the top of the fuel filter, to allow for the air to be expelled. Tighten the bleed screw, when there is no more air **(see illustration)**. Place rag over the bleed screw to soak up any fuel dispersed.

12 Raise the engine speed to about 2000 rpm several times, and then allow the engine to idle again. This should bleed the air bubbles from the filter canister, but if the engine idle is at all rough or hesitant, repeat the action until the fuel system clears itself.

2.9 litre models

13 The fuel filter is located to the left-hand side front of the cylinder head **(see illustration)**.

14 To minimise fuel spillage, position a small container underneath the filter canister and pad the surrounding area with absorbent rags.

15 Support the fuel filter with one hand, then

8.8b . . . and drain tap to new filter

8.11 Slackening the bleed screw

slacken and remove the banjo bolt from the top of the fuel filter housing. Recover both O-ring seals and discard them – new items must be used on refitting **(see illustration)**.

16 Remove the filter canister from the engine

8.9 Note the direction arrows on top of the fuel filter

8.13 Fuel filter location (2.9 litre)

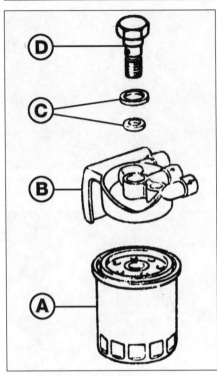

8.15 Fuel filter assembly (2.9 litre)

A Fuel filter canister   C Sealing washers
B Filter housing   D Banjo bolt

bay, keeping the mating face upwards to minimise fuel spillage. On completion, dispose of the old filter safely.

17 With the filter removed, check that the restriction orifice in the fuel return line, on the mating surface of the filter housing is clean and free from blockage.

18 Take the new filter canister and moisten the rubber seal with a little clean fuel.

19 Offer the filter up to the housing, then insert the banjo bolt (using new O-ring seals) and tighten it securely.

20 Start and run the engine at idle and check around the fuel filter for fuel leaks. **Note:** *The fuel pump is self-priming, but it may take a few seconds of cranking before the engine starts.*

21 Raise the engine speed to about 2000 rpm several times, and then allow the engine to idle again. This should bleed the air bubbles from the filter canister, but if the engine idle is at all rough or hesitant, repeat the action until the fuel system clears itself.

9 Engine compartment wiring check

1 With the vehicle parked on level ground, apply the handbrake firmly and open the bonnet. Using an inspection light or a small electric torch, check all visible wiring within and beneath the engine compartment.

2 What you are looking for is wiring that is obviously damaged by chafing against sharp edges, or against moving suspension/ transmission components and/or the auxiliary drivebelt, by being trapped or crushed between carelessly refitted components, or melted by being forced into contact with the hot engine castings, coolant pipes, etc. In almost all cases, damage of this sort is caused in the first instance by incorrect routing on reassembly after previous work has been carried out.

3 Depending on the extent of the problem, damaged wiring may be repaired by rejoining the break or splicing-in a new length of wire, using solder to ensure a good connection, and remaking the insulation with adhesive insulating tape or heat-shrink tubing, as appropriate. If the damage is extensive, given the implications for the vehicle's future reliability, the best long-term answer may well be to renew that entire section of the loom, however expensive this may appear.

4 When the actual damage has been repaired, ensure that the wiring loom is rerouted correctly, so that it is clear of other components, and not stretched or kinked, and is secured out of harm's way using the plastic clips, guides and ties provided.

5 Check all electrical connectors, ensuring that they are clean, securely fastened, and that each is locked by its plastic tabs or wire clip, as appropriate. If any connector shows external signs of corrosion (accumulations of white or green deposits, or streaks of 'rust'), or if any is thought to be dirty, it must be unplugged and cleaned using electrical contact cleaner. If the connector pins are severely corroded, the connector must be renewed; note that this may mean the renewal of that entire section of the loom – see your local Mercedes-Benz dealer for details.

6 If the cleaner completely removes the corrosion to leave the connector in a satisfactory condition, it would be wise to pack the connector with a suitable material, which will exclude dirt and moisture, preventing the corrosion from occurring again. A Mercedes-Benz dealer may be able to recommend a suitable product.

7 Use the same techniques to ensure that all earth points in the engine compartment provide good electrical contact through clean, metal-to-metal joints, and that all are securely fastened.

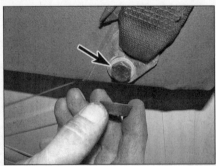

11.2 Unclip the plastic cover and check the securing bolt

10 Air conditioning system check

1 The following maintenance checks will ensure that the air conditioner operates at peak efficiency:
   a) *Check the auxiliary drivebelt (see Section 5).*
   b) *Check the system hoses for damage or leaks.*
   c) *Inspect the condenser fins for leaves, insects and other debris. Use a clean paint brush to clean the condenser.*
   d) *Check that the drain tube from the front of the evaporator is clear – note that it is normal to have clear fluid (water) dripping from this while the system is in operation, to the extent that quite a large puddle can be left under the vehicle when it is parked.*

2 It's a good idea to operate the system for about 30 minutes at least once a month, particularly during the winter. Long term non-use can cause hardening of the seals, and subsequent failure.

3 Because of the complexity of the air conditioning system and the special equipment necessary to service it, in-depth fault diagnosis and repairs are not included in this manual.

4 The most common cause of poor cooling is simply a low system refrigerant charge. If a noticeable drop in cool air output occurs, the following quick check will help you determine if the refrigerant level is low.

5 Warm the engine up to normal operating temperature.

6 Place the air conditioning temperature selector at the coldest setting, and put the blower at the highest setting. Open the doors – to make sure the air conditioning system doesn't cycle off as soon as it cools the passenger compartment.

7 With the compressor engaged – the clutch will make an audible click, and the centre of the clutch will rotate – feel the inlet and outlet pipes at the compressor. One side should be cold, and one hot. If there's no perceptible difference between the two pipes, there's something wrong with the compressor or the system. It might be a low charge – it might be something else. Take the vehicle to a dealer service department or an automotive air conditioning specialist.

11 Seat belt check

1 Check the seat belts for satisfactory operation and condition. Inspect the webbing for fraying and cuts. Check that they retract smoothly and without binding into their reels.

2 Check that the seat belt mounting bolts are tight **(see illustration)**, and if necessary tighten them to the specified torque wrench setting (Chapter 11).

12 Antifreeze concentration check

1 The cooling system should be filled with the recommended antifreeze and corrosion protection fluid. Over a period of time, the concentration of fluid may be reduced due to topping-up (this can be avoided by topping-up with the correct antifreeze mixture) or fluid loss. If loss of coolant has been evident, it is important to make the necessary repair before adding fresh fluid. The exact mixture of antifreeze-to-water, which you should use, depends on the relative weather conditions. The mixture should contain at least 40% antifreeze, but not more than 70%. Consult the mixture ratio chart on the antifreeze container before adding coolant. Use antifreeze that meets the vehicle manufacturer's specifications.

2 With the engine cold, carefully remove the cap from the expansion tank. If the engine is not completely cold, place a cloth rag over the cap before removing it, and remove it slowly to allow any pressure to escape.

3 Antifreeze checkers are available from car accessory shops. Draw some coolant from the expansion tank and observe how many plastic balls are floating in the checker. Usually, 2 or 3 balls must be floating for the correct concentration of antifreeze, but follow the manufacturer's instructions.

4 If the concentration is incorrect, it will be necessary to either withdraw some coolant and add antifreeze, or alternatively drain the old coolant and add fresh coolant of the correct concentration.

13 Steering, suspension and roadwheel check

Front suspension and steering

1 Firmly apply the handbrake, and then jack up the front of the vehicle and support it securely on axle stands (see *Jacking and vehicle support*).

2 Visually inspect the balljoint dust covers and the steering rack-and-pinion gaiters for splits, chafing or deterioration. Any wear of these components will cause loss of lubricant, together with dirt and water entry, resulting in rapid deterioration of the balljoints or steering gear.

3 Check the power steering fluid hoses for chafing or deterioration, and the pipe and hose unions for fluid leaks. Also, check for signs of fluid leakage under pressure from the steering gear rubber gaiters, which would indicate failed fluid seals within the steering gear.

4 Grasp the roadwheel at the 12 o'clock and 6 o'clock positions, and try to rock it **(see illustration)**. Very slight free play may be felt,

13.4 Check for wear in the hub bearings by grasping the wheel and trying to rock it

but if the movement is appreciable, further investigation is necessary to determine the source. Continue rocking the wheel while an assistant depresses the footbrake. If the movement is now eliminated or significantly reduced, it is likely that the hub bearings are at fault. If the free play is still evident with the footbrake depressed, then there is wear in the suspension joints or mountings.

5 Now grasp the wheel at the 9 o'clock and 3 o'clock positions, and try to rock it as before. Any movement felt now may again be caused by wear in the hub bearings or the steering track rod balljoints. If the outer track rod balljoint is worn, the visual movement will be obvious. If the inner joint is suspect, it can be felt by placing a hand over the rack-and-pinion rubber gaiter and gripping the track rod. If the wheel is now rocked, movement will be felt at the inner joint if wear has taken place.

6 Using a large screwdriver or flat bar, check for wear in the suspension mounting bushes by levering between the relevant suspension component and its attachment point. Some movement is to be expected, as the mountings are made of rubber, but excessive wear should be obvious. Also check the condition of any visible rubber bushes, looking for splits, cracks or contamination of the rubber.

7 With the car standing on its wheels, have an assistant turn the steering wheel back-and-forth, about an eighth of a turn each way. There should be very little, if any, lost movement between the steering wheel and roadwheels. If this is not the case, closely observe the joints and mountings previously described. In addition, check the steering column universal

13.9b . . . and the damper bushes

13.9a Check for wear in the spring bushes . . .

joints for wear, and also check the rack-and-pinion steering gear itself.

Rear suspension

8 Chock the front wheels, then jack up the rear of the vehicle and support securely on axle stands (see *Jacking and vehicle support*).

9 Working as described previously for the front suspension, check the rear hub bearings, the leaf spring mounting bushes and the shock absorber mountings for wear. Also check that the rear spring U-bolt nuts are tightened to the specified torque as given in Chapter 10 **(see illustrations)**.

Shock absorbers

10 Check for any signs of fluid leakage around the shock absorber body, or from the rubber gaiter around the piston rod. Should any fluid be noticed, the shock absorber is defective internally, and should be renewed.

Note: *Shock absorbers should always be renewed in pairs on the same axle.*

11 The efficiency of the shock absorber may be checked by bouncing the vehicle at each corner. Generally speaking, the body will return to its normal position and stop after being depressed. If it rises and returns on a rebound, the shock absorber is probably suspect. Also examine the shock absorber upper and lower mountings for any signs of wear.

Roadwheels

12 Periodically remove the roadwheels, and clean any dirt or mud from the inside and outside surfaces. Examine the wheel rims for signs of rusting, corrosion or other damage.

13.9c Check the U-bolt nuts for security

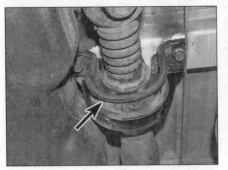

14.2 Check centre bearing – arrowed

14.3 Check universal joints – arrowed

Light alloy wheels are easily damaged by 'kerbing' whilst parking, and similarly, steel wheels may become dented or buckled. Renewal of the wheel is very often the only course of remedial action possible.

13 The balance of each wheel and tyre assembly should be maintained, not only to avoid excessive tyre wear, but also to avoid wear in the steering and suspension components. Wheel imbalance is normally signified by vibration through the vehicle's bodyshell, although in many cases it is particularly noticeable through the steering wheel. Conversely, it should be noted that wear or damage in suspension or steering components may cause excessive tyre wear. Out-of-round or out-of-true tyres, damaged wheels and wheel bearing wear/maladjustment also fall into this category. Balancing will not usually cure vibration caused by such wear.

14 Propeller shaft universal joint and centre bearing check

1 Ideally, the vehicle should be raised at the front and rear and securely supported on axle stands (see *Jacking and vehicle support*) with the rear wheels free to rotate.

2 Check around the rubber portion of the centre bearings for any signs of cracks, oil contamination or deformation of the rubber **(see illustration)**. If any of these conditions are apparent, the centre bearing(s) should be renewed as described in Chapter 8.

3 At the same time, check the condition of the universal joints by holding the propeller

15.3 Check the exhaust rubber mountings

shaft in one hand and the transmission or rear axle flange in the other **(see illustration)**. Try to twist the two components in opposite directions and look for any movement in the universal joint spiders. Repeat this check at the centre bearing(s), and in all other areas where the individual parts of the propeller shaft or universal joints connect. If any wear is evident, refer to Chapter 8 for repair procedures. If grating or squeaking noises have been heard from below the vehicle, or if there is any sign of rust-coloured deposits around the universal joint spiders, this indicates an advanced state of wear, and should be seen to immediately.

15 Exhaust system check

1 With the engine cold, check the complete exhaust system, from its starting point at the engine to the end of the tailpipe. If necessary, raise the front and rear of the vehicle and support it on axle stands (see *Jacking and vehicle support*).

2 Check the exhaust pipes and connections for evidence of leaks, severe corrosion, and damage. Make sure that all brackets and mountings are in good condition and that all relevant nuts and bolts are tight. Leakage at any of the joints or in other parts of the system will usually show up as a black sooty stain in the vicinity of the leak.

3 Rattles and other noises can often be traced to the exhaust system, especially the brackets and rubber mountings **(see illustration)**. Try to move the pipes and silencers. If the components are able to come into contact with the body or suspension parts, secure the system with new mountings. Otherwise separate the joints (if possible) and twist the pipes as necessary to provide additional clearance.

16 Underbody and fuel/brake line check

1 With the vehicle raised and supported on axle stands (see *Jacking and vehicle support*), thoroughly inspect the underbody and wheel arches for signs of damage and corrosion.

In particular, examine the bottom of the side sills, and any concealed areas where mud can collect.

2 Where corrosion and rust is evident, press and tap firmly on the panel with a screwdriver, and check for any serious corrosion, which would necessitate repairs.

3 If the panel is not seriously corroded, clean away the rust, and apply a new coating of underseal. Refer to Chapter 11 for more details of body repairs.

4 Inspect the fuel tank and filler neck for punctures, cracks and other damage. The connection between the filler neck and tank is especially critical. Sometimes a rubber filler neck or connecting hose will leak due to loose retaining clamps or deteriorated rubber.

5 Carefully check all rubber hoses and metal fuel lines leading away from the fuel tank. Check for loose connections, deteriorated hoses, crimped lines, and other damage. Pay particular attention to the vent pipes and hoses, which often loop up around the filler neck and can become blocked or crimped. Follow the lines to the front of the vehicle, carefully inspecting them all the way. Renew damaged sections as necessary. Similarly, whilst the vehicle is raised, take the opportunity to inspect all underbody brake fluid pipes and hoses.

6 From within the engine compartment, check the security of all fuel, vacuum, power steering and brake hose attachments and pipe unions, and inspect all hoses for kinks, chafing and deterioration.

17 Brake pad wear check

1 Apply the handbrake, then jack up the front (checking front brakes) or rear (checking rear brakes) of the vehicle and support it on axle stands (see *Jacking and vehicle support*). For better access to the brake calipers, remove the roadwheels.

2 Look through the inspection window in the caliper, and check that the thickness of the friction lining material on each of the pads is not less than the recommended minimum thickness given in the Specifications **(see Haynes Hint)**.

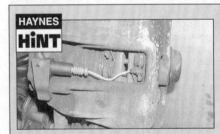

HAYNES HINT

For a quick check, the thickness of the friction material of the brake pad can be measured through the aperture in the caliper body.

17.7 Check condition of brake hoses

18.7 Handbrake adjuster wheel (disc removed for clarity)

18.8 Adjusting the handbrake adjuster through the wheel bolt hole

3 If it is difficult to determine the exact thickness of the pad linings, or if you are at all concerned about the condition of the pads, then remove them from the calipers for further inspection (refer to Chapter 9).
4 Check the caliper on the other side of the vehicle in the same way.
5 If any one of the brake pads has worn down to, or below, the specified limit, *all four* pads must be renewed as a set.
6 Check the brake discs with reference to Chapter 9.
7 Before refitting the wheels, check all brake lines and flexible hoses with reference to Chapter 9. In particular, check the flexible hoses in the vicinity of the calipers, where they are subjected to most movement. Bend them between the fingers and check that this does not reveal previously-hidden cracks, cuts or splits **(see illustration)**.
8 On completion, refit the roadwheels and lower the vehicle to the ground. Tighten the wheel bolts to the specified torque.

18 Handbrake operation and adjustment check

Note: *If the handbrake shoe clearance or cable-adjusting bolt requires a significant amount of adjustment, it is advisable to inspect the brake shoe lining thickness.*
1 With the vehicle on a slight slope, apply the handbrake lever, and check that it holds the vehicle stationary, then release the lever and check that there is no resistance to movement of the vehicle.
2 There are two areas of adjustment for the handbrake: the star wheel adjusters with the brake shoes, inside the rear brake disc and the adjusting bolt on the compensator unit under the centre of the vehicle. First you will need to carry out the adjustment at the brake shoes.
3 Slacken one of the rear wheel bolts on each rear wheel, before jacking up the car.
4 Position the vehicle on level ground, and then chock the front wheels. Jack up the rear of the vehicle and securely support it on axle stands (see *Jacking and vehicle support*).
5 Firmly apply the handbrake lever, and then release it three or four times to make sure all is working, as it should. Leave the handbrake

lever in the off position for the next part of the procedure.
6 Remove the two wheel bolts (one on each wheel), which had been slackened previously.
7 Turn the wheel so that access can be gained to the handbrake shoe adjuster **(see illustration)**, situated between the both handbrake shoes.
8 Using a long slim screwdriver engaged in the teeth of the adjuster, turn the adjuster until the handbrake shoes make contact and the wheel can no longer be turned **(see illustration)**. Repeat the procedure on the other rear wheel.
9 Noting the exact number of strokes required to do so, back off the brake shoe adjuster so that the rear wheel is completely free to turn. Repeat the procedure on the other rear wheel, turning the adjuster by exactly the same amount.
10 Check the operation of the handbrake by gradually applying it, and confirm that the rear wheels both start to 'drag' at the same point.

11 Further adjustment can be made at the adjustment bolt on the handbrake cable compensator unit under the centre of the vehicle.
12 From under the vehicle, locate the handbrake compensator plate and slacken the mounting bolts **(see illustration)**.
13 Insert a 6mm Allen key (or drill bit) between the compensator mounting bracket and handbrake lever arm **(see illustrations)**.
14 Slide the mounting bracket to the rear of the vehicle, until there is a 6 mm clearance between the mounting bracket and lever.
15 Tighten the compensator mounting bracket bolts and remove the 6 mm Allen key (or drill bit).
16 At this point apply the handbrake lever inside the passenger compartment by one notch.
17 Working back under the vehicle, slacken the clamping bolt on the eccentric adjuster, and then using an Allen key rotate the eccentric

18.12 Handbrake compensator plate mounting bolts

18.13a Insert an Allen key . . .

18.13b . . . in the gap between lever and mounting bracket – arrowed

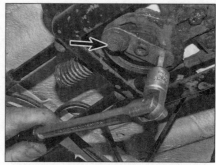

18.17 Clamping bolt – arrowed

18.18 Tighten the clamping bolt when correctly adjusted

adjuster clockwise **(see illustration)**, until the rear wheels can just be turned by hand.

18 Tighten the eccentric adjuster clamping bolt **(see illustration)**, then from inside the passenger compartment release the handbrake lever and check the wheels rotate freely.

19 On completion, lower the vehicle to the ground, refit the two wheel bolts and tighten to the specified torque.

19 Door and bonnet check and lubrication

1 Check that the doors and bonnet close securely. Check that the bonnet safety catch operates correctly. Check the operation of the door check straps.

2 Lubricate the hinges; door check straps, the striker plates and the bonnet catch sparingly with a little oil or grease.

20 Roadwheel bolt tightness check

1 Apply the handbrake, chock the wheels, and engage 1st gear.

2 Where applicable, remove the wheel bolt covers (or wheel centre cover), using the flat end of the wheel brace supplied in the tool kit.

3 Check the tightness of all wheel bolts using a torque wrench (refer to the Specifications).

21 Road test

Instruments and electrical equipment

1 Check the operation of all instruments and electrical equipment.

2 Make sure that all instruments read correctly, and switch on all electrical equipment in turn, to check that it functions properly.

Steering and suspension

3 Check for any abnormalities in the steering, suspension, handling or road 'feel'.

4 Drive the vehicle, and check that there are no unusual vibrations or noises.

5 Check that the steering feels positive, with no excessive 'sloppiness', or roughness, and check for any suspension noises when cornering and driving over bumps.

Drivetrain

6 Check the performance of the engine, clutch, transmission and driveshafts/propeller shaft.

7 Listen for any unusual noises from the engine, clutch and transmission.

8 Make sure that the engine runs smoothly when idling, and that there is no hesitation when accelerating.

9 Check that the clutch action is smooth and progressive, that the drive is taken up smoothly, and that the pedal travel is not excessive. Also listen for any noises when the clutch pedal is depressed.

10 Check that all gears can be engaged smoothly without noise, and that the gear lever action is smooth and not abnormally vague or 'notchy'.

Braking system

11 Make sure that the vehicle does not pull to one side when braking, and that the wheels do not lock when braking hard (models with ABS).

12 Check that there is no vibration through the steering when braking.

13 Check that the handbrake operates correctly, without excessive movement of the lever, and that it holds the vehicle stationary on a slope.

14 Test the operation of the brake servo unit as follows. Depress the footbrake four or five times to exhaust the vacuum, and then start the engine. As the engine starts, there should be a noticeable 'give' in the brake pedal as vacuum builds-up. Allow the engine to run for at least two minutes, and then switch it off. If the brake pedal is now depressed again, it should be possible to detect a hiss from the servo as the pedal is depressed. After about four or five applications, no further hissing should be heard, and the pedal should feel considerably harder.

Every 36 000 miles or 2 years

22 Pollen filter element renewal

1 The pollen filter element is located in the engine compartment, inside the heater ventilation box/housing.

2 Release the retaining clips and remove the soundproofing from below the pollen filter housing **(see illustrations)**.

3 Release the retaining clips at the left-hand end (as seen from the driver's seat) of the housing, and then slide the lower housing to the right and remove it from the engine compartment **(see illustrations)**.

4 Withdraw the pollen filter element, noting the position of the airflow direction arrow for

22.2a Release the securing clips . . .

22.2b . . . and remove the soundproofing

22.3a Release the retaining clips . . .

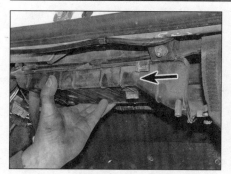

22.3b . . . and slide the cover in the direction of the arrow

22.4a Remove the pollen filter element . . .

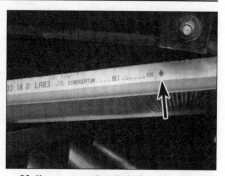

22.4b . . . note the direction arrow for refitting

refitting **(see illustrations)**. Clean out any dust or dirt particles from inside the housing.

5 If carrying out a routine service, the element must be renewed regardless of its apparent condition.

6 If you are checking the element for any other reason, inspect its lower surface; if it is very dirty, renew the element. If it is only moderately dusty, it can be re-used by blowing it clean.

7 Fit the new element using a reversal of the removal procedure.

23 Air filter element renewal

1 The air filter element is located in the air cleaner assembly on the right-hand side of the engine compartment.

2 The air filter upper housing has an air filter

service indicator. This indicates the degree of contamination of the air filter element. When this has reached 100%, the filter element will need to be renewed **(see illustration)**.

3 To make access easier, undo the retaining bolts and remove the heat shield from above the exhaust manifold **(see illustration)**.

4 Slacken the retaining clip and disconnect the air outlet hose from the air cleaner cover **(see illustration)**.

5 Release the two securing clips at rear of the air cleaner cover. Lift the air cleaner cover up at the rear, disengage it at the front and manoeuvre it out from the engine compartment **(see illustration)**.

6 Lift out the element, noting its fitted position, and then clean out the housing **(see illustration)**.

7 If carrying out a routine service, the element must be renewed regardless of its apparent condition.

8 If you are checking the element for any other reason, inspect its lower surface; if it is oily or very dirty, renew the element. If it is only moderately dusty, it can be re-used by blowing it clean.

9 Fit the new element using a reversal of the removal procedure. When new element is fitted, turn the service indicator on the upper filter housing back to zero.

24 Transmission oil level check

1 To check the oil level, raise the vehicle and support it securely on axle stands (see *Jacking and vehicle support*), making sure that the vehicle is level.

2 The filler/level plug is on the left-hand side of the transmission housing at the rear.

23.2 Service indicator on top of filter housing

23.3 Remove the heat shield

23.4 Disconnect the air hose from the filter housing

23.5a Release the securing clips . . .

23.5b . . . and remove the upper housing

23.6 Remove the filter element

24.3 Unscrew the filler/level plug

24.5 Topping-up using a plastic bottle and tube

25.2 Rear axle oil filler/level plug

25.3 Unscrew the filler/level plug

25.5 Top-up using a plastic bottle and tube . . .

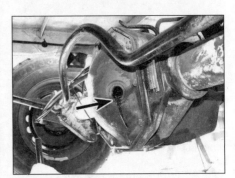

25.6 . . . until the oil level is correct

3 Using a suitable Allen key or socket, unscrew and remove the filler/level plug – take care, as it will probably be very tight **(see illustration)**.

4 If the lubricant level is correct, the oil should be up to the lower edge of the filler/level plug hole.

5 If the transmission needs topping-up, use a syringe or a plastic bottle and tube **(see illustration)** to add more lubricant of the specified type (refer to *Lubricants and fluids*).

6 Stop filling the transmission when the lubricant begins to run out of the hole, and then wait until the flow of oil ceases.

7 Refit the filler/level plug, and tighten it to the specified torque setting. Drive the vehicle a short distance, and then check for leaks.

8 A need for regular topping-up can only be due to a leak, which should be found and rectified without delay.

25 Rear axle oil level check

1 To check the oil level, raise the vehicle and support it securely on axle stands (see *Jacking and vehicle support*), making sure that the vehicle is level.

2 The filler/level plug is located on the differential housing cover at the rear **(see illustration)**.

3 Using a suitable Allen key or socket, unscrew and remove the filler/level plug – take care, as it will probably be very tight **(see illustration)**.

4 If the lubricant level is correct, the oil should be up to the lower edge of the filler/level plug hole.

5 If the axle needs topping-up, use a syringe, or a plastic bottle and tube **(see illustration)** to add more lubricant of the specified type (refer to *Lubricants and fluids*).

6 Stop filling the transmission when the lubricant begins to run out of the hole **(see illustration)**, and then wait until the flow of oil ceases.

7 Refit the filler/level plug, and tighten it to the specified torque.

8 A need for regular topping-up can only be due to a leak, which should be found and rectified without delay.

26 Brake fluid renewal

The procedure is similar to that for the bleeding of the hydraulic system as described in Chapter 9, except that the brake fluid reservoir should be emptied by siphoning, and allowance should be made for the old fluid to be removed from the circuit when bleeding a section of the circuit.

Every 10 years

27 Coolant renewal

Note: *If the antifreeze used is Mercedes-Benz antifreeze/inhibiter, or of similar quality, Mercedes-Benz state that coolant renewal is only necessary every ten years. If the vehicle's history is unknown or if the antifreeze is of lesser quality, the coolant should be changed as follows.*

 Warning: Refer to Chapter 3 and observe the warnings given. In particular, never remove the expansion tank filler cap when the engine is running, or has just been switched off, as the cooling system will be hot, and the consequent escaping steam and scalding coolant could cause serious injury. If the engine is hot, the electric cooling fan may start rotating even if the engine is not running, so be careful to keep hands, hair and loose clothing well clear when working in the engine compartment.

Warning: Wait until the engine is cold before starting this procedure.

Cooling system draining

1 To drain the system, first remove the expansion tank filler cap. Place a thick cloth over the expansion tank cap, then turn the cap anticlockwise as far as the first stop and wait for any pressure to be released, then depress it and turn it further anti-clockwise to remove it.

2 If additional working clearance is required, apply the handbrake, then jack up the front of the vehicle and support it on axle stands (see *Jacking and vehicle support*).

3 Place a large drain tray underneath the radiator, and then fit a piece of hose onto the radiator drain tube, and then unscrew the radiator drain plug **(see illustration)**. Allow the coolant to drain into the tray.

4 Depending on model, the cylinder block may also be drained by removing the drain plug located on the exhaust manifold side of the engine.

5 On completion, retighten the drain plugs securely. Where necessary, lower the vehicle to the ground.

Cooling system flushing

6 If coolant renewal has been neglected, or if the antifreeze mixture has become diluted, then in time, the cooling system may gradually lose efficiency, as the coolant passages become restricted due to rust, scale deposits, and other sediment. The cooling system efficiency can be restored by flushing the system clean.

7 The radiator should be flushed independently of the engine, to avoid unnecessary contamination.

Radiator flushing

8 Disconnect the top and bottom hoses and any other relevant hoses from the radiator, with reference to Chapter 3.

9 Insert a garden hose into the radiator top inlet. Direct a flow of clean water through the radiator, and continue flushing until clean water emerges from the radiator bottom outlet.

10 If after a reasonable period, the water still does not run clear, the radiator can be flushed with a good proprietary cleaning agent. It is important that the manufacturer's instructions are followed carefully. If the contamination is particularly bad, remove the radiator, insert the hose in the radiator bottom outlet, and reverse-flush the radiator.

Engine flushing

11 Remove the thermostat as described in Chapter 3 then, if the radiator top hose has been disconnected from the engine, temporarily refit the thermostat housing cover and reconnect the hose.

12 With the top and bottom hoses disconnected from the radiator, insert a

27.3a Fit a plastic pipe on the bottom of the radiator . . .

garden hose into the radiator top hose. Direct a clean flow of water through the engine, and continue flushing until clean water emerges from the radiator bottom hose.

13 On completion of flushing, refit the thermostat and reconnect the hoses with reference to Chapter 3.

Cooling system filling

14 Before attempting to fill the cooling system, make sure that all hoses and clips are in good condition, and that the clips are tight. Note that an antifreeze mixture must be used all year round, to prevent corrosion of the engine components.

15 Fill the system via the expansion tank, with the correct antifreeze mixture, until the coolant level reaches the MAX mark on the side of the expansion tank. Refit the expansion tank filler cap.

16 Start the engine and allow it to idle until it reaches normal operating temperature, then allow it to idle for a further 5 minutes.

17 Switch off the engine and allow it to cool for at least 30 minutes.

18 Remove the filler cap and top-up the coolant level to the MAX mark on the expansion tank. Refit and tighten the cap.

Antifreeze mixture

19 Mercedes-Benz state that, if the only antifreeze used is Mercedes-Benz antifreeze/inhibiter, it will last for ten years. This is subject to it being used in the recommended concentration, unmixed with any other type of antifreeze or additive, and topped-up when necessary using only that antifreeze type, mixed with clean water. If any other type of antifreeze is (or has been) added, the ten-year life period no longer applies; in this case, the system must be drained and thoroughly flushed before fresh coolant mixture is poured in.

20 If any antifreeze other than Mercedes-Benz

27.3b . . . and slacken the drain tap – arrowed

is to be used, the coolant must be renewed at regular intervals to provide an equivalent degree of protection. The conventional recommendation is to renew the coolant every two years.

21 If the antifreeze used is to Mercedes-Benz specification, the levels of protection it affords are indicated in the Specifications Section of this Chapter. To give the recommended *standard* mixture ratio for this antifreeze, 40% (by volume) of antifreeze must be mixed with 60% of clean, soft water. If you are using any other type of antifreeze, follow its manufacturer's instructions to achieve the correct ratio.

22 It is best to make up slightly more than the system's specified capacity, so that a supply is available for subsequent topping-up. However, note that you are unlikely to fully drain the system at any one time (unless the engine is being completely stripped), and the capacities quoted are therefore slightly academic for routine coolant renewal.

23 Before adding antifreeze, the cooling system should be completely drained, preferably flushed, and all hoses checked for condition and security. Fresh antifreeze will rapidly find any weaknesses in the system.

24 After filling with antifreeze, a label should be attached to the expansion tank, stating the type and concentration of antifreeze used, and the date installed. Any subsequent topping-up should be made with the same type and concentration of antifreeze. If topping-up using antifreeze to Mercedes-Benz specification, note that a 50/50 mixture is permissible, purely for convenience.

Caution: Do not use engine antifreeze in the windscreen washer system, as it will damage the vehicle's paintwork. A screen wash additive should be added to the washer system in its maker's recommended quantities.

2A•1

Chapter 2 Part A:
2.2 litre engine in-car repair procedures

Contents

Section number

Camshaft cover – removal and refitting 4
Camshafts, camshaft housing and hydraulic tappets – removal,
   inspection and refitting. 9
Compression and leakdown tests – description and interpretation. . 2
Crankshaft oil seals – renewal 14
Crankshaft pulley/vibration damper and hub – removal and refitting 5
Cylinder head – removal, inspection and refitting 10
Cylinder head front cover – removal and refitting 15
Engine assembly and valve timing marks – general information and
   usage 3

Section number

Engine/transmission mountings – inspection and renewal 16
Flywheel/crankshaft spigot bearing – removal, inspection and
   refitting 13
General information 1
Oil pump – removal, inspection and refitting 12
Sump – removal and refitting 11
Timing chain – inspection and renewal 7
Timing chain cover – removal and refitting. 6
Timing chain tensioner, sprockets and guides – removal, inspection
   and refitting. 8

Degrees of difficulty

Easy, suitable for novice with little experience | **Fairly easy,** suitable for beginner with some experience | **Fairly difficult,** suitable for competent DIY mechanic | **Difficult,** suitable for experienced DIY mechanic | **Very difficult,** suitable for expert DIY or professional

Specifications

General
Engine code . . . . 611.981, 611.983 or 611.987
Displacement . . . . 2148 cc
Bore . . . . 88.0 mm
Stroke. . . . . 88.3 mm
Direction of engine rotation . . . . Clockwise (viewed from front of vehicle)
No 1 cylinder location. . . . . Timing chain end
Firing order 1-3-4-2
Compression pressures:
   New compression pressure . . . . 29.0 to 35.0 bars
   Minimum compression pressure . . . . 18.0 bars (approximately)
   Maximum difference between cylinders. . . . . 3.0 bars

Cylinder head bolts
Thread diameter. M12
Length when new. . . . . 102.0 mm
Maximum length. . . . . 104.0 mm

Lubrication system
Oil pressure (at temperature 90°C):
   At idle (minimum) . . . . 0.3 bar
   At 3000 rpm (minimum) . . . . 3.0 bar

Torque wrench settings

	Nm	lbf ft
Air conditioning pump to bracket	20	15
Auxiliary drivebelt idler pulley bolt	30	22
Auxiliary drivebelt tensioner damper strut bolts:		
Lower bolt	20	15
Upper bolt	25	18
Big-end bearing cap bolts:		
Stage 1	5	4
Stage 2	25	18
Stage 3	Angle-tighten a further 90°	
Camshaft bearing cap	10	7
Camshaft cover bolts	10	7
Camshaft housing to cylinder head	15	11
Camshaft sprocket	18	13
Coolant pump to housing	10	7
Crankshaft pulley/vibration damper and hub:		
8.8 bolts:		
Stage 1	200	148
Stage 2	Angle-tighten a further 90°	
10.9 bolt:		
Stage 1	325	240
Stage 2	Angle-tighten a further 90°	
12.9 bolt:		
Stage 1	200	148
Stage 2	Angle-tighten a further 90°	
Stage 3	Angle-tighten a further 90°	
Crankshaft rear oil seal housing bolts	10	7
Cylinder block coolant drain plug	30	22
Cylinder head (M12 bolts):		
Stage 1	60	44
Stage 2	Angle-tighten a further 90°	
Stage 3	Angle-tighten a further 90°	
Cylinder head front cover	14	10
Cylinder head-to-timing cover bolts (M8 bolts)	20	15
Dipstick tube-to-cylinder head bolt	14	10
Engine cover trim bolts	10	7
Engine mountings:		
Engine mounting crossmember to underbody	40	30
Engine mounting to crossmember	25	18
Front mounting bolts:		
To axle carrier	35	26
M8	25	18
M10	40	30
Engine-to-transmission bolts:		
M10 x 40 mm bolts	55	41
M10 x 90 mm bolts	45	33
Exhaust manifold to turbocharger	30	22
Flywheel bolts:		
Stage 1	45	33
Stage 2	Angle-tighten a further 90°	
Fuel injection pipe union nuts	23	17
Fuel injector retaining plate bolt:		
Stage 1	7	5
Stage 2	Angle-tighten a further 90°	
Stage 3	Angle-tighten a further 90°	
Main bearing cap bolts:		
Stage 1	55	41
Stage 2	Angle-tighten a further 90°	
Oil drain plug	30	22
Oil feed line to cylinder head	9	7
Oil feed line to turbocharger:		
Screw fitting	30	22
Banjo bolt	18	13
Oil filter cap	25	18
Oil level sensor to crankcase	20	15
Oil pressure sensor to oil filter	15	11
Oil pump mounting bolts	18	13
Oil pump relief valve plug	50	37

Torque wrench settings (continued)

	Nm	lbf ft
Power steering pump to housing	20	15
Sump (oil pan) bolts:		
To crankcase:		
M6.	9	7
M8.	20	15
To transmission.	40	30
Timing chain cover bolts:		
M6 bolts	10	7
M8 bolts	20	15
Timing chain tensioner.	80	59
Turbocharger support bracket bolt	30	22

1 General information

How to use this Chapter

This Part of Chapter 2 describes the repair procedures that can reasonably be carried out on the engine while it remains in the vehicle. If the engine has been removed from the vehicle and is being dismantled as described in Part C, any preliminary dismantling procedures can be ignored.

Note that, while it may be possible physically to overhaul items such as the piston/ connecting rod assemblies while the engine is in the vehicle, such tasks are not usually carried out as separate operations. Usually, several additional procedures are required (not to mention the cleaning of components and oilways); for this reason, all such tasks are classed as major overhaul procedures, and are described in Part C of this Chapter.

Part C describes the removal of the engine/ transmission from the vehicle, and the full overhaul procedures that can then be carried out.

Engine description

The engine is a 4-cylinder in-line double overhead camshaft design, mounted in-line ('north-south') at the front of the vehicle with the transmission mounted on the rear of the engine.

The crankshaft is supported in five main bearing within the cast iron cylinder block. Crankshaft endfloat is controlled by thrustwashers fitted on either side of No 3 main bearing.

The connecting rods are attached to the crankshaft by horizontally split big-end bearings, and to the pistons by fully-floating gudgeon pins retained by circlips. The alloy pistons are fitted with three piston rings, two compression rings and one oil control ring.

The exhaust camshaft is driven from the crankshaft sprocket by a double-row chain, and the inlet camshaft is gear-driven from the exhaust camshaft. The camshaft also drives the fuel injection pump.

The camshaft is supported in bearings in the cylinder head, and actuates the valves directly, via hydraulic valve lifters.

The oil pump is chain-driven from the front of the crankshaft. An oil cooler is located on the oil filter housing at the left-hand front of the cylinder block.

Operations with engine in vehicle

The following operations can be carried out without having to remove the engine from the vehicle:

a) *Removal and refitting of the cylinder head.*
b) *Removal and refitting of the timing chain and sprockets.*
c) *Removal and refitting of the camshaft.*
d) *Removal and refitting of the sump.*
e) *Removal and refitting of the big-end bearings, connecting rods, and pistons.**
f) *Removal and refitting of the oil pump.*
g) *Renewal of the engine/transmission mountings.*
h) *Removal and refitting of the flywheel.*

* Although it is possible to remove these components with the engine in place, for reasons of access and cleanliness it is recommended that the engine be removed.

2 Compression and leakdown tests – description and interpretation

Compression test

Note: *A compression tester designed for diesel engines must be used for this test.*

1 When engine performance is down, a compression test can provide diagnostic clues as to the engine's condition. If the test is performed regularly, it can give warning of trouble before any other symptoms become apparent.

2 The tester is connected to an adapter, which screws into the glow plug or injector hole. On these engines, an adapter suitable for use in the injector holes is preferable. It is unlikely to be worthwhile buying such a tester for occasional use, but it may be possible to borrow or hire one – if not, have the test performed by a garage.

3 Unless specific instructions to the contrary are supplied with the tester, observe the following points.

a) *The battery must be in a good state of charge, the air filter must be clean, and the engine should be at normal operating temperature.*
b) *All the injectors should be removed before starting the test.*
c) *The stop solenoid must be disconnected, to prevent the engine from running or fuel from being discharged.*

4 There is no need to hold the accelerator pedal down during the test, because the diesel engine air inlet is not throttled.

5 Crank the engine on the starter motor. After one or two revolutions, the compression pressure should build-up to a maximum figure, and then stabilise. Record the highest reading obtained.

6 Repeat the test on the remaining cylinders, recording the pressure in each.

7 The cause of poor compression is less easy to establish on a diesel engine than on a petrol one. The effect of introducing oil into the cylinders ('wet' testing) is not conclusive, because there is a risk that the oil will sit in the swirl chamber or in the recess in the piston crown instead of passing to the rings. However, the following can be used as a rough guide to diagnosis.

8 All cylinders should produce very similar pressures; if there is a large difference, then this indicates a fault. Note that the compression should build-up quickly in a healthy engine; low compression on the first stroke, followed by gradually increasing pressure on successive strokes, indicates worn piston rings. A low compression reading on the first stroke, which does not build-up during successive strokes, indicates leaking valves or a blown head gasket (a cracked head could also be the cause). Deposits on the undersides of the valve heads can also cause low compression.

9 A low reading from two adjacent cylinders is almost certainly due to the head gasket having blown between them; the presence of coolant in the engine oil will confirm this.

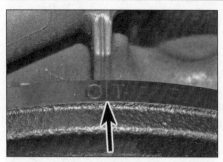

3.4 O/T (TDC) mark on crankshaft pulley/
vibration damper aligned with pointer on
timing chain cover

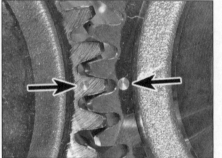

3.5b ... aligned through the centre of the
camshafts

10 If the compression reading is unusually
high, the combustion chambers are probably
coated with carbon deposits. If this is the
case, the cylinder head should be removed
and decarbonised.

11 On completion of the test, refit the
injectors or the glow plugs, and reconnect the
stop solenoid.

Leakdown test

12 A leakdown test measures the rate at
which compressed air fed into the cylinder is
lost. It is an alternative to a compression test,
and in many ways is better, since the escaping
air provides easy identification of where a
pressure loss is occurring (piston rings, valves
or head gasket).

13 The equipment needed for leakdown testing
is unlikely to be available to the home mechanic.
If poor compression is suspected, have the test
performed by a suitably-equipped garage.

3.5a Camshaft gear alignment marks ...

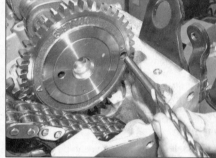

3.6 Insert drill bit to lock camshaft

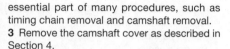

3 Engine assembly and valve timing marks – general information and usage

*Warning: When turning the engine,
do not turn the engine using the
camshaft sprocket bolts, and do
not turn the engine backwards (ie, anti-
clockwise).*

1 Top Dead Centre (TDC) is the highest point
in the cylinder that each piston reaches as
it travels up and down when the crankshaft
turns. Each piston reaches TDC at the end
of the compression stroke and again at the
end of the exhaust stroke, but for valve timing
TDC refers to the No 1 piston position on the
compression stroke. No 1 piston is at the
timing chain end of the engine.

2 Positioning No 1 piston at TDC is an

essential part of many procedures, such as
timing chain removal and camshaft removal.

3 Remove the camshaft cover as described in
Section 4.

4 Using a socket on the crankshaft pulley/
vibration damper hub bolt, turn the crankshaft
clockwise until the O/T (TDC) mark on the
crankshaft pulley/vibration damper is aligned
with the pointer on the timing chain cover (**see
illustration**). For access to the bolt, it may be
necessary to remove the fan unit and radiator
shroud as described in Chapter 3.

5 In this position the alignment indentations
(two 1.5 mm dots) on the camshaft gears
(timing chain side) should be next to each
other and aligned with the centre points of the
camshafts (**see illustrations**). The camshaft
lobes on No 1 cylinder should be facing
upwards.

6 If necessary, the camshafts can be locked in
position. The inlet camshaft gear has a timing
hole, which aligns with a hole in the camshaft
front bearing cap, and a suitable close-fitting
drill should be inserted to lock the camshaft
(**see illustration**).

*Caution: Do not use this method to lock
the engine while slackening any retaining
bolts.*

7 With the camshafts aligned as described,
No 1 piston is at TDC on its firing stroke.

4 Camshaft cover – removal and refitting

Removal

1 Disconnect the battery negative (earth) lead
and position it away from the terminal.

2 Undo the retaining bolts and remove
the heat shield from the top of the exhaust
manifold (**see illustration**).

3 Disconnect the crankcase breather hose
at the front of the camshaft cover (**see
illustration**).

4 Where applicable, disconnect the wiring
connector from the shut-off valve and
camshaft sensor (**see illustration**).

5 Remove the fuel injectors, injector pipes and
inlet manifold, as described in Chapter 4A.

6 Undo the retaining bolts and release the

4.2 Remove the heat shield

4.3 Disconnect the breather hose

4.4 Disconnect the camshaft sensor

wiring loom from the top of the camshaft cover **(see illustration)**.

7 Unscrew the bolts then lift the camshaft cover away from the cylinder head **(see illustration)**.

8 Remove the cover gaskets and discard; new ones will be required for refitting.

Refitting

9 Clean the joint surfaces of the cover and cylinder head, then locate the new gaskets in the grooves in the camshaft cover **(see illustrations)**.

10 Position the camshaft cover with gaskets on the cylinder head, then insert the bolts and tighten them progressively. Do not fully-tighten at this point as the fuel injectors will need to centralise in the cover.

11 Refit the fuel injectors and fuel lines and tighten the union nuts to the specified torque.

12 Tighten the camshaft cover bolts to their specified torque setting.

13 Complete the rest of the installation by reversing the removal procedure, referring to the relevant Chapters. When all components are refitted, start the engine and check carefully around the camshaft cover for any oil leaks.

5 Crankshaft pulley/ vibration damper and hub – removal and refitting

Removal

1 To gain better access, remove the fan and shroud from the rear of the radiator with reference to Chapter 3.

2 Remove the auxiliary drivebelt, with reference to Chapter 1.

3 Working under the front of the vehicle, undo the retaining bolts and remove the engine undershield (where fitted).

4 The crankshaft must now be held stationary while the pulley bolt is loosened. The bolt is tightened to a high torque. Mercedes-Benz technicians remove the starter motor and use a special tool which is bolted to the transmission and locks the flywheel. It may be possible to insert a wide-bladed screwdriver between the starter ring gear teeth to prevent the engine from turning.

5 Unscrew the crankshaft pulley bolt then slide the pulley from the front of the crankshaft. Note the location of the washers under the head of the bolt, as they need to be fitted in the same position on refitting **(see illustration)**. If the pulley is tight on the crankshaft, use a suitable puller to remove it. A two-legged puller, which locates in the pulley holes, is ideal.

6 If necessary, remove the Woodruff key from the groove in the nose of the crankshaft.

Inspection

7 Examine the oil seal contact surface of the pulley/vibration damper for an excessive wear groove. If evident, it is permissible to position the oil seal slightly further into the timing

4.6 Unclip the wiring harness

4.7 Remove the camshaft cover

4.9a Fit new camshaft cover gasket . . .

4.9b . . . and fuel injector recess gaskets

chain cover so that it runs on the unworn area of the pulley. Alternatively, the pulley should be renewed. The oil seal in the timing cover must be renewed as a matter of course with reference to Section 14.

Refitting

8 Locate the Woodruff key in the groove in the nose of the crankshaft. Make sure that it is firmly pressed into position, and that its outer edge is parallel with the crankshaft so that the pulley/vibration damper will engage with it easily **(see illustration)**.

9 Wipe clean and lightly oil the seal contact surface of the pulley, and then slide it fully onto the crankshaft, engaging it with the Woodruff key.

10 Lightly oil the threads of the crankshaft pulley bolt and the washers, and then locate the washer(s) correctly onto the bolt, as noted on removal. Insert the bolt and tighten it to the

specified torque while holding the crankshaft stationary as for removal. If necessary, refit the starter motor.

11 Refit the auxiliary drivebelt with reference to Chapter 1.

12 Refit the fan and shroud to the rear of the radiator with reference to Chapter 3.

13 Where applicable, refit the engine under-shield.

6 Timing chain cover – removal and refitting

Note: *The timing chain cover is located between the cylinder head and the sump; take care not to damage any of these gaskets.*

Removal

1 Disconnect the battery negative (earth) lead and position it away from the terminal.

5.5 Remove the bolt and washer

5.8 Make sure Woodruff key is located securely

6.5 Remove the air intake hose

6.12 Slacken the retaining bolts

6.14 Fasten the compressor to one side

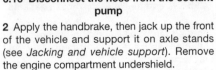

6.16 Disconnect the hose from the coolant pump

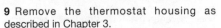

6.17a Unclip the plastic cap . . .

6.17b . . . and remove the bolt

2 Apply the handbrake, then jack up the front of the vehicle and support it on axle stands (see *Jacking and vehicle support*). Remove the engine compartment undershield.
3 Drain the engine oil from the sump and remove the oil filter as described in Chapter 1.
4 Remove the camshaft cover as described in Section 4.
5 Remove the turbocharger air ducts from between the intercooler and intake manifold **(see illustration)**.
6 Remove the cooling fan and shroud from the rear of the radiator as described in Chapter 3.
7 Refer to Section 3 and set the engine at TDC compression on No 1 cylinder. Ideally the crankshaft should be locked in this position during the removal of the timing chain cover. Mercedes-Benz technicians remove the starter motor and use a special tool to lock the teeth of the starter ring gear.
8 Drain the cooling system as described in Chapter 1.

9 Remove the thermostat housing as described in Chapter 3.
10 Remove the cover plate from the front of the cylinder head as described in Section 15.
11 Remove the high-pressure fuel pump as described in Chapter 4A.
12 Slacken the retaining bolts on the power steering pump pulley **(see illustration)**, and then remove the auxiliary drivebelt as described in Chapter 1.
13 Remove the pulley and then unbolt the power steering pump and position it to the side of the engine compartment. **Do not** disconnect the hydraulic lines from the pump. Refer to Chapter 10 for further information.
14 On models with air conditioning, disconnect the wiring connector from the compressor and then unbolt the compressor and position it to the side of the engine compartment **(see illustration)**. **Do not** disconnect the refrigerant lines from the compressor. Refer to Chapter 3 for further information.

15 Disconnect the coolant hose from the oil/water heat exchanger at the rear of the oil filter housing.
16 Disconnect the two coolant hoses from the coolant pump **(see illustration)**.
17 Remove the plastic cap and then undo the retaining bolt and remove the auxiliary belt idler pulley from the coolant pump **(see illustrations)**.
18 Remove the coolant pump as described in Chapter 3.
19 Remove the alternator with reference to Chapter 5.
20 With the engine set at TDC, slacken and remove the timing chain tensioner from the right-hand front of the engine **(see illustration)**. Discard the sealing washer, as a new one will be required for refitting.
21 Remove the plastic cap and then undo the retaining bolt and remove the auxiliary belt idler pulley from the oil filter housing **(see illustrations)**.

6.20 Timing chain tensioner

6.21a Unclip the plastic cap . . .

6.21b . . . and remove the bolt

22 Undo the retaining bolts and remove the auxiliary belt tensioner from the front cover **(see illustration)**

23 Remove the crankshaft pulley/vibration damper and hub as described in Section 5.

24 Unscrew and remove the bolts securing the sump to the bottom of the timing chain cover. Slacken the remaining sump bolts by 2 or 3 turns.

25 Working through the aperture in the top of the cylinder head, unscrew the two bolts securing the timing chain cover to the cylinder head **(see illustration)**.

26 Unscrew the bolts and remove the timing chain cover from the front of the engine, taking care not to damage the front parts of the cylinder head gasket and sump gasket. If required, to ensure the bolts are refitted in their correct locations, make a drawing of their positions, or use a dab of paint on them to identify them. If the two location dowels are loose, remove them also.

27 With the timing chain cover removed, it is recommended that the crankshaft front oil seal be renewed with reference to Section 14.

Refitting

28 Commence refitting by thoroughly cleaning away all traces of old sealant from the mating faces of the timing chain cover and cylinder block. Also clean the areas of the cylinder head gasket and sump gasket, which contact the timing chain cover.

29 Carefully check the condition of the cylinder head gasket. If the gasket has been damaged during the removal procedure, the cylinder head should be removed in order to renew the gasket, as described in Section 10.

30 Similarly, carefully check the condition of the sump gasket. If the gasket has been damaged during the removal procedure, the sump should be removed in order to renew the gasket, as described in Section 11.

31 Apply sealant to the cylinder block mating face of the timing chain cover. Make sure that the two location dowels are correctly fitted **(see illustration)**.

32 Coat the lips of the crankshaft oil seal with clean engine oil, then slide the cover into position over the crankshaft. Take care not to damage the oil seal lips or the cylinder head and sump gaskets as the cover is fitted.

33 Insert all the retaining bolts, including the two upper ones, in their original positions and hand-tighten them. First, progressively tighten the bolts securing the timing chain cover to the cylinder block to the specified torque, and then tighten the two upper bolts to the specified torque.

34 Insert the bolts securing the sump to the bottom of the timing chain cover. Progressively tighten all the sump bolts to the specified torque.

35 Complete the rest of the installation by reversing the removal procedure, referring to the relevant Chapters.

36 Refill the engine with the correct grade and quantity of oil, as described in Chapter 1.

6.22 Tensioner mounting bolts

37 Reconnect the battery negative lead.

38 When all components are refitted, start the engine and check carefully around the front of the engine for any oil leaks, or coolant leaks.

39 Where applicable, refit the engine compartment undershield and lower the vehicle to the ground.

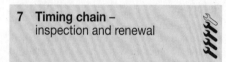

7 Timing chain –
inspection and renewal

Inspection

1 Remove the camshaft cover as described in Section 4.

2 Using a socket on the crankshaft pulley/vibration damper hub bolt, turn the engine so that the whole length of the chain can be progressively viewed at the camshaft sprocket.

3 The chain should be renewed if the sprocket is worn or if the chain is worn (indicated by excessive lateral play between the links, and excessive noise in operation). Note that the rollers on a very badly worn chain may be slightly grooved. To avoid future problems, if there is any doubt at all about the condition of the chain, renew it.

Renewal

Note 1: *This following procedure uses a chain breaker/riveter to renew the chain without removing the front timing chain cover, a second person will be required to assist fitting the timing chain. Ensure that all tools are available, as well as a new chain and new connecting link before proceeding.*

Note 2: *If the chain needs to be renewed as a complete assembly, then remove the front timing chain cover as described in Section 6.*

4 Disconnect the battery negative (earth) lead and position it away from the terminal.

5 If not already done, remove the camshaft cover as described in Section 4.

6 Remove the cover plate from the front of the cylinder head as described in Section 15.

7 Remove the fan and shroud, as described in Chapter 3.

8 Using a socket on the crankshaft pulley bolt, turn the engine until the timing marks are aligned, as described in Section 3.

6.25 Timing chain cover upper mounting bolts

9 Remove the timing chain tensioner as described in Section 8.

10 With the engine still in the TDC position, use a couple of cable-ties to keep the timing chain on the camshaft sprocket. Put some clean rag into the timing chain recess to prevent anything dropping down into the engine.

11 Use the chain breaker to press out one of the timing chain pins and split the timing chain.

12 Connect the new timing chain to the old chain and press the chain link pin back into position. **Note:** *Make sure the new chain is connected to the correct part of the old chain, as the engine has to be turned clockwise, in the direction of rotation, to feed the chain around the sprockets.*

13 With the new chain connected securely to the old chain, take a firm hold of both ends of the chain and remove the cable-ties from the camshaft sprocket. Remove the clean rag from around the timing chain before turning the engine.

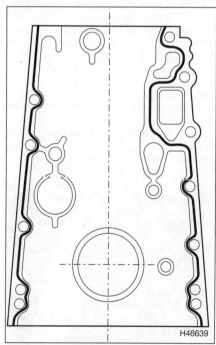

6.31 Apply sealant (2 mm bead) on the inside of the bolt holes

8.3 Remove the heat shield

8.6 Removing the tensioner

14 With the aid of an assistant, turn the engine in the direction of rotation. Keeping the timing chain taut feed it around the crankshaft sprocket, until the new chain comes all the way around to the camshaft sprocket.

15 Cable-tie both ends of the timing chain back to the camshaft sprocket, and refit the clean rag back into the timing chain recess.

16 Use the chain breaker to press out the timing chain pin and split the old timing chain from the new timing chain. **Note:** *Make sure the chain is pulled tight on the lower section of the engine, and the upper section is slack to allow for the fitting of the chain tensioner.*

17 Check that the TDC marks on the crankshaft pulley and timing chain cover are aligned, and the marks on the camshaft and camshaft bearing caps are still aligned correctly.

18 Fit the new timing chain link, using the timing chain riveter to connect the two ends of the chain securely. Always read the instructions that come with the chain riveter, as there are many different types available. The link pins need to be riveted securely, to prevent the chain coming apart.

19 Remove the clean rag from the timing chain recess, and fit the timing chain tensioner, with reference to Section 8. With the tensioner now fitted, check the timing marks are still in line.

20 Rotate the engine two complete turns and check the timing marks come back in alignment. Refer to Section 3 to check timing mark alignment is correct.

21 Refit the camshaft cover with reference to Section 4.

22 Refit the air cleaner assembly.

23 Reconnect the battery negative lead.

8 Timing chain tensioner, sprockets and guides –
removal, inspection and refitting

Timing chain tensioner

Removal

1 Disconnect the battery negative (earth) lead and position it away from the terminal.

2 Refer to Section 3 and set the engine to TDC on No 1 cylinder.

3 Undo the retaining bolts and remove the heat shield **(see illustration)**.

4 Disconnect the breather hose from the top of the camshaft cover. Undo the retaining bolt from the top of the engine oil dipstick tube and move the tube to one side.

5 Where applicable, undo the retaining bolts and remove the fuel electric shut-off valve from the front of the cylinder head and move it to one side.

6 Unscrew the tensioner from the right-hand side of the timing chain cover **(see illustration)**. Recover the sealing ring and discard; a new one will be required for refitting.

Inspection

7 Do not attempt to dismantle the tensioner assembly. If it is suspected that the tensioner is worn or faulty, the complete unit should be renewed.

Refitting

8 Locate a new sealing ring on the tensioner, then screw it into position in the cylinder head and tighten to the specified torque.

9 Refitting is the reversal of the removal procedure, referring to the relevant Chapters, where applicable. When all components are refitted, start the engine and check carefully around the tensioner for any oil leaks.

Camshaft sprocket

Removal

10 Refer to Section 3 and set the engine to TDC on No 1 cylinder. Lock the inlet camshaft as described by inserting a drill through the camshaft front bearing cap into the gear **(see illustration)**.

11 Remove the cover plate from the front of the cylinder head as described in Section 15.

12 Use a dab of paint or a marker pen to mark the timing chain and the exhaust camshaft sprocket in relation to each other. This will help ensure that the chain is refitted correctly and the valve timing maintained.

13 Remove the timing chain tensioner as described earlier in this Section.

14 Hold the exhaust camshaft (timing chain) sprocket stationary using a suitable tool located in the sprocket cut-outs, then loosen the bolts securing the sprocket to the camshaft **(see illustration)**. **Do not** rely only on the drill located in the inlet camshaft sprocket to hold the sprocket.

15 At this stage the crankshaft sprocket will still be at TDC, and the crankshaft must not be turned until the camshaft sprocket has been refitted. Use a length of wire to tie the upper part of the timing chain to the cylinder head to ensure the chain remains on the sprockets.

16 Remove the sprockets from their location dowel on the camshaft flange. Remove the timing chain sprocket from the timing chain, and if required remove the dowel from the flange in the end of the camshaft. **Note:** *The sprocket bolts must be renewed every time they are removed.*

Inspection

17 Examine the teeth on the sprockets for wear. Each tooth forms an inverted V. If worn, the side of each tooth under tension will be slightly concave in shape when compared with the other side of the tooth (ie, the teeth will have a hooked appearance). If the teeth appear worn, the sprocket must be renewed.

Refitting

18 Ensure that the camshaft and crankshaft timing marks are still aligned, as described in Section 3. If a new sprocket is being fitted, transfer the chain alignment mark from the old sprocket to the new.

19 Fit the location dowel to the hole in the exhaust camshaft flange.

20 Engage the sprocket with the chain, aligning the marks made on the chain and sprocket before removal, then locate the sprocket on the camshaft flange and engage it with the dowel.

21 Insert the bolts and tighten them to the specified torque while holding the sprocket stationary using the used tool for removal.

8.10 Lock the camshaft using a drill bit

8.14 Unbolt the sprocket from the camshaft

Remove the wire used to tie the chain to the cylinder head.

22 Refit the timing chain tensioner as described earlier in this Section.

23 Using a socket on the crankshaft pulley/vibration damper hub bolt, turn the crankshaft through two complete revolutions, and check that the crankshaft and camshaft timing marks are still aligned with No 1 piston at TDC, as described in Section 3.

24 Remove the inlet camshaft locking drill, then refit the camshaft cover with reference to Section 4.

Crankshaft sprocket

Note: *A puller may be required to remove the sprocket.*

Removal

25 Remove the timing chain cover as described in Section 6. This procedure includes removal of the crankshaft pulley/vibration damper and Woodruff key, and the setting of the engine to its TDC position.

26 Remove the sump as described in Section 11.

27 Hold the oil pump sprocket on the oil pump stationary using a suitable tool engaged with the sprocket holes, then unscrew and remove the mounting bolts. Remove the sprocket from the oil pump drive flange and unhook the drive chain from the crankshaft sprocket on the front of the crankshaft. **Note:** *The oil pump chain drive sprocket is incorporated into the crankshaft sprocket.*

28 Remove the camshaft sprocket as described previously in this Section, however, in addition to marking the timing chain in relation to the camshaft sprocket, also mark it in relation to the injection pump sprocket and crankshaft sprocket. This is necessary to ensure the valve timing and injection pump timing is maintained, since it will also be difficult to ascertain the TDC position of the crankshaft with the timing chain cover removed.

29 Unhook the timing chain from the crankshaft sprocket and injection pump sprocket.

30 Slide the crankshaft sprocket from the front of the crankshaft. If it is tight, use a suitable puller, taking care not to damage the sprocket teeth. Alternatively, use two levers against the front of the cylinder block, positioning the levers diagonally opposite each other.

31 Recover the Woodruff key from the groove in the crankshaft.

Inspection

32 Refer to paragraph 17.

Refitting

33 Locate the Woodruff key in the crankshaft groove; making sure that the upper edge is parallel with the surface of the crankshaft.

34 Slide the crankshaft sprocket onto the front of the crankshaft and engage it with the Woodruff key. If necessary, use a suitable metal tube to tap it into position.

35 Engage the timing chain with the crankshaft sprocket and injection pump sprocket, making sure that the previously-made marks are aligned with each other, then pull the chain up through the aperture at the front of the cylinder head.

36 Refit the camshaft sprocket as described earlier in this Section, making sure that the previously-made marks on the chain and sprocket are aligned with each other. Check that the alignment marks are still correctly aligned.

37 Refit the oil pump drive chain and sprocket with reference to Section 12.

38 Refit the sump with reference to Section 11.

39 Refit the timing chain cover and crankshaft pulley/vibration damper as described in Section 6.

Tensioner rail

Removal

40 Remove the cylinder head as described in Section 10.

41 Remove the timing chain cover as described in Section 6.

42 Remove the timing chain tensioner as described previously in this Section.

43 Remove the tensioner rail from its pin.

Inspection

44 Examine the tensioner rail for signs of excessive wear, damage or cracks; and renew if necessary.

Refitting

45 Locate the tensioner rail on the pin.

46 Refit the timing chain tensioner as described previously in this Section.

47 Refit the timing chain cover as described in Section 6.

48 Refit the cylinder head as described in Section 10.

---

9 Camshafts, camshaft housing and hydraulic tappets – removal, inspection and refitting

Camshafts

Removal

1 Remove the exhaust camshaft sprocket as described in Section 8. Making sure that the timing chain remains engaged with the crankshaft sprocket, using wire to tie it to one side.

2 The camshaft bearing caps are numbered from the timing chain end of the engine **(see illustration)**. Check the bearing caps to ensure that marks are present, and if necessary make suitable marks using quick-drying paint or a centre-punch.

3 The camshaft bearing cap bolts must now be slackened according to the following information, and the camshafts removed.

 Warning: It is absolutely essential to observe the correct sequence when slackening the camshaft

9.2 Check the markings on the bearing caps

bearing cap bolts, because the camshafts are very sensitive to fracturing.

  a) *Progressively slacken and then remove the bolts from bearing caps 1, 3 and 5.*

  b) *Lift off bearing caps 1, 3 and 5, keeping them in order* **(see illustration)**. *Note that the bearing caps locate on dowels – if they are stuck, tap gently using a soft-faced mallet.*

  c) *Progressively slacken the bearing cap bolts for bearing caps 2 and 4, in one-turn stages until all pressure on the camshaft is relieved. Take care not to allow uneven pressure on the camshaft, as the bolts are unscrewed.*

  d) *Lift off bearing caps 2 and 4, again keeping them in order.*

  e) *Lift the inlet and exhaust camshafts from the camshaft housing and recover the thrustwashers from No 3 bearing location.*

Inspection

4 Thoroughly clean the camshafts and the housing/caps.

5 Examine the camshaft journals and cam lobes for any sign of scoring, wear grooves or pitting, and if apparent, renew the relevant camshaft. Any damage of this nature may be attributable to a blocked oil passage in the cylinder head, and careful examination should be carried out to determine the cause.

6 Examine the bearing surfaces in the camshaft housing and bearing caps for excessive wear and scoring. If evident, renew the components together with the camshafts.

Refitting

7 Lubricate the camshaft journals and the

9.3 Note the position of the bearing caps

9.7 Lubricate the camshaft bearing housing

9.8a Lower the camshaft into position . . .

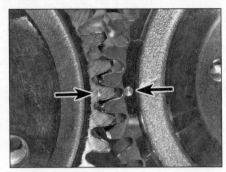

9.8b . . . and align the timing marks

bearing locations in the camshaft housing/caps with clean engine oil **(see illustration)**. Also lubricate the hydraulic tappets.

8 Locate the inlet camshaft in the left-hand side of the camshaft housing, and then locate the exhaust camshaft in the right-hand side, at the same time engaging the gears at the fronts of the camshafts so that the timing marks are aligned **(see illustrations)**, see Section 3.

9 Locate the bearing caps in position over the camshafts and tighten the securing bolts according to the following information, ensuring that the bearing caps and thrustwashers are fitted to their original locations.

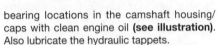 **Warning: It is absolutely essential to observe the correct sequence when tightening the camshaft bearing cap bolts, in order to avoid damage to the camshaft.**

a) Fit bearing caps 2 and 4, then insert the bolts, and tighten them progressively in one-turn stages to the specified torque. Take care not to allow uneven pressure on the camshaft as the bolts are tightened.

b) Fit bearing caps 1, 3 and 5, then insert the bolts, and tighten them progressively in one-turn stages to the specified torque.

10 Refit the exhaust camshaft sprocket as described in Section 8.

Camshaft lower housing and hydraulic tappets

Removal

11 Remove the camshafts as described earlier in this Section. This procedure includes removal of the camshaft cover and cylinder head front cover.

12 Obtain a container with 16 compartments and number the compartments to indicate the location of the hydraulic tappets. Remove each hydraulic tappet in turn from the camshaft housing and store them in the container **(see illustration)**.

13 Lift the camshaft lower housing from the cylinder head **(see illustration)**.

Inspection

14 Clean the camshaft housing and cylinder head and check for damage and wear. Also refer to paragraphs 4 to 6.

15 The operation of the removed hydraulic tappets can be checked as follows.

a) Press down firmly on the top of each tappet, using a blunt instrument such as a wooden hammer handle, for approximately 10 seconds.

b) Note how far the piston moves when depressed.

c) Repeat the operation for all the tappets in turn.

d) If any one tappet can be depressed more easily than the others, renew it.

16 Check the hydraulic tappets and the bores in the camshaft lower housing for wear and scoring. If any serious damage or wear is evident, the camshaft housing and tappets must be renewed.

Refitting

17 Locate the lower housing back into position on the cylinder head.

18 Lubricate the hydraulic tappet bores in the camshaft housing with clean engine oil, then locate each hydraulic tappet in its original position in the housing **(see illustration)**.

19 Complete the rest of the installation by reversing the removal procedure.

10 Cylinder head – removal, inspection and refitting

Note: *New cylinder head bolts may be required – see text.*

Removal

1 Ensure that the engine is cold before attempting to remove the cylinder head.

2 Apply the handbrake, then jack up the front of the vehicle and support it on axle stands (see *Jacking and vehicle support*).

3 Disconnect the battery negative (earth) lead and position it away from the terminal.

4 Raise the bonnet to the fully-open position.

5 Drain the engine oil and the coolant as described in Chapter 1.

6 Remove the camshafts, hydraulic tappets and lower housing, as described in Section 9.

7 Remove the thermostat housing from the right-hand side front of the cylinder head, as described in Chapter 3.

8 Remove the inlet manifold as described in Chapter 4A.

9 Undo the retaining bolts and remove the oil feed pipe to the turbocharger from the cylinder head **(see illustration)**.

10 Undo the retaining bolts from the turbo-

9.12 Remove the hydraulic tappets, noting their position

9.13 Removing the camshaft lower housing

9.18 Lubricate the hydraulic tappets with clean oil

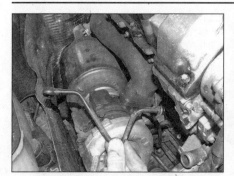

10.9 Remove the turbo oil feed pipe

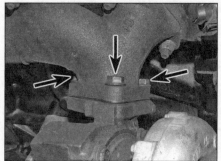

10.10 Turbo-to-manifold retaining bolts

10.11 Exhaust mounting bracket (where fitted)

charger to the exhaust manifold **(see illustration)**.

11 Depending on model, it may be necessary to undo the retaining nut from the exhaust mounting bracket at the rear of the exhaust manifold **(see illustration)**.

12 Using a socket through the cylinder head aperture, unscrew and remove the two bolts securing the timing chain cover to the cylinder head **(see illustration)**.

13 Make a final check to ensure that all relevant hoses and wires have been disconnected from the cylinder head.

14 Progressively loosen the cylinder head bolts, working in the **reverse** order to the tightening sequence **(see illustration 10.31)**. Remove all cylinder head bolts.

15 Release the cylinder head from the cylinder block and locating dowels by rocking it. Do not prise between the mating faces of the cylinder head and block, as this may damage the gasket faces.

16 With the aid of an assistant, carefully lift the cylinder head, complete with exhaust manifold, from the block, and manoeuvre it out from the engine compartment.

17 Recover the cylinder head gasket.

18 If necessary, remove the exhaust manifold from the cylinder head.

Inspection

19 Refer to Chapter 2C for details of cylinder head dismantling and reassembly.

20 The mating faces of the cylinder head and block must be perfectly clean before refitting the head. Use a scraper to remove all traces of

gasket and carbon, and also clean the tops of the pistons. Take particular care with the cylinder head, as the metal is easily damaged. Also make sure that debris is not allowed to enter the oil and water passages. Using adhesive tape and paper, seal the water, oil and bolt holes in the cylinder block. To prevent carbon entering the gap between the pistons and bores, smear a little grease in the gap. After cleaning each piston, rotate the crankshaft so that the piston moves **down** the bore, and then wipe out the grease and carbon with a cloth rag.

21 Check the block and head for nicks, deep scratches and other damage. If very slight, they may be removed from the cylinder block carefully with a file. More serious damage may be repaired by machining, but this is a specialist job.

22 If warpage of the cylinder head is suspected, use a straight-edge to check it for distortion, with reference to Chapter 2C.

23 Clean out the bolt holes in the block using a pipe cleaner or thin rag and a screwdriver. Make sure that all oil and water is removed, otherwise there is a possibility of the block being cracked by hydraulic pressure when the bolts are tightened.

24 Examine the bolt threads and the threads in the cylinder block for damage. If necessary, use the correct size tap to chase out the threads in the block.

25 The manufacturers recommend that the cylinder head bolts are measured, to determine whether renewal is necessary; however, some owners may wish to renew all the bolts as a matter of course.

26 Measure the length of each bolt from the base of the head to the end of the shank **(see illustration)**. If the bolt length is greater than the maximum specified, the bolts should be renewed.

27 Reassemble the cylinder head with reference to Chapter 2C. Where applicable, refit the exhaust manifold together with a new gasket.

Refitting

28 Locate the new cylinder head gasket on the block, making sure that it is the correct way up and positioned over the location dowels.

29 With the aid of an assistant, lower the cylinder head carefully onto the block.

30 Oil the threads and the cylinder head contact faces of the cylinder head bolts, then insert them and screw them into the cylinder block by hand. Ensure that the bolts are fitted to their correct locations as noted on removal.

31 Tighten the cylinder head bolts in the order shown **(see illustration overleaf)**, and in the stages given in the Specifications – ie, tighten all bolts to the Stage 1 torque, then tighten all bolts to the Stage 2 torque, and so on.

32 Tighten the two bolts securing the timing chain cover to the cylinder head at the front of the engine.

33 Refit the turbocharger to the exhaust manifold and tighten the retaining bolts.

34 Refit the retaining nut to the exhaust mounting bracket at the rear of the exhaust manifold.

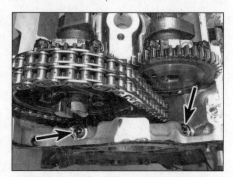

10.12 Cylinder head-to-timing chain cover bolts

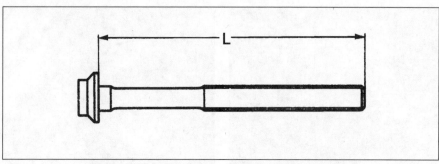

10.26 Measure the length (L) of the cylinder head bolts

See Specifications for maximum length

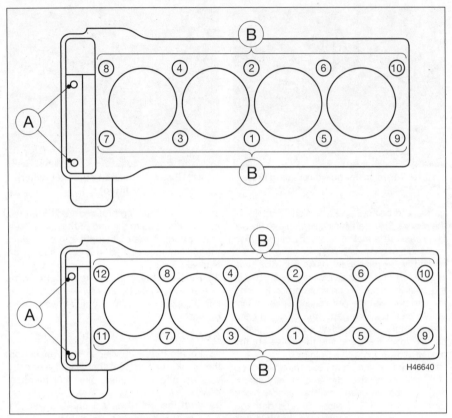

10.31 Cylinder head bolt (B) tightening sequence

A Bolts securing cylinder head to timing chain cover

35 Refit the oil feed pipe to the turbocharger from the cylinder head.
36 Refit the inlet manifold, as described in Chapter 4A.
37 Refit the thermostat housing, as described in Chapter 3.
38 Refit the camshafts, hydraulic tappets and lower housing, as described in Section 9.
39 Refill the cooling system and refill the engine with oil with reference to Chapter 1.
40 Reconnect the battery negative lead.
41 When all components are refitted, start the engine and check carefully around the engine for any oil leaks, or coolant leaks.
42 Refit the engine compartment undershield and lower the vehicle to the ground.

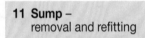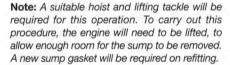

11 Sump –
removal and refitting

Note: A suitable hoist and lifting tackle will be required for this operation. To carry out this procedure, the engine will need to be lifted, to allow enough room for the sump to be removed. A new sump gasket will be required on refitting.

Removal

1 Apply the handbrake, then jack up the front of the vehicle and support it on axle stands (see *Jacking and vehicle support*). Remove both front roadwheels.

2 Drain the engine oil as described in Chapter 1. On completion, check the copper washer and renew it if necessary, then refit the drain plug and tighten to the specified torque.
3 Undo the two retaining bolts at each end of the front crossmember and move it to one side, the bonnet release cable can be disconnected if required.
4 Remove the cooling fan and shroud from the rear of the radiator, with reference to Chapter 3.
5 Refer to Chapter 4B and detach the exhaust downpipe from the manifold, then unbolt the exhaust mounting from the transmission and support the exhaust on an axle stand.
6 Disconnect the wiring from the oil level sensor. If necessary, the sensor may be removed from the sump **(see illustration)**.
7 Attach a suitable hoist to the engine and take the weight of the engine.
8 Unscrew the nuts from the bottom of the engine mountings at each side of the engine **(see illustration)**.
9 Unscrew the bolts securing the transmission to the rear engine mounting bracket. Leave the bracket attached to the underbody.
10 Raise the engine and transmission as far as possible. Make sure it is adequately supported, as the next procedure involves working beneath the engine.
11 Unscrew the bolts securing the transmission to the rear of the sump, then unscrew the remaining sump-to-engine bolts and lower the sump from the cylinder block **(see illustration)**. Note the location of the bolts as some are of different lengths. Where applicable, recover the gasket. If the sump is stuck, use a hide or wooden mallet to tap its sides in order to release it. Do not drive a screwdriver between the sump and cylinder block as this may damage the mating surfaces.
12 It is recommended that the oil and oil filter are renewed whenever the sump is removed. Before refitting the sump, it is a good idea to remove the oil filter in order to allow the oil to drain from the cylinder block oil gallery and internal oilways.

Refitting

13 Thoroughly clean the mating surfaces of the sump and cylinder block.

11.6 Disconnect the wiring connector from the oil level sensor

11.8 Engine mounting lower mounting nuts

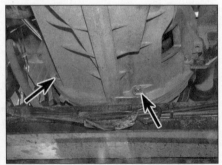

11.11 Sump-to-transmission bolts

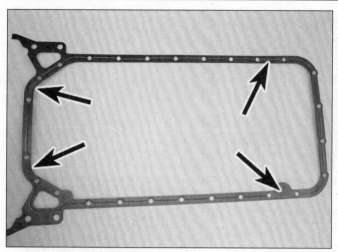

11.14a Note points where sealant is located on gasket

11.14b Fit sump using new gasket

14 Place the gasket onto the sump and align it with the bolt holes in the cylinder block **(see illustrations)**.

15 With the sump in place, insert all of the bolts finger-tight. Make sure all bolts are fitted in the correct position, some are different lengths, as noted on removal.

16 The bolts securing the transmission to the sump can now be tightened to the specified torque. This will ensure the rear of the sump is correctly aligned with the transmission, as if it is not aligned correctly, vibration and noise may occur.

17 Tighten the remaining sump bolts to the specified torque.

18 Complete the rest of the installation by reversing the removal procedure, referring to the relevant Chapters.

19 Renew the oil filter and refill the engine with clean engine oil with reference to Chapter 1.

20 When all components are refitted, start the engine and check carefully around the sump for any oil leaks.

12 Oil pump –
removal, inspection and refitting

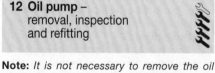

Note: *It is not necessary to remove the oil pump from the crankcase to remove the oil pressure relief valve components.*

Removal

1 Remove the sump as described in Section 11. Note that this involves suspending the engine with a hoist.

2 The sprocket must be disengaged from the chain as the oil pump is being removed.

3 Unscrew the mounting bolts, withdraw the oil pump from the bottom of the crankcase, and recover the O-ring seal. **(see illustration)**.

4 Press against the chain tensioner and disengage the sprocket from the chain as the pump is being removed **(see illustration)**.

Inspection

5 With the exception of the oil pressure relief valve components, the oil pump is a sealed unit. To remove the oil pressure relief valve components, proceed as follows.

6 Unscrew the relief valve plug, in the side of the timing chain cover **(see illustration)**. Take care, as the plug will be pushed out by the spring pressure when it reaches the end of the threads. **Note:** *If a sealing ring is present it will need to be renewed on refitting.*

7 Withdraw the spring, guide pin and piston, noting the orientation of the piston.

8 Thoroughly clean all components, and examine them for wear and damage. If there is any sign of excessive wear or damage, renew the appropriate component(s) – pay particular attention to the spring.

9 Also clean the oil pump intake strainer thoroughly, however, do not immerse the oil pump in cleaning solvent.

10 Examine the drive chain for wear and damage. If necessary, renew the chain as described later in this Section.

11 Reassemble the oil pressure relief valve using a reversal of the dismantling procedure, lubricating each component with fresh engine oil before fitting. Tighten the relief valve plug to the specified torque.

12 With the oil pump upright, pour fresh engine oil into the upper aperture while turning the pump shaft slowly. This will prime the oil pump so that normal oil pressure will be resumed as soon as possible after starting the engine.

Refitting

13 Check that the sprocket is engaged with the drive chain correctly and then locate the oil pump onto the crankcase. Insert the mounting bolts and tighten the bolts to the specified torque.

14 Refit the sump as described in Section 11.

12.3 Oil pump mounting bolts

12.4 Press against the chain tensioner

12.6 Relief valve retaining plug

13.3 Lock the flywheel in position

13.4a Remove the flywheel

13.4b Location dowel for refitting flywheel

13 Flywheel/crankshaft spigot bearing – removal, inspection and refitting

Note: *The flywheel mounting bolts must be renewed on refitting.*

Removal

1 Remove the manual transmission as described in Chapter 7.

2 Remove the clutch as described in Chapter 6.

3 The flywheel must be held stationary while the mounting bolts are loosened. To do this, have an assistant insert a wide-bladed screwdriver in the starter ring gear teeth through the access hole in the rear of the sump. Mercedes-Benz technicians use a special tool bolted to the sump incorporating serrations which engage with the ring gear teeth. Alternatively, make up a tool as shown **(see illustration)** and bolt it to a starter motor mounting hole.

4 Unscrew the mounting bolts, then lift the flywheel from the rear of the crankshaft **(see illustrations)**. Note that the location dowel ensures the flywheel can only be fitted in one position.

Inspection

5 If the teeth on the flywheel starter ring gear are badly worn, it may be possible to fit a new ring gear, however this work should be entrusted to a Mercedes-Benz dealer who will have the necessary equipment to heat the new gear to the critical temperature in order to fit it. Overheating the gear will affect its hardness, resulting in rapid wear. The old gear may be removed by drilling it and using a cold chisel to split it. Take care not to drill into the flywheel.

6 If the clutch friction face of the flywheel is deeply scored, cracked or otherwise damaged, the flywheel must be renewed. However, it may be possible to have it surface-ground, but seek the advice of an engine reconditioning specialist. Check the condition of the spigot bearing in the centre of the flywheel or in the end of the crankshaft, and renew if necessary **(see illustration)**.

7 If spigot bearing needs changing, check the fitted position of the bearing in the centre of the flywheel first. Using a puller/slide hammer, withdraw the bearing from the end of the crankshaft and then fit the new bearing to the depth noted on removal **(see illustrations)**.

8 It is recommended that the flywheel securing bolts be renewed whenever removed.

Refitting

9 Commence refitting by cleaning the mating faces of the crankshaft and flywheel.

10 Make sure that the location dowel is in position in the end of the crankshaft.

11 Locate the flywheel onto the crankshaft, then insert the new mounting bolts and hand-tighten them.

12 Lock the flywheel using the method employed during removal, then tighten the securing bolts progressively in a diagonal sequence to the specified torque first, then tighten all the bolts by the specified angle **(see illustration)**.

13 Refit the clutch as described in Chapter 6.

14 Refit the manual transmission with reference to Chapter 7.

13.6 Spigot bearing fitted in the flywheel

13.7a Insert internal puller . . .

13.7b . . . and withdraw the bearing

13.7c Use a socket to tap bearing back into position

13.12 Use an angle gauge to tighten the retaining bolts

14 Crankshaft oil seals – renewal

Front oil seal

1 Remove the crankshaft pulley/vibration damper and inspect it as described in Section 5.
2 Measure and note the fitted depth of the oil seal in the timing chain cover.
3 Prise the oil seal from the cover using a hooked instrument. Alternatively, drill a small hole in the oil seal, and use a self-tapping screw and a pair of pliers to remove it.
4 Clean the seal location in the timing cover, and also clean the oil seal contact surface on the crankshaft pulley/vibration damper. Examine the seal contact surface of the pulley/vibration damper for an excessive wear groove. If evident, refer to Section 5.
5 Dip the new oil seal in clean engine oil, and press it into the timing chain cover (open end first) to the previously-noted depth, using a suitable tube or socket.
6 Refit the crankshaft pulley/vibration damper as described in Section 5.

Rear oil seal

Note: *The rear oil seal is integral with the oil seal housing and should be renewed whenever it is removed.*

7 Remove the flywheel as described in Section 13.
8 Unscrew the retaining bolts and remove the oil seal/housing from the cylinder block (see illustration).
9 New oil seal/housings are supplied with a plastic sleeve on the inside of the seal to aid refitting of the seal over the end of the crankshaft. DO NOT remove the plastic fitting sleeve until the oil seal housing is in its fitted position.
10 Ensure that the cylinder block mating face of the oil seal housing is free from all traces of old sealant, oil and grease, and then apply a 1.5 to 2.5 mm thick bead of silicone sealant (A 003 989 98 20 or equivalent) to the oil seal housing. Note that the sealant should be run around the inside of the bolt holes in the oil seal housing. The housing must be fitted within 10 minutes of applying the sealant. Also

apply sealant at the area where the sump, oil seal housing and cylinder block meet.
11 Fit the new oil seal housing over the crankshaft and onto the cylinder block, keeping the plastic sleeve in position.
12 Fit the retaining bolts and tighten them to the specified torque setting.
13 Remove the plastic fitting sleeve from the new oil seal housing.
14 Refit the flywheel with reference to Section 13.

15 Cylinder head front cover – removal and refitting

1 Disconnect the battery negative (earth) lead and position it away from the terminal.
2 Remove the camshaft cover as described in Section 4.
3 Remove the brake vacuum pump as described in Chapter 9.
4 Remove the timing chain tensioner as described in Section 8.
5 Remove the fuel pre-delivery pump (depending on model), as described in Chapter 4A.
6 Undo the retaining bolts from cover on the front of the cylinder head.
7 Using a screwdriver release the locking ratchet in the upper timing chain slide rail, and then withdraw the cover from the front of the cylinder head.

16 Engine/transmission mountings – inspection and renewal

Inspection

1 Three engine/transmission mountings are used, one on either side of the engine, and one under the rear of the transmission.
2 For improved access, raise the front of the vehicle and support it securely on axle stands (see *Jacking and vehicle support*).
3 Check the condition of the mounting rubber to see if it is cracked, hardened or separated from the metal at any point. Renew the mounting if any such damage or deterioration is evident.

14.8 Rear crankshaft oil seal/housing bolts

4 Check that all the mounting bolts are securely tightened.
5 Using a large screwdriver or metal bar, check for wear in the mounting by carefully levering against it to check for free play. Where this is not possible, enlist the aid of an assistant to move the engine/transmission back-and-forth, or from side-to-side, while you observe the mounting. If excessive free play is found, check first that the fasteners are correctly secured, and then renew any worn components as required.

Renewal

Front engine mountings

6 Support the engine, either using a hoist and lifting tackle connected to the engine lifting brackets, or by positioning a jack and interposed block of wood under the sump. Ensure that the engine is adequately supported before proceeding.
7 Depending on which engine mounting requires removal, it may be necessary to remove the alternator or turbocharger to make access easier. See the relevant Chapters to remove any other components.
8 Unscrew and remove the engine mounting upper bolt. Depending on model, disconnect the earth cable from the top of the engine mounting (see illustrations).
9 If working on the right-hand engine mounting, below the exhaust manifold/turbo, remove the heat shield.
10 Working under the vehicle, remove the engine undershield and undo the engine mounting lower nuts (see illustration).

16.8a Upper mounting bolt (note earth cable) – left-hand mounting

16.8b Upper mounting bolt – right-hand mounting

16.10 Engine mounting lower retaining nuts

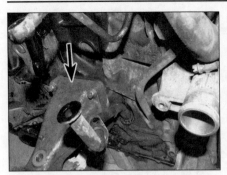

16.11a Engine mounting bracket –
right-hand side

16.11b Engine mounting bracket –
left-hand side

16.15a Unscrew the rear mounting bracket
bolts . . .

16.15b . . . and undo the mounting upper
securing nut

11 Raise the engine as necessary, taking care not to stretch any hoses or wiring, and remove the mounting. If necessary, unbolt the mounting bracket from the side of the cylinder block **(see illustrations)**.

12 Refitting is a reversal of removal, and tighten the mounting bolts to the specified torque.

Rear engine/transmission mounting

13 Raise the front of the vehicle and support it securely on axle stands (see *Jacking and vehicle support*).

14 Support the transmission using a jack and interposed block of wood.

15 Unbolt the mounting bracket from the underbody, then unscrew the bolts securing the mounting rubber to the rear of the transmission. Lower the bracket together with the mounting from the underbody **(see illustrations)**.

16 The mounting rubber can then be unbolted from the top of the mounting bracket.

17 Refitting is a reversal of removal.

Chapter 2 Part B
2.9 litre engine in-car repair procedures

Contents

Degrees of difficulty

Easy, suitable for novice with little experience	Fairly easy, suitable for beginner with some experience	Fairly difficult, suitable for competent DIY mechanic	Difficult, suitable for experienced DIY mechanic	Very difficult, suitable for expert DIY or professional

Specifications

General

Engine code	602.980
Displacement	2874 cc
Bore	89.0 mm
Stroke	92.4 mm
Direction of engine rotation	Clockwise (viewed from front of vehicle)
No 1 cylinder location	Timing chain end
Firing order	1-2-4-5-3
Compression pressures:	
Minimum compression pressure	18.0 bars (approx)
Maximum difference between cylinders	3.0 bars
Compression ratio	19.5:1

Camshaft

Endfloat:	
New engine	0.030 to 0.100 mm
Wear limit	0.150 mm
Camshaft bearing running clearance:	
New engine	0.050 to 0.091 mm
Wear limit	0.150 mm

Valve lifters

Maximum clearance between cam lobe and valve lifter (see Section 9)	0.40 mm

Cylinder head bolts

Maximum length:	
M10 x 80 mm bolts	83.6 mm
M10 x 102 mm bolts	105.6 mm
M10 x 115 mm bolts	118.6 mm

Lubrication system

Minimum oil pressure:	
At idle speed	0.3 bar
At 3000 rpm	3.0 bars

Flywheel bolts

Minimum diameter	8.0 mm
Maximum length	22.5 mm

Torque wrench settings

	Nm	lbf ft
Auxiliary drivebelt idler pulley bolt	25	18
Auxiliary drivebelt tensioner damper strut bolts:		
Upper bolt	25	18
Lower bolt	20	15
Auxiliary drivebelt tensioner pivot pin	100	74
Auxiliary drivebelt tensioner securing bolt	10	7
Big-end bearing cap bolts:		
Stage 1	40	30
Stage 2	Angle-tighten a further 90 to 100°	
Camshaft bearing cap bolts	25	18
Camshaft cover bolts	10	7
Camshaft sprocket bolt:		
M10 hexagonal head bolt	65	48
M11 splined bolt:		
Stage 1	25	18
Stage 2	Angle-tighten a further 90°	
Coolant pump pulley bolts:		
Hexagon head bolt	10	7
Torx head bolt	14	10
Crankshaft pulley/vibration damper hub bolt (see Section 5):		
Bolt with spring washers	320	236
Bolt with conical washer:		
Stage 1	200	148
Stage 2	Angle-tighten a further 90°	
Crankshaft pulley/vibration damper-to-hub bolts	25	18
Crankshaft rear oil seal housing bolts	10	7
Cylinder block coolant drain plug	30	22
Cylinder head bolts:		
Stage 1	15	11
Stage 2	35	26
Stage 3	Angle-tighten a further 90°	
Stage 4	Wait for 10 minutes	
Stage 5	Angle-tighten a further 90°	
Cylinder head-to-timing chain cover bolts	25	18
Engine mountings:		
Engine mounting bracket bolts	25	18
Engine mounting damper securing bolts	10	7
Engine mounting-to-crossmember bolts	40	30
Engine mounting-to-mounting bracket bolts	25	18
Engine/transmission mounting adjuster bolt	30	22
Engine/transmission mounting crossmember-to-underbody bolts	35	26
Engine/transmission mounting-to-crossmember bolts	25	18
Engine/transmission mounting-to-transmission nut	65	48
Engine-to-transmission bolts:		
M10 x 40 mm bolts	55	41
M10 x 90 mm bolts	45	33
Flywheel bolts:		
Stage 1:		
Standard flywheel	30	22
'Dual-mass' flywheel	40	30
Stage 2	Angle-tighten a further 90 to 100°	
Fuel filter securing bolts	16	12
Main bearing cap bolts:		
M11 bolts:		
Stage 1	55	41
Stage 2	Angle-tighten a further 90 to 100°	
M12 bolts	90	66
Oil baffle plate bolts	25	18
Oil drain plug	25	18
Oil pressure relief valve plug	50	37
Oil pump securing bolts	25	18
Oil pump sprocket bolt	32	24
Sump auxiliary section bolts	10	7
Sump bolts:		
M6 bolts	10	7
M8 bolts	25	18

Torque wrench settings (continued)

	Nm	lbf ft
Timing chain cover bolts:		
M6 bolts	10	7
M8 bolts	25	18
Timing chain tensioner body to cylinder block.	80	59
Timing chain tensioner cover plug	40	30

1 General information

How to use this Chapter

This Part of Chapter 2 describes the repair procedures that can reasonably be carried out on the engine while it remains in the vehicle. If the engine has been removed from the vehicle and is being dismantled as described in Part C, any preliminary dismantling procedures can be ignored.

Note that, while it may be possible physically to overhaul items such as the piston/connecting rod assemblies while the engine is in the vehicle, such tasks are not usually carried out as separate operations. Usually, several additional procedures are required (not to mention the cleaning of components and oilways); for this reason, all such tasks are classed as major overhaul procedures, and are described in Part C of this Chapter.

Part C describes the removal of the engine/transmission from the vehicle, and the full overhaul procedures that can then be carried out.

Engine description

The engine is a 5-cylinder in-line single overhead camshaft design, mounted in-line ('north-south') with the transmission mounted on the rear of the engine.

The crankshaft is supported in six main bearings, and the endfloat thrustwashers are fitted either side of No 4 bearing location.

The connecting rods are attached to the crankshaft by horizontally-split big-end bearings, and to the pistons by fully-floating gudgeon pins retained by circlips. The alloy pistons are fitted with three piston rings, two compression rings and one oil control ring.

The camshaft is driven from the crankshaft sprocket by a double-row chain. The timing chain also drives the fuel injection pump.

The camshaft is supported in bearings in the cylinder head, and actuates the valves directly, via hydraulic valve lifters.

The oil pump is chain-driven from the front of the crankshaft.

Operations with engine in vehicle

The following operations can be carried out without having to remove the engine from the vehicle:

a) Removal and refitting of the cylinder head.
b) Removal and refitting of the timing chain and sprockets.
c) Removal and refitting of the camshaft.
d) Removal and refitting of the sump.
e) Removal and refitting of the big-end bearings, connecting rods, and pistons.*
f) Removal and refitting of the oil pump.
g) Renewal of the engine/transmission mountings.
h) Removal and refitting of the flywheel.

* Although it is possible to remove these components with the engine in place, for reasons of access and cleanliness it is recommended that the engine be removed.

2 Compression and leakdown tests – description and interpretation

Compression test

Note: *A compression tester designed for diesel engines must be used for this test.*

1 When engine performance is down, or if misfiring occurs which cannot be attributed to the ignition or fuel systems, a compression test can provide diagnostic clues as to the engine's condition. If the test is performed regularly, it can give warning of trouble before any other symptoms become apparent.

2 The tester is connected to an adapter, which screws into the glow plug or injector hole. On these engines, an adapter suitable for use in the injector holes is preferable. It is unlikely to be worthwhile buying such a tester for occasional use, but it may be possible to borrow or hire one – if not, have the test performed by a garage.

3 Unless specific instructions to the contrary are supplied with the tester, observe the following points.

a) The battery must be in a good state of charge, the air filter must be clean, and the engine should be at normal operating temperature.
b) All the injectors should be removed before starting the test.
c) The stop solenoid must be disconnected, to prevent the engine from running or fuel from being discharged.

4 There is no need to hold the accelerator pedal down during the test, because the diesel engine air inlet is not throttled.

5 Crank the engine on the starter motor.

After one or two revolutions, the compression pressure should build-up to a maximum figure, and then stabilise. Record the highest reading obtained.

6 Repeat the test on the remaining cylinders, recording the pressure in each.

7 The cause of poor compression is less easy to establish on a diesel engine than on a petrol one. The effect of introducing oil into the cylinders ('wet' testing) is not conclusive, because there is a risk that the oil will sit in the swirl chamber or in the recess in the piston crown instead of passing to the rings. However, the following can be used as a rough guide to diagnosis.

8 All cylinders should produce very similar pressures; a difference of more than 3.0 bars between any two cylinders indicates a fault. Note that the compression should build-up quickly in a healthy engine; low compression on the first stroke, followed by gradually increasing pressure on successive strokes, indicates worn piston rings. A low compression reading on the first stroke, which does not build-up during successive strokes, indicates leaking valves or a blown head gasket (a cracked head could also be the cause). Deposits on the undersides of the valve heads can also cause low compression.

9 A low reading from two adjacent cylinders is almost certainly due to the head gasket having blown between them; the presence of coolant in the engine oil will confirm this.

10 If the compression reading is unusually high, the combustion chambers are probably coated with carbon deposits. If this is the case, the cylinder head should be removed and decarbonised.

11 On completion of the test, refit the injectors or the glow plugs, and reconnect the stop solenoid.

Leakdown test

12 A leakdown test measures the rate at which compressed air fed into the cylinder is lost. It is an alternative to a compression test, and in many ways is better, since the escaping air provides easy identification of where a pressure loss is occurring (piston rings, valves or head gasket).

13 The equipment needed for leakdown testing is unlikely to be available to the home mechanic. If poor compression is suspected, have the test performed by a suitably-equipped garage.

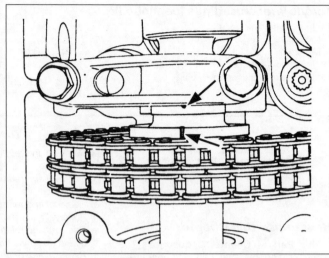

3.4a O/T (TDC) mark on crankshaft pulley/vibration damper aligned with pointer on timing chain cover

3.4b TDC notch in camshaft flange aligned with raised rib on camshaft bearing cap

3 Engine assembly and valve timing marks – general information and usage

⚠️ **Warning: When turning the engine, do not turn the engine using the camshaft sprocket bolt, and do not turn the engine backwards (ie, anti-clockwise).**

1 Top Dead Centre (TDC) is the highest point in the cylinder that each piston reaches as it travels up and down when the crankshaft turns. Each piston reaches TDC at the end of the compression stroke and again at the end of the exhaust stroke, but TDC generally refers to piston position on the compression stroke. No 1 piston is at the timing chain end of the engine.

2 Positioning No 1 piston at TDC is an essential part of many procedures, such as timing chain removal and camshaft removal.

3 Remove the camshaft cover as described in Section 4.

4 Using a suitable socket on the crankshaft pulley/vibration damper hub bolt (on some models, it may be necessary to remove the cooling fan cowl and blades for access), turn the crankshaft clockwise until the following marks are aligned (see illustrations).

a) The O/T (TDC) mark on the crankshaft pulley/vibration damper is aligned with the pointer on the timing chain cover.
b) The TDC notch in the flange at the front of the camshaft is aligned with the raised rib on the front camshaft bearing cap.

5 When the marks are aligned as described in paragraph 4, No 1 piston is at TDC on the firing stroke. If the timing chain is to be removed, do not turn the camshaft or the crankshaft until the chain has been refitted.

4 Camshaft cover – removal and refitting

Note: A new gasket may be required on refitting.

Removal

1 Open the bonnet and disconnect the battery negative lead.

2 Where applicable, disconnect and remove the turbocharger-to-inlet manifold air trunking, to allow sufficient clearance to remove the camshaft cover.

3 Disconnect the breather hose from the camshaft cover.

4 Where applicable, disconnect the throttle cable operating-lever, which runs across the top of the camshaft cover. If the lever adjuster bolt is removed, make alignment marks between the two sections of the lever before removing the bolt.

5 Unscrew the camshaft cover securing bolts and, where applicable, recover the washers.

6 Lift the camshaft cover from the cylinder head. If the cover is stuck, try rocking by hand, and if necessary tap carefully with a soft-faced mallet – take care, as the cover is easily damaged.

7 Recover the gasket.

Refitting

8 Examine the condition of the gasket, and renew if necessary.

9 Locate the gasket in the grooves in the camshaft cover, starting at the front and rear.

10 Lay the cover in position on the cylinder head, ensuring that the gasket locates correctly, then refit the securing bolts.

11 Tighten the bolts progressively to the specified torque.

12 Reconnect the breather hose.

13 Where applicable, refit the turbocharger-to-inlet manifold trunking.

14 Reconnect the battery negative lead, and close the bonnet.

5 Crankshaft pulley/ vibration damper and hub – removal and refitting

Pulley/vibration damper

Removal

1 Open the bonnet and disconnect the battery negative lead.

2 Remove the radiator as described in Chapter 3.

3 Remove the auxiliary drivebelt as described in Chapter 1.

4 Unscrew the securing bolts, and withdraw the crankshaft pulley/vibration damper. If necessary, counterhold the pulley/vibration damper using a socket or spanner on the pulley/vibration damper hub securing bolt.

Refitting

5 Refitting is a reversal of removal, refit the auxiliary drivebelt as described in Chapter 1, and refit the radiator as described in Chapter 3.

Hub

Removal

⚠️ **Warning: The hub securing bolt is very tight. A tool will be required to counterhold the hub, as the bolt is unscrewed. Do not attempt the job using inferior or poorly improvised tools; an injury or damage may result.**

Note: A torque wrench capable of providing the appropriate torque (see Specifications) will be required on refitting. A puller may be required to remove the hub.

6 Remove the crankshaft pulley/vibration damper as described previously in this Section.

7 Make up a tool to hold the hub. A suitable tool can be fabricated using two lengths of steel bar, joined by a large pivot bolt.

Bolt the holding tool to the hub using the pulley/vibration damper-to-hub bolts **(see illustration)**.

8 Using a socket and a long swing-bar, loosen the hub bolt. Note that the bolt is very tight.

9 Unscrew the hub bolt, and remove the four spring washers, or the large conical washer, as applicable.

10 Withdraw the hub from the front of the crankshaft. This may be a tight fit, so a suitable puller will be required.

Refitting

11 Align the hole in the hub with the locating pin in the crankshaft flange, and slide the hub onto the end of the crankshaft.

12 On models with spring washers fitted under the hub bolt head, oil the spring washers, then refit them with the convex side of each washer facing the hub bolt head **(see illustration)**.

13 On models with a conical washer under the hub bolt head, refit the washer with the larger diameter against the hub.

14 Oil the bolt threads, then refit the hub securing bolt.

15 Bolt the holding tool to the hub, as during removal, then tighten the hub securing bolt to the specified torque. Note the different torques for the two different types of bolt. Take care to avoid injury and/or damage.

16 Refit the crankshaft pulley/vibration damper as described previously in this Section.

6 Timing chain cover – removal and refitting

Note: *A hoist and lifting tackle will be required for this operation. Suitable sealant will be required on refitting, and it is advisable to renew the crankshaft front oil seal.*

Removal

1 Open the bonnet and disconnect the battery negative lead.

2 Where fitted, remove the engine undershield.

3 Remove the radiator and the cooling fan drive assembly as described in Chapter 3.

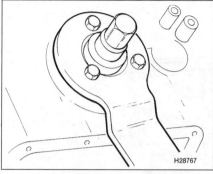

5.7 Special tool used to hold crankshaft pulley/vibration damper hub

4 Remove the crankshaft pulley/vibration damper and hub as described in Section 5.

5 Remove the auxiliary drivebelt tensioner as follows.

 a) *Pull off the plastic cover, unscrew the securing bolt, and remove the auxiliary drivebelt idler pulley.*

 b) *Unscrew the securing bolts, and remove the cooling fan pulley.*

 c) *Unscrew the securing bolts, and withdraw the tensioner damper strut. Recover any spacers and/or brackets from the bolts noting their locations.*

 d) *Using a pair of pliers, unhook the tension spring, noting its orientation to aid refitting.*

 e) *Where applicable, pull off the plastic cover, then unscrew the tensioner securing bolt and slide off the spacer sleeve (if applicable).*

 f) *Withdraw the tensioner and recover the spacer (where applicable).*

6 Remove the brake vacuum pump as described in Chapter 9.

7 Remove the alternator as described in Chapter 5.

8 Drain the engine oil as described in Chapter 1.

9 Remove the camshaft cover with reference to Section 4.

10 On models with air conditioning, place a cardboard or similar shield in front of the condenser to prevent damage during the following procedure.

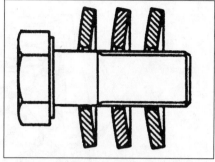

5.12 The convex side of the crankshaft pulley/vibration damper hub washers must face the bolt head

11 Where applicable, unscrew the two bolts from the front of the fuel filter/thermostat assembly.

12 Unbolt the engine oil level dipstick tube from the cylinder head.

13 Unscrew the securing bolts, and remove the alternator mounting bracket, noting the bolt locations.

14 Where applicable, mark the position of the crankshaft position sensor mounting bracket on the timing chain cover, then unbolt the sensor mounting bracket. Move the bracket to one side, clear of the working area.

15 Attach a hoist and suitable lifting tackle to the front engine lifting bracket.

16 Working under the vehicle, unscrew the lower engine mounting nuts (two on each side of the vehicle) **(see illustration)**.

17 Raise the hoist to lift the engine sufficiently for access to the sump-to-timing chain cover bolts.

18 Unscrew and remove the sump-to-timing chain cover bolts, and loosen the remaining sump bolts.

19 Lower the engine until it is again supported by the engine mountings.

20 Counterhold the nuts, and unscrew the three fuel injection pump mounting bolts from the timing chain cover **(see illustration)**. Recover the nuts.

21 Working through the aperture at the top of the cylinder head, unscrew the two bolts securing the cylinder head to the timing chain cover **(see illustration)**.

6.16 Lower engine mounting nuts (arrowed)

6.20 Counterhold the nuts and unscrew the three fuel injection pump mounting bolts (arrowed)

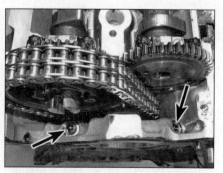

6.21 Unscrew the two bolts (arrowed) securing the cylinder head to the timing chain cover

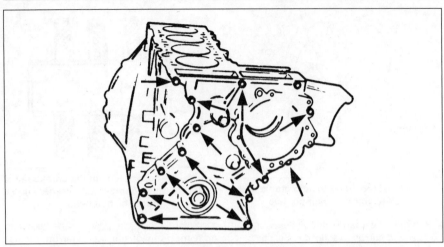

6.22 Unscrew the remaining timing chain cover securing bolts (arrowed)

22 Progressively unscrew the remaining timing chain cover securing bolts, noting their locations (see illustration).

23 Carefully pull the cover forwards from the cylinder block. If the cover is stuck, tap it around the edge gently using a soft-faced mallet – do not lever between the mating faces of the cover and the cylinder block.
Note: *Take care not to damage the cylinder head and sump gaskets as the timing chain cover is removed.*

Refitting

24 Commence refitting by thoroughly cleaning the mating faces of the timing chain cover, the cylinder block, and the cylinder head. Clean away all traces of old sealant.

25 Carefully check the condition of the cylinder head gasket. If the gasket has been damaged during the removal procedure, the cylinder head should be removed in order to renew the gasket, as described in Section 10.

26 Similarly, carefully check the condition of the sump gasket. If the gasket has been damaged during the removal procedure, the sump should be removed in order to renew the gasket, as described in Section 11.

27 It is advisable to renew the crankshaft oil seal in the in the cover as follows.

a) *Prise out the old oil seal using a screwdriver.*

b) *Clean the oil seal seating face in the timing chain cover.*

c) *Tap the new seal (dry) into position using a suitable tube or socket until the seal seats on the shoulder in the cover.*

28 A piece of thin plastic or tape wound around the front edge of the crankshaft flange is useful to prevent damage to the oil seal as the cover is fitted.

29 Apply sealant to the cylinder block mating face of the timing chain cover.

30 Coat the lips of the crankshaft oil seal with clean engine oil, then slide the cover into position over the crankshaft. Take great care not to damage the oil seal lips, or the cylinder head and sump gaskets as the cover is fitted.

31 Refit the timing chain cover-to-cylinder block securing bolts, and then tighten the bolts progressively to the specified torque.

32 Refit the cylinder head-to-timing chain cover bolts, and tighten them to the specified torque.

33 Where applicable, remove the tape from the front of the crankshaft.

34 Refit and tighten the fuel injection pump mounting bolts and nuts.

35 Raise the hoist to lift the engine sufficiently to enable the sump-to-timing chain cover bolts to be refitted.

36 Refit the sump-to-timing chain cover bolts, and tighten all the sump bolts progressively to the specified torque.

37 Lower the engine back onto the engine mountings, then refit and tighten the lower engine mounting nuts.

38 Where applicable, refit the crankshaft position sensor mounting bracket, ensuring that the bracket is aligned with the marks made before removal.

39 Refit the alternator mounting bracket, ensuring that the bolts are refitted to their correct locations.

40 Refit the bolt securing the dipstick to the cylinder head.

41 Where applicable, refit the fuel filter/thermostat assembly bolts.

42 Where applicable, remove the shield from the air conditioning condenser.

43 Refit the camshaft cover with reference to Section 4.

44 Refit the alternator with reference to Chapter 5.

45 Refit the brake vacuum pump as described in Chapter 9.

46 Refit the auxiliary drivebelt tensioner using a reversal of the procedure described in paragraph 6.

47 Refit the crankshaft pulley/vibration damper and hub as described in Section 5.

48 Refit the cooling fan drive assembly and the radiator as described in Chapter 3.

49 Refit the engine undershield.

50 Refill the engine with the correct grade and quantity of oil, as described in Chapter 1.

51 Reconnect the battery negative lead and lower the bonnet.

7 Timing chain – inspection and renewal

Inspection

1 Remove the camshaft cover as described in Section 4.

2 Using a socket on the crankshaft pulley/vibration damper hub bolt, turn the engine so that the whole length of the chain can be progressively viewed at the camshaft sprocket.

3 The chain should be renewed if the sprocket is worn or if the chain is worn (indicated by excessive lateral play between the links, and excessive noise in operation). It is wise to renew the chain in any case if the engine is to be dismantled for overhaul. Note that the rollers on a very badly worn chain may be slightly grooved. To avoid future problems, if there is any doubt at all about the condition of the chain, renew it.

Renewal

Note: *Removal of the timing chain using the following procedure entails the use of a portable electric grinder to grind off one of the chain links. Ensure that such a tool is available, as well as a new chain and new connecting link before proceeding.*

4 Disconnect the battery negative lead.

5 If not already done, remove the camshaft cover as described in Section 4.

6 Remove the fuel injectors as described in Chapter 4A.

7 Remove the cooling fan and shroud, as described in Chapter 3.

8 Remove the timing chain tensioner as described in Section 8.

9 Cover the camshaft and the chain opening in the timing cover with clean rags, but keep the rags clear of the camshaft sprocket.

10 Using a grinder, grind off the protruding lugs of one of the chain links at the camshaft sprocket – take great care not to damage the sprocket.

11 Pull off the chain link plate, then push the link out towards the rear of the chain.

12 Remove the rags, taking care not to allow any swarf to drop down into the timing chain housing.

13 Using the new link, connect one end of the new timing chain to the tail end of the old chain, in such a way that as the engine is turned (clockwise), the new chain will be drawn down, around the sprockets and guides, then up the other side. Fit the link from the rear of the sprocket, and ensure that the link is pushed firmly into position – do not fit the link plate to secure the link at this stage.

14 It is now necessary to feed the new chain around the sprockets and guides. During this procedure it is essential to observe the following points.

a) Keep tension on the new chain; ensuring that the links remain engaged with the camshaft sprocket, otherwise the valve timing will be lost.

b) Pull up on the old chain to prevent it dropping off the crankshaft sprocket, or jamming in the guides.

15 Using a suitable socket on the crankshaft pulley/vibration damper hub bolt, slowly turn the crankshaft clockwise, whilst observing the points made in the preceding paragraph.

16 When the end of the new chain appears, remove the link (ensuring that tension is kept on the new chain, and that the chain links remain engaged with the sprockets), and disconnect the old chain.

17 Engage the new chain with the camshaft sprocket, then join the two ends of the chain with the connecting link, inserted from the rear of the sprocket **(see illustration)**.

18 Fit the link plate, and then secure the plate to the link by flattening the ends of the link pins. A special tool is available for this purpose, but it should be possible to achieve a satisfactory result using a hammer, with a block of metal (or a second hammer) to

support the rear of the chain – *take great care not to damage the chain or the sprocket.*

19 Check that the chain link is secure, with no burring of the metal, or loose swarf.

20 Refit the timing chain tensioner as described in Section 8.

21 Turn the engine (clockwise) to bring No 1 piston to TDC, ensuring that crankshaft and camshaft timing marks are correctly aligned as described in Section 3.

22 It is possible that the timing chain may have slipped by one tooth on the camshaft sprocket during this operation. If this is the case, the timing can be corrected by removing the camshaft sprocket (see Section 8), and altering the position of the camshaft and sprocket by one tooth in relation to the chain. In this case, also check the fuel injection pump timing as described in Chapter 4A.

23 Refit the cooling fan and shroud as described in Chapter 3.

24 Refit the fuel injectors as described in Chapter 4A.

25 Refit the camshaft cover, with reference to Section 4.

26 Reconnect the battery negative lead.

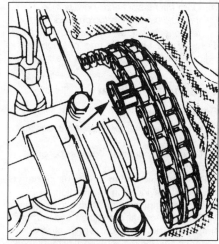

7.17 Push the chain link (arrowed) in from the rear of the chain

8 Timing chain tensioner, sprockets and guides – removal, inspection and refitting

Tensioner

Removal

1 Working at the right-hand side of the engine, unscrew the tensioner body (**do not** unscrew the tensioner cover plug) from the cylinder head (**see illustrations**). Recover the sealing ring.

Inspection

2 Do not attempt to dismantle the tensioner assembly. If it is suspected that the tensioner is worn or faulty, the complete unit should be renewed.

Refitting

3 Before refitting the tensioner, the unit must be primed with oil as follows.

a) Place the tensioner, with the plunger facing downwards in a container of engine oil. The oil level should be up to the level of the cover plug.

b) Press slowly down on the assembly (a hydraulic press may be required to achieve sufficient pressure) between seven and ten times until the plunger reaches the stop.

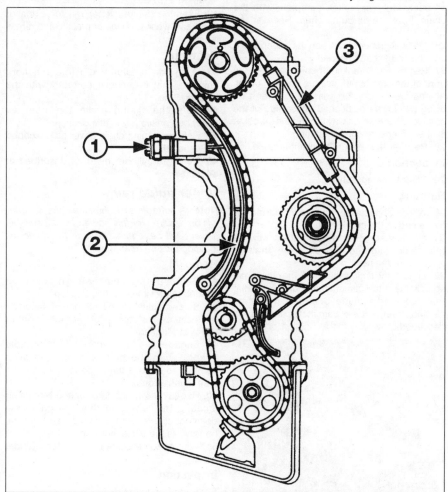

8.1a Timing chain tensioner and guide components

1 Tensioner   2 Tensioner rail   3 Upper guide rail

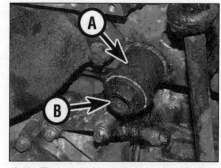

8.1b Timing chain tensioner body (A). DO NOT unscrew the cover plug (B)

c) *Once the tensioner has been primed, it should be possible to compress the tensioner slowly, evenly, and with little effort.*

4 Screw the tensioner into position in the cylinder head, and tighten to the specified torque.

Camshaft sprocket

Removal

5 Remove the auxiliary drivebelt as described in Chapter 1.
6 Remove the camshaft cover as described in Section 4.
7 Remove the timing chain tensioner as described previously in this Section.
8 Turn the engine to position No 1 piston at TDC, ensuring that crankshaft and camshaft timing marks are correctly aligned as described in Section 3. Make alignment marks on the camshaft sprocket and the timing chain.
9 The camshaft sprocket bolt must now be slackened. The camshaft must be prevented from turning as the sprocket bolt is loosened, and this can be achieved by using a screwdriver to hold the sprocket stationary by means of the holes in the sprocket – take care not to damage surrounding components.
10 Unscrew the sprocket securing bolt, and recover the washer.
11 Withdraw the sprocket from the camshaft; noting which way round it is fitted to ensure correct refitting.

Inspection

12 Examine the teeth on the sprocket for wear. Each tooth forms an inverted V. If worn, the side of each tooth under tension will be slightly concave in shape when compared with the other side of the tooth (ie, the teeth will have a 'hooked' appearance). If the teeth appear worn, the sprocket must be renewed.

Refitting

13 Ensure that the camshaft and crankshaft timing marks are still aligned, as described in Section 3. If a new sprocket is being fitted, copy the chain alignment mark from the old sprocket to the new.
14 Engage the sprocket with the chain, aligning the marks made on the chain and sprocket before removal.
15 Offer the sprocket into position on the camshaft, ensuring that it is fitted the correct way round, as noted before removal. Make sure that the locating pin on the camshaft flange engages with the hole in the sprocket.
16 Refit the securing bolt and washer, and tighten the bolt to the specified torque, holding the sprocket as during removal.
17 Refit the timing chain tensioner as described previously in this Section.
18 Using a socket on the crankshaft pulley/vibration damper hub bolts, turn the crankshaft through one complete revolution, and check that the crankshaft and camshaft timing marks are still aligned with No 1 piston at TDC, as described in Section 3.

 Warning: Do not turn the engine by means of the camshaft sprocket bolt.

19 Refit the camshaft cover as described in Section 4.
20 Refit the auxiliary drivebelt as described in Chapter 1.

Crankshaft sprocket

Note: *A puller may be required to remove the sprocket.*

Removal

21 Remove the timing chain cover as described in Section 6.
22 Remove the sump as described in Section 11.
23 Remove the camshaft sprocket as described previously in this Section. Allow the timing chain to hang down into the timing chain housing so that it disengages from the crankshaft sprocket.
24 Pull the oil pump drive chain tensioner rail and spring from the lug on the cylinder block – note the orientation of the spring to aid correct refitting.
25 Unscrew the securing bolt and remove the oil pump drive sprocket, complete with chain, from the oil pump shaft. Recover the washer.
26 Make alignment marks on the timing chain and the crankshaft sprocket.
27 Remove the crankshaft sprocket from the front of the crankshaft, using a suitable puller. Alternatively, it may be possible to lever it off using two levers positioned either side of the sprocket. Note which way around the sprocket is fitted to ensure correct refitting.
28 Recover the Woodruff key if it is loose.

Inspection

29 Refer to paragraph 12.

Refitting

30 Where applicable, refit the Woodruff key to the end of the crankshaft.
31 If a new sprocket is being fitted, transfer the chain alignment mark from the old sprocket to the new.
32 Engage the timing chain with the crankshaft sprocket and the camshaft sprocket, ensuring that the marks made before removal are aligned, then refit the camshaft sprocket, as described previously in this Section.

8.49a Using a slide hammer . . .

33 Refit the oil pump sprocket and chain (the convex side of the sprocket should face the oil pump). Tighten the securing bolt to the specified torque, ensuring that the washer is in place.
34 Refit the oil pump drive chain tensioner rail bush, spring, and then the tensioner rail. Ensure that the spring is orientated as noted before removal.
35 Refit the sump as described in Section 11.
36 Refit the timing chain cover as described in Section 6.

Fuel injection pump sprocket

37 The procedure is described in Chapter 4A.

Tensioner rail

Removal

38 Remove the cylinder head as described in Section 10.
39 Remove the timing chain cover as described in Section 6.
40 Remove the timing chain tensioner as described previously in this Section.
41 Pull the tensioner rail from its locating lugs.

Inspection

42 Examine the tensioner rail for signs of excessive wear, damage or cracks, and renew if necessary.

Refitting

43 Push the tensioner rail into position, ensuring that it engages correctly with the locating lugs.
44 Refit the timing chain tensioner as described previously in this Section.
45 Refit the timing chain cover as described in Section 6.
46 Refit the cylinder head as described in Section 10.

Upper guide rail

Note: *A suitable slide hammer and adapter will be required for this operation, and suitable sealant will be required to coat the guide rail locating pins on refitting.*

Removal

47 Remove the camshaft sprocket as described previously in this Section.
48 Screw a suitable bolt into one of the guide rail locating pins (accessible from the front of the cylinder head).
49 Engage a slide hammer and suitable adapter with the bolt, and use the slide hammer to remove the guide rail locating pin **(see illustrations)**.
50 Repeat the procedure for the remaining locating pin, ensuring that the guide rail does not slide down the timing chain into the housing as the pin is removed.
51 Withdraw the guide rail from the cylinder head.

Inspection

52 Refer to paragraph 42.

Refitting

53 Offer the guide rail into position in the

housing, then position the locating pins in their holes in the cylinder head, and tap them into position sufficiently to retain the guide rail.

54 Apply sealant to the outer collar of each locating pin, where it seats in the cylinder head, then tap the pins fully into the cylinder head.

55 Refit the camshaft sprocket as described previously in this Section.

Lower guide rail

Removal

56 Remove the timing chain cover as described in Section 6.

57 Remove the timing chain tensioner as described previously in this Section.

58 Pull the guide rail from its locating pin.

Inspection

59 Refer to paragraph 42.

Refitting

60 Push the guide rail into position on the locating pin.

61 Refit the timing chain tensioner as described previously in this Section.

62 Refit the timing chain cover as described in Section 6.

9	Camshaft and valve lifters – removal, inspection and refitting

Removal

Note: *If desired, before removing the camshaft, the condition of the valve lifters can be checked as described in paragraphs 10 to 18. A new camshaft endfloat control thrustwasher may be required on refitting.*

1 Remove the camshaft sprocket as described in Section 8.

2 The camshaft bearing caps are numbered from the timing chain end of the engine. Check

8.49b . . . to extract a locating pin . . .

the bearing caps to ensure that marks are present, and if necessary make suitable marks using quick-drying paint or a centre-punch.

3 The camshaft bearing cap bolts must now be slackened, according to the following information **(see illustration)**.

⚠️ *Warning: It is absolutely essential to observe the correct sequence when slackening the camshaft bearing cap bolts, in order to avoid damage to the camshaft.*

a) *Progressively slacken and then remove the bolts from bearing caps 1, 2 and 6.*

b) *Lift off bearing caps 1, 2 and 6, keeping them in order. Note that the bearing caps locate on dowels – if they are stuck, tap gently using a soft-faced mallet.*

c) *Progressively slacken the bearing cap bolts for bearing caps 3, 4 and 5, in one-turn stages until all pressure on the camshaft is relieved. Take great care not to allow uneven pressure on the camshaft, as the bolts are unscrewed.*

d) *Fully unscrew the remaining bearing cap bolts, and lift off the bearing caps (3, 4 and 5), again keeping them in order.*

e) *Lift the camshaft from the cylinder head.*

4 Lift out the camshaft endfloat control thrustwasher from the rear bearing location **(see illustration)**.

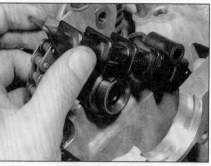
8.49c . . . and then withdraw the guide rail

5 Withdraw the hydraulic valve lifters from the bores in the cylinder head. This is most easily done using a suction valve-grinding tool – push the tool onto the top of the valve lifter, and pull out the valve lifter – **do not** use a magnet to remove the lifters, as this may cause damage to the cam lobe contact faces. Identify the lifters for location, and store them upright in a container of clean engine oil to prevent the oil from draining from inside the lifters.

Inspection

Camshaft

6 Examine the camshaft bearings and cam lobes for any sign of scoring, wear grooves or pitting, and if apparent, renew the camshaft. Any damage of this nature may be attributable to a blocked oil passage in the cylinder head, and careful examination should be carried out to determine the cause.

Valve lifters removed

7 Inspect the valve lifters and spacer washers for obvious signs of wear or damage, and renew if necessary.

8 The operation of the valve lifters can be checked as follows.

a) *Press down firmly on the top of each*

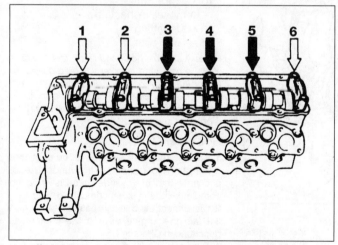
9.3 Camshaft bearing cap loosening sequence
Remove bearing caps 1, 2 and 6 (light arrows), and then slacken the bolts for bearing caps 3, 4 and 5 (dark arrows) in one-turn stages

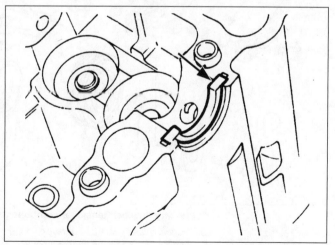
9.4 Lift out the camshaft endfloat control thrustwasher (arrowed)

valve lifter piston, using a blunt instrument such as a wooden hammer handle, for approximately 10 seconds.

b) Note how far the piston moves when depressed.

c) Repeat the operation for all the valve lifters in turn.

d) If any one of the valve lifter pistons can be depressed more easily than the others, renew the relevant lifter.

9 Check the valve lifter bores in the cylinder head for wear and scoring. If any serious damage or wear is evident, the cylinder head must be renewed.

Valve lifters in position

10 Run the engine until it reaches normal operating temperature.

11 Check the engine oil level, ensuring that the engine has not been overfilled.

12 Remove the camshaft cover as described in Section 4 – take care, as the engine will be hot!

13 Turn the engine to position No 1 piston at TDC, ensuring that crankshaft and camshaft timing marks are correctly aligned as described in Section 3.

14 Ensure that the valves are fully closed – ie, the cam lobes are pointing upwards, then, using a soft metal or strong wooden rod, push down lightly on the top of the No 1 valve lifter at the front of the cylinder head (see illustration).

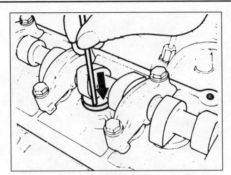

9.14 Pressing a valve lifter down to check the clearance between the lifter and the cam lobe

15 Keep the valve lifter pressed down, and measure the clearance between the top of the valve lifter and the camshaft lobe, using a feeler blade.

16 If the clearance is greater than specified, the valve lifter should be renewed. Note that it is possible to dismantle the valve lifters for further checking, but this is best entrusted to a Mercedes-Benz dealer or a suitably-qualified engineer.

17 Turn the crankshaft using a socket on the crankshaft pulley/vibration damper hub bolt, and repeat the checking procedure for the remaining valve lifters. Each clearance must be checked with the relevant valve fully-closed – ie, the cam lobe pointing upwards.

Warning: When turning the engine, do not turn the engine using the camshaft sprocket bolt, and do not turn the engine backwards (ie, anti-clockwise).

18 When all the valve lifters have been checked, refit the camshaft cover with reference to Section 4.

Refitting

19 Lubricate the external surfaces of the valve lifters with clean engine oil, then refit the lifters to their original locations in the cylinder head. Check that the lifters slide freely in their bores.

20 Check the condition of the camshaft endfloat control thrustwasher and if necessary renew. Refit the washer to the rear bearing location.

21 Lubricate the camshaft and the bearing locations in the cylinder head with clean engine oil, then lay the camshaft in position on the cylinder head. The timing notch in the flange at the front of the camshaft should point vertically upwards.

22 Lay the bearing caps in position over the camshaft and tighten the securing bolts according to the following information, ensuring that the bearing caps are fitted to their original locations.

Warning: It is absolutely essential to observe the correct sequence when tightening the camshaft bearing cap bolts, in order to avoid damage to the camshaft.

a) Fit bearing caps 3, 4 and 5, then fit the bolts, and tighten them progressively in one-turn stages to the specified torque. Take care not to allow uneven pressure on the camshaft as the bolts are tightened.

b) Fit bearing caps 1, 2 and 6, and tighten the bolts to the specified torque.

23 Refit the camshaft sprocket as described in Section 8.

10 Cylinder head – removal, inspection and refitting

Note: A suitable hoist and lifting tackle, and a slide hammer and adapter will be required for this operation. A new cylinder head gasket and a new coolant elbow O-ring will be required on refitting. New cylinder head bolts may be required – see text.

Removal

1 Ensure that the engine is cold before attempting to remove the cylinder head, and note that the cylinder head is removed complete with the exhaust manifold.

2 Disconnect the battery negative lead.

3 Drain the engine oil and the coolant as described in Chapter 1.

4 Remove the camshaft as described in Section 9.

5 Remove the fuel injectors as described in Chapter 4A.

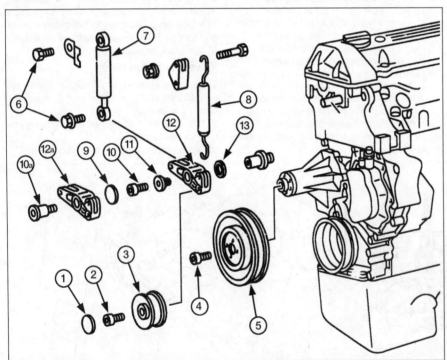

10.7 Auxiliary drivebelt tensioner components

1	Plastic cover	5	Cooling fan pulley	8	Tension spring	11	Spacer sleeve
2	Bolt	6	Bolts	9	Plastic cover	12	Tensioner
3	Idler pulley	7	Tensioner damper strut	10	Bolt	12a	Alternative tensioner type
4	Bolt			10a	Alternative bolt type	13	Spacer

10.10 Disconnect the fuel lines (arrowed)

10.13 Disconnect the hose and EGR pipe from the valve

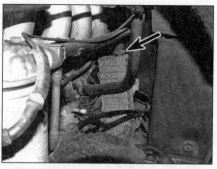

10.16 Disconnect the hose from the oil cooler

6 Remove the radiator as described in Chapter 3.

7 Remove the auxiliary drivebelt tensioner as follows **(see illustration)**.

a) Pull off the plastic cover, unscrew the securing bolt, and remove the auxiliary drivebelt idler pulley.

b) Unscrew the securing bolts, and remove the cooling fan pulley.

c) Unscrew the securing bolts, and withdraw the tensioner damper strut. Recover any spacers and/or brackets from the bolts noting their locations.

d) Using a pair of pliers, unhook the tension spring, noting its orientation to aid refitting.

e) Where applicable, pull off the plastic cover, then unscrew the tensioner securing bolt and slide off the spacer sleeve (if applicable).

f) Withdraw the tensioner, and recover the spacer (where applicable).

8 On non-turbo models, remove the air cleaner cover, inlet hose and air filter element, as described in Chapter 4A.

9 On turbo models, carry out the following operations.

a) Remove the turbocharger inlet air hose.

b) Unbolt the turbocharger support bracket.

c) Unscrew the union nut, and disconnect the turbocharger oil return pipe from the cylinder block.

10 Place a wad of rags beneath the fuel line connections at the fuel filter, then unscrew the union nuts, and disconnect the fuel lines, noting their locations to aid refitting **(see illustration)** Plug the open ends of the unions and pipes to prevent dirt entry and further fuel loss.

11 Unbolt the fuel filter from the cylinder head, and remove the filter.

12 Unbolt the engine oil level dipstick tube from the cylinder head.

13 On models with exhaust gas recirculation, disconnect the pipe and hose from the exhaust gas recirculation valve **(see illustration)**.

14 Working under the vehicle, unscrew the bolts securing the exhaust mounting bracket to the transmission, then unscrew the bolts securing the mounting bracket to the exhaust system.

15 Disconnect the exhaust front section from the manifold with reference to Chapter 4B.

16 Disconnect the coolant connection from the oil cooler assembly **(see illustration)**.

17 Unscrew the elbow from the oil filter assembly, then pull the elbow from the connector.

18 Unscrew the securing nuts, and disconnect the wiring connector bar from the glow plugs.

19 Remove the inlet manifold as described in Chapter 4A.

20 Remove the upper timing chain guide as described in Section 8.

21 Working in the timing chain housing, unscrew the two bolts securing the cylinder head to the timing chain cover.

22 Make a final check to ensure that all relevant hoses and wires have been disconnected to allow cylinder head removal.

23 Progressively loosen the cylinder head bolts, working in the **reverse** order to that shown in illustration 10.42.

24 Remove the cylinder head bolts, noting their locations, as different lengths of bolts are used.

25 Attach a hoist and lifting tackle to the lifting bracket at the front left of the cylinder head, and the rear right of the exhaust manifold. Raise the hoist to just take the weight of the cylinder head.

26 Release the cylinder head from the cylinder block and locating dowels by rocking it. Do not prise between the mating faces of the cylinder head and block, as this may damage the gasket faces.

27 Carefully lift the cylinder head, complete with exhaust manifold, from the block, and manoeuvre it out from the engine compartment.

28 Recover the cylinder head gasket.

Inspection

29 Refer to Chapter 2C for details of cylinder head dismantling and reassembly. If desired, the exhaust manifold can be removed with reference to Chapter 4B.

30 The mating faces of the cylinder head and block must be perfectly clean before refitting the head. Use a scraper to remove all traces of gasket and carbon, and also clean the tops of the pistons. Take particular care with the cylinder head, as the metal is easily damaged. Also make sure that debris is not allowed to enter the oil and water passages. Using adhesive tape and paper, seal the water, oil and bolt holes in the cylinder block. To prevent carbon entering the gap between the pistons and bores, smear a little grease in the gap. After cleaning each piston, rotate the crankshaft so that the piston moves down the bore, and then wipe out the grease and carbon with a cloth rag.

31 Check the block and head for nicks, deep scratches and other damage. If very slight, they may be removed from the cylinder block carefully with a file. More serious damage may be repaired by machining, but this is a specialist job.

32 If warpage of the cylinder head is suspected, use a straight-edge to check it for distortion, with reference to Chapter 2C.

33 Clean out the bolt holes in the block using a pipe cleaner or thin rag and a screwdriver. Make sure that all oil and water is removed, otherwise there is a possibility of the block being cracked by hydraulic pressure when the bolts are tightened.

34 Examine the bolt threads and the threads in the cylinder block for damage. If necessary, use the correct size tap to chase out the threads in the block.

35 The manufacturers recommend that the cylinder head bolts be measured to determine whether renewal is necessary; however, some owners may wish to renew all the bolts as a matter of course.

36 Measure the length of each bolt from the base of the head to the end of the shank **(see illustration)**. If the bolt length is greater than

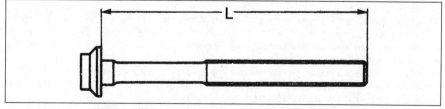

10.36 Measure the length (L) of the cylinder head bolts

See Specifications for maximum length

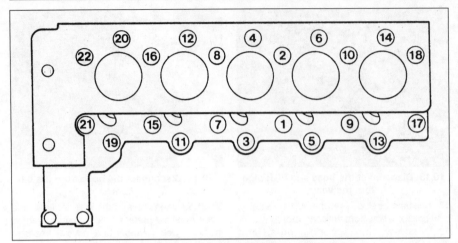

10.42 Cylinder head bolt tightening sequence

the maximum specified, the bolts should be renewed.

Refitting

37 Where applicable, refit the exhaust manifold with reference to Chapter 4B.
38 Check that the camshaft and crankshaft timing marks are still aligned with No 1 piston at TDC, as described in Section 3.
39 Fit the gasket over the dowels in the cylinder block, ensuring that it is fitted the correct way round.
40 Support the cylinder head using the hoist and lifting tackle, then lower the cylinder head onto the block.
41 Oil the threads and the cylinder head contact faces of the cylinder head bolts (see paragraphs 35 and 36), then insert them and screw them into the cylinder block by hand. Ensure that the bolts are fitted to their correct locations as noted before removal.
42 Tighten the cylinder head bolts in the order shown **(see illustration)**. Tighten the bolts in the stages given in the Specifications – ie, tighten all bolts to the Stage 1 torque, then tighten all bolts to the Stage 2 torque, and so on.
43 Refit and tighten the bolts securing the cylinder head to the timing chain cover.
44 Refit the upper timing chain guide rail as described in Section 8.
45 Refit the inlet manifold as described in Chapter 4A.
46 Reconnect the wires to the glow plugs, and tighten the securing nuts.
47 Refit the coolant elbow to the oil cooler assembly, using a new O-ring. Lubricate the O-ring with clean coolant before fitting. Refit the locking clip.
48 Reconnect the exhaust front section to the manifold with reference to Chapter 4B.
49 Refit the exhaust-to-transmission mounting bracket, and tighten the securing bolts, ensuring that the exhaust system is mounted free from stress.
50 Further refitting is a reversal of removal, bearing in mind the following points.

a) *Ensure that the fuel lines are correctly reconnected to the fuel filter, as noted before removal.*
b) *Refit the auxiliary drivebelt tensioner using a reversal of the procedure described in paragraph 8.*
c) *Refit the radiator with reference to Chapter 3.*
d) *Refit the fuel injectors as described in Chapter 4A.*
e) *Refit the camshaft as described in Section 9.*
f) *Refill the cooling system and refill the engine with oil as described in Chapter 1.*

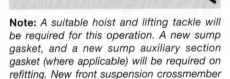

11 Sump –
removal and refitting

Note: *A suitable hoist and lifting tackle will be required for this operation. A new sump gasket, and a new sump auxiliary section gasket (where applicable) will be required on refitting. New front suspension crossmember bolts will be required.*

Removal

1 Disconnect the battery negative lead.
2 Where applicable, remove the engine undershield.
3 Remove the front anti-roll bar as described in Chapter 10. Note that the anti-roll bar can be left in position under the vehicle, provided that the mounting bolts have been removed.
4 Drain the engine oil with reference to Chapter 1.
5 Where applicable, unscrew the two bolts securing the engine mounting damper to the body member on the left-hand side of the vehicle.
6 Unclip the cooling fan shroud, and lay it in position over the fan blades as described in Chapter 3.
7 Disconnect the starter motor earth strap from the body and, where applicable, unbolt the engine speed sensor.

8 Where applicable, disconnect the wiring from the engine oil level sensor.
9 Disconnect the engine oil cooler hoses from the rigid pipes. Plug or clamp the open ends of the hoses, and plug the pipes to prevent dirt entry.
10 Attach an engine hoist and lifting tackle to the front engine lifting eye.
11 Unbolt the left- and right-hand engine mountings from the crossmember.
12 Carefully raise the engine as far as possible, until the rear of the cylinder head touches the engine compartment bulkhead. Take care not to damage any of the components in the engine compartment.
13 Remove the front suspension coil springs, as described in Chapter 10.
14 Remove the steering column-to-coupling upper clamp bolt, and disconnect the steering column from the coupling, with reference to Chapter 10.
15 Support the front suspension cross-member using a jack and a suitable large block of wood, then unscrew the four securing bolts (unbolt the plastic covers for access to the rear bolts), and lower the crossmember assembly until it is supported by the shock absorbers – see *Front suspension lower arm – removal and refitting* in Chapter 10. Discard the crossmember securing bolts – new bolts must be used on refitting, and take care not to strain any pipes, hoses or wiring as the crossmember is lowered.
16 On models with an auxiliary section bolted to the right-hand side of the sump, unscrew the securing bolts, and remove the sump side section. Recover the washers and the gasket.
17 Where applicable, unscrew the two lower engine-to-transmission bolts, which secure the transmission to the sump.
18 Working progressively, in a diagonal sequence, unscrew and remove the sump securing bolts. Note the locations of the bolts to aid refitting, as various lengths of bolts may be used. Also note the locations of any brackets secured by the bolts (note that some of the bolts may already have been removed in order to release the transmission fluid and oil cooler pipes from the sump).
19 Lower the sump forwards from under the vehicle, and recover the gasket. If necessary, turn the crankshaft using a socket on the pulley/vibration damper hub bolt to move the crankshaft webs, allowing clearance for the sump to be withdrawn.

Refitting

20 Commence refitting by cleaning the remains of the gasket from the sump and cylinder block, and wipe dry.
21 Position a new gasket on the sump, then lift the sump into position, and insert the bolts in their original locations.
22 Tighten the bolts progressively to the specified torque.
23 Where applicable, refit the lower engine-to-transmission bolts, which secure the transmission to the sump.

24 On models with an auxiliary side section bolted to the sump, refit the side section using a new gasket, and tighten the securing bolts, ensuring that the washers are in place.
25 Raise the front suspension crossmember, and secure it in position using new bolts, as described in *Front lower arm – removal and refitting* in Chapter 10. Tighten the bolts to the specified torque.
26 Reconnect the steering column to the coupling, ensuring that the column and coupling are correctly aligned, as described in Chapter 10.
27 Refit the front suspension coil springs as described in Chapter 10.
28 Carefully lower the engine into position, and refit the engine mounting bolts. Tighten the bolts to the specified torque. Disconnect the lifting tackle and hoist.
29 Reconnect the engine oil cooler hoses to the rigid pipes, and tighten the clamp bolts.
30 Where applicable, reconnect the wiring to the engine oil level sensor.
31 Reconnect the starter motor earth strap to the body and, where applicable, refit the engine speed sensor.
32 Refit the cooling fan shroud as described in Chapter 3.
33 Refit the front anti-roll bar as described in Chapter 10.
34 Ensure that the engine oil drain plug has been tightened, and then refit the engine undershield.
35 Reconnect the battery negative lead, then fill the engine with oil as described in Chapter 1.

12 Oil pump and drive chain – removal, inspection and refitting

Oil pump

Removal

1 Remove the sump as described in Section 11.
2 Unscrew the oil pump sprocket securing bolt, and recover the washer. Withdraw the oil pump sprocket, complete with the drive chain, from the oil pump shaft.
3 Unscrew the bolt securing the oil pick-up pipe to the support bracket.
4 Unscrew the three bolts securing the oil pump to the cylinder block, and recover the washers. Where applicable, unscrew the securing bolts, and withdraw the oil pump baffle plate.
5 Lift the oil pump from the cylinder block, noting that it locates on two dowels.

Inspection

6 With the exception of the oil pressure relief valve components, the oil pump is a sealed unit. To remove the oil pressure relief valve components, proceed as follows.
7 Unscrew the relief valve plug. Take care, as the plug will be pushed out by the spring pressure when it reaches the end of the threads.

8 Withdraw the spring, guide pin and piston (see illustration).
9 Thoroughly clean all components, and examine them for wear and damage. If there is any sign of excessive wear or damage, renew the appropriate component(s) – pay particular attention to the spring.
10 Refit the components using a reversal of the removal procedure, and tighten the plug to the specified torque.
11 On models with an oil baffle plate fitted to the cylinder block, when the oil pump is removed, it is advisable to remove and clean the baffle plate. Simply unbolt the baffle plate, clean it, and refit.

Refitting

12 Refitting is a reversal of removal, bearing in mind the following points.
a) Prime the oil pump by filling it with clean engine oil.
b) Ensure that the pump locates correctly on the dowels.
c) Tighten the pump securing bolts to the specified torque.
d) Fit the pump sprocket with the convex side of the sprocket facing the pump.
e) Tighten the pump sprocket securing bolt to the specified torque.
f) Refit the sump as described in Section 11.

Drive chain renewal

Note: *Removal of the oil pump drive chain using the following procedure entails the use of a portable electric grinder to grind off one of the chain links. Ensure that such a tool is available, as well as a new chain and new*

connecting link before proceeding. The oil pump sprocket should be renewed whenever the chain is renewed.
13 Remove the sump as described in Section 11.
14 Slacken the oil pump sprocket securing bolt.
15 Using a grinder, grind off the protruding lugs of one of the chain links at the bottom of the sprocket – take great care not to damage the sprocket.
16 Pull off the chain link plate, then push the link out towards the rear of the chain.
17 Unscrew the oil pump sprocket securing bolt, and recover the washer, then withdraw the sprocket from the pump shaft.
18 Using the new link, connect one end of the new chain to the tail end of the old chain, in such a way that as the engine is turned (clockwise), the new chain will be drawn up, around the crankshaft sprocket, then down the other side. Fit the link from the rear of the sprocket, and ensure that the link is pushed firmly into position – do not fit the link plate to secure the link at this stage.
19 It is now necessary to feed the new chain around the crankshaft sprocket. During this procedure it is essential to observe the following points.
a) Keep tension on the new chain, ensuring that the links of the chains remain engaged with the crankshaft sprocket.
b) Pull down on the old chain as it appears from the timing chain cover to prevent it dropping off the crankshaft sprocket, or jamming in the casing.

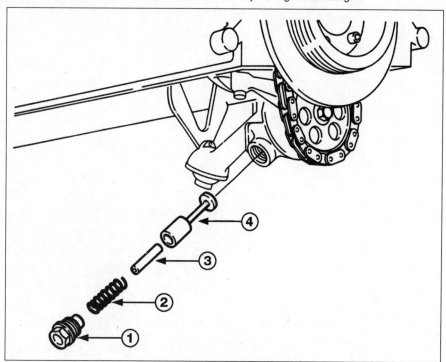

12.8 Oil pressure relief valve components

1 Plug   2 Spring   3 Guide pin   4 Piston

20 Using a suitable socket on the crankshaft pulley/vibration damper hub bolt, slowly turn the crankshaft clockwise, whilst observing the points made in the preceding paragraph.

21 When the end of the new chain appears, remove the link (ensuring that tension is kept on the new chain, and that the chain links remain engaged with the crankshaft sprocket), and disconnect the new chain from the old chain. Remove the old chain.

22 Join the two ends of the chain with the connecting link, inserted from the rear of the sprocket.

23 Fit the link plate, and then secure the plate to the link by flattening the ends of the link pins. A special tool is available for this purpose, but it should be possible to achieve a satisfactory result using a hammer, with a block of metal (or a second hammer) to support the rear of the chain – *take great care not to damage the chain or the sprocket.*

24 Check that the chain link is secure, with no burring of the metal, or loose swarf.

25 Engage the chain with the new oil pump sprocket.

26 Fit the new sprocket to the pump shaft, with the convex side of the sprocket facing the pump.

27 Tighten the oil pump sprocket bolt to the specified torque.

28 Refit the sump as described in Section 11.

13 Flywheel/crankshaft spigot bearing – removal, inspection and refitting

The procedure is identical to that described in Chapter 2A, Section 13.

14 Crankshaft oil seals – renewal

The procedure is identical to that described in Chapter 2A, Section 14.

15 Engine/transmission mountings – inspection and renewal

The procedure is identical to that described in Chapter 2A, Section 16.

Chapter 2 Part C:
Engine removal and engine overhaul procedures

Contents

Degrees of difficulty

Easy, suitable for novice with little experience	Fairly easy, suitable for beginner with some experience	Fairly difficult, suitable for competent DIY mechanic	Difficult, suitable for experienced DIY mechanic	Very difficult, suitable for expert DIY or professional

Specifications

Cylinder head

Maximum gasket face distortion:
   Longitudinal . . . . 0.08 mm
   Transverse . . . . 0.00 mm
Swirl chamber protrusion . . . . 7.6 to 8.1 mm

Cylinder block

Maximum cylinder bore ovality . . . . 0.07 mm
Maximum cylinder bore taper . . . . 0.07 mm
Maximum gasket face distortion . . . . 0.03 mm

Valves

Valve seat width . . . . 0.9 to 1.1 mm
Valve seat angle . . . . 45°

Pistons

Piston protrusion:
   Minimum . . . . 0.38 mm
   Maximum . . . . 0.62 mm
Gudgeon pin clearance in small end bush . . . . 0.007 to 0.018 mm

Piston rings

End gaps:
   Top compression ring . . . . 0.22 to 0.42 mm
   Second compression ring . . . . 0.20 to 0.40 mm
   Oil control ring . . . . 0.20 to 0.40 mm
Clearance in grooves:
   Top compression ring . . . . 0.12 to 0.16 mm
   Second compression ring . . . . 0.05 to 0.09 mm
   Oil control ring . . . . 0.03 to 0.07 mm

Big-end bearing cap bolts

2.2 litre engines:
   Maximum length . . . . 48.0 mm
2.9 litre engines . . . . N/A

Crankshaft main bearing cap bolts

2.2 litre engines:
Length when new . . . . 62.0 mm
Maximum length . . . . 63.8 mm
2.9 litre engines:
Maximum length . . . . 63.8 mm

Crankshaft

Endfloat . . . . 0.300 mm
Endfloat thrustwasher thicknesses . . . . 2.15, 2.20, 2.25, 2.35 and 2.40 mm
Main bearings clearance on crankshaft . . . . 0.080 mm
Big-end bearings clearance on crankshaft . . . . 0.080 mm

Torque wrench settings

See Chapters 2A (2.2 litre engine) and 2B (2.9 litre engine).

1 General information

Included in this Part of Chapter 2 are details of removing the engine from the vehicle and general overhaul procedures for the cylinder head, cylinder block/crankcase and all other engine internal components.

The information given ranges from advice concerning preparation for an overhaul and the purchase of parts, to detailed step-by-step procedures covering removal, inspection, renovation and refitting of engine internal components.

After Section 9, all instructions are based on the assumption that the engine has been removed from the vehicle. For information concerning in-car engine repair, as well as the removal and refitting of those external components necessary for full overhaul, refer to Part A or B of this Chapter, as applicable, and to Section 6. Ignore any preliminary dismantling operations described in Parts A or B that are no longer relevant once the engine has been removed from the vehicle.

2 Engine overhaul – general information

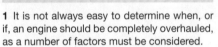

1 It is not always easy to determine when, or if, an engine should be completely overhauled, as a number of factors must be considered.
2 High mileage is not necessarily an indication that an overhaul is needed, while low mileage does not preclude the need for an overhaul. Frequency of servicing is probably the most important consideration. An engine, which has had regular and frequent oil and filter changes, as well as other required maintenance, should give many thousands of miles of reliable service. Conversely, a neglected engine may require an overhaul very early in its life.
3 Excessive oil consumption is an indication that piston rings, valve seals and/or valve guides are in need of attention. Make sure that oil leaks are not responsible before deciding that the rings and/or guides are worn. Perform a compression test, as described in Part A or

B of this Chapter (as applicable), to determine the likely cause of the problem.
4 Check the oil pressure with a gauge fitted in place of the oil pressure switch, and compare it with that specified in Part A or B. If it is extremely low, the main and big-end bearings, and/or the oil pump, are probably worn out.
5 Loss of power, rough running, knocking or metallic engine noises, excessive valve gear noise, and high fuel consumption may also point to the need for an overhaul, especially if they are all present at the same time. If a complete service does not remedy the situation, major mechanical work is the only solution.
6 A full engine overhaul involves restoring all internal parts to the specification of a new engine. During a complete overhaul, the pistons and the piston rings are renewed, and the cylinder bores are reconditioned. New main and big-end bearings are generally fitted; if necessary, the crankshaft may be reground, to compensate for wear in the journals. The valves are also serviced as well, since they are usually in less-than-perfect condition at this point. Always pay careful attention to the condition of the oil pump when overhauling the engine, and renew it if there is any doubt as to its serviceability. The end result should be an as-new engine that will give many trouble-free miles.
7 Critical cooling system components such as the hoses, thermostat and coolant pump should be renewed when an engine is overhauled. The radiator should be checked carefully, to ensure that it is not clogged or leaking.
8 Before beginning the engine overhaul, read through the entire procedure, to familiarise yourself with the scope and requirements of the job. Overhauling an engine is not difficult if you follow carefully all of the instructions, have the necessary tools and equipment, and pay close attention to all specifications. It can, however, be time-consuming. Plan on the vehicle being off the road for a minimum of two weeks, especially if parts must be taken to an engineering works for repair or reconditioning. Check on the availability of parts and make sure that any necessary special tools and equipment are obtained in advance. Most work can be done with typical hand tools, although a number of precision measuring tools are required for inspecting parts to determine if they must be

renewed. Often the engineering works will handle the inspection of parts and offer advice concerning reconditioning and renewal.
9 Always wait until the engine has been completely dismantled, and until all components (especially the cylinder block/crankcase and the crankshaft) have been inspected, before deciding what service and repair operations must be performed by an engineering works. The condition of these components will be the major factor to consider when determining whether to overhaul the original engine, or to buy a reconditioned unit. Do not, therefore, purchase parts or have overhaul work done on other components until they have been thoroughly inspected. As a general rule, time is the primary cost of an overhaul, so it does not pay to fit worn or sub-standard parts.
10 As a final note, to ensure maximum life and minimum trouble from a reconditioned engine, everything must be assembled with care, in a spotlessly clean environment.

3 Engine removal – methods and precautions

1 If you have decided that the engine must be removed for overhaul or major repair work, several preliminary steps should be taken.
2 Locating a suitable place to work is extremely important. Adequate workspace, along with storage space for the vehicle, will be needed. If a workshop or garage is not available, at the very least, a flat, level, clean work surface is required.
3 Cleaning the engine compartment and engine/transmission before beginning the removal procedure will help keep tools clean and organised.
4 An engine hoist will also be necessary. Make sure the equipment is rated in excess of the weight of the engine (and transmission if both are being removed). Safety is of primary importance, considering the potential hazards involved in lifting the engine out of the vehicle.
5 If this is the first time you have removed an engine, an assistant should ideally be available. Advice and aid from someone more experienced would also be helpful. There are many instances

when one person cannot simultaneously perform all of the operations required when lifting the engine out of the vehicle.

6 Plan the operation ahead of time. Before starting work, arrange for the hire of or obtain all of the tools and equipment you will need. Some of the equipment necessary to perform engine removal and installation safely and with relative ease (in addition to an engine hoist) is as follows: a heavy duty trolley jack, complete sets of spanners and sockets (see *Tools and working facilities*), wooden blocks, and plenty of rags and cleaning solvent for mopping-up spilled oil, coolant and fuel. If the hoist must be hired, make sure that you arrange for it in advance, and perform all of the operations possible without it beforehand. This will save you money and time.

7 Plan for the vehicle to be out of use for quite a while. An engineering works will be required to perform some of the work which the do-it-yourselfer cannot accomplish without special equipment. These places often have a busy schedule, so it would be a good idea to consult them before removing the engine, in order to accurately estimate the amount of time required to rebuild or repair components that may need work.

8 Always be extremely careful when removing and refitting the engine. Serious injury can result from careless actions. Plan ahead and take your time, and a job of this nature, although major, can be accomplished successfully.

9 On all models, the engine is removed by lifting the assembly out from the front of the vehicle (see illustration).

4 Engine – removal and refitting

Note: *A suitable hoist and lifting tackle will be required for this operation.*

Removal

1 Disconnect the battery negative (earth) lead and position it away from the terminal.

2 Apply the handbrake, then jack up the front of the vehicle and support it on axle stands (see *Jacking and vehicle support*). Allow sufficient height for the hoist to lift the engine out of the engine compartment. Alternatively, the vehicle can be lowered to the ground just before

attaching the hoist. With the vehicle raised, remove the engine compartment undershield.

3 On turbocharged models, disconnect and remove the left- and right-hand air ducts to the intercooler. If necessary, remove the intercooler as described in Chapter 4A.

4 Drain the cooling system, and then remove the radiator and cooling fan as described in Chapters 1 and 3.

5 If necessary, drain the oil from the engine as described in Chapter 1.

6 Remove the auxiliary drivebelt as described in Chapter 1.

7 On air conditioning models, position a piece of strong card or similar over the condenser to protect it as the engine is being removed.

8 Identify then disconnect the vacuum hoses from the brake vacuum pump, inlet manifold, brake servo unit, and vacuum control valve.

9 Loosen the clips and disconnect the coolant hoses from the rear of the cylinder head and from the thermostat housing on the front, left-hand side of the cylinder head (2.2litre models), or right-hand side above the alternator (2.9 litre models).

10 Refer to Chapter 10 and unbolt the power steering pump from the left-hand side of the engine. Tie the pump to one side, in an upright position to prevent the fluid escaping (see illustration).

11 On the left-hand rear of the engine compartment, disconnect the engine main wiring, and position the connectors on the engine (see illustration).

12 Briefly remove the filler cap from the fuel tank to relieve any pressure or vacuum, then

3.9 Lifting the engine out from the vehicle

unscrew the union nuts and disconnect the fuel supply and return lines from the injection pump.

13 On models with air conditioning, unbolt the compressor from the mounting bracket on the left-hand side of the engine, and support it to one side (see illustration). **Do not** disconnect the refrigerant line from the compressor.

⚠️ *Warning: The refrigeration circuit contains pressurised liquid refrigerant. For this reason, disconnection of any part of the system without specialised knowledge and equipment is not recommended.*

14 Remove the front section of the exhaust system as described in Chapter 4B (see illustration).

15 Remove the intake manifold as described in Chapter 4A (see illustration).

16 Remove the starter motor as described in Chapter 5.

4.10 Tie the power steering pump to one side

4.11 Disconnect the engine wiring connectors (2.2 litre shown)

4.13 Secure the compressor to one side

4.14 Disconnect the exhaust front pipe

4.15 Remove the intake upper manifold (2.2 litre engine)

4.22 Lifting the engine from the engine compartment

Without transmission

17 Support the weight of the transmission with a trolley jack and interposed piece of wood.

18 Attach a suitable hoist to the two lifting eyes, and take the weight of the engine.

19 Unscrew and remove the bolts securing the engine mountings to the suspension crossmember. Alternatively, the mountings can be removed completely.

20 Unscrew the bolts securing the transmission to the rear of the engine, noting the location of any mounting brackets or earth cables. Access to the upper mounting bolts is best achieved from the rear of the transmission with an extensions and a socket.

21 Check around the engine for any wiring or hoses that may still be connected to the engine. Make a note of their position and then disconnect.

22 With the help of an assistant, draw the engine forwards from the transmission until the transmission input shaft is clear of the clutch, then lift the engine from the engine compartment, taking care not to damage the surrounding components and wiring. Move the hoist forwards and lower the engine to the ground **(see illustration)**.

With transmission (2.2 litre models only)

23 Unbolt the front of the propeller shaft from the rear of the transmission (refer to Chapter 8).

24 Unbolt the earth cable from the transmission. Also disconnect all wiring plugs from the transmission.

25 Fit a hose clamp to the hydraulic line leading to the clutch slave cylinder on the transmission (see Chapter 6). Remove the retaining clip and

5.3a Remove the engine mounting brackets, wiring . . .

4.28 Remove the rear mounting bracket

detach the hydraulic line from the slave cylinder. Tape over or plug the line and slave cylinder to prevent entry of dust and dirt.

26 Disconnect the gearchange lever from the transmission as described in Chapter 7.

27 Attach a suitable hoist to the two lifting eyes, and take the weight of the engine and transmission. The hoist chains should be positioned so that the front of the engine will be tilted upwards slightly.

28 Temporarily support the transmission, then unscrew the bolts securing the engine rear mounting bracket to the underbody. If necessary, the complete bracket may be removed from the transmission **(see illustration)**.

29 Unscrew the lower nuts from the engine front mountings (see Chapter 2A).

30 Check around the engine for any wiring or hoses that may still be connected to the engine. Make a note of their position and then disconnect.

31 With the help of an assistant, lift and tilt the engine and transmission to withdraw it from the engine compartment, taking care not to damage the surrounding components and wiring. It will be necessary to move the hoist forwards and guide the engine and transmission up through the engine compartment, taking care not to damage the surrounding components. Move the hoist forwards and lower the engine/transmission assembly to the ground.

32 To remove the transmission from the engine, refer to Chapter 7.

Refitting

33 Before refitting the engine and trans-

5.3b . . . and remove the dipstick tube

mission, check the condition of the engine/transmission mountings. In particular, check if they are compressed, are damaged or split, or have signs of oil leakage. If necessary, renew them with reference to Chapter 2A.

34 The reconnection and refitting procedures are a reversal of removal, noting the following additional information.

a) *Tighten all nuts and bolts to the specified torque wrench settings, where given.*

b) *Bleed the clutch hydraulic system as described in Chapter 6.*

c) *Reconnect the propeller shaft to the flange on the rear of the transmission with reference to Chapter 8.*

d) *Refill the power steering fluid reservoir with fresh fluid and bleed the system as described in Chapter 10.*

e) *Ensure that all wiring, hoses and brackets are positioned and routed as noted before removal.*

f) *Refit the intake manifold with reference to Chapter 4A.*

g) *On completion, refill the engine with oil, and refill the cooling system as described in Chapter 1.*

5 Engine overhaul – dismantling sequence

1 It is much easier to dismantle and work on the engine if it is mounted on a portable engine stand. These stands can often be hired from a tool hire shop. Before the engine is mounted on a stand, the flywheel should be removed, so that the stand bolts can be tightened into the end of the cylinder block/crankcase.

2 If a stand is not available, it is possible to dismantle the engine with it blocked up on a sturdy workbench, or on the floor. Be extra careful not to tip or drop the engine when working without a stand.

3 If you are going to obtain a reconditioned engine, all the external components around the engine must be removed first, so that they can be transferred to the new engine (just as they will if you are doing a complete engine overhaul yourself). These components include the following **(see illustrations)**.

a) *Ancillary unit mounting brackets (oil filter,*

5.3c Where fitted remove the crankshaft sensor

alternator, power steering pump, engine mountings, crankcase breather housing, etc).

b) Thermostat and housing (Chapter 3).
c) Dipstick tube.
d) All electrical switches and sensors.
e) Inlet and exhaust manifolds (Chapters 4A and 4B).
f) Injectors and fuel pipes (Chapter 4A)

Note: *When removing the external components from the engine, pay close attention to details that may be helpful or important during refitting. Note the fitted position of gaskets, seals, spacers, pins, washers, bolts, and other small items.*

4 If you are obtaining a 'short' engine (which consists of the engine cylinder block/ crankcase, crankshaft, pistons and connecting rods all assembled), then the cylinder head, sump, oil pump, and timing chain will have to be removed also.

5 If you are planning a complete overhaul, the engine can be dismantled, and the internal components removed, in the order given below, referring to Part A or B of this Chapter unless otherwise stated.

a) Inlet and exhaust manifolds (Chapter 4A and 4B).
b) Timing chain, sprockets and tensioner.
c) Cylinder head.
d) Flywheel.
e) Sump.
f) Oil pump.
g) Piston/connecting rod assemblies (Section 9).
h) Crankshaft (Section 10).

6 Before beginning the dismantling and overhaul procedures, make sure that you have all of the correct tools necessary. Refer to *Tools and working facilities* for further information.

6 Cylinder head – dismantling

Note: *New and reconditioned cylinder heads are available from the manufacturer, and from engine overhaul specialists. Be aware that some specialist tools are required for the dismantling and inspection procedures, and new components may not be readily available. It may therefore be more practical and economical for the home mechanic to purchase a reconditioned head, rather than dismantle, inspect and recondition the original head. A valve spring compressor tool will be required for this operation.*

1 Remove the cylinder head as described in Part A or B of this Chapter.
2 Remove the exhaust manifold as described in Chapter 4B.
3 If desired, remove the glow plugs as described in Chapter 5.
4 Using a valve spring compressor, compress the spring on each valve in turn until the split collets can be removed. Release the compressor, and lift off the spring cap and

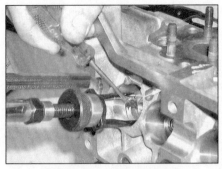
6.4a Remove the split collets

6.4b . . . and spring

6.4b Removing the valve spring cap . . .

6.5 Removing the valve spring seat

spring **(see illustrations)**. If, when the valve spring compressor is screwed down, the spring cap refuses to free and expose the split collets, gently tap the top of the tool, directly over the spring cap, with a light hammer. This will free the retainer.
5 Using a pair of pliers or special removal tool, carefully extract the valve stem oil seal from the top of the guide, then lift off the spring seat **(see illustration)**.
6 Withdraw the valve through the combustion chamber **(see illustration)**.
7 It is essential that each valve is stored with its collets, cap, spring, and spring seat. The valves should also be kept in their correct sequence, unless they are so badly worn that they are to be renewed. If they are going to be kept and used again, place each valve assembly in a labelled polythene bag or similar small container **(see illustration)**. Label each bag No 1 inlet, No 1 exhaust, No 2 inlet, No 2

exhaust, etc, noting that No 1 valve is nearest to the timing chain end of the engine.

7 Cylinder head and valves – cleaning and inspection

1 Thorough cleaning of the cylinder head and valve components, followed by a detailed inspection, will enable you to decide how much valve service work must be carried out during the engine overhaul. **Note:** *If the engine has been severely overheated, it is best to assume that the cylinder head is warped – check carefully for signs of this.*

Cleaning

2 Scrape away all traces of old gasket material from the cylinder head, taking care not to damage the cylinder head.
3 Scrape away the carbon from the

6.6 Removing a valve from the combustion chamber

6.7 Store the valve components in a labelled bag

7.6 Use a straight-edge and feeler blade to check the cylinder head gasket face for distortion

combustion chambers and ports, then wash the cylinder head thoroughly with paraffin or a suitable solvent.

4 Scrape off any heavy carbon deposits that may have formed on the valves, then use a power-operated wire brush to remove deposits from the valve heads and stems.

Inspection

Note: *Be sure to perform all the following inspection procedures before concluding that the services of a machine shop or engine overhaul specialist are required. Make a list of all items that require attention.*

Cylinder head

5 Inspect the head very carefully for cracks, evidence of coolant leakage, and other damage. If cracks are found, a new cylinder head should be obtained.

6 Use a straight-edge and feeler blade to check that the cylinder head gasket surface is not distorted **(see illustration)**. If it is, it may be possible to have it machined, provided that the cylinder head is not reduced to less than the specified height; refer to a dealer or engine specialist. Note also that the swirl chamber protrusion must be checked whenever the cylinder head surface is machined – see paragraphs 11 to 13.

7 Examine the valve seats in each of the combustion chambers. If they are severely pitted, cracked, or burned, they will need to be renewed or recut by an engine overhaul specialist. If they are only slightly pitted, this can be removed by grinding-in the valve heads and seats with fine valve grinding compound, as described later in this Section. If the valve

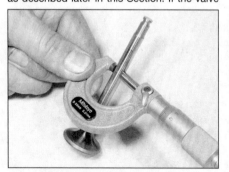

7.15 Measuring a valve stem diameter

seats are recut, check that the valve recess dimensions, measured between the plane of the cylinder head sealing face and the centre of the valve head, are maintained within the specified limits.

8 Check the valve guides for wear by inserting the relevant valve, and checking for side-to-side motion of the valve. A very small amount of movement is acceptable. If the movement seems excessive, remove the valve. Measure the valve stem diameter (see later in this Section), and renew the valve if it is worn. If the valve stem is not worn, the wear must be in the valve guide, and the guide must be renewed. The renewal of new valve guides should be entrusted to a Mercedes-Benz dealer or engine overhaul specialist, who will have the necessary tools available.

9 If renewing the valve guides, the valve seats should be recut or reground only *after* the guides have been fitted.

10 Examine the camshaft bearing surfaces in the cylinder head and the bearing caps for signs of wear or damage. If the bearings are excessively worn, consult a Mercedes-Benz dealer, or an engine overhaul specialist for further advice.

Swirl chambers

11 When inspecting the cylinder head, the swirl chamber protrusion should be checked – this is particularly important if the cylinder head face has been machined. If the swirl chamber protrusion is too great, the pistons may hit the swirl chambers when the engine is running, causing expensive damage.

12 Measure the protrusion of the swirl chamber from the sealing face of the cylinder head. If the protrusion is greater than the specified maximum, the protrusion can be altered by removing the swirl chamber and fitting sealing spacers of varying thickness to achieve the specified protrusion.

13 Removal and refitting of the swirl chambers, and fitting of the appropriate spacers should be entrusted to a Mercedes-Benz dealer, or an engine overhaul specialist, due to the special tools required.

Valves

 Warning: The exhaust valves on most engines are filled with sodium to improve their heat transfer.

7.18 Using a suction valve-grinding tool to grind in a valve

Sodium is a highly reactive substance, and will ignite or explode spontaneously on contact with water (including water vapour in the air). These valves must NOT be disposed of as ordinary scrap. Seek advice from a Mercedes-Benz dealer when disposing of the valves.

14 Examine the head of each valve for pitting, burning, cracks, and general wear. Check the valve stem for scoring and wear ridges. Rotate the valve, and check for any obvious indication that it is bent. Look for pits or excessive wear on the tip of each valve stem. Renew any valve that shows any such signs of wear or damage.

15 If the valve appears satisfactory at this stage, measure the valve stem diameter at several points using a micrometer **(see illustration)**. Any significant difference in the readings obtained indicates wear of the valve stem. Should any of these conditions be apparent, the valve(s) must be renewed.

16 If the valves are in satisfactory condition, they should be ground (lapped) into their respective seats, to ensure a smooth, gas-tight seal. If the seat is only lightly pitted, or if it has been recut, fine grinding compound should be used to produce the required finish. Coarse valve-grinding compound should not be used, unless a seat is badly burned or deeply pitted. If this is the case, the cylinder head and valves should be inspected, to decide whether seat recutting, or even the renewal of the valve or seat insert (where possible) is required.

17 Valve grinding is carried out as follows. Place the cylinder head upside-down on a bench.

18 Smear a trace of (the appropriate grade of) valve-grinding compound on the seat face, and press a suction grinding tool onto the valve head **(see illustration)**. With a semi-rotary action, grind the valve head to its seat, lifting the valve occasionally to redistribute the grinding compound. A light spring placed under the valve head will greatly ease this operation.

19 If coarse grinding compound is being used, work only until a dull, matt even surface is produced on both the valve seat and the valve, then wipe off the used compound, and repeat the process with fine compound. When a smooth unbroken ring of light grey matt finish is produced on both the valve and seat, the grinding operation is complete. *Do not grind-in the valves any further than absolutely necessary, or the seat will be prematurely sunk into the cylinder head.*

20 When all the valves have been ground-in, carefully wash off *all* traces of grinding compound using paraffin or a suitable solvent, before reassembling the cylinder head.

Valve components

21 Examine the valve springs for signs of damage and discoloration. Compare the length of the valve springs with that of a new component, where possible, and if necessary renew the springs.

22 Stand each spring on a flat surface, and check it for squareness. If any of the springs are damaged, distorted or have lost their tension, obtain a complete new set of springs. It is normal to renew the valve springs as a matter of course if a major overhaul is being carried out.

23 Renew the valve stem oil seals regardless of their apparent condition.

Hydraulic tappets

24 Refer to Part A or B of this Chapter for further details.

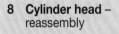
8 Cylinder head – reassembly

Note: *New valve stem oil seals should be fitted.*

1 Lubricate the stems of the valves, and insert the valves into their original locations **(see illustration)**. If new valves are being fitted, insert them into the locations to which they have been ground.

2 Refit the spring seat.

3 Working on the first valve, dip the new valve stem seal in fresh engine oil. New seals are normally supplied with protective sleeves, which should be fitted to the tops of the valve stems to prevent the collet grooves from damaging the oil seals. If no sleeves are supplied, wind a little thin tape round the top of the valve stems to protect the seals. Carefully locate the seal over the valve and onto the guide. Take care not to damage the seal as it is passed over the valve stem. Use a suitable socket or tube to press the seal firmly onto the guide **(see illustrations)**. Remove the sleeve from the valve stem.

4 Locate the valve spring on top of the seat, then refit the spring cap. On engines where the spring is tapered, make sure that the large diameter end of the spring locates on the seat.

5 Fit the compressor tool, then compress the valve spring and locate the split collets in the recess in the valve stem **(see illustration)**. Release the compressor, then repeat the procedure on the remaining valves.

6 With all the valves installed, support the cylinder head on blocks of wood and, using a hammer and interposed block of wood, tap the end of each valve stem to settle the components.

7 Where applicable, refit the glow plugs as described in Chapter 5.

8 Refit the exhaust manifold as described in Chapter 4B.

9 Refit the cylinder head as described in Part A or B of this Chapter.

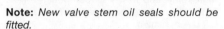
9 Piston/connecting rod assembly – removal

1 Remove the cylinder head, sump and oil pump as described in Part A or B of this Chapter (as applicable). Where fitted, unbolt

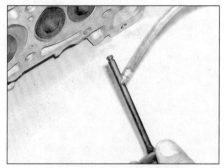
8.1 Lubricate the stems of the valves before inserting them

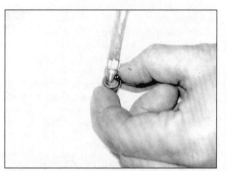
8.3b . . . then oil the new valve stem seal . . .

8.5 Fitting the split collets

and remove the oil baffle plate from the crankcase.

2 If there is a pronounced wear ridge at the top of any bore, it may be necessary to remove it with a scraper or ridge reamer, to avoid piston damage during removal. Such a ridge indicates excessive wear of the cylinder bore.

3 Check the connecting rods and big-end caps for identification marks. Both rods and caps should be marked with the cylinder number on the inlet manifold side of each assembly. Note that No 1 cylinder is at the timing chain end of the engine. If no marks are present, using a hammer and centre-punch, paint or similar, mark each connecting rod and big-end bearing cap with its respective cylinder number on the flat-machined surface provided – note on which side of the connecting rods the marks are made.

4 Similarly, check the piston crowns for a

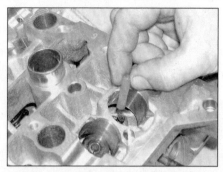
8.3a Locate the protective sleeve on the valve stem . . .

8.3c . . . and press it onto the valve guide

direction marking. An arrow on each piston crown should point towards the timing chain end of the engine. On some engines, this mark may be obscured by carbon build-up, in which case the piston crown should be cleaned to check for a mark. In some cases, the direction arrow may have worn off, in which case a suitable mark should be made on the piston crown using a scriber – do not deeply score the piston crown, but ensure that the mark is easily visible.

5 Turn the crankshaft to bring piston Nos 1 and 4 (4-cylinder engines) or No 1 (5-cylinder engine), as applicable, to BDC (bottom dead centre).

6 Unscrew the bolts from No 1 piston big-end bearing cap. Take off the cap, and recover the bottom half bearing shell. If the bearing shells are to be re-used, tape the cap and the shell together.

7 Using a hammer handle, push the piston up through the bore, and remove it from the top of the cylinder block. Take care not to damage the piston cooling oil spay jets in the cylinder block as the piston/connecting rod assembly is removed. Recover the bearing shell, and tape it to the connecting rod for safekeeping.

8 Loosely refit the big-end cap to the connecting rod, and secure with the bolts – this will help to keep the components in their correct order.

9 On 4-cylinder engines, remove No 4 piston assembly in the same way before turning the crankshaft.

10 Turn the crankshaft as necessary to bring the remaining pistons to BDC, and remove them in the same manner.

10.2 Crankshaft rear oil seal housing

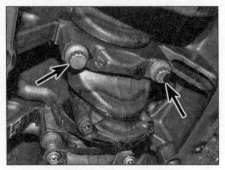

10.6 Main bearing cap bolts

10 Crankshaft –
removal

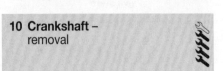

1 Remove the sump, the timing chain cover, timing chain, crankshaft sprocket, and the flywheel, as described in Part A or B of this Chapter.
2 Unbolt the crankshaft rear oil seal housing from the cylinder block **(see illustration)**.
3 Remove the pistons and connecting rods, as described in Section 9. If no work is to be done on the pistons and connecting rods, there is no need to remove the cylinder head, or to push the pistons out of the cylinder bores. The pistons should just be pushed far enough up the bores so that they are positioned clear of the crankshaft journals.
4 Check the crankshaft endfloat as described in Section 13, then proceed as follows.
5 On 4-cylinder engines, the crankshaft main bearing caps should be numbered 1 to 5 on the inlet side of the engine, starting from the timing chain end of the engine. Similarly, on the 5-cylinder engine, the main bearing caps should be numbered 1 to 6. If the bearing caps are not marked, mark them accordingly using a centre-punch. Note the orientation of the markings to ensure correct refitting.
6 Unscrew and remove the main bearing cap retaining bolts, and lift off each bearing cap **(see illustration)**. Recover the lower bearing shells, and tape them to their respective caps for safekeeping.
7 Recover the lower endfloat control thrustwasher halves from either side of the

appropriate bearing cap, noting their positions, as follows.

> *4-cylinder engine – centre (No 3) main bearing.*
> *5-cylinder engine – No 4 main bearing.*

8 Lift the crankshaft from the crankcase.
9 Recover the upper bearing shells from the cylinder block, and tape them to their respective caps for safekeeping. Similarly, recover the upper thrustwasher halves, noting their orientation.

11 Cylinder block/crankcase –
cleaning and inspection

Cleaning

1 Remove all external components, brackets and electrical switches/sensors from the block. Note the position of any mounting brackets before removal. For complete cleaning, the core plugs should ideally be removed. Drill a small hole in the plugs, and then insert a self-tapping screw into the hole. Pull out the plugs by pulling on the screw with a pair of grips, or by using a slide hammer.
2 Scrape all traces of gasket from the cylinder block/crankcase, taking care not to damage the gasket/sealing surfaces.
3 Where applicable, remove the oil gallery plugs, and use new plugs when the engine is reassembled.
4 If the castings are extremely dirty, they should be steam-cleaned.
5 After the castings have been steam-cleaned,

clean all oil holes and oil galleries one more time. Flush all internal passages with warm water until the water runs clear. Dry thoroughly, and apply a light film of oil to all mating surfaces, to prevent rusting. Also oil the cylinder bores. If you have access to compressed air, use it to speed up the drying process, and to blow out all the oil holes and galleries.

> **Warning: Wear eye protection when using compressed air.**

6 If the castings are not very dirty, you can do an adequate cleaning job with hot (as hot as you can stand!), soapy water and a stiff brush. Take plenty of time, and do a thorough job. Regardless of the cleaning method used, be sure to clean all oil holes and galleries very thoroughly, and to dry all components well. Protect the cylinder bores as described above, to prevent rusting.
7 Where applicable, the piston oil spray jets can be removed from the cylinder block for cleaning, however a special tool is required and it is recommended that an engine overhaul specialist carry out the work **(see illustration)**. The tool for removing the jets consists of an adapter, which engages the base of the jet, and a slide hammer screwed into the adapter. Renew any jets which show signs of damage. Check the oil spray hole and oil passages for blockage.
8 All threaded holes must be clean, to ensure accurate torque readings during reassembly. To clean the threads, run the correct-size tap into each of the holes to remove rust, corrosion, thread sealant or sludge, and to restore damaged threads **(see illustration)**. If possible, use compressed air to clear the holes of debris produced by this operation.
9 Ensure that all threaded holes in the cylinder block are dry.
10 After coating the mating surfaces of the new core plugs with suitable sealant, fit them to the cylinder block. Make sure that they are driven in straight and seated correctly, or leakage could result.
11 Where applicable, fit the new oil gallery plugs.
12 If the engine is not going to be reassembled right away, cover it with a large plastic bag to keep it clean; protect all mating surfaces and the cylinder bores as described above, to prevent rusting.

Inspection

13 Visually check the cylinder block/ crankcase for cracks and corrosion. Look for stripped threads in the threaded holes. If there has been any history of internal water leakage, it may be worthwhile having an engine overhaul specialist check the cylinder block/ crankcase with special equipment. If defects are found, have them repaired if possible, or renew the assembly.
14 Check each cylinder bore for scuffing and scoring. Check for signs of a wear ridge at the top of the cylinder, indicating that the bore is excessively worn.

11.7 Piston oil spray jet – where fitted

11.8 Clean damaged threads using a tap

15 If the cylinder walls are badly scored or scuffed, then the cylinders will have to be rebored by a suitably qualified specialist, and new oversize pistons will have to be fitted. A Mercedes-Benz dealer or engineering workshop will normally be able to supply suitable oversize pistons when carrying out the reboring work.

16 Inspect the upper surface of the cylinder block for damage. Use a straight-edge and feeler blade to check that the cylinder head gasket surface is not distorted. Note also that the piston protrusion must be checked whenever the cylinder head surface is machined – see paragraph 18.

17 After checking the cylinder block/crankcase, refit the items removed in paragraph 1.

Piston protrusion

18 When inspecting the cylinder block, the piston protrusion should be checked – this is particularly important if the cylinder head face has been machined. If the piston protrusion is too great, the pistons may hit the swirl chambers when the engine is running, causing expensive damage.

19 Measure the protrusion of the piston from the sealing face of the cylinder head (a dial gauge should be used if possible). If the protrusion is greater than the specified maximum, consult a Mercedes-Benz dealer or an engine-reconditioning specialist for advice – it is likely that the cylinder block will have to be renewed.

12 Piston/connecting rod assembly – cleaning and inspection

Cleaning

1 Before the inspection process can begin, the piston/connecting rod assemblies must be cleaned, and the original piston rings removed from the pistons.

2 Carefully expand the old rings over the top of the pistons. The use of two or three old feeler blades will be helpful in preventing the rings dropping into empty grooves (**see illustration**). Be careful not to scratch the piston with the ends of the ring. The rings are brittle, and will snap if they are spread too far. They are also very sharp – protect your hands and fingers. Note that the third ring incorporates an expander. Always remove the rings from the top of the piston. Keep each set of rings with its piston if the old rings are to be re-used. Note which way up each ring is fitted to ensure correct refitting.

3 Scrape away all traces of carbon from the top of the piston. A hand-held wire brush (or a piece of fine emery cloth) can be used, once the majority of the deposits have been scraped away.

4 Remove the carbon from the ring grooves in the piston, using an old ring. Break the ring

in half to do this (be careful not to cut your fingers – piston rings are sharp). Be careful to remove only the carbon deposits – do not remove any metal, and do not nick or scratch the sides of the ring grooves.

5 Once the deposits have been removed, clean the piston/connecting rod assembly with paraffin or a suitable solvent, and dry thoroughly. Make sure that the oil return holes in the ring grooves are clear.

Inspection

6 If the pistons and cylinder bores are not damaged or worn excessively, and if the cylinder block does not need to be rebored, the original pistons can be refitted. Measure the piston diameters, and check that they are within limits for the corresponding bore diameters. If the piston-to-bore clearance is excessive, the block will have to be rebored, and new pistons and rings fitted. Normal piston wear shows up as even vertical wear on the piston thrust surfaces, and slight looseness of the top ring in its groove. New piston rings should always be used when the engine is reassembled. Note that the piston and bore size grades are stamped on the piston crowns, and on the adjacent cylinder head mating face of the cylinder block.

7 Carefully inspect each piston for cracks around the skirt, around the gudgeon pin holes, and at the piston ring 'lands' (between the ring grooves).

8 Look for scoring and scuffing on the piston skirt, holes in the piston crown, and burned areas at the edge of the crown. If the skirt is scored or scuffed, the engine may have been suffering from overheating, and/or abnormal combustion, which caused excessively high operating temperatures. The cooling and lubrication systems should be checked thoroughly. Scorch marks on the sides of the pistons show that blow-by has occurred. A hole in the piston crown, or burned areas at the edge of the piston crown, indicates that abnormal combustion (pre-ignition, knocking or detonation) has been occurring. If any of the above problems exist, the causes must be investigated and corrected, or the damage will occur again. The causes may include incorrect ignition/injection pump timing, inlet air leaks or a faulty fuel injector.

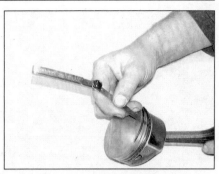

12.2 Using a feeler blade to help remove a piston ring

9 Corrosion of the piston, in the form of pitting, indicates that coolant has been leaking into the combustion chamber and/or the crankcase. Again, the cause must be corrected, or the problem may persist in the rebuilt engine.

10 New pistons can be purchased from a Mercedes-Benz dealer or motor factor.

11 Examine each connecting rod carefully for signs of damage, such as cracks around the big-end and small-end bearings. Check that the rod is not bent or distorted. Damage is highly unlikely, unless the engine has been seized or badly overheated. Detailed checking of the connecting rod assembly can only be carried out by a Mercedes-Benz dealer or engine repair specialist with the necessary equipment.

12 The gudgeon pins are of the floating type, secured in position by two circlips. The pistons and connecting rods can be separated as follows.

13 Using a small screwdriver, prise out the circlips, and push out the gudgeon pin (**see illustrations**). Hand pressure should be sufficient to remove the pin. Identify the piston and rod to ensure correct reassembly. Discard the circlips – new ones must be used on refitting.

14 Examine the gudgeon pin and connecting rod small-end bearing for signs of wear or damage. It should be possible to push the gudgeon pin through the connecting rod bush by hand, without noticeable play. Wear can be cured by renewing both the pin and bush. Bush renewal, however, is a specialist job – press facilities are required, and the new bush must be reamed accurately.

12.13a Prise out the circlips . . .

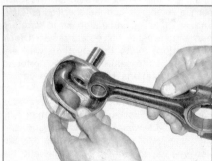

12.13b . . . then press out the gudgeon pin and separate the connecting rod

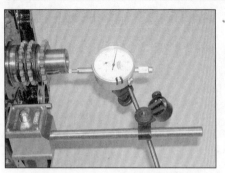

13.2 Checking the crankshaft endfloat using a dial gauge

13.10 Measuring a big-end bearing journal diameter with a micrometer

15 The connecting rods themselves should not be in need of renewal, unless seizure or some other major mechanical failure has occurred. Check the alignment of the connecting rods visually, and if the rods are not straight, take them to an engine overhaul specialist for a more detailed check.

16 Examine all components, and obtain any new parts from your Mercedes-Benz dealer. If new pistons are purchased, they will be supplied complete with gudgeon pins and circlips. These circlips can also be purchased individually.

17 Position the piston in relation to the connecting rod as noted on removal.

18 Apply a smear of clean engine oil to the gudgeon pin. Slide it into the piston and through the connecting rod small-end. Check that the piston pivots freely on the rod, then secure the gudgeon pin in position with two new circlips. Ensure that each circlip is correctly located in its groove in the piston.

13 Crankshaft – inspection

Checking crankshaft endfloat

1 If the crankshaft endfloat is to be checked, this must be done when the crankshaft is still installed in the cylinder block/crankcase, but is free to move.

2 Check the endfloat using a dial gauge in contact with the end of the crankshaft. Push the crankshaft fully one way, and then zero the gauge. Push the crankshaft fully the other way, and check the endfloat. The result can be compared with the specified amount, and will give an indication as to whether new thrustwasher halves are required **(see illustration)**. Note that all thrustwashers must be of the same thickness – refer to the Specifications for the thicknesses of thrustwashers available.

3 If a dial gauge is not available, feeler blades can be used. First push the crankshaft fully towards the flywheel end of the engine, and then use feeler blades to measure the gap between the web of No 3 crankpin and the thrustwasher halves on 4-cylinder engines, or between the web of No 4 crankpin and the thrustwasher halves on the 5-cylinder engine.

Inspection

4 Clean the crankshaft using paraffin or a suitable solvent, and dry it, preferably with compressed air if available. Be sure to clean the oil holes with a pipe cleaner or similar probe, to ensure that they are not obstructed.

 Warning: Wear eye protection when using compressed air.

5 Check the main and big-end bearing journals for uneven wear, scoring, pitting and cracking.

6 Big-end bearing wear is accompanied by distinct metallic knocking when the engine is running (particularly noticeable when the engine is pulling from low speed) and some loss of oil pressure.

7 Main bearing wear is accompanied by severe engine vibration and rumble – getting progressively worse as engine speed increases – and again by loss of oil pressure.

8 Check the bearing journal for roughness by running a finger lightly over the bearing surface. Any roughness (which will be accompanied by obvious bearing wear) indicates that the crankshaft requires regrinding (where possible) or renewal.

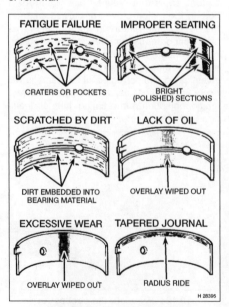

14.2 Typical bearing failures

9 If the crankshaft has been reground, check for burrs around the crankshaft oil holes (the holes are usually chamfered, so burrs should not be a problem unless regrinding has been carried out carelessly). Remove any burrs with a fine file or scraper, and thoroughly clean the oil holes.

10 Using a micrometer, measure the diameter of the main and big-end bearing journals **(see illustration)**. By measuring the diameter at a number of points around each journal's circumference, you will be able to determine whether or not the journal is out-of-round. Take the measurement at each end of the journal, near the webs, to determine if the journal is tapered.

11 Check the oil seal contact surfaces of the crankshaft for wear and damage. If the seal has worn a deep groove in the surface of the crankshaft, refer to Part A or B of this Chapter.

12 If the crankshaft journals have not previously been reground, it may be possible to have the crankshaft reconditioned, and to fit undersize shells (see Section 17). If no undersize shells are available and the crankshaft has worn beyond repair, it will have to be renewed. Consult your Mercedes-Benz dealer or engine specialist for further information on parts availability.

13 Where the transmission input shaft spigot bearing is located in the end of the crankshaft, examine it for smooth running. If necessary renew it as described in Part A or B of this Chapter.

14 Main and big-end bearings, and bearing cap bolts – inspection

Bearings

1 Even though the main and big-end bearings should be renewed during the engine overhaul, the old bearings should be retained for close examination, as they may reveal valuable information about the condition of the engine. The bearing shells are graded by thickness.

2 Bearing failure can occur due to lack of lubrication, the presence of dirt or other foreign particles, overloading the engine, or corrosion **(see illustration)**. Regardless of the cause of bearing failure, the cause must be corrected before the engine is reassembled to prevent it from happening again.

3 When examining the bearing shells, remove them from the cylinder block/crankcase, the connecting rods and the connecting rod big-end bearing caps. Lay them out on a clean surface in the same general position as their location in the engine. This will enable you to match any bearing problems with the corresponding crankshaft journal. Do not touch any shell's bearing surface with your fingers while checking it, or the delicate surface may be scratched.

4 Dirt and other foreign matter get into the engine in a variety of ways. It may be left in the engine during assembly, or it may pass through filters or the crankcase ventilation system. It may get into the oil, and from there into the bearings. Metal chips from machining operations and normal engine wear are often present. Abrasives are sometimes left in engine components after reconditioning, especially when parts are not thoroughly cleaned using the proper cleaning methods. Whatever the source, these foreign objects often end up embedded in the soft bearing material, and are easily recognised. Large particles will not embed in the bearing, and will score or gouge the bearing and journal. The best prevention for this cause of bearing failure is to clean all parts thoroughly, and keep everything spotlessly clean during engine assembly. Frequent and regular engine oil and filter changes are also recommended.

5 Lack of lubrication (or lubrication breakdown) has a number of interrelated causes. Excessive heat (which thins the oil), overloading (which squeezes the oil from the bearing face) and oil leakage (from excessive bearing clearances, worn oil pump or high engine speeds) all contribute to lubrication breakdown. Blocked oil passages, which may be the result of misaligned oil holes in a bearing shell, will also oil-starve a bearing, and destroy it. When lack of lubrication is the cause of bearing failure, the bearing material is wiped or extruded from the steel backing of the bearing. Temperatures may increase to the point where the steel backing turns blue from overheating.

6 Driving habits can have a definite effect on bearing life. Full-throttle, low-speed operation (labouring the engine) puts very high loads on bearings, tending to squeeze out the oil film. These loads cause the bearings to flex, which produces fine cracks in the bearing face (fatigue failure). Eventually, the bearing material will loosen in pieces, and tear away from the steel backing.

7 Short-distance driving leads to corrosion of bearings, because insufficient engine heat is produced to drive off the condensed water and corrosive gases. These products collect in the engine oil, forming acid and sludge. As the oil is carried to the engine bearings, the acid attacks and corrodes the bearing material.

8 Incorrect bearing installation during engine assembly will lead to bearing failure as well. Tight-fitting bearings leave insufficient bearing running clearance, and will result in oil starvation. Dirt or foreign particles trapped behind a bearing shell result in high spots on the bearing, which lead to failure.

9 *Do not* touch any shell's bearing surface with your fingers during reassembly; there is a risk of scratching the delicate surface, or of depositing particles of dirt on it.

10 As mentioned at the beginning of this Section, the bearing shells should be renewed as a matter of course during engine overhaul;

to do otherwise is false economy. Refer to Sections 17 and 18 for details of bearing shell selection.

Main bearing cap bolts

11 On some models, the manufacturers recommend that the main bearing cap bolts are measured to determine whether renewal is necessary; however, some owners may wish to renew all the bolts as a matter of course.
12 Where applicable, measure the length of each bolt from the base of the head to the end of the shank **(see illustration)**. If the bolt length is greater than the maximum specified, the bolts should be renewed.

Big-end bearing cap bolts

13 On some models, the manufacturers recommend that the big-end bearing cap bolts are measured to determine whether renewal is necessary, however, some owners may wish to renew all the bolts as a matter of course. It is strongly recommended that the bolts be renewed when reassembling the engine.
14 Press or tap the bolts out from the connecting rods.
15 Where applicable, measure the length of each bolt from the base of the head to the end of the shank. If the bolt length is greater than the maximum specified, the bolts should be renewed.

15 Engine overhaul –
reassembly sequence

1 Before reassembly begins, ensure that all new parts have been obtained, and that all necessary tools are available. Read through the entire procedure to familiarise yourself with the work involved, and to ensure that all items necessary for reassembly of the engine are at hand. In addition to all normal tools and materials, thread-locking compound will be needed. A suitable tube of liquid sealant will also be required for the joint faces that are fitted without gaskets.
2 In order to save time and avoid problems, engine reassembly can be carried out in the following order, referring to Part A or B of this Chapter unless otherwise stated. Where applicable, use new gaskets and seals when refitting the various components.
  a) *Crankshaft (Section 17).*
  b) *Piston/connecting rod assemblies (Section 18).*
  c) *Oil pump.*
  d) *Sump.*
  e) *Flywheel.*
  f) *Cylinder head.*
  g) *Timing chain, tensioner and sprockets.*
  h) *Engine external components.*
3 At this stage, all engine components should be absolutely clean and dry, with all faults repaired. The components should be laid out (or in individual containers) on a completely clean work surface.

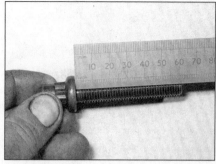
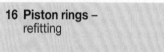

14.12 Measuring a main bearing cap bolt

16 Piston rings –
refitting

1 Before fitting new piston rings, the ring end gaps must be checked as follows.
2 Lay out the piston/connecting rod assemblies and the new piston ring sets, so that the ring sets will be matched with the same piston and cylinder during the end gap measurement and subsequent engine reassembly.
3 Insert the top ring into the first cylinder, and push it down the bore using the top of the piston. This will ensure that the ring remains square with the cylinder walls. Position the ring near the bottom of the cylinder bore, at the lower limit of ring travel. Note that the top and second compression rings are different. The second ring is easily identified by the step on its lower surface.
4 Measure the end gap using feeler blades.
5 Repeat the procedure with the ring at the top of the cylinder bore, at the upper limit of its travel **(see illustration)**, and compare the measurements with the figures given in the Specifications.
6 If the gap is too small (unlikely if genuine Mercedes-Benz parts are used), it must be enlarged, or the ring ends may contact each other during engine operation, causing serious damage. Ideally, new piston rings providing the correct end gap should be fitted. As a last resort, the end gap can be increased by filing the ring ends very carefully with a fine file. Mount the file in a vice equipped with soft

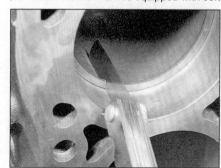

16.5 Measuring a piston ring end-gap

16.10 Fitting the oil control ring expander

jaws, slip the ring over the file with the ends contacting the file face, and slowly move the ring to remove material from the ends. Take care, as piston rings are sharp, and are easily broken.

7 With new piston rings, it is unlikely that the end gap will be too large. If the gaps are too large, check that you have the correct rings for your engine and for the particular cylinder bore size.

8 Repeat the checking procedure for each ring in the first cylinder, and then for the rings in the remaining cylinders. Remember to keep rings, pistons and cylinders matched up.

9 Once the ring end gaps have been checked and if necessary corrected, the rings can be fitted to the pistons.

10 Fit the piston rings using the same technique as for removal. Fit the bottom (oil control) ring first, and work up. When

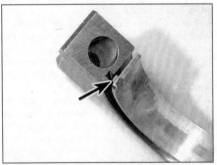

17.5 Ensure that the tab on each bearing shell (arrowed) engages with the notch in the cap

17.9b ... and lubricate them with clean engine oil

fitting the oil control ring, first insert the wire expander, then fit the ring with its gap positioned 180° from the protruding wire ends of the expander. Ensure that the rings are fitted the correct way up – the top surface of the rings is normally marked TOP **(see illustration)**. Arrange the gaps of the top and second compression rings 120° either side of the oil control ring gap, but make sure that none of the rings gaps are positioned over the gudgeon pin hole. **Note:** *Always follow any instructions supplied with the new piston ring sets – different manufacturers may specify different procedures. Do not mix up the top and second compression rings, as they have different cross-sections.*

17 Crankshaft – refitting and main bearing running clearance check

Selection of new bearing shells

1 If the original crankshaft is in good condition and is being refitted, new main bearing shells, which are the same size as the removed shells, should be fitted.

2 If the crankshaft has been reground, undersize bearing shells must be fitted. The engine-reconditioning specialist normally supplies the appropriate shells.

Main bearing clearance check

3 The running clearance check can be carried out using the original bearing shells. However,

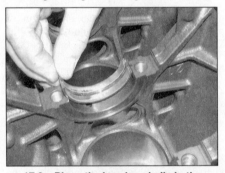

17.9a Place the bearing shells in the crankcase ...

17.10 Fitting the upper thrustwasher halves

it is preferable to use a new set, since the results obtained will be more conclusive in determining wear of the crankshaft journals.

4 Clean the backs of the bearing shells, and the bearing locations in both the cylinder block/crankcase and the main bearing caps.

5 Press the bearing shells into their locations, ensuring that the tab on each shell engages in the notch in the cylinder block/crankcase or bearing cap **(see illustration)**. Take care not to touch any shell's bearing surface with your fingers. If the original bearing shells are being used for the check, ensure that they are refitted in their original locations. Note that the bearings shells with oil grooves fit in the cylinder block, and the plain bearing shells fit in the bearing caps.

6 The running clearance can be checked, although this will be difficult to achieve without a range of internal micrometers or internal/external expanding calipers. Refit the main bearing caps to the cylinder block/crankcase, with bearing shells in place. With the original cap retaining bolts tightened to the specified torque, measure the internal diameter of each assembled pair of bearing shells. If the diameter of each corresponding crankshaft journal is measured and then subtracted from the bearing internal diameter, the result will be the main bearing running clearance.

Final crankshaft refitting

Note: *It is recommended that new main bearing cap bolts be used when finally refitting the crankshaft.*

7 Carefully lift the crankshaft out of the cylinder block once more, and wipe off the surfaces of the bearing shells in the crankcase and bearing caps.

8 Where applicable, ensure that the oil spray jets are fitted to the cylinder block.

9 Place the bearing shells in their locations as described earlier. If new shells are being fitted, ensure that all traces of protective grease are cleaned off using paraffin. Wipe dry the shells and connecting rods with a lint-free cloth. Liberally lubricate each bearing shell in the cylinder block/crankcase and cap with clean engine oil **(see illustrations)**.

10 Fit the upper thrustwasher halves to the appropriate bearing location in the cylinder block as follows **(see illustration)**.
4-cylinder engine – centre (No 3) main bearing.
5-cylinder engine – No 4 main bearing.
Ensure that the oil grooves in the thrustwasher halves face out towards the crankshaft journals.

11 The crankshaft can now be lowered into position.

12 Lubricate the lower bearing shells in the main bearing caps with clean engine oil. Make sure that the locating lugs on the shells engage with the corresponding recesses in the caps **(see illustrations)**.

13 Fit the main bearing caps to their correct locations, ensuring that they are fitted the correct way round. Ensure that

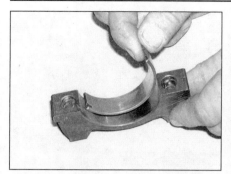

17.12a Locate the main bearing shells in the caps . . .

17.12b . . . and lubricate them with clean engine oil

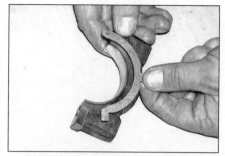

17.13a Fitting a thrustwasher half to a main bearing cap (use a little grease to hold the washer in position)

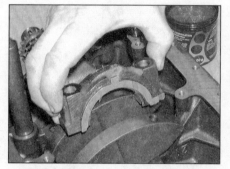

17.13b Fitting No 3 main bearing cap

17.14a Lightly lubricate the main bearing cap bolts . . .

17.14b . . . then insert them

the thrustwasher halves are in place on the appropriate bearing cap (see illustrations).

14 Lightly lubricate the bolt threads, then fit the main bearing cap bolts (see illustrations). Where applicable, ensure that the oil pick-up pipe support bracket is in place on the relevant bolts, as noted before removal. Tighten the bolts by hand only at this stage.

15 Progressively tighten the main bearing cap bolts to the specified torque, starting with the centre bearing cap and working outwards. Observe the two tightening stages given in the Specifications (see illustrations). If the bolts are angle-tightened, it is recommended that an angle-measuring gauge be used during this stage of the tightening, to ensure accuracy. If a gauge is not available, use a dab of white paint to make alignment marks between the bolt and bearing cap prior to tightening; the marks can then be used to check that the bolt has been rotated sufficiently during tightening.

16 Check that the crankshaft rotates freely.

17 Fit a new crankshaft rear oil seal to the housing, then refit the housing, using a new gasket, or suitable sealant, as applicable.

18 Refit the piston/connecting rod assemblies as described in Section 18.

19 Refit the flywheel, crankshaft sprocket, timing chain, timing chain cover and sump, as described in Part A or B of this Chapter.

18 Piston/connecting rod assembly – refitting and big-end bearing running clearance check

Selection of new bearing shells

1 If the big-end journals on the crankshaft are in good condition, new big-end bearing shells, which are the same size as the removed shells, should be fitted.

2 If the crankshaft has been reground,

undersize bearing shells must be fitted. The engine-reconditioning specialist normally supplies the appropriate shells.

Big-end bearing clearance check

3 Clean the backs of the bearing shells, and the bearing locations in both the connecting rod and bearing cap.

4 Press the bearing shells into their locations, ensuring that the tab on each shell engages in the notch in the connecting rod and cap (see illustrations). Take care not to touch the bearing surface of the shell with your fingers. If the original bearing shells are being used for the check, ensure that they are refitted in their original locations.

5 The running clearance can be checked, although this will be difficult to achieve without a range of internal micrometers or internal/external expanding calipers. Refit the big-end

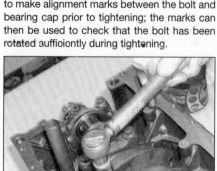

17.15a Torque-tightening the main bearing cap bolts

17.15b Angle-tightening the main bearing cap bolts

18.4a Inserting the bearing shells in the conrod . . .

18.4b ... and big-end bearing cap

18.7a Lubricating the pistons and rings ...

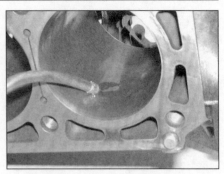
18.7b ... and cylinder bores

18.8 Fitting a piston ring compressor to the piston

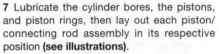
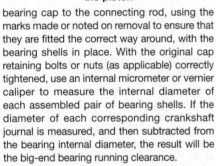
18.9 Inserting a piston in its cylinder bore

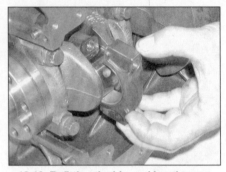
18.10 Refitting the big-end bearing cap

bearing cap to the connecting rod, using the marks made or noted on removal to ensure that they are fitted the correct way around, with the bearing shells in place. With the original cap retaining bolts or nuts (as applicable) correctly tightened, use an internal micrometer or vernier caliper to measure the internal diameter of each assembled pair of bearing shells. If the diameter of each corresponding crankshaft journal is measured, and then subtracted from the bearing internal diameter, the result will be the big-end bearing running clearance.

Piston/connecting rod refitting

Note: *A piston ring compressor tool will be required for this operation. Note that the following procedure assumes that the main bearing caps are in place.*

6 Ensure that the bearing shells are correctly fitted as described earlier. If new shells are being fitted, ensure that all traces of the

protective grease are cleaned off using paraffin. Wipe dry the shells and connecting rods with a lint-free cloth.
7 Lubricate the cylinder bores, the pistons, and piston rings, then lay out each piston/connecting rod assembly in its respective position **(see illustrations)**.
8 Start with assembly No 1. Make sure that the piston rings are still spaced as described in Section 16, and then clamp them in position with a piston ring compressor **(see illustration)**.
9 Insert the piston/connecting rod assembly into the top of cylinder No 1. Ensure that the arrow on the piston crown points towards the timing chain end of the engine, and that the identifying marks on the connecting rods and big-end caps are positioned as noted before removal. Using a block of wood or hammer handle against the piston crown, tap the assembly into the cylinder until the piston crown is flush with the top of the cylinder **(see**

illustration). Where applicable, take care not to damage the piston cooling oil spray jets as the piston/connecting rod assemblies are refitted.
10 Ensure that the bearing shell is still correctly installed. Liberally lubricate the crankpin and both bearing shells. Taking care not to mark the cylinder bores or damage the piston oil jets (where fitted), pull the piston / connecting rod assembly down the bore and onto the crankpin. Refit the big-end bearing cap **(see illustration)**. Note that the bearing shell locating tabs must abut each other.
11 Lightly lubricate the bolt threads, then screw the big-end bearing cap bolts by hand into position in the connecting rods **(see illustration)**.
12 Progressively tighten the bolts to the specified torque and angle, observing the two tightening stages given in the Specifications **(see illustrations)**. It is recommended

18.11 Fitting the big-end bearing cap bolts

18.12a Torque-tightening the big-end bearing bolts

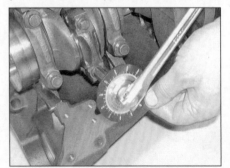
18.12b Angle-tightening the big-end bearing bolts

that an angle-measuring gauge is used to angle-tighten the bolts. If a gauge is not available, use a dab of white paint to make alignment marks between the bolt and bearing cap prior to tightening; the marks can then be used to check that the bolt has been rotated sufficiently during tightening.

13 Once the bearing cap bolts have been correctly tightened, rotate the crankshaft and check that it turns freely. Some stiffness is to be expected if new components have been fitted, but there should be no signs of binding or tight spots.

14 Refit the remaining piston/connecting rod assemblies in the same way.

15 Refit the oil pump, sump and cylinder head as described in Part A or B of this Chapter (as applicable).

19 Engine – initial start-up after overhaul

1 Refit the remainder of the engine components in the correct order listed in this Chapter. Refit the engine to the vehicle as described in the relevant Section of this Chapter. Double-check the engine oil and coolant levels, and make a final check that everything has been reconnected. Make sure that there are no tools or rags left in the engine compartment.

2 Where necessary, reconnect the battery leads with reference to *Disconnecting the battery* at the rear of this manual.

3 Disconnect the injector harness wiring plug at the left-hand rear of the engine compartment – refer to Chapter 4A for details.

4 Turn the engine using the starter motor until the oil pressure warning lamp goes out.

5 If the lamp fails to extinguish after several seconds of cranking, check the engine oil level and oil filter security. Assuming these are correct, check the security of the oil pressure switch cabling – do not progress any further until you are satisfied that oil is being pumped around the engine at sufficient pressure.

6 Reconnect the injector wiring plug.

7 Start the engine, but be aware that as fuel system components have been disturbed, the cranking time may be a little longer than usual.

8 While the engine is idling, check for fuel, water and oil leaks. Don't be alarmed if there are some odd smells and the occasional plume of smoke as components heat up and burn off oil deposits.

9 Assuming all is well; keep the engine idling until hot water is felt circulating through the top hose.

10 After a few minutes, recheck the oil and coolant levels, and top-up as necessary.

11 There is no need to retighten the cylinder head bolts once the engine has been run following reassembly.

12 If new pistons, rings or crankshaft bearings have been fitted, the engine must be treated as new, and run-in for the first 600 miles. *Do not* operate the engine at full-throttle, or allow it to labour at low engine speeds in any gear. It is recommended that the engine oil and filter be changed at the end of this period.

Notes

Chapter 3
Cooling, heating and ventilation systems

Contents

Degrees of difficulty

Easy, suitable for novice with little experience	Fairly easy, suitable for beginner with some experience	Fairly difficult, suitable for competent DIY mechanic	Difficult, suitable for experienced DIY mechanic	Very difficult, suitable for expert DIY or professional

Specifications

System type .... Sealed cooling system with auxiliary belt driven coolant pump. The system also has a thermostat and a thermostatically controlled thermo-viscous cooling fan.

General

Pressure cap opening pressure	1.4 bar
Thermostat:	
Opening commences.................................	80 ± 2°C
Fully open	100°C
Coolant type.......................................	See *Lubricants and fluids*
Cooling system total capacity	See Chapter 1

Air conditioning system

Refrigerant	R134a

Torque wrench settings

	Nm	lbf ft
Air conditioning compressor bolts.........................	20	15
Air conditioning refrigerant pipes-to-compressor bolts.............	20	15
Alternator mounting bracket bolts...........................	45	33
Cooling fan blades to viscous coupling......................	10	7
Coolant pump mounting bolts	10	7
Coolant pump pulley bolts:		
2.2 litre	10	7
2.9 litre:		
Hexagon head bolt.................................	10	7
Torx head bolt....................................	14	10
Cylinder block drain plug................................	30	22
Thermostat housing mounting bolts	10	7
Viscous fan coupling to coolant pump/bearing body	54	40

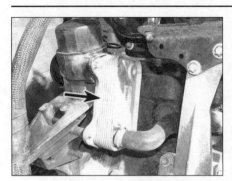

1.7a Oil cooler (2.2 litre engine)

1.7b Oil cooler (2.9 litre engine)

1.8 Power steering fluid cooler

1 General information and precautions

The cooling system is of pressurised type, comprising a pump, an aluminium crossflow radiator, temperature-conscious thermo-viscous cooling fan, and a thermostat. Cold coolant from the radiator passes through the hose to the coolant pump, where it is pumped around the cylinder block and head passages. After cooling the cylinder bores, combustion surfaces and valve seats, the coolant reaches the underside of the thermostat, which is initially closed. The coolant passes through the heater and is returned through the cylinder block to the coolant pump.

When the engine is cold, the coolant circulates only through the cylinder block, cylinder head, expansion tank and heater. When the coolant reaches a predetermined temperature, the thermostat opens and the coolant passes through to the radiator. As the coolant circulates through the radiator, it is cooled by the inrush of air when the car is in forward motion. Airflow is supplemented by the action of the cooling fan as necessary. Upon reaching the bottom of the radiator, the coolant is now cooled and the cycle is repeated.

The coolant pump is mounted externally on the front of the engine, and is driven by the auxiliary drivebelt.

Coolant temperature information for the gauge mounted in the instrument panel, and for the fuel system, is provided by temperature sensors mounted in the thermostat housing or in the cylinder head, depending on model. A coolant level switch is fitted to bottom of the radiator expansion tank.

The thermo-viscous cooling fan is controlled by the temperature of air behind the radiator. When the air temperature reaches a predetermined level, a bi-metallic coil opens a valve within the unit, and silicon fluid is fed through a system of vanes. Half of the vanes are driven directly by the coolant pump pulley by the auxiliary drivebelt, and the remaining half are connected to the fan blades. The vanes are arranged so that drive is transmitted to the fan blades in relation to the drag, or

viscosity of the fluid, and this in turn depends on ambient temperature and engine speed. The fan is therefore only operated when required.

All models have a coolant expansion tank, which is built into the top, left-hand side of the radiator and collects the coolant, which is displaced from the system as it expands due to the rise in temperature. The displaced coolant is returned to the radiator as the system cools.

All models are equipped with a heat exchanger attached to either the oil filter housing (2.2 litre engines) or on the rear of the cylinder block (2.9 litre engines). A supply of coolant is fed to the heat exchanger to cool the oil **(see illustrations)**.

Although not strictly part of the cooling system, note that the power steering fluid rigid pipes pass in front of the radiator **(see illustration)**, and are cooled by the inrush of air when the car is moving, thus cooling the fluid.

The vehicle interior heater operates by means of coolant from the engine cooling system. Coolant flow through the heater matrix is regulated by a valve, which is controlled by a temperature sensor in the heater unit. Temperature control is further achieved by blending cool air from outside the vehicle (or from the air conditioning system) with the warm air from the heater matrix, in the desired ratio.

Refer to Sections 9 and 10 for information on the air conditioning system.

⚠ **Warning: Do not attempt to remove the pressure cap, or disturb any part of the cooling system, while the engine is hot, as there is a high risk of scalding. If the pressure cap must be removed before the engine and radiator have fully cooled (even though this is not recommended), the pressure in the cooling system must first be relieved. Cover the cap with a thick layer of cloth, to avoid scalding, and slowly unscrew the pressure cap until a hissing sound is heard (be prepared to refit the cap quickly if bubbling noises are heard and hot coolant starts to come out). When the hissing stops, indicating that the pressure has reduced, slowly unscrew the pressure cap until it can be removed; if**

more hissing sounds are heard, wait until they have stopped before unscrewing the cap completely. At all times, keep your face well away from the pressure cap opening, and protect your hands.

⚠ **Warning: Do not allow antifreeze to come into contact with your skin, or with the painted surfaces of the vehicle. Rinse off spills immediately with plenty of water. Never leave antifreeze lying around in an open container, or in a puddle in the driveway or on the garage floor. Children and pets are attracted by its sweet smell, but antifreeze can be fatal if ingested.**

⚠ **Warning: The cooling fan could cut in even if the engine is not running (if the ignition is on). Be careful to keep your hands, hair, and any loose clothing well clear when working in the engine compartments.**

2 Cooling system hoses – disconnection and renewal

1 The number, routing and pattern of hoses will vary according to model, but the same basic procedure applies. Before commencing work, make sure that the new hoses are to hand, along with new hose clips if needed. It is good practice to renew the hose clips at the same time as the hoses.

2 Drain the cooling system as described in Chapter 1, saving the coolant if it is fit for re-use. Squirt a little penetrating oil onto the hose clips if they are corroded.

3 Release the hose clips from the hose concerned. The clip most commonly used on the Mercedes-Benz is a spring clip, which is released by squeezing its tags together with pliers, at the same time working the clip away from the hose stub. A worm-drive clip is released by turning its screw anti-clockwise **(see illustration)**. The 'sardine-can' clips are not re-usable, and are best cut off with snips or side-cutters.

4 Unclip any wires, cables or other hoses, which may be attached to the hose being removed. Make notes for reference when reassembling, if necessary.

2.3 Coolant hoses with worm-drive clip

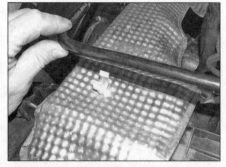

3.2 Unclip the brake vacuum pipe . . .

3.3 . . . and remove the heat shield

5 Release the hose from its stubs with a twisting motion. Be careful not to damage the stubs on delicate components such as the radiator, or thermostat housings. If the hose is stuck fast, the best course is often to cut it off using a sharp knife, but again be careful not to damage the stubs.

6 Before fitting the new hose, smear the stubs with washing-up liquid or a suitable rubber lubricant to aid fitting. Do not use oil or grease, which may attack the rubber.

7 Fit the hose clips over the ends of the hose, and then fit the hose over its stubs. Work the hose into position. When satisfied, locate and tighten the hose clips.

8 Refill the cooling system as described in Chapter 1. Run the engine, and check that there are no leaks.

9 Recheck the tightness of the hose clips on any new hoses after a few hundred miles.

10 Top-up the coolant level if necessary (see *Weekly checks*).

3.6a Undo the two mounting bolts

3.6b Release the upper radiator retaining clips

8 Move the radiator away from the cross-member to access the two upper retaining screws, and then remove them from the top of the radiator **(see illustration)**.

9 If required, remove the plastic upper trim

panel from under the front of the crossmsmber **(see illustration)**.

10 On turbo models, undo the retaining bolts from the intercooler and disconnect it from the front of the radiator **(see illustration)**.

---

3 Radiator –
removal, inspection
and refitting

Removal

1 Refer to Chapter 1 and drain the cooling system.

2 Open the bonnet and unclip the vacuum pipe from the top of the heat shield **(see illustration)**.

3 Undo the retaining bolts and withdraw the heat shield from the top of the exhaust manifold **(see illustration)**.

4 Removo the front grille as described Chapter 11, Section 22.

5 Remove the headlight units as described in Chapter 12, Section 10.

Models up to 2000

6 Undo the two retaining bolts and remove the air intake hose from across the front of the crossmember. Then release the two upper radiator retaining clips **(see illustrations)**.

7 Release the four retaining clips (two each side) from the cooling fan cowling and then unclip it from the radiator and move it towards the engine **(see illustration)**. Leave it in place around the cooling fan.

3.7 Cowling retaining clips – one side shown

3.9 Removing the upper plastic trim

3.8 Two upper retaining screws

3.10 Intercooler securing bolts – one side shown

3.14 Carefully lift out the radiator

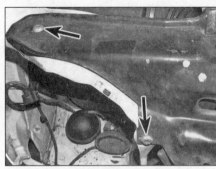

3.15a Undo the crossmember retaining bolts – one side shown . . .

3.15b . . . release the radiator upper retaining clips . . .

3.15c . . . and remove the crossmember

3.16a Remove the plastic trim from the right . . .

3.16b . . . and left-hand side of the radiator

11 Disconnect the wiring connector from the sensor in the expansion tank **(see illustration 3.20).**

12 Slacken the retaining clips and disconnect the top hose from the radiator and the smaller hose from the expansion tank **(see illustration 3.21).**

13 Slacken the retaining clip and disconnect the bottom hose from the coolant pump **(see illustration 3.22).**

14 Carefully lift the radiator upwards out of its lower mountings, and withdraw it from the vehicle **(see illustration)**. Take care not to damage the radiator fins as the radiator is removed. If required lift out the cowling from around the cooling fan.

Models from 2000

15 Undo the two retaining bolts from each end of the front upper crossmember and release the two upper radiator retaining clips **(see illustrations)**. Move the crossmember to one side or disconnect the bonnet release cable from the catch to remove completely.

16 Undo the retaining bolts and remove the plastic trim panels from each side of the radiator **(see illustrations)**.

17 On turbo models, slacken the retaining clips and disconnect the air hoses from each side of the intercooler. Undo the two retaining bolts and two retaining screws from across the top of the intercooler, and then withdraw it from the front of the vehicle **(see illustrations)**. **Note:** *The lower mounting bolts for the intercooler where removed when the plastic side trim panels where removed in paragraph 7.*

18 Undo the retaining screws and remove the plastic trim panel and power steering fluid cooling pipes from across the top of the radiator **(see illustrations)**.

19 On air conditioned models, unclip the radiator from the condenser and carefully remove the condenser out of the way, taking care not to damage the refrigerant lines. Fasten the condenser to one side securely to prevent any damage.

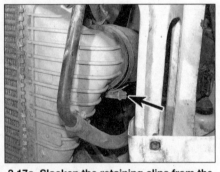

3.17a Slacken the retaining clips from the air hoses . . .

3.17b . . . undo the retaining screws . . .

3.17c . . . and remove the intercooler

3.18a Undo the retaining screws . . .

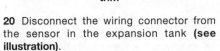

3.18b . . . and remove the upper plastic trim

3.20 Disconnect the wring connector

3.21 Slacken the retaining clips

20 Disconnect the wiring connector from the sensor in the expansion tank **(see illustration)**.
21 Slacken the retaining clips and disconnect the top hose from the radiator and the smaller hose from the expansion tank **(see illustration)**.
22 Slacken the retaining clip and disconnect the bottom hose from the coolant pump **(see illustration)**.
23 Carefully lift the radiator upwards out of its lower mountings, and withdraw it from the vehicle **(see illustration)**. Take care not to damage the radiator fins as the radiator is removed.

Inspection

24 Clear the radiator core of flies, small leaves or other debris by brushing or hosing. Check the condition of all hoses, clips, mountings and retaining spring clips, and renew as necessary.
25 Carefully examine the radiator/expansion tank for signs of leaks, corrosion of the alloy core, or damage to the plastic side, top or bottom compartments, as applicable. Should the radiator/expansion tank require attention, this work should be left to a specialist due to the nature of its construction.

Refitting

26 Refitting the radiator is the reverse sequence to removal, noting the following points:
  a) *Ensure that the lower mounting lugs properly engage with the rubber mountings, and that (where applicable) the locating studs are pressed fully home.*
  b) *Make sure that the radiator retaining clips are a secure fit.*
  c) *On turbo models, make sure the hoses are tightened securely.*
  d) *After fitting, fill the cooling system as described in Chapter 1.*

4 Thermostat – removal, testing and refitting

1 As the thermostat ages, it will become slower to react to changes in water temperature. Ultimately, the unit may stick in the open or

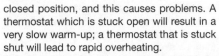

3.22 Disconnect the hose from the coolant pump

closed position, and this causes problems. A thermostat which is stuck open will result in a very slow warm-up; a thermostat that is stuck shut will lead to rapid overheating.
2 Before assuming that the thermostat is to blame for a cooling system problem, check the coolant level. If the system is draining due to a leak, or has not been properly filled, there may be an airlock in the system (refer to the coolant renewal procedure in the relevant part of Chapter 1).
3 If the engine seems to be taking a long time to warm up (based on heater output or temperature gauge operation), the thermostat is probably stuck open.
4 Equally, a lengthy warm-up period might suggest that the thermostat is missing – it may have been removed or inadvertently omitted by a previous owner or mechanic. Don't drive the vehicle without a thermostat – the engine management system's ECU will then stay in warm-up mode for longer than necessary, causing emissions and fuel economy to suffer.
5 If the engine runs hot, use your hand to check the temperature of the radiator top hose. If the hose isn't hot, but the engine is, the thermostat is probably stuck closed, preventing the coolant inside the engine from escaping to the radiator – renew the thermostat. Again, this problem may also be due to an airlock (refer to the coolant renewal procedure in the relevant part of Chapter 1).
6 If the radiator top hose is hot, it means that the coolant is flowing and the thermostat is open. Consult the *Fault finding* section at the

3.23 Remove the radiator from the vehicle

end of this manual to assist in tracing possible cooling system faults.
7 To gain a rough idea of whether the thermostat is working properly when the engine is warming-up, without dismantling the system, proceed as follows.
8 With the engine completely cold, start the engine and let it idle, while checking the temperature of the radiator top hose. Periodically check the temperature indicated on the coolant temperature gauge – if overheating is indicated, switch the engine off immediately.
9 The top hose should feel cold for some time as the engine warms-up, and should then get warm quite quickly as the thermostat opens.
10 The above is not a precise or definitive test of thermostat operation, but if the system does not perform as described, remove and test the thermostat as described below.

Removal

11 Disconnect the battery negative cable and position it away from the terminal.
12 Remove the engine plastic covers (where applicable) and drain the cooling system as described in Chapter 1.
13 Depending on model, it may be necessary to remove air inlet trunking from across the front of the engine to gain better access **(see illustration)**

2.2 litre engines

14 The thermostat is located in a housing which is bolted to front left-hand side of the cylinder head. On some models, the thermostat and cover are one unit – do not

4.13 Disconnect the air intake trunking

4.15a Disconnect the hoses . . .

4.15b . . . from the thermostat housing

4.16 Disconnect the wiring from the temperature sensor

4.17 Remove the thermostat housing

attempt to separate the thermostat from the cover, or it will be damaged.

15 Slacken the clips and detach the coolant hoses from the thermostat housing **(see illustrations)**.

16 Disconnect the wiring connector from the temperature sensor in the thermostat housing **(see illustration)**.

17 Unscrew the securing bolts, and remove the thermostat housing. Take care not to damage the bypass pipe below the housing as it is removed. Recover the O-ring seal from the bypass pipe and discard; a new one will be required when refitting **(see illustration)**.

2.9 litre engines

18 The thermostat is located in a housing which is bolted to the right-hand side of the cylinder block behind the alternator **(see illustration)**.

19 Slacken the clip and detach the air intake

hose from the air filter housing to the turbo **(see illustration)**. Then undo the retaining clip and disconnect the coolant hose from the thermostat cover.

20 Unscrew the securing bolts, and remove the thermostat cover from the housing. If the cover is stuck to the housing, tap it gently, or carefully rock it back and forth to free it – do not lever between the mating surfaces.

21 Recover the seal, then lift the thermostat from its housing, noting its orientation. Discard the O-ring seal; a new one will be required for refitting.

Testing

22 Check the temperature marking stamped on the thermostat, or refer to the opening temperature quoted in this Chapter's Specifications.

23 Using a thermometer and container of water, heat the water until the temperature

corresponds with the temperature marking stamped on the thermostat.

24 Suspend the (closed) thermostat on a length of string in the water, and check that maximum opening occurs within two minutes.

25 Remove the thermostat and allow it to cool down; check that it closes fully.

26 If the thermostat does not open and close as described, or if it sticks in either position, it must be renewed. If there is any question about the operation of the thermostat, renew it.

Refitting

27 Commence refitting by thoroughly cleaning the mating faces of the cover and the housing.

28 Lay a new seal in position on the housing, ensuring that it is correctly seated **(see illustration)**.

29 If removed, refit the thermostat to the housing, noting the correct fitted position.

30 Fit the thermostat and housing (where applicable), then refit the securing bolts, and tighten to the specified torque.

31 Further refitting is a reversal of removal. Refill the cooling system as described in Chapter 1.

5 Cooling fan – removal and refitting

Note: *It is recommended that the correct Mercedes-Benz locking tool be obtained, to avoid damaging the fan pulley and its associated components.*

4.18 Thermostat housing (2.9 litre engines)

4.19 Disconnect the inlet air pipe

4.28 Fit new seal to housing

5.3 Counterhold the pulley and slacken the securing bolt

5.4 Remove the complete fan

5.5 Securing bolts for fan blades

Removal

1 Disconnect the battery negative cable and position it away from the terminal.

2 On models up to 2000, remove the radiator and cooling fan cowling as described in Section 3. On models from 2000, unbolt the crossmember from across the front of the engine compartment and move it to one side. Move the radiator assembly as far forward as possible, taking care not to damage the hoses or radiator fins. Prise off the metal spring clips, then detach the fan shroud from the radiator and remove it from the engine bay.

3 The fan pulley shaft should be counterheld with a special Mercedes-Benz tool which grips the edge of the fan pulley with the auxiliary belt still in place. It may be possible to hold the pulley in position using an oil filter strap while slackening the centre bolt **(see illustration)**.

4 Remove the centre bolt, and then detach the fan assembly from the pulley shaft **(see illustration)**.

5 To remove the fan blades from the centre viscous clutch unit, slacken and remove the three retaining bolts **(see illustration)**.

Refitting

6 Refitting is a reversal of removal. Ensure that all bolts are tightened to the specified torque **(see illustration)**.

6   Cooling system electrical switches – removal and refitting

Coolant level sensor

1 The sensor is mounted in the top of the coolant expansion tank **(see illustration)**.

2 Refer to the relevant part of Chapter 1 and partially drain the expansion tank, so that the level is below the position of the sensor.

3 Ensure that the ignition is switched off, and then unplug the wiring from the coolant level switch at the connector.

4 Turn the sensor clockwise a quarter of a turn, and pull to remove it from the expansion tank. Check the sealing ring, renew it if required.

5 Refit the level sensor by following the removal procedure in reverse, noting the following points:

a) Fit a new O-ring seal to the sensor body, if required.
b) On completion, top-up the expansion tank.

Engine coolant temperature (ECT) sensor

Removal

2.2 litre engines

6 The coolant temperature sensor is located in the thermostat housing, on the left-hand side of the engine, at the front **(see illustration)**.

7 Ensure that the engine is cold, then refer to Chapter 1 and partially drain the cooling system.

8 Ensure that the ignition is switched off, and then unplug the wiring from the sensor at the connector **(see illustration)**.

9 Release the retaining clip and pull the

6.1 Coolant level sensor

6.8 Disconnect the wiring connector

sensor to remove it from the thermostat housing. Recover the sealing ring.

2.9 litre engines

10 The sensor for the temperature gauge is threaded into the cylinder head, on the left hand side of the engine**(see illustration)**.

11 Ensure that the engine is cold, then refer to Chapter 1 and partially drain the cooling system.

12 Ensure that the ignition is switched off, and then unplug the wiring from the sensor at the connector.

13 Unscrew the sensor from the cylinder head and recover the sealing ring.

Refitting

14 Refitting is a reversal of removal, noting the following points:
a) Use a new sealing ring, where fitted.
b) On completion, top-up the cooling system as described in Chapter 1 or Weekly checks.

6.6 Coolant temperature sensor (2.2 litre engines)

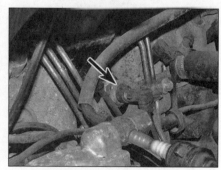

6.10 Coolant temperature sensor (2.9 litre engines)

7.4 Coolant pulley retaining bolts

7.7a Unclip the plastic cap . . .

7.7b . . . and remove the idler pulley

7.8 Coolant pump retaining bolts – note the different sizes

7.11 Removing the coolant pump

7.13 Fit new coolant pump gasket

7 Coolant pump – removal and refitting

Removal

1 Disconnect the battery negative cable and position it away from the terminal.
2 Refer to Chapter 1 and drain the cooling system.
3 Remove the viscous-coupled cooling fan, as described in Section 5.
4 Slacken the four retaining bolts **(see illustration)** on the pulley before removing the auxiliary belt to help prevent the pulley from turning.
5 Remove the auxiliary drivebelt as described in Chapter 1, and then remove the bolts and detach the pulley from coolant pump.
6 Slacken the hose clips and disconnect the

8.3 Undo the two retaining screws

coolant hoses from the ports on the coolant pump, noting their fitted position.

2.2 litre engines

7 Remove the plastic cap and remove the guide pulley from the top of the coolant pump housing **(see illustrations)**. **Note:** *One of the coolant pump retaining bolts is positioned behind the guide pulley.*
8 Loosen and remove the bolts securing the coolant pump, noting their locations, as they are of different lengths and sizes **(see illustration)**.

2.9 litre engines

9 Unbolt the heater return pipe from the pump at the union and recover the O-ring seal.
10 With reference to Chapter 5, remove the alternator, and then unbolt the alternator mounting bracket from the engine block.

All engines

11 Withdraw the pump, and recover the gasket **(see illustration)**. Discard the gasket, as a new one will be required when refitting.

Refitting

12 Carefully clean the coolant pump and cylinder block mating surfaces, removing all traces of the old gasket or sealant. Take care to avoid scoring the surfaces, as this will cause leakage.
13 Refit the coolant pump by following the removal procedure in reverse, noting these points:
  a) *If the pump is to be refitted using a bead of sealant instead of a gasket, apply the sealant in an even bead to the pump body*

only. *Do not apply an excessive amount, as any excess may enter the pump and then the cooling system itself, which could block the radiator passages.*
  b) *Fit a new gasket when refitting the pump* **(see illustration)**.
  c) *Tighten the pump bolts in a diagonal sequence to the correct torque, noting the different figures for the different size bolts used.*
  d) *Refit and tension the auxiliary drivebelt with reference to Chapter 1.*
  e) *On completion, refill the cooling system with reference to Chapter 1.*

8 Heater/ ventilation components – removal and refitting

1 Before working on any of the heater ventilation components, disconnect the battery negative cable and position it away from the terminal.

Heater control panel

2 Remove the centre console (models from 2000) or instrument panel surround (models up to 2000), as described in Chapter 11.
3 On models from 2000, remove the four screws (two at each side), from the heater control panel **(see illustration)**.
4 Carefully prise the heater control panel out of the facia panel.
5 Noting their locations, disconnect the wiring connectors from the rear of the heater control panel **(see illustrations)**.

8.5a Disconnect the wiring connectors (models from 2000)

8.5b Disconnect the wiring connectors (models up to 2000)

8.6a Disconnect the control cables (models from 2000)

8.6b Disconnect the control cables (models up to 2000)

8.8a Release the securing clips . . .

8.8b . . . and remove the soundproofing

6 Noting their fitted position (and colour), disconnect the heater control cables from the rear of the heater control panel **(see illustrations)**. The heater control panel can now be removed from the facia.

7 Refitting is a reversal of removal, making sure the wiring connectors and control cables are fitted correctly.

Ventilation box/ heater blower motor

Note: *The heater blower motor and resistor unit are situated inside the ventilation box in the engine compartment.*

8 Open the bonnet, release the securing clips and remove the insulation from below the heater ventilation box **(see illustrations)**.

9 Unscrew the four heater ventilation box retaining nuts, and withdraw it slightly from the vehicle bulkhead **(see illustrations)**.

10 Disconnect the wiring connector from the heater motor resistor **(see illustration)**.

11 Disconnect the vacuum pipe from the heater control valve **(see illustration)**.

12 The heater ventilation box can now be

removed completely from the vehicle **(see illustration)**.

13 To remove the blower motor out from the lower housing, remove the insulation from the housing, and then disconnect the wiring

8.9a Undo the bolts . . .

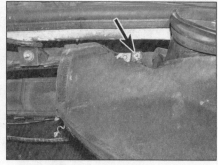

8.9b . . . securing the . . .

8.9c . . . heater ventilation box . . .

8.9d . . . to the bulkhead

8.10 Disconnect the wiring connector(s)

8.11 Disconnect the vacuum pipe

8.12 Remove the heater ventilation box

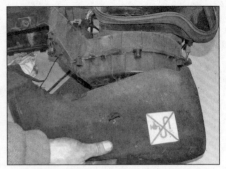

8.13a Remove the insulation . . .

8.13b . . . disconnect the wiring connector . . .

8.13c . . . undo the retaining screws . . .

8.13d . . . and remove the heater fan and motor

connector and undo the retaining screws **(see illustrations)**. The fan and motor can now be removed from the lower housing.

14 To remove the resistor unit from the housing, disconnect the wiring connectors

(if not already done), undo the two retaining screws, and withdraw it from the housing **(see illustrations)**.

15 Refitting is a reversal of removal, making sure that all wiring connections are securely

remade. Operate the fan before refitting the lower trim panel to check it is fitted correctly.

Heater housing

⚠ **Warning: On models fitted with air conditioning, the air conditioning refrigerant MUST be discharged prior to removal – see Section 9.**

16 Drain the cooling system as described in the relevant part of Chapter 1.

17 Remove the radio, speakers, glove compartment, instrument panel and facia trim panels, as described in Chapter 11.

18 Working inside the engine compartment, release the securing clips on the heater hoses into the heater matrix **(see illustration)**, and then carefully disconnect the hoses.

19 On models with air conditioning, working inside the engine compartment (with the system discharged), unscrew the two nuts securing the air conditioning pipe union to the bulkhead. Separate the pipes from the evaporator and quickly seal the pipe and evaporator unions to prevent the entry of moisture into the refrigerant circuit. Discard the sealing rings, new ones must be used on refitting.

⚠ **Warning: Failure to seal the refrigerant pipe unions will result in the dehydrator reservoir to become saturated, necessitating its renewal.**

20 Remove the ventilation box/heater blower unit, as described previously (paragraphs 8 to 12).

21 Undo the retaining screws and disconnect the ventilation air ducts from the heater housing **(see illustrations)**.

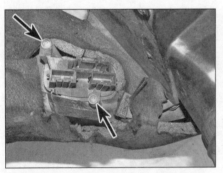

8.14a Undo the retaining screws . . .

8.14b . . . and remove the resistor from the housing

8.18 Disconnect the heater hoses

8.21a Disconnect the heater ducts . . .

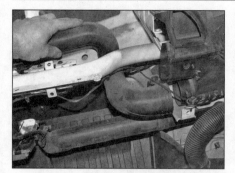

8.21b . . . from the heater housing

8.22a Unclip the wiring loom . . .

8.22b . . . and disconnect the wiring connectors

8.23a Undo the lower mounting screw . . .

8.23b . . . and the three upper mounting screws

8.24 Withdraw the heater housing from the bulkhead

22 Unclip the wiring loom from across the front of the heater housing and disconnect the wiring connector, noting their fitted positions for refitting **(see illustrations)**.

23 Undo the four retaining screws from the heater housing **(see illustrations)**.

24 With all the screws removed, withdraw the heater housing from inside the vehicle. Take care not to damage the heater matrix pipes as they are withdrawn through the bulkhead **(see illustration)**. **Note:** *The wiring loom also passes through the aperture in the bulkhead for the heater matrix pipes.*

25 Refitting is a reversal of removal, making sure that all connections are securely remade.

Heater regulating valve

26 Remove the heater housing, as described previously (paragraphs 16 to 24).

27 Peel the foam seal from the bulkhead end of the heater matrix pipes, taking care not to damage it.

28 Undo the valve mounting bolts from the pipes to the heater matrix **(see illustration)**.

29 Undo the mounting bolt securing the valve to the heater housing **(see illustration)**, and then withdraw the valve from the housing.

30 Refitting is a reversal of removal, making sure that all connections are securely remade.

Heater matrix

31 Remove the heater housing, as described previously (paragraphs 16 to 24).

32 Remove the regulating valve, as described previously (paragraphs 26 to 29).

33 Remove or cut through the foam gasket on the bulkhead side of the heater housing **(see illustration)**.

34 Working around the outer edge of the heater housing, undo the retaining screws, and then lift the upper part of the housing from the lower part **(see illustration)**.

35 The heater matrix can now be withdrawn

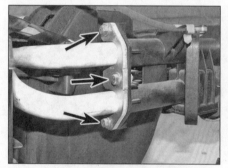

8.28 Remove the heater regulating valve . . .

8.29 . . . and mounting bolts

8.33 Carefully cut through the foam seal

8.34 Remove the upper part of the housing . . .

8.35 . . . and withdraw the heater matrix

8.39a Facia trim panel and vents (models from 2000)

8.39b Facia trim panel and vents (models up to 2000)

from the lower part of the heater housing **(see illustration)**. **Note:** *On models with air conditioning, the evaporator can also be removed at this point.*

36 Refitting is a reversal of removal, noting the following points:

a) *On completion, refill the cooling system as described in the relevant part of Chapter 1.*

b) *Run the engine and check the heater operation. It is not unknown for a heater not to work initially, due to the formation of an airlock (especially when a new heater matrix has been fitted).*

Facia air vents

Driver's side vents

37 The driver's side air vents are built into the instrument panel surround trim panel.

38 Remove the steering instrument panel surround as described in Chapter 11, Section 26.

39 Carefully pull the trim panel (including air vents) to release it from the facia panel **(see illustrations)**. As the trim panel is removed, disconnect the wiring connectors from the switches.

40 Refitting is a reversal of removal.

Passenger side vents (from 2000)

41 Unclip the upper trim panel from the top of the facia **(see illustration)**.

42 Undo the two retaining screws and remove the support bar from above the storage compartment **(see illustration)**.

43 Carefully pull the storage compartment (complete with air vents), to release it from the facia panel **(see illustration)**.

44 Refitting is a reversal of removal.

Centre vents (from 2000)

45 Unclip the air vent trim panel from the top of the facia panel **(see illustration)**.

46 Refitting is a reversal of removal.

Heater control cables

47 Depending on model, there are a number of control cables fitted to the heater housing behind the facia panel. To access these, remove the relevant panels as described in Chapter 11.

48 Remove the heater control panel, as described previously (paragraphs 2 to 6).

49 Release the securing clip holding the outer cable to the housing, and then disconnect the inner cable from the relevant control lever **(see illustrations)**. Withdraw the cable from behind the facia, noting its fitted position (and colour).

50 Refitting is a reversal of removal.

8.41 Unclip the upper tray panel . . .

8.42 . . . and remove the support bracket

8.43 Using a piece of wire to release the securing clips

8.45 Unclip the upper air vents from the facia

8.49a Unclip the outer cable from the retaining clip

8.49b Releasing the outer cable from the heater valve

9 Air conditioning system – general information and precautions

An air conditioning system is fitted as standard equipment on later high specification models, and was available as an optional extra on some lower specification models. In conjunction with the heater, the system enables any reasonable air temperature to be achieved inside the vehicle, it also reduces the humidity of the incoming air, aiding demisting even when cooling is not required.

The refrigeration circuit of the air conditioning system functions in a similar way to a domestic refrigerator. A compressor, belt-driven from the crankshaft pulley, draws refrigerant in its gaseous state from an evaporator. The refrigerant heats up as a result of being compressed, but is then passed through a condenser (mounted in front of the engine radiator) where it loses heat and enters its liquid state. After dehydration, the refrigerant is passed through an evaporator (mounted inside the heater housing) where it is allowed to expand and reverts to being gas. This change of state has the effect of absorbing heat from the air passing over the evaporator fins, reducing its temperature. This cool air is mixed with warm air from the heater unit to achieve the desired cabin temperature. The refrigerant is directed back to the compressor and the cycle is then repeated.

Various subsidiary controls and sensors protect the system against excessive temperature and pressures. Additionally, engine idle speed is increased when the system is in use to compensate for the additional load imposed by the compressor. Electronic sensors detect the rotational speed differential between the engine and the compressor – if this becomes too great (due to a malfunctioning compressor), the compressor clutch is disengaged, to preserve the drivebelt.

The air conditioning electronic control system can only be tested using dedicated equipment. For this reason, it is recommended that problems with the operation of the air conditioning system be referred to a Mercedes-Benz dealer for diagnosis.

⚠ **Warning: The refrigeration circuit contains pressurised liquid refrigerant. The refrigerant is potentially dangerous, and should only be handled by qualified persons. Refrigerant that is allowed to come into contact with the skin will cause severe frostbite. It is not itself poisonous, but in the presence of a naked flame (including inhalation through a lighted cigarette), it forms a poisonous gas. Uncontrolled discharging of the refrigerant is dangerous and is also extremely damaging to the environment. For these reasons, disconnection of any part of the system without specialised knowledge and equipment is not recommended.**

• *Do not allow refrigerant lines to be exposed to temperatures in excess of 110°C, for example during welding or paint-drying operations.*
• *Do not operate the air conditioning system if it is known to be short of refrigerant, or component damage may result.*

10 Air conditioning system components – removal and refitting

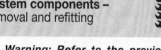

⚠ **Warning: Refer to the previous Section before proceeding. Before carrying out any of the procedures detailed below, the air conditioning system MUST be professionally discharged by a garage or air conditioning specialist.**
Note: *The car may be driven once the system has been discharged, but the air conditioning system should NOT be switched on, as this will cause damage to the compressor. The safest option is to have the system discharged where the car is to be worked on, and not move the car until the system has been recharged. With air conditioning becoming an increasingly common fitment, mobile air conditioning specialists are becoming more widespread.*

Evaporator

1 The evaporator is situated inside the heater housing behind the facia panel along side the heater matrix. To remove the evaporator, follow the procedures as described for removing the heater matrix in Section 8 of this Chapter.

Receiver/drier

2 The receiver/drier stores refrigerant and removes moisture from the system. When any major air conditioning component (compressor, condenser or evaporator) is renewed, or the system has been apart and exposed to air for any length of time, the receiver/drier must be renewed. This is to ensure correct functioning of the air conditioning system.
3 The receiver/dryer is mounted at the rear of the engine compartment.
4 Gloves must be worn when disconnecting the refrigerant lines, even though the system will have been discharged at this point (refer to the warning at the start of this Section). Where applicable, recover the O-ring seals – new ones must be used when refitting. Cover the pipe ends, to prevent the entry of foreign matter.
5 Open the bonnet and disconnect the wiring connector from the top of the receiver/dryer.
6 With the system discharged, undo the two retaining screws and disconnect the refrigerant lines from the receiver/drier. Plug the end of the lines to prevent the ingress of dirt and moisture.
7 Slacken the clamp screw on the mounting bracket and withdraw the receiver/drier out from the engine compartment.

10.11 Undo the pipe retaining nut

8 Refitting is a reversal of removal, noting the following points:
 a) Use new O-ring seals when reconnecting the refrigerant lines, and tighten the unions securely.
 b) Lubricate the O-ring seals with clean refrigerant oil.
 c) If the receiver/drier is being renewed, add 20 cc of clean refrigerant oil to the new receiver/drier. This will maintain the correct oil level in the system after the repairs are completed.
 d) Have the system professionally recharged before attempting to use it.

Condenser

9 Follow the procedures for removing the radiator, as described in Section 3.
10 Gloves must be worn when disconnecting the refrigerant lines, even though the system will have been discharged at this point (refer to the warning at the start of this Section).
11 Unscrew the unions on the two pipes at the side of the condenser, and disconnect them **(see illustration)**. Recover the O-ring seals – new ones must be used when refitting. Cover the pipe ends to prevent the entry of foreign matter.
12 Carefully lift the condenser out of its lower mountings and remove it from the car, taking care not to damage the fins or pipework.
13 Refitting is a reversal of removal, noting the following points:
 a) Use new O-ring seals when reconnecting the refrigerant lines, and tighten the unions securely.
 b) Lubricate the O-ring seals with clean refrigerant oil.
 c) Renew the receiver/drier, see paragraph 2 in this Section.
 d) Have the system professionally recharged before attempting to use it.

Compressor

14 Disconnect the battery negative cable and position it away from the terminal.
15 Apply the handbrake, then jack up the front of the vehicle and support it on axle stands (see *Jacking and vehicle support*). Where fitted, remove the plastic shield from under the engine.
16 Remove the auxiliary drivebelt as described in the relevant part of Chapter 1.
17 Undo the retaining bolt and disconnect the

10.19 Fasten the compressor to one side

10.21 Disconnect the wiring connector

refrigerant line bracket from the transmission housing.

18 Support the compressor (it is a heavy unit) and remove the mounting bolts. Depending on the exact type of compressor, and on the engine to which it is fitted, there will be either three or four mounting bolts. Lift the compressor and move it forward to access the refrigerant lines and wiring connector.

19 If the compressor is being removed as part of another procedure (such as engine removal), it is sufficient to remove the mounting bolts and tie the compressor up to one side without disconnecting the refrigerant lines **(see illustration)**. If the compressor is being removed completely, proceed as follows.

20 Gloves must be worn when disconnecting the refrigerant lines, even though the system will have been discharged at this point (refer to the warning at the start of this Section). Unscrew the unions on the two pipes on the compressor, and disconnect them. Recover the O-ring seals – new ones must be used when refitting.

21 Disconnect the wiring plug from the top of the compressor **(see illustration)**.

22 It is advisable to cover the openings on the compressor while it is removed, to reduce oil loss and to prevent foreign matter from entering.

23 Refitting is a reversal of removal, noting the following points:

a) *Use new O-ring seals when reconnecting the refrigerant lines, and tighten the unions securely.*

b) *Tighten the mounting bolts securely.*

c) *Renew the receiver/drier, see paragraph 2 in this Section.*

d) *Have the system professionally recharged before attempting to use it.*

Chapter 4 Part A: Fuel system

Contents

Section number

Degrees of difficulty

Easy, suitable for novice with little experience	**Fairly easy,** suitable for beginner with some experience	**Fairly difficult,** suitable for competent DIY mechanic	**Difficult,** suitable for experienced DIY mechanic	**Very difficult,** suitable for expert DIY or professional

Specifications

General

Injection	Indirect
Idle speed (electronic idle speed control):	
2.2 litre engine	690 to 790 rpm
2.9 litre engine	630 to 730 rpm
Smoke test opacity	1.5
Fuel pressure at idle (2.2 litre engines)	2.0 bar
Vacuum at idle (2.2 litre engines)	100 to 150 mbar
Vacuum reading at maximum rpm (2.2 litre engines)	220 to 300 mbar

Torque wrench settings

	Nm	lbf ft
2.2 litre engines		
Camshaft bearing cap	10	7
Camshaft cover	10	7
Camshaft sprocket	18	13
Fuel gauge sender unit retaining ring	50	37
Fuel injection high-pressure pipe union nuts	14	10
Fuel injection high-pressure pump mounting bolts	14	10
Fuel injector clamp retaining bolt:		
Stage 1	7	5
Stage 2	Angle-tighten a further 90°	
Stage 3	Angle-tighten a further 90°	
Fuel pipe union nuts to fuel rail	23	17
Fuel pipe union nuts to injectors	42	31
Fuel pre-delivery pump mounting bolts	9	7
Fuel pressure control valve to fuel rail mounting bolts:		
Stage 1	3	2
Stage 2	5	4
Fuel pressure sensor in fuel rail	22	16
Fuel rail mounting bolts	14	10
Fuel shut-off valve mounting bolts	9	7
Fuel temperature sensor in fuel rail	25	18
Inlet manifold bolts:		
Upper section	9	7
Lower section	16	12
Inlet manifold support bracket bolts	10	7

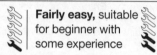

Torque wrench settings (continued)

	Nm	lbf ft
2.9 litre engines		
Fuel gauge sender unit retaining ring	50	37
Fuel injector clamp retaining bolt:		
Stage 1	7	5
Stage 2	Angle-tighten a further 180°	
Fuel injection pipe mounting bracket bolts	10	7
Fuel injection pipe union nuts	18	13
Fuel injection pump drivegear securing nut	83	61
Fuel injection pump support bracket bolts	15	11
Fuel injection pump support bracket to engine bolts	10	7
Fuel injection pump to intermediate flange bolts	23	17
Inlet manifold bolts	15	11

1 General information and precautions

The major components of the fuel system are a fuel tank, a gauge sender unit, fuel lift and injection pumps, engine-bay mounted filter, fuel supply and return lines and one fuel injector per cylinder.

On 2.9 litre engines, the distributor fuel injection pump is driven at half crankshaft speed by the timing chain. Fuel is drawn from the fuel tank, through the filter, to the injection pump, which then distributes the fuel under very high pressure to the injectors via separate delivery pipes. The basic injection timing is set by the position of the injection pump on its mounting bracket. When the engine is running, the injection timing is advanced and retarded electronically. In addition, an injection-timing device is incorporated in the pump drive sprocket. The injectors are spring-loaded mechanical valves, which open when the pressure of the fuel supplied to them exceeds a specific limit. Fuel is then sprayed from the injector nozzle into the cylinder via a pre-chamber (indirect injection).

On 2.2 litre engines, the high-pressure fuel injection pump is driven directly off the end of the camshaft. Fuel is drawn from the fuel tank, through the filter, to the injection pump, which then forces the fuel under very high pressure to the injectors via a fuel rail (common rail) that maintains a constant pressure. The basic injection timing is set by the electronic control module (ECM), which is given information from sensors positioned in the fuel system and engine components. The fuel injectors are also controlled by the ECM.

Engine idle speed is controlled electronically, responding to engine load. The system increases the idle speed when the power steering or air conditioning systems are operative, in addition to increased idle speed under cold start conditions. The engine speed is monitored by an electronic control unit via a sensor mounted at the flywheel, and coolant temperature via a sensor threaded into the cylinder head. The ECM compares the actual engine speed with a mapped value stored in memory. If the two are different, the ECM drives an electromagnetic actuator, which mechanically preloads the injection pump governor to alter the engine idle speed accordingly.

On turbocharged models, the operation of the diesel fuel injection system is identical to that of the normally aspirated engines, however, the inlet charge pressure (turbo-boost) and exhaust gas recirculation systems are also controlled by the ECM. Air inlet temperature is monitored by a sensor inside the air duct.

⚠ *Warning: Many of the procedures in this Chapter require the removal of fuel lines and connections, which may result in some fuel spillage. Before carrying out any operation on the fuel system, refer to the precautions given in Safety first! at the beginning of this manual, and follow them implicitly. Always switch off the ignition before working on the fuel system.*

⚠ *Warning: When working on any part of the fuel system, avoid direct skin contact with diesel fuel – wear protective clothing and gloves when handling fuel system components. Ensure the work area is well ventilated. Fuel injectors operate at extremely high pressures and the jet of fuel produced at the nozzle is capable of piercing skin, with potentially fatal results. When working with pressurised injectors, take great care to avoid exposing any part of the body to the fuel spray. It is recommended that any pressure testing of the fuel system components should be carried out by a diesel fuel injection specialist.*

Caution: Do not allow diesel fuel to come into contact with coolant hoses – wipe off accidental spillage immediately. Hoses that have been contaminated with fuel for an extended period should be renewed. Diesel fuel systems are particularly sensitive to contamination from dirt, air and water. Pay particular attention to cleanliness when working on any part of the fuel system, to prevent the ingress of dirt. Thoroughly clean the area around fuel unions before disconnecting them. Store dismantled components in sealed containers to prevent contamination and the formation of condensation. Only use lint-free cloths and clean fuel for component cleansing.

2 Air cleaner housing and filter element – removal and refitting

1 Undo the retaining bolts and remove the heat shield from above the exhaust manifold **(see illustration)**.

2 Slacken the hose clip and detach the ducting from the front of the air cleaner housing **(see illustration)**.

3 Release the retaining clips from around the edge of the air cleaner housing and remove the upper part of the housing **(see illustrations)**.

4 Remove the air filter from the air cleaner housing **(see illustration)**.

5 Undo the retaining bolt from the lower part

2.1 Remove the heat shield

2.2 Disconnect the air intake hose

2.3a Release the securing clips . . .

2.3b . . . and remove the upper filter housing

2.4 Remove the air filter element

2.5a Undo the retaining bolt . . .

2.5b . . . disconnect the air ducting . . .

2.6 . . . and remove the lower housing

of the housing and then unclip the air ducting **(see illustrations)**.
6 Remove the lower housing from the engine compartment **(see illustration)**.
7 Refitting is a reversal of removal.

3 Fuel gauge/ pump sender unit – removal and refitting

⚠ *Warning: Observe the precautions in Section 1 before working on any component in the fuel system.*

Removal

1 Disconnect the battery negative (earth) lead and position it away from the terminal.
2 Remove the fuel tank as described in Section 4.
3 If not already done, disconnect the fuel gauge wiring from the sender unit, and then release the retaining clips and disconnect the fuel lines, noting which way around they are fitted. **Note:** *Depending on model, there maybe a different number of fuel lines and wiring connectors.*
4 The retaining rings must now be loosened and removed. To do this, Mercedes-Benz technicians use a special tool which engages with the outer part of the ring. Ideally, this tool should be obtained, however it should be possible to fabricate a homemade version.
5 Make note of the markings on the locking ring and fuel tank to aid refitting **(see illustration)**, with the ring removed, carefully withdraw the sender unit from the fuel tank.

Recover the sealing gaskets, taking care not to damage the fuel sender unit.

Refitting

6 Refitting is a reversal of removal, but always renew the sender unit sealing gaskets, and tighten the retaining rings to the specified torque. Making sure that the marks noted on removal are aligned.

4 Fuel tank – removal and refitting

⚠ *Warning: Observe the precautions in Section 1 before working on any component in the fuel system.*

Removal

1 The fuel tank must be emptied before

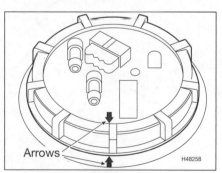

3.5 Alignment marks for sender unit locking ring

the operation can be started. This is best achieved by waiting until the tank is almost empty through the course of normal driving.
2 Park the vehicle on a level surface and chock the front roadwheels. Raise the rear of the vehicle, support it securely on axle stands (see *Jacking and vehicle support*) and remove the rear roadwheels.

⚠ *Warning: The use of an inspection pit is not advised; fuel vapours are heavier than air and can quickly build-up on the floor of the pit, causing a potential hazard.*

3 Disconnect the battery negative (earth) lead and position it away from the terminal.
4 Slacken the securing nuts on the two straps that support the fuel tank, do not remove completely at this point **(see illustration)**. These are prone to corrosion, so use a wire brush and some penetrating oil to release the retaining nuts.

4.4 Fuel tank securing strap retaining nuts

4.6 Fuel spiral cooling pipe

4.7 Fuel tank filler neck securing clip

5.2 Disconnect the air intake hose

5.7 Remove the upper section of the intake manifold

5 Reaching to the top of the fuel tank, disconnect the wiring connector from the fuel tank sender unit. Also disconnect the fuel lines from the sender unit, noting their fitted positions. Plug the ends of the fuel lines to prevent dirt ingress.

6 On 2.2 litre engines, disconnect the fuel line to the cooling spiral pipe on the rear of the fuel tank **(see illustration)**.

7 Slacken the hose clips from the filler neck (and vent hose, where fitted) and disconnect the hose(s) from the fuel tank **(see illustration)**.

8 With the aid of an assistant, support the fuel tank and completely remove the securing nuts from the straps under the fuel tank.

9 Lower the tank and check that there are no more hoses or wiring still attached, then

remove the fuel tank out from the side of the vehicle.

10 If required, remove the fuel gauge/pump sender unit as described in Section 3.

11 Swill the tank out with clean fuel. If the tank shows signs of leakage, it should be renewed.

⚠ *Warning: Do not attempt to repair the tank yourself by welding, soldering or brazing. The tank will contain an explosive mixture of air and fuel vapour, even when emptied of liquid fuel.*

Refitting

12 Refit the fuel tank by reversing the removal procedure, but tighten all fixings to the correct torque, where specified.

5 Inlet manifold – removal and refitting

1 Disconnect the battery negative (earth) lead and position it away from the terminal.

2.2 litre engines

Upper section

2 Slacken the hose clip and detach the air intake hose from the front of the inlet manifold **(see illustration)**.

3 Disconnect the vacuum pipe from the rear of the inlet manifold.

4 Undo the two retaining bolts from the support bracket at the front of the inlet manifold.

5 Undo the two retaining bolts from the support bracket at the rear of the inlet manifold.

6 Undo the retaining nuts at the rear left-hand side of the manifold to disconnect the EGR valve.

7 Progressively unscrew the upper inlet manifold mounting bolts, and then lift it away from the lower part **(see illustration)**. Discard the O-ring seals, as new seals will be required for refitting.

8 Refitting is a reversal of removal, but fit new O-ring seals. Tighten the upper inlet manifold securing bolts to the specified torque in the correct sequence **(see illustration)**.

Lower section

9 Remove the upper section of the inlet manifold as described previously, in paragraphs 2 to 7.

10 To remove the lower part of the inlet manifold, it will be necessary to remove the wiring loom, which passes up through the manifold.

11 Disconnect the wiring connections from the starter motor, glow plug relay and the positive and negative posts on the battery **(see illustration)**.

12 Trace the wiring back through the bulkhead and disconnect the wiring connectors from the engine control module

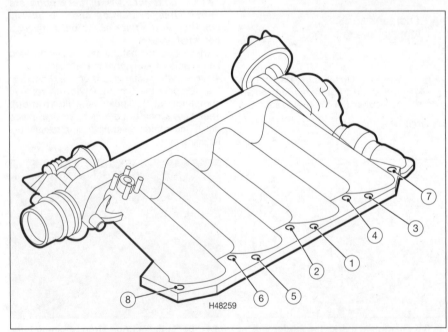

5.8 Tightening sequence for the intake manifold

H48259

inside the passenger compartment, below the glove compartment on the left-hand side **(see illustration)**.

13 Withdraw the wiring loom through into the engine compartment and free it from the retaining clips as it is removed **(see illustration)**. Note the routing of the wiring loom for refitting.

14 Undo the retaining bolts from the support bracket under the inlet manifold **(see illustration)**. Depending on model, it may be necessary to detach the fuel pressure sensor from the support bracket.

15 Release the securing clips and disconnect the fuel lines from across the top of the lower inlet manifold.

16 Progressively unscrew the lower inlet manifold mounting bolts, and then lift it away from the cylinder head. Withdraw the wiring loom through the manifold, noting the routing for refitting. Discard the O-ring seals, as new seals will be required for refitting.

17 Refitting is a reversal of removal, but fit new O-ring seals. Tighten the inlet manifold securing bolts to the specified torque.

2.9 litre engines

18 Slacken the hose clips and detach the air intake hose from the top of the manifold **see illustration)**.

19 Disconnect the vacuum pipe from the vacuum capsule on the top of the inlet manifold **(see illustration)**.

20 Slacken the securing clamp and disconnect the corrugated EGR pipe from the manifold **(see illustration)**.

21 Disconnect the two wiring connectors from the top of the injector fuel pipes and move them to one side, noting their fitted position **(see illustration)**.

 Warning: Observe the precautions in Section 1 before working on any component in the fuel system.

22 Slacken the fuel pipe unions and disconnect them from the top of the injectors **(see illustration)**. Be prepared for an amount of fuel loss – pad the surrounding area with absorbent rags. Tape over or plug the apertures in the injection pump and the fuel pipe to prevent entry of dust and dirt.

23 Undo the retaining bolts and remove the lifting eye from the rear of the cylinder head.

5.11 Disconnecting the glow plug relay connection

5.13 Cut retaining clips from wiring loom

24 Progressively unscrew the inlet manifold mounting bolts, and then lift it away from the cylinder head. Discard the manifold gasket, as a new one will be required for refitting.

5.18 Remove the air intake hose

5.20 Disconnect the EGR pipe

5.12 Disconnecting the engine control module connection

5.14 Remove the support bracket from the manifold

25 Refitting is a reversal of removal, but fit new manifold gasket. Tighten the inlet manifold securing bolts to the specified torque.

5.19 Disconnect the vacuum pipe

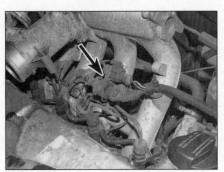

5.21 Disconnect the wiring connectors

5.22 Slacken the injector union pipes

6.5 Disconnect the wiring connector

6.6 Disconnect the high-pressure pipe

6.8a Undo the mounting bolts . . .

6.8b . . . remove the fuel pump . . .

6.8c . . . and the drivegear

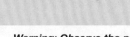

6 Fuel injection pump –
removal and refitting

⚠ **Warning: Observe the precautions in Section 1 before working on any component in the fuel system.**

Removal

1 Disconnect the battery negative (earth) lead and position it away from the terminal.
2 Remove the auxiliary drivebelt, as described in Chapter 1.
3 Remove the cooling fan, as described in Chapter 3.

2.2 litre engines (high-pressure type)

4 Remove the electric fuel shut-off valve, as described in Section 10 of this Chapter.

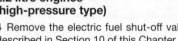

6.9 Fit new O-ring seal

5 Disconnect the wiring connector from the lower part of the high-pressure fuel pump **(see illustration)**.
6 Disconnect the high-pressure fuel pipe from the left-hand side of the pump **(see illustration)**. Be prepared for an amount of fuel loss – pad the surrounding area with absorbent rags. Tape over or plug the apertures in the injection pump and the fuel pipe to prevent entry of dust and dirt. **Note:** *Where applicable, slacken the fuel pipe retaining nut by using a spanner on the nut nearest the pump to hold the pipe in position while slackening the fuel pipe union.*
7 Undo the retaining bolt and remove the bracket to disengage the fuel return pipe from the right-hand side of the fuel pump.
8 Undo the retaining bolts and remove the high-pressure fuel pump from the front of the cylinder head. As the pump is removed,

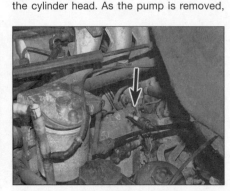

6.13 Disconnect the fuel pipes from the pump

retrieve the drivegear from the end of the shaft **(see illustrations)**.
9 Recover the O-ring seal from the rear of the injection pump and discard it – a new one must be used on refitting **(see illustration)**.
10 Refit the pump by following the removal procedure in reverse, noting these points:
  a) *Fit a new O-ring seal to the injection pump mating face and lubricate it lightly with clean engine oil.*
  b) *Make sure the drivegear is located correctly on the shaft before refitting.*
  c) *Counterhold the fuel pump nut when tightening the high-pressure fuel pipe.*
  d) *Tighten the injection pump mounting bolts to the specified torque.*

2.9 litre engines (distributor type)

Note: *The final adjustment of the distributor type injection pump will need to be done by special equipment, this is best done by a Mercedes-Benz dealer or specialist with the right equipment.*
11 Remove the cylinder head cover as described in Chapter 2B.
12 Set the engine at 12° before TDC (ignition of cylinder 1). **Note:** *The two cams of the camshaft on cylinder one should be pointing upwards.*
13 Disconnect the fuel pipe feed and return pipes from the distributor injection pump **(see illustration)**. Be prepared for an amount of fuel loss – pad the surrounding area with absorbent rags. Tape over or plug the apertures in the injection pump and the fuel pipe to prevent entry of dust and dirt. **Note:** *Where applicable, slacken the fuel pipe retaining nut by using a spanner on the nut nearest the pump to hold the pipe in position while slackening the fuel pipe union.*
14 Disconnect the wiring connector from the fuel shut-off valve on the rear of the injection pump.
15 Disconnect the wiring connectors from the two temperature sensors in the cylinder head.
16 Disconnect the two wiring connectors from the top of the injector fuel pipes and move them to one side, noting their fitted position.
17 Undo the retaining bolts and disconnect

7.3a Release the securing clips

7.3b Noting the direction arrows for refitting

7.4 Pre-delivery pump mounting bolts

the fuel injector pipe mounting brackets from the top of the inlet manifold.

18 Slacken the fuel pipe union nuts at the injectors and the fuel pump, and then remove them from the engine compartment. **Note:** *Where applicable, slacken the fuel pipe retaining nut by using a spanner on the nut nearest the pump to hold the pipe in position while slackening the fuel pipe union.*

19 Undo the retaining bolts and remove the support bracket from behind the fuel injection pump.

20 Undo the three retaining nuts and withdraw the fuel injection pump from the intermediate flange.

21 If a new pump is to be fitted, special tools will be required to hold the drivegear on the end of the pump while the retaining nut is slackened. Also a puller will be required to withdraw the drivegear from the end of the shaft. Retrieve the Woodruff key from the shaft, as the drivegear is removed.

22 At this point it is advisable to renew the seal in the back of the intermediate flange, while the pump is removed. Note the fitted position of the seal in the housing for refitting, and then carefully lever the seal out from the flange. Using a special tool (or large socket), carefully drift the seal back into position in the intermediate flange.

23 Before refitting the fuel pump check the engine is still set at 12° before TDC (ignition of cylinder 1) as noted in paragraph 12.

24 When refitting the fuel pump, make sure the markings (gap in the teeth on the drivegear), faces towards the connection of the injection pipe for cylinder 1. After this is done, turn the injection pump shaft clockwise as far as the pressure point and then fit the pump into position.

25 Refit the pump by following the removal procedure in reverse, noting these points:
a) Fit a new seal to the injection pump intermediate flange (see paragraph 22).
b) If removed, make sure the drivegear is located correctly on the shaft before refitting.
c) Counterhold the fuel pump/injector union nuts when tightening the fuel pipes.
d) Tighten the injection pump mounting bolts to the specified torque.

7 Fuel pre-delivery pump (2.2 litre engines) – removal and refitting

Warning: Observe the precautions in Section 1 before working on any component in the fuel system.

Removal

1 Disconnect the battery negative cable and position it away from the terminal.

2 Remove the brake vacuum pump from the front of the cylinder head as described in Chapter 9.

3 Release the retaining clips and disconnect the feed and return fuel pipes from the pre-delivery pump **(see illustrations)**. Be prepared for an amount of fuel loss – pad the surrounding area with absorbent rags. Tape over or plug the apertures in the injection pump and the fuel pipe to prevent entry of dust and dirt. Note their fitted position for refitting.

4 Slacken and withdraw the retaining bolts, then pull the lift pump away from the front of the cylinder head **(see illustration)**. Recover the sealing gasket.

Refitting

5 Refitting is a reversal of removal, noting the following points:
a) Use a new sealing gasket when refitting the pre-delivery pump.
b) Refit the brake vacuum pump with reference to Chapter 9.

c) On completion, tighten the pump retaining bolts to their specified torque setting.

8 Fuel rail (2.2 litre engines) – removal and refitting

Warning: Observe the precautions in Section 1 before working on any component in the fuel system.

Note: *Take care not to allow dirt into the fuel rail, injectors or fuel pipes during this procedure. Keep the fuel pipes identified for position to ensure correct refitting. As the fuel pipes are removed, plug the ends of the pipes, injectors and fuel rail to prevent dirt ingress.*

1 Disconnect the battery negative cable and position it away from the terminal.

2 Remove the upper part of the inlet manifold as described in Section 5.

3 Disconnect the wiring connectors from the pressure sensor and the pressure regulator valve at each end of the fuel rail **(see illustrations)**. If required, the sensors can be unscrewed from the ends of the fuel rail.

4 Slacken and disconnect the injector fuel pipes from the fuel rail, it may be necessary to slacken the pipes at the injectors, to allow for better movement. Make a note of their fitted position, as they will need to be refitted in the same position on refitting **(see illustration)**. Be prepared for an amount of fuel loss – pad the surrounding area with absorbent rags. Tape over or plug the apertures in the injectors

8.3a Disconnect the rear sensor wiring connector

8.3b Disconnect the front sensor wiring connector

8.4 Disconnect the fuel injector pipes

8.5a Unbolt the mounting bracket . . .

8.5b . . . and undo the fuel pipe from the pump

8.6 Undo the banjo bolt from the rail

8.8 Removing the fuel rail

and fuel pipes to prevent entry of dust and dirt.

5 Undo the retaining bolt from the fuel pipe retaining bracket and disconnect the high-pressure fuel pipe from the pump **(see illustrations)**. Be prepared for an amount of fuel loss – pad the surrounding area with absorbent rags. Tape over or plug the apertures in the injection pump and the fuel pipe to prevent entry of dust and dirt. **Note:** *Undo the fuel pipe retaining nut and not the nut nearest the fuel pump. Use a spanner on the nut nearest the pump to hold the pipe in position, while slackening the fuel pipe retaining nut.*

6 Undo the banjo bolt and disconnect the fuel return pipe and leak-off pipes from the rear the fuel rail **(see illustration)**. Discard sealing rings, as new ones will be required for refitting.

7 Working your way along the fuel rail, unclip

and disconnect any wiring or pipes that are still attached to the fuel rail. Note their fitted position to aid refitting.

8 Undo the retaining bolts and withdraw the fuel rail from the top of the engine compartment **(see illustration)**.

9 Refitting is a reversal of removal, using new O-ring seals/washers where applicable. Tighten the mounting bolts and union nuts to the specified torque.

9 Fuel injectors – removal and refitting

⚠️ *Warning: Exercise extreme caution when working on the fuel injectors. Never expose the hands or any part of the body to injector spray, as the high working pressure can cause the*

fuel to penetrate the skin, with possibly fatal results. You are strongly advised to have any work which involves testing the injectors under pressure carried out by a dealer or fuel injection specialist. Refer to the precautions given in Section 1 of this Chapter before proceeding.

Caution: The injector clamping-bracket retaining bolt can be tight and thread damage or bolt breaking can occur. Bolt repair or Helicoil may be required; this may need to be done by a specialist. A puller will also be required for pulling the injectors out from the cylinder head.

Note 1: *Take care not to allow dirt into the injectors or fuel pipes during this procedure. Keep the fuel pipes and injectors identified for position to ensure correct refitting. As the fuel pipes are removed, plug the ends of the pipes and injectors to prevent dirt ingress.*

Note 2: *Injectors deteriorate with prolonged use, and it is reasonable to expect them to need reconditioning after 60 000 miles or so. Accurate testing, overhaul and calibration of the injectors must be left to a specialist. Do not drop the injectors or allow the needles at their tips to become damaged. The injectors are precision-made to fine limits, and must not be handled roughly.*

2.2 litre engine

1 Disconnect the battery negative cable and position it away from the terminal.

2 Remove the upper part of the inlet manifold as described in Section 5.

3 Remove the trim panel from the top of the cylinder head cover.

4 Disconnect the wiring connectors from each of the fuel injectors **(see illustration)**.

5 Slacken and disconnect the fuel pipes from the top of the injectors, it may be necessary to slacken the pipes at the fuel rail to allow for better movement. Make a note of their fitted position, as they will need to be refitted in the same position on refitting **(see illustration)**. Be prepared for an amount of fuel loss – pad the surrounding area with absorbent rags. Tape over or plug the apertures in the injectors and fuel pipes to prevent entry of dust and dirt.

6 Release and disconnect the fuel leak-off pipes from the top of the four injectors **(see**

9.4 Disconnect the fuel injector wiring connectors

9.5 Remove the injector fuel pipe

illustrations). Discard the securing clips, as new ones will be required on refitting.

7 Slacken and remove the injector clamp mounting bracket retaining bolts (see *Caution* above) from between the injectors **(see illustrations)**. Discard the mounting bolts, as new ones will be required when refitting.

8 If required use a slide hammer/puller to withdraw the injectors from the cylinder head, making sure it is in the vertical position **(see illustration)**. Recover the sealing rings/washers and discard. New ones must be used for refitting.

9 Refitting is a reversal of removal, using new sealing rings. Fit new clamp mounting bracket retaining bolts and tighten them to the specified torque. Apply special high-temperature grease from Mercedes-Benz to prevent the injectors from getting tight in the bore **(see illustrations)**.

2.9 litre engine

10 Disconnect the battery negative cable and position it away from the terminal.

11 Disconnect the two wiring connectors from the top of the injector fuel pipes and move them to one side, noting their fitted position **(see illustration)**.

12 Slacken and disconnect the fuel pipes from the top of the injectors, it may be necessary to slacken the pipes at the fuel pump, to allow for better movement. Make a note of their fitted position, as they will need to be refitted in the same position on refitting. Be prepared for an amount of fuel loss – pad the surrounding area with absorbent rags. Tape over or plug the apertures in the injectors

and fuel pipes to prevent entry of dust and dirt.

13 Release and disconnect the fuel leak-off pipes from the four injectors **(see illustration)**.

14 Slacken and remove the claw mounting-bracket retaining bolt, clamp and spherical

washer from the fuel injector nozzle **(see illustration)**. Discard the mounting bolts, clamps and spherical washers, as new ones will be required when refitting.

15 If required use a puller to withdraw the injectors from the cylinder head. Recover the

9.6a Release the retaining clips . . .

9.6b . . . and remove the fuel return pipes

9.7a Injector retaining bolts – two shown

9.7b Remove the injector clamps

9.8 Withdraw the injectors

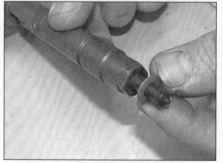
9.9a Fit new sealing washer . . .

9.9b . . . and apply high-temperature grease

9.11 Disconnect the wiring connectors

9.13 Release the fuel leak-off pipes

9.14 Undo the injector mounting bolt

11.1 Electronic control module (ECM) – 2.2 litre engines

11.2 Disconnect the wiring connectors

sealing rings/washers and discard. New ones must be used for refitting.
16 Refitting is a reversal of removal, using new sealing rings. Fit new spherical washers, clamps and mounting bolts, and then tighten them to the specified torque. Apply special high-temperature grease from Mercedes-Benz to prevent the injectors from getting tight in the bore **(see illustrations 9.9a and 9.9b).**

10 Electric fuel shut-off valve – removal and refitting

 Warning: Observe the precautions in Section 1 before working on any component in the fuel system.

1 Disconnect the battery negative cable and position it away from the terminal.

2.2 litre engine

Note: *The electric fuel shut-off valve (where fitted) is fitted below the vacuum pump, on the front of the cylinder head.*
2 Undo the retaining bolts and remove the heat shield from above the exhaust manifold.
3 Disconnect the wiring connector from the fuel shut-off valve.
4 Release the retaining clip and disconnect the fuel pipe from the valve. Be prepared for an amount of fuel loss – pad the surrounding area with absorbent rags. Tape over or plug the apertures in the injection pump and the fuel pipe to prevent entry of dust and dirt.
5 Slacken and withdraw the retaining bolts from the valve and mounting bracket.

6 Pull the valve away from the cylinder head, disconnecting the intermediate pipe connection to the fuel pump. Recover the sealing ring(s).
7 Refitting is a reversal of removal, noting the following points:
  a) *Use a new sealing ring when refitting the valve to the fuel pump.*
  b) *On completion, tighten the retaining bolts to their specified torque setting.*

2.9 litre engine

Note: *The electric fuel shut-off valve is fitted to the rear of the fuel pump, above the fuel feed pipe connections.*
8 Undo the retaining nut and disconnect the wiring connector from the fuel shut-off valve.
9 Slacken and then unscrew the valve from the rear of the fuel pump.
10 Refitting is a reversal of removal.

11 Electronic control module (ECM) – removal and refitting

Caution: Electronic Control Modules (ECMs) contain components that are sensitive to the levels of static electricity generated by a person during normal activity. Once the multiway harness connectors has been unplugged, the exposed ECM connector pins can freely conduct stray static electricity to these components, damaging or even destroying them – the damage will be invisible and may not manifest itself immediately. Expensive repairs can be

avoided by observing the following basic handling rules:
• *Handle a disconnected ECM by its case only; do not allow fingers or tools to come into contact with the pins.*
• *When carrying an ECM, earth yourself from time to time by touching a metal object such as an unpainted water pipe, this will discharge any potentially damaging static that may have built-up.*
• *Do not leave the ECM unplugged from its connector for any longer than is absolutely necessary.*

2.2 litre engine

1 The electronic control module (ECM) is located under the facia below the passenger glove compartment **(see illustration)**. First, make sure that the ignition is switched off, and the earth lead is disconnected from the battery negative terminal.
2 Working inside the passenger footwell, release the securing clips and disconnect the wiring connectors from the control module **(see illustration)**. Usually the connectors can only be fitted one way, but it is best to note their fitted position for refitting.
3 Release the retaining clips at each side of the control module, and then unclip it from the retaining bracket **(see illustrations)**. The control module can now be withdrawn from under the facia.
4 Refitting is a reversal of removal.

2.9 litre engine

5 The electronic control module (ECM) is located under the battery tray inside the engine compartment **(see illustration)**. First, make sure that the ignition is switched off, and the earth lead is disconnected from the battery negative terminal.
6 Working inside the engine compartment, unclip the plastic cover from the front of the control module to access the wiring connectors
7 Release the securing clips and disconnect the wiring connectors from the control module. Usually the connectors can only be fitted one way, but it is best to note their fitted position for refitting.
8 Release the control module from the retaining bracket and withdraw it out from under the battery tray.
9 Refitting is a reversal of removal.

11.3a Release the securing clips . . .

11.3b . . . and remove the ECM from under the facia

11.5 Electronic control module (ECM) – 2.9 litre engines

12.7a Disconnect the air hoses . . .

12.7b . . . from each side of the intercooler

12.8a Undo the retaining screws . . .

12.8b . . . and remove the intercooler (models from 2000)

12.9 Removing the intercooler (models up to 2000)

13.2 Diagnostic socket location

12 Intercooler – removal, inspection and refitting

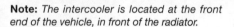

Note: *The intercooler is located at the front end of the vehicle, in front of the radiator.*

Removal

1 Undo the retaining bolts and withdraw the heat shield from the top of the exhaust manifold.

2 Remove the front grille as described Chapter 11, Section 22.

3 Remove the headlight units as described in Chapter 12, Section 10.

4 On models up to 2000, remove the radiator as described in Chapter 3, Section 3.

5 On models from 2000, undo the two retaining bolts from each end of the front upper crossmember and release the two upper radiator retaining clips. Move the crossmember to one side or disconnect the bonnet release cable from the catch to remove completely.

6 Undo the retaining bolts and remove the plastic trim panels from each side of the radiator (see Chapter 3).

7 Slacken the retaining clips and disconnect the air hoses from each side of the intercooler **(see illustrations)**.

8 On models up to 2000, undo the retaining bolts and two retaining screws from across the top of the intercooler, and then withdraw it from the front of the vehicle **(see illustrations)**.
Note: *The lower mounting bolts for the intercooler where removed, when the plastic side trim panels where removed.*

9 On models from 2000, withdraw the intercooler up and out of the top of the engine compartment **(see illustration)**.

Inspection

10 Clear the intercooler core of flies, small leaves or other debris by brushing or hosing. Check the condition of all hoses, clips, mountings and retaining spring clips, and renew as necessary.

11 Carefully examine the intercooler for signs of cracks, splits, corrosion of the alloy core, or damage to the plastic side sections. Should the intercooler require attention, this work should be left to a specialist due to the nature of its construction.

Refitting

12 Refitting the intercooler is the reverse sequence to removal, noting the following points:

a) *Ensure that the mounting bolts are secure.*
b) *Make sure that the intercooler hose clips are a secure fit.*

13 Idle speed, exhaust CO content and fault diagnosis

Experienced home mechanics equipped with an accurate tachometer and a carefully-calibrated exhaust gas analyser may be able to check the exhaust gas CO content and the engine idle speed, although the vehicle must be taken to a suitably-equipped Mercedes-Benz dealer or fuel injection specialist for assessment. Neither the air/fuel mixture (exhaust gas CO content) nor the engine idle speed are manually-adjustable.

A diagnostics socket, located under the passenger side facia panel **(see illustration)**, next to the bonnet release lever, is incorporated in the engine management system wiring harness, to which dedicated electronic test equipment can be connected. The test equipment is capable of 'interrogating' the engine management system ECM electronically and accessing its internal fault log. In this manner, faults can be pinpointed quickly and simply, even if their occurrence is intermittent. Testing all the system components individually in an attempt to locate the fault by elimination is a time consuming operation that is unlikely to be fruitful (particularly if the fault occurs dynamically), and also carries high risk of damage to the ECM's internal components.

Notes

Chapter 4 Part B:
Emission control and exhaust systems

Contents

Degrees of difficulty

Easy, suitable for novice with little experience	**Fairly easy,** suitable for beginner with some experience	**Fairly difficult,** suitable for competent DIY mechanic	**Difficult,** suitable for experienced DIY mechanic	**Very difficult,** suitable for expert DIY or professional

Specifications

Torque wrench settings	Nm	lbf ft
Exhaust manifold studs in cylinder head	12	9
Exhaust manifold to cylinder head:		
2.2 litre engines	30	22
2.9 litre engines:		
Stage 1	21	15
Stage 2	Wait 5 minutes	
Stage 3	23	17
Exhaust manifold to front pipe	20	15
Exhaust mounting to transmission	20	15
Lambda (oxygen) sensor	50	37
Turbocharger hose clips	3	2
Turbocharger to exhaust manifold:		
2.2 litre engines	30	22
2.9 litre engines	25	18
Turbocharger to front exhaust pipe	23	17

1 General information

All models are designed to meet strict emission requirements. The engines are fitted with a crankcase emission control system and a catalytic converter to keep exhaust emissions down to a minimum. An exhaust gas recirculation (EGR) system is also fitted to further decrease exhaust emissions.

The emissions control systems function as follows.

Crankcase emission control

To reduce the emission of unburned hydrocarbons from the crankcase into the atmosphere, the engine is sealed and the blow-by gases and oil vapour are drawn from inside the crankcase, through an oil separator, into the inlet tract to be burned by the engine during normal combustion.

Under all conditions the gases are forced out of the crankcase by the (relatively) higher crankcase pressure; if the engine is worn, the raised crankcase pressure (due to increased blow-by) will cause some of the flow to return under all manifold conditions.

The components of this system require no attention other than to check that the hose(s) are clear and undamaged at regular intervals.

Exhaust emission control

To minimise the level of exhaust pollutants released into the atmosphere, an unregulated catalytic converter is fitted in the exhaust system.

The catalytic converter consists of a canister containing a fine mesh impregnated with a catalyst material, over which the hot exhaust gases pass. The catalyst speeds up the oxidation of harmful carbon monoxide, unburned hydrocarbons and soot, effectively reducing the quantity of harmful products released into the atmosphere via the exhaust gases.

Exhaust gas recirculation (EGR) system

This system is designed to recirculate small quantities of exhaust gas into the inlet tract, and therefore into the combustion process. This process reduces the level of unburnt hydrocarbons present in the exhaust gas before it reaches the catalytic converter. The system is controlled by the electronic control module (ECM), using the information from its various sensors, via the EGR valve.

Exhaust systems

The exhaust system comprises the exhaust manifold (and turbocharger on turbo-diesel engines), downpipe and catalytic converter, and tailpipe and silencers. On some models the downpipe and catalytic converter are integral. The system is suspended beneath the vehicle by rubber mountings.

The turbocharger fitted to turbo-diesel engine models is oil-cooled and has an integral charge pressure-limiting valve.

2 Exhaust Gas Recirculation (EGR) system – testing and component renewal

Testing

EGR valve

1 Start the engine and allow it to idle.
2 Detach the vacuum hose from the EGR valve, and attach a hand vacuum pump in its place.

2.6 Remove the air intake hose

2.7 Disconnect the vacuum pipe

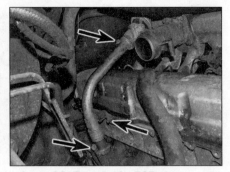

2.8 Remove the EGR pipe

3 Apply vacuum to the EGR valve. Vacuum should remain steady, and the engine should run poorly or stall.

   a) *If the vacuum doesn't remain steady and the engine doesn't run poorly, renew the EGR valve and recheck it.*

   b) *If the vacuum remains steady but the engine doesn't run poorly, remove the EGR valve, and check the valve and the inlet manifold for blockage. Clean or renew parts as necessary, and recheck.*

EGR system

4 Any further checking of the system requires special tools and test equipment. Take the vehicle to a dealer service department for checking.

EGR valve renewal

2.2 litre engines

5 The EGR valve is fitted at the rear of the inlet manifold (upper section). See the procedure for removing the upper section of the inlet manifold, in Chapter 4A, Section 5.

2.9 litre engines

6 Slacken the retaining clips and disconnect the charge air pipe from the EGR mixing housing **(see illustration)**.

7 Disconnect the vacuum hose from the top of the EGR valve **(see illustration)**.

8 Slacken the retaining clamps and disconnect the EGR pipe from the EGR valve and the exhaust manifold **(see illustration)**. Undo the mounting bracket securing bolt and remove the EGR pipe from the engine compartment.

9 Undo the EGR valve/mixing housing to the inlet manifold mounting bolts and remove it from the engine compartment.

10 Refitting is a reversal of removal, making sure that the hoses/pipes are correctly refitted. **Note:** *Check the condition of the hoses/pipes and renew them if necessary.*

4.2a Undo the securing bolt . . .

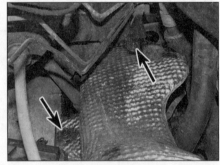

4.2b . . . and nuts . . .

4.2c . . . then remove the heat shield

4.3 Manifold-to-turbo retaining bolts

3 Crankcase emission control system – general information

The crankcase emission control system consists of hoses (depending on model) that connects the crankcase vent to the inlet ports of the cylinder head and the camshaft cover to the inlet air duct, a restrictor valve and an oil separator unit. When the engine is operating in the idle speed to mid part-load speed, the blow-by gases in the crankcase are drawn through an oil separator and hose with a restrictor to the inlet ports of the cylinder head, where it is mixed with fresh air entering the engine through the inlet manifold. When the engine is operating at mid part-load to full-load speed, the blow-by gases are drawn through the camshaft cover through a hose into the inlet air duct leading to the throttle body.

The components of this system require no attention other than to check at regular intervals that the hoses are free of blockages and undamaged.

4 Exhaust manifold – removal and refitting

Removal

1 Apply the handbrake, then jack up the front of the vehicle and support it on axle stands (see *Jacking and vehicle support*). Where fitted, remove the engine compartment undershield.

2 Undo the retaining bolts/nuts and remove the heat shield from above the exhaust manifold **(see illustration)**.

2.2 litre engines

3 Undo the bolts securing the exhaust manifold to the turbocharger **(see illustration)**. **Note:** it may be necessary to slacken the bolts from the mounting bracket at the rear of the turbocharger/exhaust to allow for some movement. Refer to Section 5.

4 Progressively unscrew the nuts securing the exhaust manifold to the cylinder head. Discard the nuts, as new ones will be required for refitting.

5 Withdraw the exhaust manifold from the studs on the cylinder head, and recover the gasket.

2.9 litre engines

6 Undo the nuts securing the exhaust manifold to the turbocharger.

7 Undo the bolts from the mounting bracket at the rear of the turbocharger/exhaust, and disconnect the mounting bracket from the transmission bolts.

8 Slacken the retaining clamp and disconnect the EGR pipe from the exhaust manifold. Undo the mounting bracket securing bolt and move the EGR pipe away from manifold **(see illustration)**.

9 Progressively unscrew the nuts securing the exhaust manifold to the cylinder head. Discard the nuts, as new ones will be required for refitting **(see illustration)**.

10 Carefully move the turbocharger to one side, and then withdraw the exhaust manifold from the studs on the cylinder head, and recover the gasket. Make sure the oil feed pipe on the turbo does not get damaged.

Refitting

11 Before refitting the exhaust manifold, check the studs in the cylinder head and renew them if necessary. The nuts should be renewed as a matter of course.

12 Refitting is a reversal of removal, but fit a new gasket and progressively tighten the new mounting nuts to the specified torque.

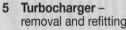

5 Turbocharger – removal and refitting

General information

1 The turbocharger is mounted on the exhaust manifold. Lubrication is provided by a dedicated oil supply pipe that runs from a tapping on the cylinder head **(see illustration)**. Oil is returned to the sump via a return pipe that connects to the side of the cylinder block. The turbocharger unit has an integral wastegate valve, which is controlled through a vacuum reservoir **(see illustration)** which is bolted to the inner wing panel below the right-hand side headlamp unit.

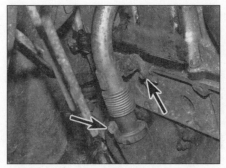

4.8 Disconnect the EGR pipe from the manifold

2 The turbocharger's internal components rotate at very high speed and as such are very sensitive to contamination; a great deal of damage can be caused by small particles of dirt, particularly if they strike the delicate turbine blades. Refer to the **Caution** and **Warning** notes given below before working on or removing the turbocharger unit.

Caution: Thoroughly clean the area around all oil pipe unions before disconnecting them, to prevent the ingress of dirt. Store dismantled components in a sealed container to prevent contamination. Cover the turbocharger air inlet ducts to prevent debris entering and clean using lint-free cloths only.

⚠ *Warning: Do not run the engine with the turbocharger air inlet hose disconnected, since the depression at the inlet can build up very suddenly if the engine speed is raised, and*

5.1a Turbo oil supply pipe

4.9 Undo the manifold-to-cylinder head retaining nuts

there is the risk of foreign objects being sucked in and then ejected at very high speed.

Removal

3 Disconnect the battery negative (earth) lead and position it away from the terminal.

4 Apply the handbrake, then jack up the front of the vehicle and support it on axle stands (see *Jacking and vehicle support*). Where fitted, remove the engine compartment undershield.

5 Undo the retaining bolts/nuts and remove the heat shield from above the exhaust manifold **(see illustration 4.2c)**.

6 Undo the retaining bolt from the exhaust front pipe retaining clamp, and then undo the mounting bracket retaining nuts and disconnect the front pipe from the turbocharger **(see illustrations)**.

7 Slacken the securing clip and disconnect

5.1b Turbo vacuum reservoir and valve

5.6a Undo the retaining clamp . . .

5.6b . . . and undo the mounting bracket bolts (2.2 litre engine)

5.6c Undo the front pipe retaining nuts . . .

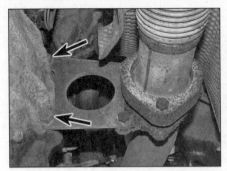

5.6d . . . and undo the mounting bracket bolts (2.9 litre engine)

5.7 Disconnect the air intake hose from the turbo

5.8 Disconnect the charge air hose from the turbo

5.9 Disconnect the vacuum pipe

5.10a Undo the banjo bolt . . .

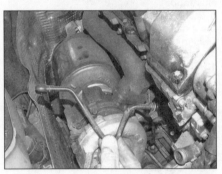

5.10b . . and remove the oil supply pipe

the air intake hose from the turbocharger (see illustration).

8 Slacken the securing clip and disconnect the intercooler charge air hose from the turbocharger (see illustration).

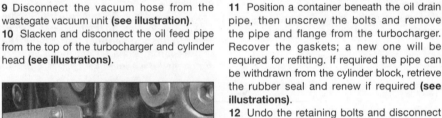

5.11a Oil drain pipe gasket . . .

5.11b . . . and cylinder block seal

9 Disconnect the vacuum hose from the wastegate vacuum unit (see illustration).
10 Slacken and disconnect the oil feed pipe from the top of the turbocharger and cylinder head (see illustrations).

11 Position a container beneath the oil drain pipe, then unscrew the bolts and remove the pipe and flange from the turbocharger. Recover the gaskets; a new one will be required for refitting. If required the pipe can be withdrawn from the cylinder block, retrieve the rubber seal and renew if required (see illustrations).
12 Undo the retaining bolts and disconnect the mounting bracket from the turbocharger (see illustration).
13 Undo the bolts securing the exhaust manifold to the turbocharger, and then manoeuvre the turbocharger from the engine compartment (see illustrations). Recover the gasket; a new one will be required for refitting.

Refitting

14 Refitting is a reversal of removal, but before reconnecting the oil supply pipe to the turbocharger, prime the oil inlet port with

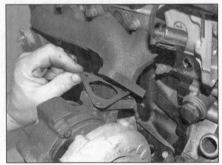

5.12 Undo the support bracket bolt

5.13a Manifold-to-turbo bolts

5.13b New gasket will be required

clean engine oil. Tighten all nuts and bolts securely, and to the specified torque where given. When the engine is first started, allow it to idle for at least one minute to allow the oil to circulate around the turbocharger bearings. Fit new seals and gaskets, where required **(see illustration)**.

6 Exhaust system – general information and component renewal

General information

1 Depending on model, the exhaust system is made up of an exhaust manifold, a catalytic converter, front silencer, a front pipe and a rear tailpipe incorporating one or two silencers.
2 The exhaust system is suspended along its entire length by rubber mountings **(see illustration)** which are secured to the underside of the vehicle. The downpipe is secured to the transmission by means of a mounting bracket attached to the side of the transmission housing.
3 The catalytic converter (where fitted) is part of the front pipe and attached to the exhaust manifold either by a flange joint or by a joint and sealing ring secured by a clamp.

Removal

4 Each exhaust section can be removed individually or, alternatively, the complete system can be removed as a unit.
5 Before removing any part of the system, first jack up the front or rear of the vehicle, as applicable, and support it on axle stands (see *Jacking and vehicle support*). Alternatively (or if the complete exhaust system is being removed) position the vehicle over an inspection pit or on ramps.

Front pipe/silencer/catalytic converter

6 Open the bonnet and undo the retaining bolts and remove the heat shield from above the exhaust manifold **(see illustration)**.
7 Remove the clamp securing the front pipe/silencer to the exhaust manifold **(see illustrations)**. Recover the sealing gasket.
8 Working under the vehicle, remove the clamp securing the front pipe to the middle section.

5.14 Fit new sealing ring

9 Unbolt the front pipe from the bracket on the rear of the transmission, and then withdraw the pipe/silencer from under the vehicle.

Middle and rear pipes/silencers

10 Unscrew the retaining bolts/nuts from the securing clamps and separate the front and rear sections of the exhaust system.
11 Support the rear pipe and silencers, and then release the rubber mountings **(see illustration)**. Lower the exhaust and remove it from under the vehicle.

Complete system

12 Unscrew and remove the clamp bolts securing the catalytic converter/front pipe to the exhaust manifold/turbocharger, separate and, where necessary, recover the gasket.
13 Release the rubber mounting along the length of the exhaust, and then unbolt the mounting bracket from the transmission.

6.2 Exhaust rubber mountings

6.7a Undo the retaining clamp (2.2 litre engine)

6.7b Undo the front pipe retaining nuts (2.9 litre engine)

14 With the help of an assistant, support the rear of the exhaust system, then unhook the rubber mountings and lower the system to the floor. Slide the system forwards from over the rear axle and withdraw it from under the vehicle.

Refitting

15 Each section is refitted by a reverse of the removal sequence, noting the following points.
  a) *Ensure that all traces of corrosion have been removed from the flanges and renew all necessary gaskets.*
  b) *Inspect the rubber mountings for signs of damage or deterioration and renew as necessary.*
  c) *Renew the sealing rings/gaskets between the front pipe/front silencer and catalytic converter.*
  d) *Make sure all mounting brackets are refitted securely.*
  e) *Prior to tightening the exhaust system joints, ensure that all rubber mountings are correctly located and that there is adequate clearance between the exhaust system and vehicle under-body.*

7 Catalytic converters – general information and precautions

The catalytic converter is a reliable and simple device, with no moving parts and as such requires no maintenance. There are,

6.6 Remove the upper heat shield

6.11 Exhaust rubber mountings

4B•6 Emission control and exhaust systems

however, some facts of which an owner should be aware if the converter is to function properly for its full service life.

a) DO NOT use fuel or engine oil additives – these may contain substances harmful to the catalytic converter.

b) DO NOT continue to use the car if the engine burns oil to the extent of leaving a visible trail of blue smoke.

c) Remember that the catalytic converter operates at very high temperatures. DO NOT, therefore, park the car in dry undergrowth, over long grass or piles of dead leaves after a long run.

d) Remember that the catalytic converter is FRAGILE – do not strike it with tools during servicing work.

e) The catalytic converter, used on a well-maintained and well-driven car, should last for between 50 000 and 100 000 miles – if the converter is no longer effective it must be renewed.

Chapter 5
Starting and charging systems

Contents

Degrees of difficulty

Easy, suitable for novice with little experience	**Fairly easy,** suitable for beginner with some experience	**Fairly difficult,** suitable for competent DIY mechanic	**Difficult,** suitable for experienced DIY mechanic	**Very difficult,** suitable for expert DIY or professional

Specifications

General
Electrical system type . . . . 12 volt negative earth

Battery
Charge condition:
    Poor . . . . 12.5 volts
    Normal . . . . 12.6 volts
    Good . . . . 12.7 volts

Alternator
Minimum brush length . . . . 5.0 mm

Glow plugs
Nominal operating voltage . . . . 11.5 V
Electrical resistance . . . . 0.75 to 1.5 ohms (approximately at operating temperature)
Current consumption . . . . 14 to 16 amps (per glow plug, after approximately 8 seconds of operation)
Post-heating . . . . 180 seconds up to maximum coolant temperature of 40°C

Torque wrench settings

	Nm	lbf ft
Alternator mounting bolts	45	33
Glow plugs	20	15
Glow plug wiring terminal	4	3
Starter motor main cable nut	14	10
Starter motor mounting bolts	42	31

1 General information, precautions and battery disconnection

General information

The engine electrical system consists mainly of the charging and starting systems. Because of their engine-related functions, these components are covered separately from the body electrical devices such as the lights, instruments, etc (which are covered in Chapter 12).

The electrical system is of 12 volt negative earth type.

The battery may be of the low maintenance or maintenance-free (sealed for life) type and is charged by the alternator, which is belt-driven from the crankshaft pulley.

The starter motor is of pre-engaged type incorporating an integral solenoid. On starting, the solenoid moves the drive pinion into engagement with the flywheel ring gear before the starter motor is energised. Once the engine has started, a one-way clutch prevents the motor armature being driven by the engine until the pinion disengages from the flywheel.

To assist cold starting, models are fitted with a preheating system, which comprises four glow plugs (one per cylinder), a glow plug control unit, a facia-mounted warning lamp, a coolant temperature sensor and the associated electrical wiring.

The glow plugs are miniature electric heating elements, encapsulated in a metal case with a probe at one end and electrical connection at the other. Each combustion chamber has one glow plug threaded into it. When the glow plug is energised, it heats up rapidly causing the temperature of the air charge drawn into each of the combustion chambers to rise. The glow plug probe is positioned directly in line with the incoming spray of fuel from the injectors. Hence the fuel passing over the glow plug probe is also heated, allowing its optimum combustion temperature to be achieved more readily. In addition, small particles of the fuel passing over the glow plugs are ignited and this helps to trigger the combustion process.

The duration of the preheating period is

governed by the glow plug control unit, which is fitted to the left-hand inner wing panel, below the battery tray. This device monitors the temperature of the engine coolant via a sensor threaded into the cylinder head and then alters the preheating time (the length for which the glow plugs are supplied with current) to suit the conditions.

A facia-mounted warning lamp informs the driver that preheating is taking place. The lamp extinguishes when sufficient preheating has taken place to allow the engine to be started, but power will still be supplied to the glow plugs for a further period until the engine is started. If no attempt is made to start the engine, the power supply to the glow plugs is switched off to prevent battery drain and glow plug burnout. Note that the warning lamp will also illuminate during normal driving if a preheating system malfunction occurs. The system employs post-heating (after-heating), which operates as follows. After the engine has been started, the glow plugs continue to operate for a further period of time as given in this Chapter's Specifications. This helps to improve fuel combustion whilst the engine is warming-up, resulting in quieter, smoother running and reduced exhaust emissions. The duration of the post-heating period is dependent on the coolant temperature.

Precautions

Further details of the various systems are given in the relevant Sections of this Chapter. While some repair procedures are given, the usual course of action is to renew the component concerned.

It is necessary to take extra care when working on the electrical system to avoid damage to semi-conductor devices (diodes and transistors), and to avoid the risk of personal injury. In addition to the precautions given in *Safety first!* at the beginning of this manual, observe the following when working on the system:

• Always remove rings, watches, etc, before working on the electrical system. Even with the battery disconnected, capacitive discharge could occur if a component's live terminal is earthed through a metal object. This could cause a shock or nasty burn.
• Do not reverse the battery connections. Components such as the alternator, electronic control units, or any other components having semi-conductor circuitry could be irreparably damaged.
• If the engine is being started using jump leads and a slave battery, connect the batteries positive-to-positive and negative-to-negative (see *Jump starting*). This also applies when connecting a battery charger but in this case both of the battery terminals should first be disconnected.
• Never disconnect the battery terminals, the alternator, any electrical wiring or any test instruments when the engine is running.
• Do not allow the engine to turn the alternator when the alternator is not connected.

• Never test for alternator output by flashing the output lead to earth.
• Never use an ohmmeter of the type incorporating a hand-cranked generator for circuit or continuity testing.
• Always ensure that the battery negative lead is disconnected when working on the electrical system.
• Before using electric arc welding equipment on the car, disconnect the battery, alternator and components such as the engine control module (ECM) to protect them from the risk of damage.

Battery disconnection

The radio/CD unit fitted as standard equipment by Mercedes-Benz is equipped with a built-in security code to deter thieves. If the power source to the unit is cut, the anti-theft system will activate. Even if the power source is immediately reconnected, the radio/CD unit will not function until the correct security code has been entered. Therefore, if you do not know the correct security code for the radio/CD unit, do not disconnect the battery negative terminal of the battery or remove the radio/CD unit from the vehicle. Refer to your Mercedes-Benz dealer for further information on whether the unit fitted to your vehicle has a security code.

Refer to the precautions listed in *Disconnecting the battery* in the Reference Chapter.

2 Battery – testing and charging

Testing

Standard and low maintenance battery

1 If the vehicle covers a small annual mileage, it is worthwhile checking the specific gravity of the electrolyte every three months to determine the state of charge of the battery. Use a hydrometer to make the check and compare the results with the following table. The temperatures quoted in the table are ambient (air) temperatures. Note that the specific gravity readings assume an electrolyte temperature of 15°C. For every 10°C below 15°C subtract 0.007. For every 10°C above 15°C add 0.007.

	Ambient temperature	
	Above 25°C	Below 25°C
Fully-charged	1.210 to 1.230	1.270 to 1.290
70% charged	1.170 to 1.190	1.230 to 1.250
Discharged	1.050 to 1.070	1.110 to 1.130

2 If the battery condition is suspect, first check the specific gravity of electrolyte in each cell. A variation of 0.040 or more between any cells indicates loss of electrolyte or deterioration of the internal plates.

3 If the specific gravity variation is 0.040 or more, the battery should be renewed. If the cell variation is satisfactory but the battery is

discharged, it should be charged as described later in this Section.

Maintenance-free battery

4 Where a 'sealed for life' maintenance-free battery is fitted, topping-up and testing of the electrolyte in each cell is not possible. The condition of the battery can therefore only be tested using a battery condition indicator or a voltmeter.

5 Certain models may be fitted with a maintenance-free battery with a built-in charge condition indicator. The indicator is located in the top of the battery casing, and indicates the condition of the battery from its colour. If the indicator shows green, then the battery is in a good state of charge. If the indicator turns darker, eventually to black, then the battery requires charging, as described later in this Section. If the indicator shows clear/yellow, then the electrolyte level in the battery is too low to allow further use, and the battery should be renewed. **Do not** attempt to charge, load or jump-start a battery when the indicator shows clear/yellow.

All battery types

6 If testing the battery using a voltmeter, connect the voltmeter across the battery and compare the result with those given in the Specifications under 'charge condition'. The test is only accurate if the battery has not been subjected to any kind of charge for the previous six hours. If this is not the case, switch on the headlights for 30 seconds, then wait four to five minutes before testing the battery after switching off the headlights. All other electrical circuits must be switched off, so check that the doors are fully shut when making the test.

7 If the voltage reading is less than 12.2 volts, then the battery is discharged, whilst a reading of 12.2 to 12.4 volts indicates a partially discharged condition.

8 If the battery is to be charged, remove it from the vehicle and charge it as described later in this Section.

Charging

Note: *The following is intended as a guide only. Always refer to the manufacturer's recommendations (often printed on a label attached to the battery) before charging a battery.*

Standard and low maintenance battery

9 Charge the battery at a rate equivalent to 10% of the battery capacity (eg, for a 46 Ah battery charge at 4.6 A) and continue to charge the battery at this rate until no further rise in specific gravity is noted over a four hour period.

10 Alternatively, a trickle charger charging at the rate of 1.5 amps can safely be used overnight.

11 Specially rapid 'boost' charges, which are claimed to restore the power of the battery in 1 to 2 hours are not recommended, as they

3.3 Disconnect the battery positive (+) connection

3.4a Undo the retaining nuts . . .

3.4b . . . and remove the securing plates

can cause serious damage to the battery plates through overheating.
12 While charging the battery, note that the temperature of the electrolyte should never exceed 38ºC.

Maintenance-free battery

13 This battery type takes considerably longer to fully recharge than the standard type, the time taken being dependent on the extent of discharge, but it will take anything up to three days.
14 A constant voltage type charger is required, to be set, when connected, to 13.9 to 14.9 volts with a charger current below 25 amps. Using this method, the battery should be usable within three hours, giving a voltage reading of 12.5 volts, but this is for a partially discharged battery and, as mentioned, full charging can take considerably longer.
15 If the battery is to be charged from a fully discharged state (condition reading less than 12.2 volts), have it recharged by your dealer or local automotive electrician, as the charge rate is higher and constant supervision during charging is necessary.

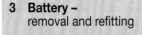

3 Battery – removal and refitting

Note: *Refer to 'Disconnecting the battery' in the Reference Chapter before proceeding.*

Removal

1 The battery is located at the left-hand side of the engine compartment.
2 Loosen the clamp bolt and disconnect the battery negative cable from the terminal.
3 Loosen the clamp bolt and disconnect the battery positive cable from the terminal **(see illustration)**.
4 Unscrew the bolt and remove the clamp plate securing the battery to the inner wing panel **(see illustration)**.
5 The battery can now be lifted out from the engine compartment.

Refitting

Note: *As a precaution, before refitting the battery check that the doors are open. On models with central door locking, connecting*

the battery could energise the solenoids and lock the doors.
6 Refitting is a reversal of removal, but smear petroleum jelly on the terminals after reconnecting the leads to reduce corrosion, and always reconnect the positive lead(s) first, followed by the negative lead(s). Tighten the battery clamp plate bolt securely.

4 Alternator/charging system – testing

Note: *Refer to the precautions given in 'Safety first!' and in Section 1 of this Chapter before starting work.*

1 If the ignition warning light fails to illuminate when the ignition is switched on, first check the alternator wiring connections for security. If satisfactory, check that the warning light bulb has not blown, and that the bulb holder is secure in its location in the instrument panel. If the light still fails to illuminate, check the continuity of the warning light feed wire from the alternator to the bulb holder. If all is satisfactory, the alternator is at fault and should be renewed or taken to an auto-electrician for testing and repair.
2 If the ignition warning light illuminates when the engine is running, stop the engine and check that the drivebelt is intact and that the alternator connections are secure. If all is so far satisfactory, check the alternator brushes and slip-rings as described in Section 6. If the fault persists, the alternator should be renewed, or taken to an auto-electrician for testing and repair.
3 If the alternator output is suspect even though the warning light functions correctly, the regulated voltage may be checked as follows.
4 Connect a voltmeter across the battery terminals, and start the engine.
5 Increase the engine speed until the voltmeter reading remains steady. The reading should be approximately 12 to 13 volts, and no more than 14 volts.
6 Switch on as many electrical accessories (eg, the headlights and heater blower) as possible, and check that the alternator maintains the regulated voltage at around 13 to 14 volts.

7 If the regulated voltage is not as stated, the fault may be due to worn brushes, weak brush springs, a faulty voltage regulator, a faulty diode, a severed phase winding, or worn or damaged slip-rings. The brushes and slip-rings may be checked (see Section 6), but if the fault persists, the alternator should be renewed or taken to an auto-electrician for testing and repair.

5 Alternator – removal and refitting

Removal

1 The alternator is bolted to the right-hand side of the engine block and is driven by the auxiliary belt.
2 Disconnect the battery negative (earth) lead and position it away from the terminal.
3 Apply the handbrake, then jack up the front of the vehicle and support it on axle stands (see *Jacking and vehicle support*). Where fitted, remove the engine compartment undershield.
4 Undo the retaining bolts and remove the heat shield from above the exhaust manifold **(see illustration)**.
5 Detach the auxiliary drivebelt from the alternator pulley with reference to Chapter 1.
6 Unscrew and remove the alternator lower and upper mounting bolt(s) **(see illustrations)**.
7 Withdraw the alternator forwards to access the wiring connectors on the rear of the alternator.

5.4 Remove the upper heat shield

5.6a Alternator mounting bolts (2.2 litre engine)

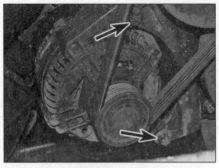

5.6b Alternator mounting bolts (2.9 litre engine)

5.8a Remove the plastic cap . . .

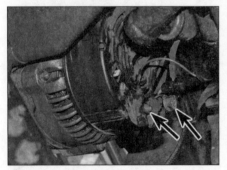

5.8b . . . and undo the wiring securing nut(s)

5.9 Disconnect the wiring connectors

8 Prise off the protective cap (where fitted) and unscrew the nut securing the battery positive lead to the alternator terminal **(see illustrations)**. Position the lead to one side.
9 Release the locking clip and disconnect the

wiring connector from the alternator terminal **(see illustration)**.
10 If necessary, remove the brush holder/voltage regulator module as described in Section 6.

6.3a Undo the retaining bolts . . .

6.3b . . . and remove the rear cover

Refitting

11 Refitting is a reversal of removal. Refer to Chapter 1 for details of refitting the auxiliary drivebelt.

6 Alternator brush holder/ regulator module – renewal

Note: *This procedure may vary slightly depending on type of alternator fitted.*
1 Remove the alternator as described in Section 5.
2 Place the alternator on a clean work surface, with the pulley facing down.

Valeo type

3 Undo the two screws, then remove the plastic cover from the rear of the alternator **(see illustrations)**.
4 Undo the three screws securing the brush holder/voltage regulator module to the alternator, then withdraw the module **(see illustration)**.

Bosch type

5 Undo the two screws securing the brush holder/voltage regulator module to the alternator, then withdraw the module **(see illustrations)**.

All types

6 Measure the free length of the brush contacts, check the measurement with the *Specifications*; renew the module if the brushes are worn below the minimum limit.

6.4 Voltage regulator/brush module retaining screws

6.5a Undo the retaining screws . . .

6.5b . . . and remove the voltage regulator/ brush module

7 Inspect the surfaces of the slip-rings through the brush holder/regulator aperture. If they are dirty, carefully clean them with fine glasspaper, however, if they are excessively worn, burnt or pitted, renewal of the complete alternator may be necessary.

8 Carefully locate the new brush holder/regulator on the alternator, taking care not to break the carbon brushes, then insert and tighten the retaining screws. The new holder may incorporate pins which retain the brushes retracted while the holder is being fitted and the screws inserted, after which the pins are removed to release the brushes against the slip-rings.

9 Refit the plastic cover to the alternator and retain with the three screws.

10 Refit the alternator with reference to Section 5.

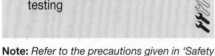

7 Starting system – testing

Note: *Refer to the precautions given in 'Safety first!' and in Section 1 of this Chapter before starting work.*

1 If the starter motor fails to operate during the normal starting procedure, the possible causes are as follows:

  a) *The engine immobiliser is faulty.*
  b) *The battery is faulty.*
  c) *The electrical connections between the switch, solenoid, battery and starter motor are somewhere failing to pass the necessary current from the battery through the starter to earth.*
  d) *The solenoid is faulty.*
  e) *The starter motor is mechanically or electrically defective.*

2 To check the battery, switch on the headlights. If they dim after a few seconds, this indicates that the battery is discharged – recharge (see Section 3) or renew the battery. If the headlights glow brightly, operate the starter switch while watching the headlights. If they dim, then this indicates that current is reaching the starter motor, therefore the fault must lie in the starter motor. If the lights continue to glow brightly (and no clicking sound can be heard from the starter motor

8.4 Disconnect the wiring connectors from the starter motor solenoid

solenoid), this indicates that there is a fault in the circuit or solenoid – see the following paragraphs. If the starter motor turns slowly when operated, but the battery is in good condition, then this indicates either that the starter motor is faulty, or there is considerable resistance somewhere in the circuit.

3 If a fault in the circuit is suspected, disconnect the battery leads (including the earth connection to the body), the starter/solenoid wiring and the engine/transmission earth strap. Thoroughly clean the connections, and reconnect the leads and wiring. Use a voltmeter or test light to check that full battery voltage is available at the battery positive lead connection to the solenoid. Smear petroleum jelly around the battery terminals to prevent corrosion – corroded connections are among the most frequent causes of electrical system faults.

4 If the battery and all connections are in good condition, check the circuit by disconnecting the ignition switch supply wire from the solenoid terminal. Connect a voltmeter or test lamp between the wire end and a good earth (such as the battery negative terminal), and check that the wire is live when the ignition switch is turned to the 'start' position. If it is, then the circuit is sound – if not the circuit wiring can be checked as described in Chapter 12.

5 The solenoid contacts can be checked by connecting a voltmeter or test light between the battery positive feed connection on the starter side of the solenoid and earth. When the ignition switch is turned to the 'start' position, there should be a reading or lighted

bulb, as applicable. If there is no reading or lighted bulb, the solenoid is faulty.

6 If the circuit and solenoid are proved sound, the fault must lie in the starter motor. In this event, it may be possible to have the starter motor overhauled by a specialist, but check on the cost of spares before proceeding, as it may prove more economical to obtain a new or exchange motor.

8 Starter motor – removal and refitting

Removal

1 The starter motor is bolted to the transmission bellhousing, at the rear of the engine on the left-hand side. Access may be best achieved from under the front of the vehicle

2 Disconnect the battery negative (earth) lead and position it away from the terminal.

3 Apply the handbrake, then jack up the front of the vehicle and support it on axle stands (see *Jacking and vehicle support*). Where fitted, remove the engine compartment undershield.

4 Where fitted, unclip the plastic cover, and then undo the securing nuts and disconnect the two wiring connectors from the terminals on the starter solenoid **(see illustration)**.

5 If required, release the wiring loom from the securing clips/cable-ties on the starter motor.

6 Working under the vehicle, use a socket and extension to remove the starter motor-to-transmission mounting bolts **(see illustrations)**. Note: *On 2.9 litre models, there is an earth cable secured to the transmission on the upper mounting bolt.*

7 Where necessary, unbolt the wiring loom support bracket from the transmission housing, noting its fitted position **(see illustration)**.

8 Remove the starter motor from the transmission bellhousing and withdraw from under the car.

Refitting

9 Refitting is a reversal of removal, tightening the mounting bolts to the specified torque. Ensure all wiring is correctly routed and the retaining nuts are securely tightened.

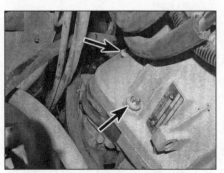

8.6a Starter motor securing bolts (2.2 litre engine)

8.6b Starter motor securing bolts (2.9 litre engine)

8.7 Unbolt the cable support bracket

10.1a Glow plug control unit (2.2 litre engines)

10.1b Glow plug control unit (2.9 litre engines)

10.3 Disconnect the wiring connector securing nut

9 Starter motor – overhaul

If the starter motor is thought to be defective, it should be removed from the vehicle and taken to an auto-electrician for assessment. In the majority of cases, new starter motor brushes can be fitted at a reasonable cost. However, check the cost of repairs first as it may prove more economical to purchase a new or exchange motor.

10 Glow plug control unit – removal and refitting

Removal

1 The control unit is located in the front left-hand side of the engine compartment, on the inner wing panel, below the battery tray **(see illustrations)**.
2 Disconnect the battery negative (earth) lead and position it away from the terminal.
3 Disconnect the wiring connectors from the control unit and move them to one side. On 2.9 litre engines, the lower cable is held on by a securing nut **(see illustration)**.
4 Undo the retaining bolts/nuts and withdraw the control unit from the engine compartment.

Refitting

5 Refitting is a reversal of removal.

11 Glow plugs – testing, removal and refitting

Testing

1 If the system malfunctions, testing is ultimately by substitution of known good units, but some preliminary checks may be made as follows.
2 Connect a voltmeter or 12 volt test lamp between the glow plug supply cable and good earth point on the engine or vehicle bodywork.
Caution: Make sure that the live connection is kept well clear of the engine and bodywork.
3 Have an assistant activate the preheating system with the ignition key and check that battery voltage is applied to the glow plug supply cable. Note that the voltage will drop to zero when the preheating period ends.
4 If no supply voltage can be detected at the glow plug supply cable, then either the glow plug relay or the supply cabling must be faulty.
5 To locate a faulty glow plug, first disconnect the supply cabling from all of the glow plug terminals. Connect an ohmmeter between the first glow plug terminal and a good earthing point on the cylinder head and measure the electrical resistance of the glow plug. A reading of anything more than a few ohms indicates that the plug is defective. Repeat the test on the remaining glow plugs.

6 If a suitable ammeter is available, connect it between the glow plug and its supply cable and measure the steady state current consumption (ignore the initial current surge which will be about 50% higher). Compare the result with this Chapter's Specifications – high current consumption (or no current draw at all) indicates a faulty glow plug.
7 As a final check, remove the glow plugs and inspect them visually, as described in the following paragraphs.

Removal

Caution: If the pre/post-heating system has just been energised, or if the engine has just been running, the glow plugs will be very hot.
8 Disconnect the battery negative (earth) lead and position it away from the terminal.
9 On 2.2 litre engines, remove the upper section of the inlet manifold as described in Chapter 4A, Section 5.
10 Depending on type of glow plug fitted, either pull the wiring connectors from the top of the glow plug terminals or undo the securing nut from the top of the glow plug to disconnect **(see illustrations)**.
11 Unscrew and remove the glow plug from the cylinder head.
12 Inspect the glow plug probe for signs of damage. A badly burned or charred probe indicates a faulty fuel injector (refer to Chapter 4A) – consult a diesel specialist for advice if necessary. Otherwise, if one plug is found to be faulty and the engine has completed a high mileage, it is probably worth renewing all four plugs as a set.

Refitting

13 Refitting is a reversal of removal, noting the following points:
 a) Apply a little anti-seize compound (or copper brake grease) to the glow plug threads.
 b) Tighten the glow plugs to the specified torque.
 c) Make sure when remaking the glow plug wiring connections that the contact surfaces are clean.
 d) Where applicable, refit the upper section of the inlet manifold as described in Chapter 4A.

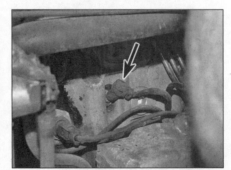

11.10a Glow plug wiring connector (2.2 litre engine)

11.10b Glow plug wiring connector (2.9 litre engine)

Chapter 6
Clutch

Contents

Degrees of difficulty

Easy, suitable for novice with little experience	**Fairly easy,** suitable for beginner with some experience	**Fairly difficult,** suitable for competent DIY mechanic	**Difficult,** suitable for experienced DIY mechanic	**Very difficult,** suitable for expert DIY or professional

Specifications

Friction disc
Lining thickness:
  New . . . . 3.6 to 4.0 mm
  Wear limit . . . . 2.6 to 3.0 mm
Lining face run-out . . . . 0.5 mm maximum

Torque wrench settings

	Nm	lbf ft
Master cylinder to pedal mounting bracket	10	7
Pressure plate-to-flywheel bolts.	25	18
Release bearing/slave cylinder bleed screw	16	12
Release bearing/slave cylinder bolts (2.2 litre model)	9	7
Slave cylinder bolts (2.9 litre model).	23	17
Slave cylinder hydraulic hose (2.9 litre model)	16	12
Pedal mounting bracket retaining nuts	23	17

---

1 General information and precautions

All models are fitted with a single dry plate clutch system. The main components consist of a friction disc, pressure plate (or cover), hydraulic master cylinder, release bearing and slave cylinder.

The clutch pressure plate is bolted to the rear face of the flywheel, and the friction disc is located between the pressure plate and the flywheel friction surface. The friction disc is splined to the transmission input shaft and is free to slide along the splines. Friction lining material is riveted to each side of the disc, and the disc hub incorporates cushioning springs to absorb transmission shocks and ensure a smooth take-up of drive. The pressure plate incorporates an internal diaphragm spring mounted on a fulcrum ring. When the inner fingers of the spring are depressed, the outer perimeter draws the pressure plate away from the friction disc.

On 2.2 litre models, the release bearing is part of the slave cylinder and is operated by the clutch pedal, using hydraulic pressure. The pedal acts on the hydraulic master cylinder

pushrod, and hydraulic pressure operates the slave cylinder and release bearing.

On 2.9 litre models, the release bearing is located on a guide sleeve at the front of the transmission, and the bearing is free to slide on the sleeve, under the action of the release arm, which pivots inside the clutch bellhousing. The release mechanism is operated by the clutch pedal, using hydraulic pressure. The pedal acts on the hydraulic master cylinder pushrod and the slave cylinder, mounted on the transmission bellhousing, operates the clutch release lever via a pushrod.

When the clutch pedal is depressed, the release bearing is pushed forwards, to bear against the centre of the diaphragm spring, thus pushing the centre of the diaphragm spring inwards.

When the clutch pedal is released, the diaphragm spring forces the pressure plate into contact with the friction linings on the friction disc, and simultaneously pushes the friction disc forwards on its splines, forcing it against the flywheel. The friction disc is now firmly sandwiched between the pressure plate and the flywheel, and drive is taken up.

The clutch is self-adjusting. As wear takes place on the friction disc over a period of time, the pressure plate automatically moves closer to the friction plate to compensate.

Warning: Dust created by clutch wear and deposited on the clutch components may contain asbestos, which is a health hazard. DO NOT blow it out with compressed air, or inhale any of it. DO NOT use petrol (or petroleum-based solvents) to clean off the dust. Brake system cleaner or methylated spirit should be used to flush the dust into a suitable receptacle. After the clutch components are wiped clean with rags, dispose of the contaminated rags and cleaner in a sealed, marked container.

Warning: Hydraulic fluid is poisonous; wash off immediately and thoroughly in the case of skin contact, and seek immediate medical advice if any fluid is swallowed or gets into the eyes. Certain types of hydraulic fluid are inflammable, and may ignite when allowed into contact with hot components; when servicing any hydraulic system, it is safest to assume that the fluid is inflammable, and to take precautions against the risk of fire as though it is petrol that is being handled. Hydraulic fluid is also an effective paint stripper, and will attack plastics; if any is spilt, it should be washed off immediately, using copious quantities of fresh water. Finally, it is hygroscopic (it

2.2 Marking the pressure plate-to-flywheel

2.3 Pressure plate retaining bolts

2.4 Withdraw the pressure plate and friction disc

absorbs moisture from the air) – old fluid may be contaminated and unfit for further use. When topping-up or renewing the fluid, always use the recommended type, and ensure that it comes from a freshly-opened, sealed container.

2 Clutch assembly –
removal, inspection and refitting

Removal

1 Remove the transmission, as described in Chapter 7.

 Warning: Refer to the precautions given in Section 1 regarding dust.

2 If the original clutch is to be refitted, make alignment marks between the clutch pressure plate assembly and the flywheel, so that the

clutch can be refitted in its original position **(see illustration)**.
3 Progressively unscrew the bolts securing the clutch pressure plate assembly to the flywheel, and recover the washers (where fitted) **(see illustration)**.
4 Withdraw the clutch pressure plate assembly (cover) and disc from the flywheel **(see illustration)**. Be prepared to catch the friction disc, and note which way round the friction disc is fitted – the two sides of the disc may be marked *Engine side* and *Transmission side*, or the side with the part number on faces the flywheel. The greater projecting side of the hub faces away from the flywheel.

Inspection

5 Clean the cover, disc, and flywheel. Do not inhale the dust, as it may contain asbestos, which is dangerous to health.
6 Examine the fingers of the diaphragm spring

for wear or scoring. If the depth of any scoring is excessive, a new cover assembly must be fitted.
7 Examine the pressure plate for scoring, cracking and discoloration. Light scoring is acceptable, but if excessive, a new assembly must be fitted.
8 Examine the friction disc linings for wear cracking, and for contamination with oil or grease. Using vernier calipers, check the thickness of the linings and compare with the details given in the Specifications. Check the disc hub and splines for wear by temporarily fitting it on the transmission input shaft. Renew the friction disc as necessary.
9 Examine the flywheel friction surface for scoring, cracking and discoloration (caused by overheating). If excessive, it may be possible to have the flywheel machined by an engineering works, otherwise it should be renewed.
10 Ensure that all parts are clean, and free of oil or grease, before reassembling. Apply just a small amount of high melting-point grease to the splines of the friction disc hub. Note that a new pressure plate may be coated with protective grease. It is only permissible to clean the grease away from the friction disc lining contact area. Removal of the grease from other areas will shorten the service life of the clutch.
11 Check the spigot bearing in the end of the crankshaft or in the centre of the flywheel. Make sure that it turns smoothly and quietly. If the transmission input shaft contact face on the bearing is worn or damaged, fit a new bearing, as described in the relevant part of Chapter 2A.

Refitting

12 If you are re-using the pressure plate, the adjustment ring will need to be reset. Position the pressure plate in a hydraulic press (Mercedes-Benz technicians use a special tool, with a block of wood placed under the central portion of the pressure plate, directly below the diaphragm spring fingers, not on the friction face). Apply pressure to the diaphragm spring fingers until the adjusting ring is loose. While still applying pressure, use a screwdriver to rotate the adjusting ring anti-clockwise **(see illustrations)**. Hold the adjustment ring in place, and then release the pressure on the diaphragm spring fingers.
13 It is important to ensure that no oil or grease

2.12a Special tool to adjust pressure plate . . .

2.12b . . . which presses down on the diaphragm spring fingers

2.12c Turn the adjusting ring anti-clockwise . . .

2.12d . . . and release the pressure on the diaphragm

gets onto the friction disc linings, or the pressure plate and flywheel faces. It is advisable to refit the clutch assembly with clean hands, and to wipe down the pressure plate and flywheel faces with a clean rag before assembly begins.

14 Apply a smear of molybdenum disulphide grease to the splines of the friction disc hub, then offer the disc to the flywheel, with the greater projecting side of the hub facing away from the flywheel (most friction discs will have an *Engine side* marking which should face the flywheel). Hold the friction disc against the flywheel while the pressure plate assembly is offered into position, or alternatively use the centralising tool described in paragraph 16 to hold the disc on the flywheel.

15 Fit the clutch pressure plate assembly, where applicable aligning the marks with those on the flywheel. Ensure that the pressure plate assembly locates over the dowels on the flywheel. Insert the securing bolts and washers, and tighten them finger-tight, so that the friction disc is gripped, but can still be moved.

16 The friction disc must now be centralised, to ensure correct alignment of the transmission input shaft with the spigot bearing in the crankshaft/flywheel **(see illustrations)**. To do this, a proprietary tool may be used, or alternatively, use a wooden mandrel made to fit inside the friction disc hub and spigot bearing. Insert the tool through the friction disc into the spigot bearing, and make sure that it is central.

17 Tighten the clutch pressure plate bolts progressively and in diagonal sequence, until the specified torque setting is achieved, and then remove the centralising tool.

18 Check the release bearing in the front of the transmission for smooth operation, and if necessary renew it with reference to Section 3 or 4, depending on model.

19 Refit the transmission with reference to Chapter 7.

3 Clutch release bearing (2.9 litre models) – removal, inspection and refitting

Note: *On 2.2 litre models, the release bearing is part of the slave cylinder; see Section 4.*

Release bearing

Removal

1 Remove the transmission, as described in Chapter 7.

⚠ **Warning: Refer to the precautions given in Section 1 regarding dust.**

2 Rotate the bearing to disengage it from the release fork, then pull the bearing forwards, and slide it from the guide sleeve in the transmission housing **(see illustration)**.

Inspection

3 Spin the release bearing, and check it for excessive roughness. Hold the outer race, and attempt to move it laterally against the inner

2.16a Centralise the clutch friction disc . . .

2.16b . . . and fit the assembly onto the flywheel

race. If any excessive movement or roughness is evident, renew the bearing. If a new clutch has been fitted, it is wise to renew the release bearing as a matter of course.

Refitting

4 Clean and then lightly grease the release bearing contact surfaces on the release lever. Similarly lightly grease the guide sleeve.

5 Slide the bearing into position on the guide sleeve, then rotate the bearing until it snaps into position in the release lever.

6 Refit the transmission as described in Chapter 7.

Release lever

Removal

7 Remove the release bearing, as described previously in this Section.

8 Pull the slave cylinder end of the release lever forwards, then slide the lever sideways to

release it from the pivot pin, and withdraw the lever over the guide sleeve **(see illustration)**.

Inspection

9 Inspect the release bearing, pivot and slave pushrod contact faces on the release lever for wear. Renew it if excessive wear is evident.

10 Check the condition of the release lever retaining spring clip, and the lever if necessary.

Refitting

11 Clean and then lightly grease the release bearing contact surfaces on the release lever and the pivot pin. Similarly lightly grease the guide sleeve **see illustration)**.

12 Slide the release lever into position over the guide sleeve, then slide the end of the lever over the pivot pin, ensuring that the retaining spring clip engages around the rear of the pivot pin **(see illustration)**.

13 Refit the release bearing as described previously in this Section.

3.2 Removing the clutch release bearing

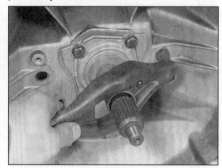
3.8 Removing the clutch release lever

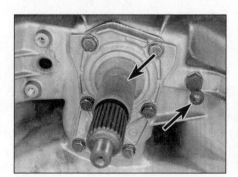
3.11 Lightly grease the pivot pin and the guide sleeve

3.12 Ensure that the spring clip (arrowed) engages with the pivot pin

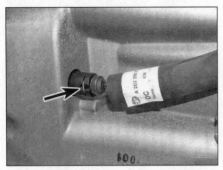

4.2 Clutch fluid line retaining clip

4.3a Undo the mounting bolts . . .

4.3b . . . and remove the release bearing/ slave cylinder

4.8 Flexible hose mounting bracket

4.9 Clutch slave cylinder mounting bolts

4 Hydraulic slave cylinder – removal, inspection and refitting

2.2 litre models

Note: *The release bearing is part of the slave cylinder.*

Removal

1 Remove the transmission, as described in Chapter 7.

⚠ **Warning: Refer to the precautions given in Section 1 regarding dust.**

2 If not already disconnected, release the retaining clip from the clutch fluid hose on the outside of the transmission housing, and remove the hose **(see illustration)**.

3 Undo the retaining bolts and withdraw the release bearing/slave cylinder from the transmission housing, complete with bleed screw connection **(see illustrations)**.

Inspection

4 Spin the release bearing, and check it for excessive roughness. If any excessive movement or roughness is evident, renew the bearing. If a new clutch has been fitted, it is wise to renew the release bearing as a matter of course.

Refitting

5 Slide the bearing/slave cylinder into position, and then tighten the retaining bolts to the specified torque setting.

6 Refit the transmission as described in Chapter 7.

2.9 litre models

Removal

7 Apply the handbrake, then jack up the front of the vehicle and support securely on axle stands (see *Jacking and vehicle support*).

⚠ **Warning: Refer to the precautions given in Section 1 regarding dust.**

8 Working on the left-hand side of the vehicle, place a suitable container beneath the slave cylinder, then unscrew the fluid pipe union, and disconnect the fluid pipe from the rear of the cylinder. Alternatively, the flexible hose can be disconnected at its other end, from the rigid metal fluid pipe **(see illustration)**. Plug the open ends of the pipe/hose and slave cylinder to prevent dirt ingress.

9 Undo the two retaining bolts securing the slave cylinder to the transmission bellhousing, and then withdraw the cylinder, complete with

5.4 Clutch fluid supply hose

pushrod **(see illustration)**. Remove the shim from the transmission housing, where fitted.

Refitting

10 Commence refitting by placing the shim into position on the transmission housing, with the grooved side facing towards the housing.

11 Offer the cylinder and pushrod to the housing, ensuring that the pushrod engages with the spherical recess in the clutch release lever.

12 Refit and tighten the slave cylinder securing bolts.

13 Reconnect the pipe/hose, and then bleed the clutch hydraulic system as described in Section 6.

5 Hydraulic master cylinder – removal and refitting

Note: *Refer to the precautions given in Section 1 regarding the use of hydraulic fluid.*

Removal

1 The clutch master cylinder is located inside the vehicle, attached to the pedal mounting bracket. Hydraulic fluid for the unit is supplied by a flexible rubber hose connected to the brake fluid reservoir in the engine compartment.

2 Disconnect the battery negative (earth) lead and position it away from the terminal.

3 To reduce fluid loss, draw off as much fluid as possible from the appropriate chamber of the brake fluid reservoir, using a clean syringe, until the fluid level is below the level of the clutch master cylinder supply pipe. Alternatively, fit a hose clamp to the supply pipe.

4 Place a suitable container beneath the clutch master cylinder to catch any spilt fluid, and disconnect the supply pipe **(see illustration)**. Plug the open ends of the pipe to prevent dirt entry and further fluid loss.

5 Release the securing clip from the hydraulic pipe union, and carefully withdraw the pipe from the master cylinder **(see illustration)**. Plug the open ends of the pipe and master cylinder to prevent dirt entry and further fluid loss.

6 If required, remove the lower facia trim

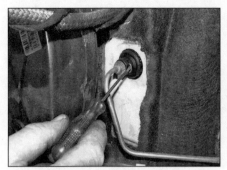

5.5 Release the clutch fluid line retaining clip

5.7 Turn the switch to release it from the mounting bracket

5.8a Release the retaining clip . . .

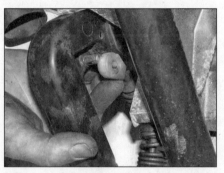

5.8b . . . and disconnect the clutch pushrod from the pedal

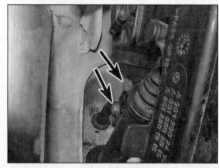

5.9 Clutch master cylinder mounting bolts

panel from under the steering column for easier access to the master cylinder and pedal assembly, with reference to Chapter 11.

7 Disconnect the wiring connector from the switch, and then turn the switch to remove it from the mounting bracket **(see illustration)**.

8 Release the circlip and disconnect the clutch master cylinder pushrod from the pin on the pedal **(see illustrations)**.

9 Unscrew the two mounting bolts securing the master cylinder to the pedal mounting bracket **(see illustration)**, and then withdraw the master cylinder from the driver's footwell.

Refitting

10 Refitting is a reversal of removal, making sure that retaining bolts are tightened securely. Finally bleed the hydraulic system as described in Section 6.

6 Hydraulic system – bleeding

Note: *Refer to the precautions given in Section 1 regarding the use of hydraulic fluid.*

1 The correct operation of the hydraulic system is only possible after removing all air from the circuit, and this is achieved by bleeding the system.

2 During the bleeding procedure, add only clean, unused hydraulic fluid of the recommended type. Never re-use fluid that has already been bled from the system. Ensure that sufficient fluid is available before starting work.

3 If there is any possibility of incorrect fluid being already in the system, both the clutch and brake circuits must be flushed completely with uncontaminated, correct fluid, and new seals should be fitted to the various components.

4 If hydraulic fluid has been lost from the system, or air has entered because of a leak, ensure that the fault is cured before proceeding further.

5 Apply the handbrake, then jack up the front of the vehicle and support it on axle stands (see *Jacking and vehicle support*).

6 Where applicable, remove the underbody shield for access to the transmission bellhousing.

7 Remove the dust cap from the slave

cylinder bleed screw, and clean away any dirt **(see illustration)**.

8 Note that the brake fluid reservoir feeds both the brake and clutch hydraulic systems.

9 Mercedes-Benz recommended that pressure-bleeding equipment be used to bleed the system. Some pressure-bleeding kits are operated by the reservoir of pressurised air contained in a spare tyre; however, note that it will probably be necessary to reduce the pressure to a lower level than normal. Refer to the instructions supplied with the kit. If a pressure-bleeding kit is not available, use the normal bleeding method described for the brake hydraulic circuit in Chapter 9.

10 By connecting a pressurised, fluid-filled container to the brake fluid reservoir, bleeding can be carried out simply by opening the bleed screw on the clutch slave cylinder, and allowing the fluid to flow out until no more air bubbles can be seen in the expelled fluid.

6.7 Clutch slave cylinder bleed screw

This method has the advantage that the large reservoir of fluid provides an additional safeguard against air being drawn into the system during bleeding.

11 Collect a clean glass jar, a suitable length of plastic or rubber tubing which is a tight fit over the bleed screw, and a ring spanner to fit the screw.

12 Fit the spanner and tube to the slave cylinder bleed screw **(see illustration)**, place the other end of the tube in the jar, and pour in sufficient fluid to cover the end of the tube.

13 Connect the pressure-bleeding equipment to the brake/clutch fluid reservoir in accordance with its manufacturer's instructions.

14 Loosen the bleed screw half a turn using the spanner, and allow fluid to drain into the jar until no more air bubbles emerge.

15 When bleeding is complete, tighten the bleed screw, and disconnect the hose and the pressure bleeding equipment.

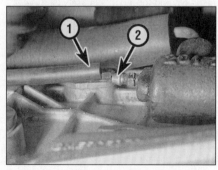

6.12 Fit tube (1) to the slave cylinder bleed screw (2)

7.3 Turn the switch to release it from the mounting bracket

7.4a Release the retaining clip . . .

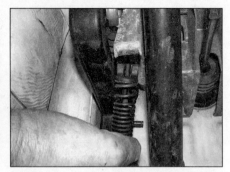

7.4b . . . and remove the spring assembly from the pedal

7.6a Release the retaining clip . . .

7.6b . . . remove the washer . . .

7.6c . . . and slide the clutch pedal from the pivot pin

7.7 Make sure the upper part of the spring assembly locates in the mounting bracket

16 Wash off any spilt fluid, check once more that the bleed screw is tightened securely, and refit the dust cap.

17 Check the hydraulic fluid level in the reservoir, and top-up if necessary (see *Weekly checks*).

18 Discard any hydraulic fluid that has been bled from the system, as it will not be fit for re-use.

19 Check the feel of the clutch pedal. If it feels at all spongy, air must still be present in the system, and further bleeding is required. Failure to bleed satisfactorily after a reasonable repetition of the bleeding procedure may be due to worn master or slave cylinder seals.

20 On completion, lower the vehicle to the ground.

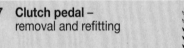

7 Clutch pedal – removal and refitting

Removal

1 Disconnect the battery negative (earth) lead and position it away from the terminal.

2 If required, remove the lower facia trim panel from under the steering column for easier access to the pedal assembly, with reference to Chapter 11.

3 Disconnect the wiring connector from the switch, and then turn the switch to remove it from the mounting bracket **(see illustration)**.

4 Remove the securing clip and release the lower end of the spring assembly from the clutch pedal, then move it to the rear of the pedal assembly to disengage it from its upper pivot point **(see illustrations)**.

Caution: The clutch spring assembly is under pressure, so will need to be removed carefully.

5 Release the circlip and disconnect the clutch master cylinder pushrod from the pin on the pedal **(see illustrations 5.8a and 5.8b)**.

6 Release the circlip, remove the shim/washer and withdraw the clutch pedal from the pivot pin on the pedal mounting bracket **(see illustrations)**.

Refitting

7 Refitting is a reversal of removal, but make sure the clutch spring upper pivot is located correctly **(see illustration)**.

Chapter 7
Manual transmission

Contents

Degrees of difficulty

Easy, suitable for novice with little experience	Fairly easy, suitable for beginner with some experience	Fairly difficult, suitable for competent DIY mechanic	Difficult, suitable for experienced DIY mechanic	Very difficult, suitable for expert DIY or professional

Specifications

General

Type	5 forward speeds and reverse. Synchromesh on all forward and reverse gears

Transmission codes:

2.2 litre models	711.605 and 711.620
2.9 litre models	711.612

Lubrication

Transmission capacity	See Chapter 1
Lubricant type	See *Lubricants and fluids*

Torque wrench settings

	Nm	lbf ft
Gearchange lever base to bulkhead bracket (2.2 litre models)	20	15
Gearchange lever base to transmission (2.9 litre models)	63	46
Input shaft bearing guide sleeve-to-transmission bolts (2.9 litre models)	10	8
Oil filler and drain plugs	60	44
Output shaft flange retaining bolt*	110	81
Propeller shaft intermediate bearing-to-floor retaining bolts	105	77
Propeller shaft safety bracket to floor retaining bolts	100	74
Propeller shaft universal joint flange to output shaft flange*	70	52
Reversing light switch (2.9 litre models)	40	30
Speedo sensor to transmission housing	14	10
Transmission mounting to crossmember	89	66
Transmission to engine	38	28

* Use new nuts/bolts

1   General information

A 5-speed manual transmission is bolted to the rear of the engine. Drive is transmitted from the crankshaft via the clutch to the input shaft, which has a splined extension to accept the clutch friction disc. The transmission output shaft transmits the drive via the propeller shaft to the rear differential. The input shaft runs in-line with the output shaft. The input shaft and output shaft gears are in constant mesh with the lay-shaft gear cluster. Selection of gears is by sliding synchromesh hubs, which lock the appropriate output shaft gears to the output shaft.

Gear selection is via a floor-mounted lever bolted directly to the top of the transmission on 2.9 litre models, or a facia-mounted lever and selector mechanism incorporating cables to the transmission on 2.2 litre models. The selector mechanism causes the appropriate selector fork to move its respective synchro-sleeve along the shaft, to lock the gear pinion to the synchro-hub. Since the synchro-hubs are splined to the output shaft, this locks the pinion to the shaft, so that the drive can be transmitted. To ensure that gearchanging can be made quickly and quietly, a synchromesh system is fitted to all the gears, consisting of baulk rings and spring-loaded fingers, as well as the gear pinions and synchro-hubs. The synchromesh cones are formed on the mating faces of the baulk rings and gear pinions.

Because of the complexity, possible unavailability of parts and special tools necessary, internal repair procedures for the transmission are not recommended for the home mechanic. The bulk of the information in this Chapter is therefore devoted to removal and refitting procedures.

2.1a Pull back the rubber gaiter . . .

2.1b . . . remove the foam insulation . . .

2.2 . . . and undo the retaining bolt

2 Gear lever (models up to 2000) – removal and refitting

Removal

1 From inside the vehicle, disengage the rubber gaiter from the locating flange on the floor panel. Withdraw the soundproofing foam and then slide the gaiter up the gearchange lever **(see illustrations)**.

2 Undo the bolt securing the gear lever to the transmission bracket, and withdraw the gear lever from inside the vehicle **(see illustration)**.

Refitting

3 Refitting is a reversal of removal.

3 Gear lever and cables (models from 2000) – removal, refitting and adjusting

Removal

1 From inside the vehicle, unclip the gear lever gaiter from the facia panel, and slide it up the gear lever **(see illustration)**.

2 With the gear lever in the neutral position press down on the securing clamp to lock the gear lever in the neutral position **(see illustration)**. **Note:** *On models up to 2003, the lever is locked in position by inserting a 6 mm rod (Allen key or drill bit) into the holes provided at the base of the lever.*

3 Firmly apply the handbrake, and then jack up the front of the vehicle and support

it securely on axle stands (see *Jacking and vehicle support*). Where fitted, remove the engine undershield.

4 Working under the vehicle, lever the cable ball sockets from the selector levers on the side of the transmission, and then unclip the outer cables from the mounting bracket **(see illustration)**. Note the fitted position of the cables for refitting (blue at the top and black at the bottom).

5 Working inside the vehicle, remove the lower trim panels from around the centre bulkhead and floor mats with reference to Chapter 11.

6 Undo the two retaining screws and remove the retaining plate from the gear selector cables **(see illustrations)**. Withdraw the cables up through the floor panel.

7 Remove the trim panel from the centre of the facia panel **(see illustration)**, with reference to Chapter 11, Section 26.

3.1 Unclip the rubber gaiter from the facia

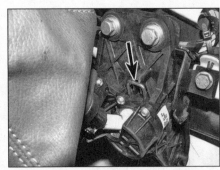
3.2 Push down on clip to lock the gear lever in position

3.4 Disconnect the cables from the transmission

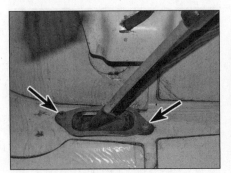
3.6a Undo the two screws . . .

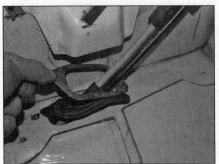
3.6b . . . remove the retaining plate . . .

3.6c . . . and withdraw the cables

3.7 Remove the facia centre panel

3.8a Undo the two upper mounting bolts . . .

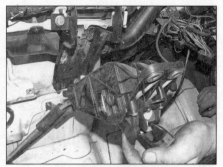
3.8b . . . and unclip the lower part from the mounting bracket

3.9a Unclip the balljoints . . .

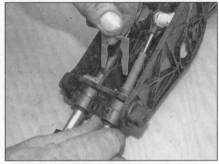
3.9b . . . withdraw the retaining clips . . .

3.9c . . . and slide the cables out from the mounting bracket

8 Undo the bolts securing the gear lever to the mounting bracket, and withdraw the assembly, complete with cables from the vehicle **(see illustrations)**.
9 To release the cables from the gear lever assembly, carefully unclip the balljoints from the gear lever and then withdraw the retaining clips from the outer cables **(see illustrations)**. Note the fitted position of the cables for refitting (one cable is blue and the other black).

Refitting

10 Refitting is a reversal of removal, noting the following points:
 a) *Tighten the gear lever base retaining bolts to the specified torque.*
 b) *Check the condition of the cables and bushes, and renew if required.*
 c) *Make sure the cables are fitted securely and the correct way around, as noted on removal.*

 d) *Adjust the cables as described in paragraphs 11 to 15 of this section.*

Adjusting

11 From inside the vehicle, unclip the gear lever gaiter from the facia panel, and slide it up the gear lever **(see illustration 3.1)**.
12 With the gear lever in the neutral position press down on the securing clamp to lock the gear lever in the neutral position **(see illustration 3.2)**. *Note: On models up to 2003, the lever is locked in position by inserting a 6 mm rod (Allen key or drill bit) into the holes provided at the base of the lever.*
13 Working under the vehicle, release the securing clips from the gearchange cables, then make sure the transmission is in the neutral position **(see illustration)**.
14 With the gear lever in the neutral position and the transmission in neutral, secure the cables in position by pressing the securing

clips back in position on the gear change cables **(see illustration)**.
15 When completed, release the locking clamp (or 6 mm locking peg) from the base of the gear lever, before refitting the gear lever gaiter.

4 Vehicle speed sensor – removal and refitting

Note: *On later models, the speed of the vehicle is monitored by the wheel speed sensors, which give information to the ECM.*

Removal

1 On early models, the vehicle speed sensor is located on the left-hand side rear of the transmission, above the oil filler plug **(see illustration)**.
2 Firmly apply the handbrake, and then

3.13 Using a screwdriver to unclip the outer cover

3.14 Press the outer cover firmly into place to secure the cable

4.1 Vehicle speed sensor – where fitted

5.1 Reversing light switch (2.2 litre models)

5.3 Undo the switch mounting bolt

5.5 Reversing light switch (2.9 litre models)

jack up the front of the vehicle and support it securely on axle stands (see *Jacking and vehicle support*). Where fitted, remove the engine undershield.

3 Trace the wiring from the vehicle speed sensor and disconnect the wiring connector.

4 Unscrew the retaining bolt and remove the sensor from the transmission.

Refitting

5 Refitting is a reversal of the removal procedure. On completion, check and if necessary top-up the transmission oil level with reference to Section 9.

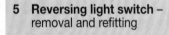

5 Reversing light switch – removal and refitting

2.2 litre models

Removal

1 The reversing light circuit is controlled by a plunger-type switch, which is screwed into the upper left-hand side rear of the selector transmission casing **(see illustration)**.

2 Firmly apply the handbrake, and then jack up the front of the vehicle and support it securely on axle stands (see *Jacking and vehicle support*). Where fitted, remove the engine undershield.

3 Disconnect the wiring from the reversing light switch, then unscrew the securing bolt and withdraw the switch from the transmission **(see illustration)**. Discard the O-ring oil seal, as a new one will be required for refitting.

Refitting

4 Refitting is a reversal of the removal procedure, ensuring that the bolt is tightened securely and a new seal is fitted. On completion, check and if necessary, top-up the transmission oil level with reference to Section 9.

2.9 litre models

Removal

5 The reversing light circuit is controlled by a plunger-type switch screwed into the upper right-hand side of the transmission casing, at the base of the gear lever mounting housing **(see illustration)**.

6 Firmly apply the handbrake, and then jack up the front of the vehicle and support it securely on axle stands (see *Jacking and vehicle support*). Where fitted, remove the engine undershield.

7 Disconnect the wiring from the reversing light switch, then unscrew the switch from the housing and withdraw it from the transmission. If required the plunger (thrust piece) can also be withdrawn from the housing to check its condition.

Refitting

8 Refitting is a reversal of the removal procedure, ensuring that the switch is tightened securely. On completion, check and if necessary, top-up the transmission oil level with reference to Section 9.

6 Oil seals – renewal

Front (input shaft) oil seal

Note: *The following procedures require the use of a Mercedes-Benz tool (711 589 00 33 00), to remove and refit the input shaft oil seal. Ensure that this tool, or a suitable alternative (see paragraph 4 or 11), is available before proceeding.*

1 Remove the transmission from the vehicle as described in Section 7, of this Chapter.

2.2 litre models

2 Remove the hydraulic slave cylinder, as described in Chapter 6, Section 4.

3 Thoroughly clean the transmission assembly, paying particular attention to the area inside the clutch housing.

4 Using the special tool, withdraw the oil seal from the transmission. If the tool is not available, carefully punch or drill two small holes opposite each other in the oil seal. Screw a self-tapping screw into each and pull on the screws with pliers to extract the seal. Take care not to damage the transmission housing as the oil seal is removed. Note the fitted position of the seal in the housing before removal to aid refitting.

5 Clean the seal housing and polish off any burrs or raised edges that may have caused the seal to fail in the first place.

6 Lubricate the lip of the new oil seal with a smear of multipurpose grease, then ease the seal into position on the end of the input shaft. Press the seal a little way into the housing by hand, making sure that it is square to its seating then, using suitable tubing, carefully drive the oil seal into the housing. Take great care not to damage the seal lips during fitting, and ensure that the seal lips face inwards and the seal is fitted in the position noted on removal.

7 Refit the clutch release cylinder as described in Chapter 6. Then refit the transmission as described in Section 7.

2.9 litre models

8 Remove the clutch release bearing and lever, as described in Chapter 6, Section 3.

9 Thoroughly clean the transmission assembly, paying particular attention to the area inside the clutch housing.

10 Undo the three retaining bolts and withdraw the bearing guide sleeve from over the input shaft.

11 Using the Mercedes-Benz special tool 711 589 00 33 00, withdraw the oil seal from the transmission. If the tool is not available, carefully punch or drill two small holes opposite each other in the oil seal. Screw a self-tapping screw into each and pull on the screws with pliers to extract the seal. Take care not to damage the transmission housing as the oil seal is removed. Note the fitted position of the seal in the housing before removal to aid refitting.

12 Clean the seal housing and polish off any burrs or raised edges that may have caused the seal to fail in the first place.

13 Lubricate the lip of the new oil seal with a smear of multipurpose grease, then ease the seal into position on the end of the input shaft. Press the seal a little way into the housing by hand, making sure that it is square to its seating then, using suitable tubing, carefully drive the oil seal into the housing. Take great care not to damage the seal lips during fitting, and ensure that the seal lips face inwards and the seal is fitted in the position noted on removal.

14 Refit the bearing guide sleeve over the input shaft and tighten the three retaining bolts to the specified torque setting.

15 Refit the clutch release bearing and lever,

6.18 Mark the position of the prop shaft-to-flange

6.19 Remove the safety bracket from around the prop shaft

6.21a Slacken the retaining bolt . . .

6.21b . . . and then remove complete with washer

6.22 Slide the flange from the splines

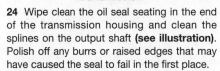

6.23 Prise the oil seal from the transmission

as described in Chapter 6. Then refit the transmission as described in Section 7.

Rear (output shaft) oil seal

Note: *A new output shaft flange retaining bolt, new propeller shaft retaining bolts will be required for refitting.*

16 Firmly apply the handbrake, and then jack up the front of the vehicle and support it securely on axle stands (see *Jacking and vehicle support*). Where fitted, remove the engine undershield.

17 Drain the transmission oil as described in Section 9.

18 Mark the relative positions of the propeller shaft universal joint flange and transmission output shaft flange **(see illustration)**.

19 Undo the two retaining bolts and remove the safety bracket from around the propeller shaft **(see illustration)**.

20 Undo the four bolts securing the propeller shaft to the output shaft flange, and then

separate the flanges and position the propeller shaft to one side. Discard the bolts, as a new ones will be required when refitting.

21 Using a bar or suitable forked tool bolted to the output shaft flange holes, hold the flange stationary and unscrew the retaining bolt **(see illustrations)**. Discard the bolt, as a new one will be required when refitting.

22 Withdraw the flange from the end of the output shaft splines **(see illustration)**. **Note:** *If the flange is tight on the splines, it may be necessary to use a puller to withdraw the flange from the output shaft.*

23 Using a screwdriver, carefully prise the old oil seal out of its location in the transmission housing **(see illustration)**. Alternatively, screw two self-tapping screws into the face of the oil seal, 180° apart. Using pliers, pull or lever on each screw alternately to withdraw the oil seal. Note the fitted position of the seal in the housing before removal to aid refitting.

24 Wipe clean the oil seal seating in the end of the transmission housing and clean the splines on the output shaft **(see illustration)**. Polish off any burrs or raised edges that may have caused the seal to fail in the first place.

25 Press the new seal a little way into the housing by hand, making sure that it is square to its seating **(see illustration)**. Apply a small amount of grease between the sealing lip and dust lip on the seal before fitting.

26 Using suitable tubing or a large socket, carefully drive the oil seal fully into the housing. Take great care not to damage the seal lips during fitting and ensure that the seal lips face inwards and the seal is fitted in the position noted on removal.

27 Refit the flange to the output shaft using a new securing bolts, and then tighten to the specified torque. Whilst tightening, prevent the output shaft flange from turning by holding it as described on removal **(see illustration)**.

6.24 Clean out the recess in the rear of the transmission

6.25 Press the new seal into place

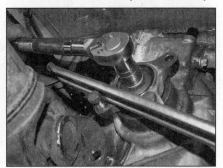

6.27 Tighten the bolt to the specified torque

7.13a Using a clamp on the clutch fluid hose

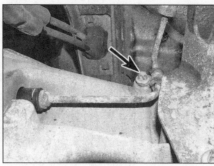

7.13b Clutch fluid pipe mounting bracket bolt

28 Align the marks made on removal and refit the propeller shaft to the transmission output flange, using new retaining bolts, and then tighten to the specified torque.

29 Refit the safety bracket around the propeller shaft and then tighten the bolts to the specified torque setting.

30 Refill the transmission with oil as described in Section 9, then lower the vehicle to the ground.

7 Transmission – removal and refitting

Note 1: *The transmission can be removed as a unit with the engine as described in Chapter 2C, then separated from the engine on the bench. However, if work is only necessary on the transmission or clutch unit, it is better*

to remove the transmission on its own from underneath the vehicle. The latter method is described in this Section. The aid of an assistant will be required during the removal and refitting procedures.
Note 2: *New propeller shaft universal joint/ rubber coupling retaining bolts will be required for refitting.*

Removal

1 Open the bonnet and disconnect the battery negative terminal (refer to *Disconnecting the battery* in the Reference Chapter).

2 On 2.9 litre models, remove the gearchange lever as described in Section 2.

3 Firmly apply the handbrake, and then jack up the front of the vehicle and support it securely on axle stands (see *Jacking and vehicle support*). Where fitted, remove the engine undershield. **Note:** *There must be sufficient clearance below the vehicle for the*

transmission to be lowered and removed from under the vehicle.

4 If any work is to be carried out on the transmission after removal, it is advisable, at this stage, to drain the transmission oil as described in Section 9.

5 Where applicable, undo the retaining bolts and remove the exhaust heat shield from under the vehicle.

6 On 2.2 litre models, working under the vehicle, release the securing clips and lever the ball sockets from the selector levers. Unclip the outer cables from the mounting bracket on the side of the transmission and fasten the cables to one side away from the transmission housing **(see illustration 2.4)**. Note the fitted position of the cables for refitting (blue at the top and black at the bottom).

7 Mark the relative positions of the propeller shaft universal joint flange and transmission output shaft flange **(see illustration 6.18)**.

8 Undo the two retaining bolts and remove the safety bracket from around the propeller shaft **(see illustration 6.19)**.

9 Undo the four bolts securing the propeller shaft to the output shaft flange, and then separate the flanges and position the propeller shaft to one side. Discard the bolts, as a new ones will be required when refitting.

10 On early models, disconnect the wiring connector to the speed sensor on the rear of the transmission.

11 Disconnect the wiring connector to the reversing light switch (see Section 5).

12 On 2.9 litre models, remove the clutch hydraulic slave cylinder, as described in Chapter 6, Section 4.

13 On 2.2 litre models, working on the left-hand side of the vehicle, place a suitable container beneath the slave cylinder, and clamp the flexible hose to prevent fluid draining from reservoir. Release the retaining clip from the clutch fluid hose on the outside of the transmission housing, undo the retaining bolt and disconnect the clutch hydraulic fluid pipe from the transmission **(see illustrations)**. Plug the open ends of the pipe/hose and slave cylinder to prevent dirt ingress.

14 Remove the starter motor as described in Chapter 5.

15 Undo the two retaining bolts on the right-hand side of the transmission casing and disconnect the exhaust mounting bracket from the transmission **(see illustrations)**.

16 Support the engine by positioning a wooden block of suitable thickness between the sump and the engine crossmember.

17 Position a trolley jack beneath the centre of the transmission and just support the weight **(see illustration)**.

18 Undo the two bolts at each side of the rear crossmember that secures the transmission to the vehicle underbody **(see illustration)**. Discard the retaining nuts, as new ones will be required for refitting.

19 Undo the rear transmission mounting retaining nut and withdraw the crossmember

7.15a Undo the exhaust mounting bracket retaining bolts (2.2 litre engine)

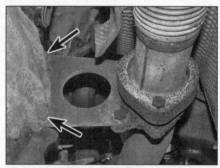

7.15b Undo the exhaust mounting bracket retaining bolts (2.9 litre engine)

7.17 Support the weight of the transmission with a trolley jack

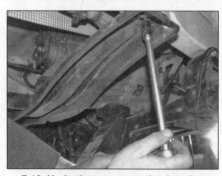

7.18 Undo the rear mounting bracket securing bolts

complete with mounting from under the rear of the vehicle **(see illustrations)**.

20 Lower the jack and transmission slightly, until the engine is supported with the piece of wood put between the engine sump and crossmember, see paragraph 16.

21 With the aid of an assistant to help steady the transmission, work around the outer edge of the transmission casing and slacken and remove the transmission-to-engine securing bolts. Note the fitted position of any earth cables or mounting brackets for refitting.

22 Check that all fixings are fully disconnected and positioned out of the way, then pull the transmission rearwards and detach it from the engine. Where applicable, it may be necessary to initially prise free the clutch housing from the engine location dowels. At no time during its removal (and subsequent refitting), allow the weight of the transmission to rest on the input shaft.

23 When the unit is fully clear of the engine, lower it, and withdraw it from underneath the vehicle **(see illustration)**.

24 The clutch components can now be inspected with reference to Chapter 6, and renewed if necessary. Unless they are virtually new, it is worth renewing the clutch components as a matter of course, even if the transmission has been removed for some other reason.

Refitting

25 Before lifting the unit into position, check that the clutch release bearing is correctly positioned, and apply a thin smear of high melting-point grease to the transmission input shaft.

26 With the aid of an assistant, lift the transmission into position, and then carefully slide it onto the rear of the engine, at the same time engaging the input shaft with the clutch friction disc splines. Do not use excessive force to refit the transmission – if the input shaft does not slide into place easily, turn the input shaft so that the splines engage properly with the disc. If problems are still experienced, check that the clutch friction disc is correctly centred (Chapter 6).

27 Once the transmission is fully engaged with the engine, insert the retaining bolts and tighten them to the specified torque.

28 Raise the trolley jack and refit the rear crossmember back into position on the rear of the transmission and tighten the rear mounting retaining nut. Refit the retaining nuts at each side of the crossmember and tighten to the specified torque. With the transmission in position, remove the trolley jack and the wooden block positioned under the sump.

29 Refit the two retaining bolts on the right-hand side of the transmission casing securing the exhaust mounting bracket to the transmission.

30 Refit the starter motor as described in Chapter 5.

31 On 2.2 litre models, refit the hydraulic clutch fluid hose to the transmission, making

7.19a Undo the mounting upper retaining nut . . .

sure the retaining clip is secure and the pipe securing bracket bolt is tight. Remove the clamp from the flexible hose.

32 On 2.9 litre models, refit the clutch hydraulic slave cylinder, as described in Chapter 6.

33 Reconnect the wiring connector to the reversing light switch (see Section 5).

34 On early models, reconnect the wiring connector to the speed sensor on the rear of the transmission.

35 Refit the propeller shaft to the output shaft flange on the rear of the transmission, noting the marks made on removal. Fit new retaining bolts.

36 Refit the safety bracket around the propeller shaft to the vehicle underbody **(see illustration)**.

37 On 2.2 litre models, refit the gear selector cables to the transmission, with reference to Section 2 of this Chapter.

38 If removed, refit the exhaust heat shield under the vehicle.

39 On 2.9 litre models, refit the gearchange lever as described in Section 2.

40 Refill/top-up the transmission oil with reference to Section 9, then lower the vehicle to the ground and reconnect the battery negative terminal.

8 Transmission overhaul – general information

Overhauling a manual transmission unit is

7.19b . . . and remove the rear mounting bracket

a difficult and involved job for the DIY home mechanic. In addition to dismantling and reassembling many small parts, clearances must be precisely measured and, if necessary, changed by selecting shims and spacers. Internal transmission components are also often difficult to obtain, and in many instances, extremely expensive. Because of this, if the transmission develops a fault or becomes noisy, the best course of action is to have the unit overhauled by a specialist repairer, or to obtain an exchange reconditioned unit.

Nevertheless, it is not impossible for the more experienced mechanic to overhaul the transmission, provided the special tools are available, and the job is done in a deliberate step-by-step manner, so that nothing is overlooked.

The tools necessary for an overhaul include internal and external circlip pliers, bearing pullers, slide hammer, set of pin punches, dial test indicator, and possibly a hydraulic press. In addition, a large, sturdy workbench and a vice will be required.

During dismantling of the transmission, make careful notes of how each component is fitted, to make reassembly easier and more accurate.

Before dismantling the transmission, it will help if you have some idea what area is malfunctioning. Certain problems can be closely related to specific areas in the transmission, which can make component examination and renewal easier. Refer to the *Fault finding* Section of this manual for more information.

7.23 Support the transmission on the trolley jack and remove

7.36 Make sure the safety bracket is bolted securely

9.2 Transmission oil drain plug

9.5 Transmission oil filler/level plug

9 Transmission oil – draining and refilling

Caution: If this procedure is to be carried out on a hot transmission unit, take care not to burn yourself on the hot exhaust or the transmission/engine unit.

1 Firmly apply the handbrake, and then jack up the front and rear of the vehicle and support it securely on axle stands (see *Jacking and vehicle support*). Make sure the vehicle is kept level to get the correct oil level. Where fitted, remove the undershields from under the transmission.

2 Wipe clean the area around the drain plug at the base of the transmission and position a suitable container underneath **(see illustration)**.

3 Unscrew the drain plug and allow the transmission oil to drain completely into the container. If the oil is hot, take precautions against scalding.

4 Once the oil has finished draining, ensure the drain plug is clean and refit it to the transmission with a new washer. Tighten the drain plug to the specified torque. Lower the vehicle to the ground.

5 The transmission is refilled through the filler/level plug hole on the side of the transmission casing **(see illustration)**. Wipe clean the area around the filler/level plug and unscrew it from the casing. Refill the transmission with the specified type and amount of oil given in the specifications, until the oil begins to trickle out of the level hole. Refit the plug and tighten it to the specified torque.

6 When completed. Lower the vehicle to the ground and take the vehicle on a short journey, so that the new oil is distributed fully around the transmission components.

7 On your return, park on level ground and check the transmission oil level is up to the filler level plug hole. Further transmission oil level checks can be carried out as described in Chapter 1, Section 24.

Chapter 8
Propeller shaft and rear axle

Contents

Degrees of difficulty

Easy, suitable for novice with little experience	**Fairly easy,** suitable for beginner with some experience	**Fairly difficult,** suitable for competent DIY mechanic	**Difficult,** suitable for experienced DIY mechanic	**Very difficult,** suitable for expert DIY or professional

Specifications

Propeller shaft

Type . . . . Two- or three-piece with centre support bearing(s), and universal joints at each end

Rear axle

Type . . . . Semi-floating axle supported on semi-elliptic leaf spring(s)
Gear backlash . . . . 0.10 to 0.15 mm
Lubricant type . . . . See *Lubricants and fluids*
Lubricant capacity . . . . See Chapter 1

Torque wrench settings	Nm	lbf ft
Anti-roll bar clamp-to-rear axle bolts	25	18
Anti-roll bar link arm-to-chassis securing bolts	95	70
Brake actuator rod to axle	34	25
Brake caliper mounting bracket-to-axle bolts:		
M12 bolts	105	77
M14 bolts	170	125
Differential housing cover bolts	65	48
Halfshaft bearing cover retaining bolts*	72	53
Haltshaft retaining nut (slotted nut)*	500	369
Oil drain plug	100	74
Oil filler plug	100	74
Propeller shaft centre bearing housing-to-underbody bolts*	105	77
Propeller shaft flange retaining bolt (3-piece shaft)*	95	70
Propeller shaft safety bracket-to-underbody bolts	100	74
Propeller shaft-to-rear axle final drive coupling flange bolts*	70	52
Propeller shaft-to-transmission output shaft flange bolts*	70	52
Rear spring-to-axle U-bolt nuts*	170	125
Roadwheel nuts	190	140
Shock absorber lower mounting bolt/nuts:		
M12 x 1.5 (8.8 bolts)	70	52
M12 x 1.5 (10.9 bolts)	110	81

* *Use new nuts/bolts*

2.2 Remove the safety bracket

2.3 Mark the position of the front prop shaft flange . . .

1 General information

Propeller shaft

The drive is transmitted from the transmission to the rear axle by a finely balanced two- or three-piece tubular propeller shaft, supported at the centre by one or two rubber-mounted bearings.

Fitted at the front, centre and rear of the propeller shaft assembly are universal joints, which cater for movement of the rear axle with suspension travel, and slight movement of the power unit on its mountings.

Rear axle

The rear axle is a live axle suspended on semi-elliptic leaf spring(s) and utilising telescopic shock absorbers to provide the damping for the axle assembly. Drive to the wheels is by two solid steel halfshafts, which are secured in the rear axle housing by a retaining plate. This plate also supports the rear wheel bearing on the inside of the axle housing, which is held in place on the shaft by a large 'slotted' retaining nut. The brake backplate and discs are then fitted to the outer flange of the halfshaft.

The oil filler plug is located on the rear differential cover, and the drain plug in the lower right-hand side of the differential housing. The internal final drive and differential components are supported on taper-roller bearings and are housed within the axle casing itself. Access to the differential is by means of a removable cover bolted to the rear of the axle.

2 Propeller shaft – removal and refitting

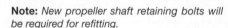

Note: *New propeller shaft retaining bolts will be required for refitting.*

Removal

1 Chock the front wheels then jack up the rear of the vehicle and securely support it on axle stands (see *Jacking and vehicle support*). Where applicable, undo the retaining bolts and remove the undershields.
2 Undo the two retaining bolts and remove the safety bracket from around the propeller shaft **(see illustration)**.
3 Mark the front universal joint and transmission flanges in relation to each other **(see illustration)**.
4 Also mark the rear universal joint and final drive coupling flanges in relation to each other **(see illustration)**.
5 Unscrew the four bolts securing the propeller shaft to the final drive coupling flange. If required, hold the shaft stationary with a long lever inserted inside the universal joint. Support the rear of the propeller shaft on an axle stand after disconnecting the flanges. Note that new flange retaining bolts will be required for refitting.
6 Undo the four bolts securing the universal joint flange to the transmission output flange, then separate the flanges and support the front of the propeller shaft on an axle stand. Note that new flange retaining bolts will be required for refitting.
7 With the aid of an assistant to support the propeller shaft, undo the two bolts securing the propeller shaft centre bearing to the underbody **(see illustrations)**. Note on 3-piece driveshafts, there will be two centre bearing mounting brackets to remove.
8 Lower the propeller shaft assembly to the ground and remove it from under the vehicle. Noting its fitted position for refitting. New centre bearing retaining bolts will be required for refitting.
9 On 3-piece propeller shafts, if required undo the centre flange retaining bolts to split the front part of the propeller shaft from the rear. Make sure the flanges are marked in relation to each other for correct refitting. New flange retaining bolts will be required for refitting.

Refitting

10 Slide the propeller shaft into position under the vehicle making sure it the correct way around as noted on removal.
11 Align the front flange mark (made on removal) with the mark made on the transmission flange and fit the new retaining bolts. Do not fully tighten the bolts at this stage.
12 Raise the propeller shaft centre section, and fit the new retaining bolts to the centre bearing(s) (both bearings on 3-piece propeller shafts). Do not fully tighten the bolts at this stage.
13 Raise the propeller shaft rear section, align the coupling flange marks made on removal, and fit the new flange retaining bolts. Do not fully tighten the bolts at this stage.
14 With the propeller shaft in position, tighten all the retaining bolts to the specified torque in the following sequence:
   a) *Front universal joint flange bolts.*
   b) *Front centre bearing retaining bolts.*
   c) *Rear centre bearing retaining bolts (3-piece shafts).*
   d) *Final drive coupling flange bolts.*
15 Lower the vehicle to the ground and road test to check for any noise or vibration.

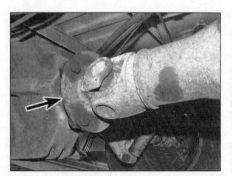

2.4 . . . and the position of the rear prop shaft flange

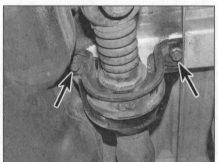

2.7a Undo the mounting bolts . . .

2.7b . . . and remove the prop shaft centre bearing

3.2 Undo the two retaining clips

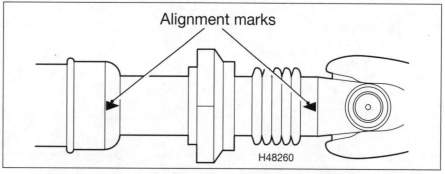

Alignment marks

H48260

3.3 Check for alignment marks on the two parts of the shaft

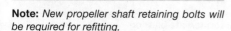

3 Propeller shaft centre bearing(s) – renewal

Note: *New propeller shaft retaining bolts will be required for refitting.*

Centre bearing (2-piece shaft)

Removal

1 Remove the propeller shaft, as described in Section 2 of this Chapter.
2 Release the retaining clips and pull back the rubber gaiter **(see illustration)**.
3 Check the shaft for alignment marks, if no marks are found, mark the shafts in relation with each other **(see illustration)**.

4 Pull the two shafts apart, leaving the centre bearing fitted to the front part of the propeller shaft. The gaiter and retaining clips can now be removed from over the rear shaft splines. Discard the gaiter, as new one will be required for refitting.
5 Using circlip pliers remove the circlip from the end of the front propeller shaft.
6 The centre bearing can now be removed from the front propeller shaft, complete with protective caps and washer. If required use a suitable puller to withdraw the centre bearing from the shaft, noting its fitted position **(see illustrations)**.

Refitting

7 Locate the new centre bearing (including washers and protective caps) on the propeller

shaft and drive it fully into position. Make sure it is fitted in the position noted on removal.
8 Refit the new circlip to the end of the front shaft, to secure the bearing in place.
9 Refit the new gaiter complete with securing clips to the rear propeller shaft, and coat the splines with multipurpose grease.
10 Slide the two parts of the propeller shaft together and secure the gaiter in position using the retaining clips. Make sure the marks on the shaft are aligned as noted on removal **(see illustration 3.3)**.
11 Refit the propeller shaft, as described in Section 2 of this Chapter.

Front centre bearing (3-piece shaft)

Removal

12 Remove the propeller shaft, as described in Section 2 of this Chapter.
13 If not already done undo the centre flange retaining bolts to split the front part of the propeller shaft from the rear. Make sure the flanges are marked in relation to each other for correct refitting. New flange retaining bolts will be required for refitting.
14 Slacken the retaining bolt from the rear of the front propeller shaft and remove it complete with washer. Discard the retaining bolt, as a new one will be required for refitting.
15 Check the shaft for alignment marks, if no marks are found, mark the flange in relation with the shaft **(see illustration)**.
16 The centre bearing can now be removed from the propeller shaft, complete with flange.

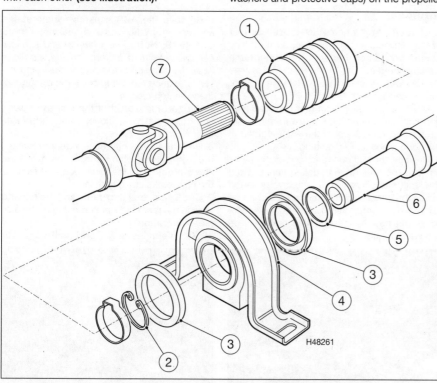

3.6a Exploded view of the centre bearing

1 *Rubber boot*	3 *Protective cap*	6 *Front propeller shaft*
2 *Circlip*	4 *Intermediate bearing*	7 *Rear propeller shaft*
	5 *Washer*	

3.6b Propeller shaft intermediate bearing fitting kit

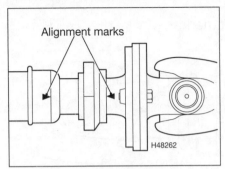

3.15 Check for alignment marks on the two parts of the shaft

If required use a suitable puller to withdraw the flange from the splined shaft **(see illustration)**.

Refitting

17 Locate the new centre bearing on the propeller shaft and drive it fully into position with the flange. Make sure the marks on the shaft are aligned as noted on removal **(see illustration 3.15)**.

18 Refit the new bolt, together with washer to the end of the shaft, and tighten to the specified torque setting.

19 Refit the propeller shaft, as described in Section 2 of this Chapter.

Rear centre bearing (3-piece shaft)

20 The removal and refitting procedure for the rear centre bearing is the same as the centre bearing on the 2-piece propeller shaft, see paragraphs 1 to 11.

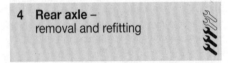

| 4 | Rear axle – |
| | removal and refitting |

Note 1: *The rear axle removal/refitting details described below are for the removal of the unit on its own. If required, it can be removed together with the roadwheels and rear leaf springs as a combined unit, although this method requires the vehicle to be raised and supported at a greater height (to allow the roadwheels to clear the body during withdrawal of the unit). If the latter method is*

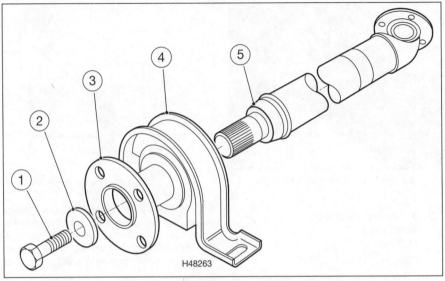

3.16 Propeller shaft intermediate bearing

| 1 Hexagon bolt | 3 Flange | 5 Propeller shaft |
| 2 Washer | 4 Intermediate bearing | |

used, follow the instructions given, but ignore the references to removal of the roadwheels and detaching the springs from the axle. Refer to Chapter 10 for details on detaching the springs from the underbody.

Note 2: *New spring-to-axle U-bolt retaining nuts, and new propeller shaft final drive coupling flange retaining bolts will be required for refitting.*

Removal

1 Chock the front wheels then jack up the rear of the vehicle and securely support it on axle stands positioned beneath the underframe sidemembers in front of the rear springs (see *Jacking and vehicle support*). Remove the rear roadwheels on both sides.

2 Mark the propeller shaft rear universal joint and final drive coupling flanges in relation to each other, to make sure the shaft is fitted in the correct position on refitting.

3 Unscrew the four bolts securing the propeller shaft to the final drive coupling flange. Hold the shaft stationary with a long lever inserted inside the universal joint. Support the shaft on an axle stand after disconnecting the flanges. Note that new flange retaining bolts will be required for refitting.

4 Undo the retaining bolts and remove the rear brake calipers **(see illustration)**. Using a piece of wire, fasten them to the underbody of the vehicle.

5 Disconnect the handbrake cables from the handbrake shoes, with reference to Chapter 9. Trace the handbrake cables back across the axle housing, and then disconnect it from any brackets or cable-ties.

6 Remove the ABS sensors (wheel speed sensors), from the rear axle housing; refer to Chapter 9. **Note:** *The wheel speed sensors can be a tight fit in the housing, and can easily be damaged. To prevent damaging the sensors, trace the wiring back and disconnect the wiring connectors.*

7 Support the weight of the rear axle, using two trolley jacks, positioned beneath the axle at each side.

8 Undo the two bolts each side and release the anti-roll bar clamps from the axle **(see illustration)**. Note the lower bolt also secures the handbrake cable bracket.

9 Undo the retaining nuts and bolts, and detach the rear shock absorbers from the axle **(see illustration)**.

10 On vehicles equipped with a load-

4.4 Remove the rear brake caliper

4.8 Undo the rear anti-roll bar mounting bracket bolts

4.9 Undo the lower shock absorber mounting bolts

apportioning valve in the brake hydraulic circuit, undo the retaining bolts and detach the valve operating rod from the rear axle **(see illustration)**.

11 Where fitted, disconnect the vent hose from the top of the differential casing.

12 With the axle still supported, undo the retaining nuts, and remove the spring-to-axle U-bolts and upper mounting plate **(see illustrations)**.

13 Check around the axle to make sure all various fittings and attachments are disconnected, and tied up out of the way.

14 Check that the axle unit is securely supported, by the two trolley jacks. Have an assistant available to steady the axle each side as it is lowered from the vehicle.

Refitting

15 Refitting is a reversal of the removal procedure, noting the following points:
  a) *Tighten all retaining nuts and bolts to the specified torque (where given).*
  b) *Use new retaining nuts on the spring-to-axle U-bolts.*
  c) *If the propeller shaft rear section was separated from the centre section, align the marks made on removal and re-engage the sliding spline connection.*
  d) *Align the marks made on removal when refitting the propeller shaft flange, and use new retaining bolts.*
  e) *Final tightening of the rear axle U-bolt nuts, and shock absorber mounting nuts should be carried out with the weight of the vehicle resting on the roadwheels.*
  f) *Refer to the procedures contained in Chapter 9 for the brake-related procedures, then adjust the handbrake as described in Chapter 1, Section 18.*
  g) *If the axle has been dismantled during removal, top-up the oil level as described in Chapter 1.*
  h) *When all is completed, refit the roadwheels, and then tighten the wheel nuts to the specified torque. Lower the vehicle to the ground and check the brake operation.*

5 Rear axle halfshaft – removal and refitting

Removal

1 Chock the front wheels then jack up the rear of the vehicle and securely support it on axle stands (see *Jacking and vehicle support*). Remove the appropriate rear wheel.

2 Remove the rear brake caliper, brake disc and handbrake shoes, as described in Chapter 9.

3 Undo the retaining bolt and disconnect the handbrake cable from the axle housing **(see illustration)**, with reference to Chapter 9.

4 Remove the ABS sensors (wheel speed sensors), from the rear axle housing; refer to

4.10 Disconnect the load sensitive linkage from the top of the axle

4.12b . . . remove the U-bolts . . .

Chapter 9. **Note:** *The wheel speed sensors can be a tight fit in the housing, and can easily be damaged. To prevent damaging the sensors, trace the wiring back and disconnect the wiring connectors.*

5 Working through the holes in the flange

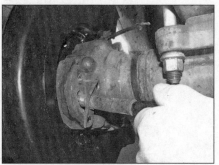
5.3 Disconnect the handbrake cable from the backplate

5.6a Withdraw the halfshaft from the axle . . .

4.12a Undo the retaining nuts . . .

4.12c . . . and remove the mounting plate

on the outer end of the halfshaft, undo the retaining bolts from the bearing cover **(see illustration)**.

6 Withdraw the halfshaft from the axle housing and recover the oil seal **(see illustrations)**. Be prepared for some oil spillage. Discard the

5.5 Undo the bearing cover retaining bolts

5.6b . . . and recover the oil seal

5.7 Fit new oil seal to the axle housing

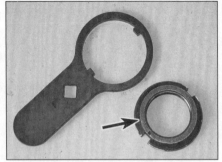

6.0 Special Mercedes tool to tighten the slotted retaining nut (arrowed)

6.3 Tap the locking washer in the direction of the arrow

oil seal, as a new one will be required when refitting.

Refitting

7 Lubricate the oil seal with multipurpose grease, then carefully insert into the axle housing **(see illustration)**.

8 If a new bearing is to be fitted to the halfshaft.

9 Insert the halfshaft into the axle housing and tighten the bearing cover mounting bolts to the specified torque setting.

10 Refer to the procedures contained in Chapter 9 for the brake-related procedures, then adjust the handbrake as described in Chapter 1, Section 18.

11 If the axle has lost some oil during this procedure, top-up the oil level as described in Chapter 1, Section 24.

12 When all is completed, refit the roadwheel, and then tighten the wheel nuts to the specified torque. Lower the vehicle to the ground and check the brake operation.

6 Rear wheel bearings – removal and refitting

Note 1: *The bearing is held in place on the halfshaft with a special 'slotted' nut, which requires a special tool (see illustration). The nut is tightened to 500 Nm (369 lbf ft).*

Note 2: *The nut on the left-hand halfshaft has a **left-hand thread**, and the nut on the right-hand halfshaft has a right-hand thread.*

1 Chock the front wheels then jack up the rear of the vehicle and securely support it on axle stands (see *Jacking and vehicle support*). Remove the appropriate rear wheel.

2 Remove the rear axle halfshaft on the side concerned as described in Section 5.

3 Using a thin punch, tap the locking tab washer to clear it of the slot in the retaining nut **(see illustration)**.

4 Using the special Mercedes-Benz tool (No 460 589 01 07 00) slacken and remove the slotted nut from the halfshaft **(see illustration 6.13c)**. To prevent the halfshaft from turning, insert two wheel bolts into the halfshaft flange and clamp them in the vice.

5 Withdraw the locking tab washer from the halfshaft. Discard, as a new locking tab washer will be required on refitting **(see illustration)**. Note which way up the locking tab washer is for refitting, as it is stepped.

6 Using a two-legged puller, fit long threaded bar through the bearing retainer and draw the bearing of the halfshaft, complete with bearing cover and brake backplate **(see illustration)**.

7 Using a thin punch, tap the shaft oil seal from the bearing cover **(see illustration)**. Noting its fitted position.

8 Obtain a new oil seal and bearing kit for refitting, as the original components will have been damaged during removal **(see**

6.5 Remove the tab washer from the shaft

6.6 Using a two-legged puller to remove the bearing

6.7 Tap the old seal from the bearing cover

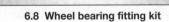

6.8 Wheel bearing fitting kit

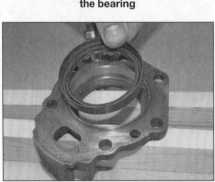

6.9a Fit the new seal to the bearing cover . . .

6.9b . . . by carefully tapping it squarely into place

6.10 Fit the bearing cover and gasket onto the shaft

6.12a Use retaining nut to press bearing onto shaft . . .

6.12b . . . and then tap it fully onto the shaft

6.12c Slide the outer bearing race over the shaft . . .

6.12d . . . and then the inner bearing

6.12e Use retaining nut to press the inner bearing onto the shaft

6.13a Fit the new tab washer onto the shaft . . .

6.13b . . . and then fit the new retaining nut

6.13c Using the special tool to tighten the retaining nut

6.13d Lock the nut in place with the tab washer

illustration). Check and clean all components before reassembly, including ABS target ring on halfshaft.

9 Press the new oil seal squarely into the bearing cover, and then tap it into the fitted position noted during removal **(see illustrations)**.

10 Slide the bearing cover over the shaft taking care not to damage the oil seal, and then fit the new bearing cover gasket **(see illustration)**.

11 Fit the brake backplate into position over the halfshaft, making sure all the holes in the

backplate are aligned with the holes in the bearing cover and gasket.

12 To fit the bearing to the halfshaft, we found that by removing the inner tapered roller bearing races from the double bearing, we could use the bearing retaining nut to press the bearing into position **(see illustrations)**.

13 With the bearing fitted in place on the half-shaft, fit new locking tab washer and bearing retaining nut **(see illustrations)**. Tighten the slotted nut to the torque setting specified and then using a small punch, stake the locking tab washer to prevent the nut from undoing.

14 Refit the halfshaft as described in Section 5. Making sure a new seal is fitted to the axle housing **(see illustration 5.7)**, before refitting the halfshaft.

7 Differential unit – overhaul

1 The design and layout of the axle is such that any attempt to remove the differential unit or pinion assembly from the axle housing will upset their preset meshing.

2 Since special tools and skills are required to set up the crownwheel and pinion mesh, the removal, overhaul and assembly of these differential types is not recommended, and should be entrusted to a dealer.

3 If the drive pinion radial seal is leaking, it will need to be carried out by a specialist, as there is a compression washer fitted on the pinion shaft. If the flange is removed from the shaft to access the oil seal a new compression washer

will need to be fitted, so that the retaining nut can be tightened to the correct friction torque.
4 If required, an inspection inside the differential unit can be made to assess for excessive wear or damage to any component parts. To do this, place a large container beneath the differential to catch the oil, and then remove the differential drain plug. Unbolt and remove the differential housing cover, and check inside for wear.

5 Before refitting the rear cover, clean the cover and axle case mating surfaces, and remove the remains of the old gasket. Also clean the threads of the retaining bolts with a wire brush, and the threaded holes in the casing with a suitable cleaning solvent.

6 Locate the new gasket and the cover, smear the retaining bolt threads with sealant, and fit them. Tighten the bolts in an alternate and progressive sequence to the specified torque setting. Refit the differential drain plug.
7 Referring to Chapter 1, refill the rear axle with the correct grade of oil, then refit and tighten the filler plug.

Chapter 9
Braking system

Contents

Degrees of difficulty

Easy, suitable for novice with little experience	**Fairly easy,** suitable for beginner with some experience	**Fairly difficult,** suitable for competent DIY mechanic	**Difficult,** suitable for experienced DIY mechanic	**Very difficult,** suitable for expert DIY or professional

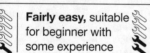

Specifications

Front brakes

Type	Ventilated disc, with single-piston sliding caliper
Disc thickness:	
New	22.0 mm
Minimum	19.0 mm
Maximum disc run-out	0.05 mm
Maximum disc thickness variation	0.02 mm
Brake pad friction material minimum thickness	2.0 mm

Rear brakes

Type	Solid disc with single-piston sliding caliper. Handbrake shoes incorporated inside the disc centre hub
Disc thickness:	
Early models:	
New	12.0 mm
Minimum	10.0 mm
Later models:	
New	16.0 mm
Minimum	14.0 mm
Maximum disc run-out	0.05 mm
Maximum disc thickness variation	0.02 mm
Brake pad friction material minimum thickness	2.0 mm
Handbrake shoe lining minimum thickness	1.0 mm

Torque wrench settings

	Nm	lbf ft
ABS pressure sensor to hydraulic unit	20	15
Brake fluid pipe connections to ABS unit	16	12
Brake fluid pipe unions	14	10
Caliper guide pins/bolts:		
M8 bolt	25	18
M10 bolt	30	22
Caliper mounting bracket bolts:		
M12 bolts	105	77
M14 bolts	170	125
Handbrake compensator-to-underbody retaining bolts	25	18
Handbrake lever-to-seat frame retaining bolts	25	18
Master cylinder retaining nuts	28	21
Pedal mounting bracket bolts/nuts	23	17
Roadwheel nuts	190	140
Vacuum pump-to-cylinder head bolts (2.2 litre engines)	14	10
Vacuum pump-to-timing case cover bolts (2.9 litre engines)	9	7
Vacuum servo unit hose to pump (2.9 litre models)	30	22
Vacuum servo unit mounting nuts	23	17

* Use new nuts/bolts

1 General information

The braking system is of servo-assisted, dual-circuit hydraulic type split diagonally. The arrangement of the hydraulic system is such that each circuit operates one front and one rear brake from a tandem master cylinder. Under normal circumstances, both circuits operate in unison. However, in the event of hydraulic failure in one circuit, full braking force will still be available at two wheels.

All models are fitted with front and rear disc brakes. An Anti-lock Braking System (ABS) is fitted as standard or an optional extra to all vehicles covered in this manual. Refer to Section 20 for further information on ABS operation.

The front brake discs are of the ventilated type and the rear brake discs are of the solid type. Both front and rear brakes are fitted with single-piston sliding pin type brake calipers.

The rear brake discs incorporate handbrake shoes, which are actuated by a cable through the inside of the axle housing. The cable-operated handbrake provides an independent mechanical means of rear brake application. A self-adjust mechanism is incorporated to automatically compensate for brake shoe wear. As the brake shoe linings wear, the handbrake operation automatically operates the adjuster mechanism, which effectively lengthens the shoe strut, and repositions the brake shoes to maintain the lining-to-drum clearance.

A vacuum servo unit is fitted between the master cylinder and the bulkhead, its function being to reduce the amount of pedal pressure required to operate the brakes. Since there is no throttling as such of the inlet manifold on diesel engines, the manifold is not a suitable source of vacuum to operate the vacuum servo unit. The servo unit is therefore connected to a separate engine-mounted vacuum pump. On 2.2 litre engines, the pump is bolted to the front of the cylinder head and is driven by the end of the camshaft. On 2.9 litre engines, the pump is attached to the timing case cover and driven by the timing chain.

A load-apportioning valve (LAV) is incorporated in the rear brake hydraulic circuit on some models. The valve function is to regulate the braking force available at each rear wheel, to reduce the possibility of the rear wheels locking up under heavy braking.

⚠️ *Warning: When servicing any part of the system, work carefully and methodically; also observe scrupulous cleanliness when overhauling any part of the hydraulic system. Always renew components (in axle sets, where applicable) if in doubt about their condition, and use only genuine parts, or at least those of known good quality. Note the warnings given in 'Safety first!' and at relevant points in this Chapter concerning the dangers of asbestos dust and hydraulic fluid.*

2 Hydraulic system – bleeding

⚠️ *Warning: Hydraulic fluid is poisonous. Wash off immediately and thoroughly in the case of skin contact, and seek immediate medical advice if any fluid is swallowed or gets into the eyes. Certain types of hydraulic fluid are inflammable, and may ignite when allowed into contact with hot components. When servicing any hydraulic system, it is safest to assume that the fluid is inflammable, and to take precautions against the risk of fire as though it is petrol that is being handled. Hydraulic fluid is also an effective paint stripper, and will attack plastics; if any is spilt, it should be washed off immediately, using copious quantities of fresh water. Finally, it is hygroscopic (it absorbs moisture from the air) therefore old fluid may be contaminated and unfit for further use. When topping-up or renewing the fluid, always use the recommended type, and ensure that it comes from a freshly-opened sealed container.*

General

1 The correct operation of any hydraulic system is only possible after removing all air from the components and circuit; this is achieved by bleeding the system.

2 During the bleeding procedure, add only clean, unused hydraulic fluid of the recommended type; never re-use fluid that has already been bled from the system. Ensure that sufficient fluid is available before starting work.

3 If there is any possibility of incorrect fluid being already in the system, the brake components and circuit must be flushed completely with uncontaminated, correct fluid, and new seals should be fitted to the various components.

4 If hydraulic fluid has been lost from the system, or air has entered because of a leak, ensure that the fault is cured before proceeding further.

5 When bleeding the brakes on vehicles with a load-apportioning valve in the rear brake hydraulic circuit, it is important to note that the vehicle must be standing on its wheels. If the rear of the vehicle is jacked up and the axle is in a 'wheel free' state, the load-apportioning valve will prevent complete bleeding of the system.

6 Check that all pipes and hoses are secure, unions tight and bleed screws closed. Clean any dirt from around the bleed screws.

7 Unscrew the master cylinder reservoir cap, and top-up the master cylinder reservoir to the MAX level line. Refit the cap loosely, and remember to maintain the fluid level at least above the MIN level line throughout the

procedure, otherwise there is a risk of further air entering the system.

8 There are a number of one-man, do-it-yourself brake bleeding kits currently available from motor accessory shops. It is recommended that one of these kits is used whenever possible, as they greatly simplify the bleeding operation, and also reduce the risk of expelled air and fluid being drawn back into the system. If such a kit is not available, the basic (two-man) method must be used, which is described in detail below.

9 If a kit is to be used, prepare the vehicle as described previously, and follow the kit manufacturer's instructions, as the procedure may vary slightly according to the type being used. Generally, they are as outlined below in the relevant sub-Section.

10 If the system has been only partially disconnected, and suitable precautions were taken to minimise fluid loss, it should only be necessary to bleed that part of the system (ie, the primary or secondary circuit). If the master cylinder or main brake lines have been disconnected, then the complete system must be bled.

Bleeding

Basic (two-man) method

11 Collect together a clean glass jar, a suitable length of plastic or rubber tubing, which is a tight fit over the bleed screw, and a ring spanner to fit the screw. The help of an assistant will also be required.

12 Remove the dust cap from the bleed screw at the wheel to be bled **(see illustration)**. Fit the spanner and tube to the screw, place the other end of the tube in the jar, and pour in sufficient fluid to cover the end of the tube.

13 Ensure that the master cylinder reservoir fluid level is maintained at least above the MIN level line throughout the procedure.

14 Have the assistant fully depress the brake pedal several times to build-up pressure, and then maintain it on the final downstroke.

15 While pedal pressure is maintained, unscrew the bleed screw (approximately one turn) and allow the compressed fluid and air to flow into the jar. The assistant should maintain pedal pressure, following it down to the floor if necessary, and should not release it until instructed to do so. When the flow stops, tighten the bleed screw again, have the assistant release the pedal slowly, and recheck the reservoir fluid level.

16 Repeat the steps given in paragraphs 14 and 15 until the fluid emerging from the bleed screw is free from air bubbles. If the master cylinder has been drained and refilled, and air is being bled from the first bleed screw, allow approximately five seconds between cycles for the master cylinder passages to refill.

17 When no more air bubbles appear, securely tighten the bleed screw, remove the tube and spanner, and refit the dust cap. Do not overtighten the bleed screw.

18 Repeat the procedure on the remaining

2.12 Rear brake caliper bleed screw

bleed screws, until all air is removed from the system and the brake pedal feels firm again.

Using a one-way valve kit

19 As the name implies, these kits consist of a length of tubing with a one-way valve fitted, to prevent expelled air and fluid being drawn back into the system. Some kits include a translucent container, which can be positioned so that the air bubbles can be more easily seen flowing from the end of the tube **(see illustration)**.

20 The kit is connected to the bleed screw, which is then opened. The user returns to the driver's seat, depresses the brake pedal with a smooth, steady stroke, and slowly releases it; this is repeated until the expelled fluid is clear of air bubbles.

21 Note that these kits simplify work so much that it is easy to forget the master cylinder reservoir fluid level, therefore ensure that this is maintained at least above the MIN level line at all times.

Using a pressure-bleeding kit

22 These kits are usually operated by a reservoir of pressurised air contained in the spare tyre. However, note that it will probably be necessary to reduce the pressure to a lower level than normal. Refer to the instructions supplied with the kit.

23 By connecting a pressurised, fluid-filled container to the master cylinder reservoir, bleeding can be carried out simply by opening each bleed screw in turn, and allowing the fluid to flow out until no more air bubbles can be seen in the expelled fluid.

24 This method has the advantage that the

3.2 Brake hose retaining clip

2.19 Bleeding a front brake caliper

large reservoir of fluid provides an additional safeguard against air being drawn into the system during bleeding.

25 Pressure-bleeding is particularly effective when bleeding 'difficult' systems, or when bleeding the complete system at the time of routine fluid renewal.

All methods

26 When bleeding is complete, and firm pedal feel is restored, wash off any spilt fluid, securely tighten the bleed screws, and refit the dust caps.

27 Check the hydraulic fluid level in the master cylinder reservoir, and top-up if necessary (see *Weekly checks*).

28 Discard any hydraulic fluid that has been bled from the system as it will not be fit for re-use.

29 Check the feel of the brake pedal. If it feels at all spongy, air must still be present in the system, and further bleeding is required. Failure to bleed satisfactorily after a reasonable repetition of the bleeding procedure may be due to worn master cylinder seals.

3 Hydraulic pipes and hoses – renewal

Note: *Before starting work, refer to the note at the beginning of Section 2 concerning the dangers of hydraulic fluid.*

1 If any pipe or hose is to be renewed, minimise fluid loss by first removing the master cylinder reservoir cap and screwing it down onto a piece of polythene. Alternatively, flexible hoses can be sealed, if required, using a proprietary brake hose clamp. Metal brake pipe unions can be plugged (if care is taken not to allow dirt into the system) or capped immediately they are disconnected. Place a wad of rag under any union that is to be disconnected, to catch any spilt fluid.

2 If a flexible hose is to be disconnected, unscrew the brake pipe union nut(s) before removing the spring clip (or retaining bolt) which secures the hose to its mounting bracket **(illustration)**. Where applicable, unscrew the banjo union bolt securing the hose to the caliper and recover the copper washers. When removing the front flexible hose, undo the retaining bolt and release the hose support bracket from the suspension strut.

3 To unscrew union nuts, it is preferable to obtain a brake pipe spanner of the correct size; these are available from most motor accessory shops. Failing this, a close-fitting open-ended spanner will be required, though if the nuts are tight or corroded, their flats may be rounded-off if the spanner slips. In such a case, a self-locking wrench is often the only way to unscrew a stubborn union, but it follows that the pipe and the damaged nuts must be renewed on reassembly. Always clean a union and surrounding area before disconnecting it. If disconnecting a component with more than one union, make a careful note of the connections before disturbing any of them.

4 If a brake pipe is to be renewed, it can be obtained, cut to length and with the union nuts and end flares in place, from dealers. All that is

then necessary is to bend it to shape, following the line of the original, before fitting it to the vehicle. Alternatively, most motor accessory shops can make up brake pipes from kits, but this requires very careful measurement of the original, to ensure that the new one is of the correct length. The safest answer is usually to take the original to the shop as a pattern.

5 On refitting, do not overtighten the union nuts.

6 When refitting hoses to the front calipers, always use new copper washers and tighten the banjo union bolts to the specified torque. Make sure that the hoses are positioned so that they will not touch surrounding bodywork or the roadwheels.

7 Ensure that the pipes and hoses are correctly routed, with no kinks, and that they are secured in the clips or brackets provided. After fitting, remove the polythene from the reservoir, and bleed the hydraulic system as

described in Section 2. On completion, wash off any spilt fluid, and check carefully for fluid leaks.

4 Front brake pads – renewal

Warning: Renew BOTH sets of front brake pads at the same time – NEVER renew the pads on only one wheel, as uneven braking may result. Note that the dust created by wear of the pads may contain asbestos, which is a health hazard. Never blow it out with compressed air, and do not inhale any of it. An approved filtering mask should be worn when working on the brakes. DO NOT use petroleum-based solvents to clean brake parts – use brake cleaner or methylated spirit only.

1 Apply the handbrake, then jack up the front of the vehicle and support it on axle stands (see Jacking and vehicle support). Remove the front roadwheels.

2 Follow the accompanying photos (illustrations 4.2a to 4.2g) for the actual pad renewal procedure, bearing in mind the additional points given in the following paragraphs. Be sure to stay in order and read the caption under each illustration. Note that if the old pads are to be refitted, ensure that they are identified so that they can be returned to their original positions.

3 If the original brake pads are still serviceable, carefully clean them using a clean, fine wire brush or similar, paying particular attention to the sides and back of the metal backing plate. Clean out the grooves in the friction material, and pick out any large embedded particles of dirt or debris. Carefully clean the pad locations in the caliper mounting bracket (see illustration).

4 Prior to fitting the pads (reversal of the removal procedure), check that the guide pins are a snug fit in the caliper. Inspect the dust seals around the pistons for damage, and the pistons for evidence of fluid leaks, corrosion or damage.

5 If new brake pads are to be fitted, the caliper pistons must be pushed back into the

4.2b ... and disconnect the brake pad warning light wiring

4.2c Remove the two plastic caps ...

4.2d ... and undo the two guide pins

4.2e Withdraw the caliper ...

4.2f ... and remove the inner brake pad from the piston ...

4.2g ... then remove the outer brake pad from the mounting bracket

4.2a Release the retaining clip ...

cylinder to allow for the extra pad thickness **(see illustration)**. Either use a G-clamp or similar tool, or use suitable pieces of wood as levers. Clamp off the flexible brake hose leading to the caliper then connect a brake bleeding kit to the caliper bleed screw. Open the bleed screw as the pistons are retracted, the surplus brake fluid will then be collected in the bleed kit vessel. Close the bleed screw just before the caliper pistons are pushed fully into the caliper. This should ensure no air enters the hydraulic system.

Caution: The ABS unit contains hydraulic components that are very sensitive to impurities in the brake fluid. Even the smallest particles can cause the system to fail through blockage. The pad retraction method described here prevents any debris in the brake fluid expelled from the caliper from being passed back to the ABS hydraulic unit, as well as preventing any chance of damage to the master cylinder seals.

6 With the brake pads installed, depress the brake pedal repeatedly, until normal (non-assisted) pedal pressure is restored, and the pads are pressed into firm contact with the brake disc.

7 Repeat the above procedure on the remaining front brake caliper.

8 Refit the roadwheels, then lower the vehicle to the ground and tighten the roadwheel nuts to the specified torque setting.

9 Check the hydraulic fluid level as described in *Weekly checks*.

Caution: New pads will not give full braking efficiency until they have bedded-in. Be prepared for this, and avoid hard braking as far as possible for the first hundred miles or so after pad renewal.

5 Front brake disc – inspection, removal and refitting

Note: *Before starting work, refer to the warning at the beginning of Section 4 concerning the dangers of asbestos dust. If either disc requires renewal, both should be renewed at the same time together with new pads, to ensure even and consistent braking.*

Inspection

1 Firmly apply the handbrake, and then jack up the front of the vehicle and support it securely on axle stands (see *Jacking and vehicle support*). Remove the roadwheel.

2 Rotate the brake disc, and examine it for deep scoring or grooving. Light scoring is normal, but if excessive, the disc should be removed and either renewed or machined (within the specified limits) by an engineering works. The minimum thickness is given in the Specifications at the start of this Chapter.

3 Using a dial gauge, or a flat metal block and feeler blades, check that the disc run-out does not exceed the figure given in the Specifications

4.3 Apply a small amount of copper grease to the areas shown

(see illustration). Measure the run-out 10.0 mm in from the outer edge of the disc.

4 If the disc run-out is excessive, remove the disc as described later, and check that the disc-to-hub surfaces are perfectly clean. Refit the disc and check the run-out again.

5 If the run-out is still excessive, the disc should be renewed.

6 To remove a disc, proceed as follows.

Removal

7 Firmly apply the handbrake, and then jack up the front of the vehicle and support it securely on axle stands (see *Jacking and vehicle support*). Remove the relevant front roadwheel.

8 Undo the two bolts securing the brake caliper mounting bracket to the steering knuckle **(see illustration)**. Slide the caliper and mounting bracket, complete with brake pads, off the disc and suspend the assembly from the coil spring using a cable-tie.

5.3 Using a dial gauge to check the run-out of the disc

5.9a Undo the retaining screw . . .

4.5 Using a special tool for pushing the piston back into the caliper

9 Undo the retaining screw and withdraw the brake disc from the hub assembly **(see illustrations)**. If necessary, tap the rear of the brake disc with a soft-faced mallet to free it from the hub assembly.

Refitting

10 Thoroughly clean the mating surfaces of the brake disc and hub flange ensuring that all traces of dirt and corrosion are removed.

11 Place the disc in position on the hub flange, aligning the holes in the centre part of the brake disc. Then fit the retaining screw to secure the brake disc to the hub and tighten.

12 Slide the brake caliper assembly over the disc and into position on the steering knuckle. Refit the two mounting bracket retaining bolts and tighten them to the specified torque.

13 Refit the roadwheel, tighten the wheel nuts to the specified torque, and then lower the vehicle to the ground.

5.8 Caliper mounting bracket bolts

5.9b . . . and remove the brake disc

6.4 Brake pad warning light wire securing bolt

6 Front brake caliper – removal and refitting

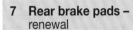

Note: *Before starting work, refer to the note at the beginning of Section 2 concerning the dangers of hydraulic fluid, and to the warning at the beginning of Section 4 concerning the dangers of asbestos dust.*

Removal

1 Apply the handbrake, then jack up the front of the vehicle and support it on axle stands (see *Jacking and vehicle support*). Remove the roadwheel.
2 Minimise fluid loss by first removing the master cylinder reservoir cap and screwing it down onto a piece of polythene. Alternatively,

use a brake hose clamp to clamp the flexible hose leading to the brake caliper.
3 Clean the area around the caliper brake hose union. Unscrew and remove the union, where fitted, recover the sealing washers from the hose union. Discard the washers, as new ones must be used on refitting. Plug the hose end and caliper hole, to minimise fluid loss and prevent the ingress of dust and dirt into the hydraulic system.
4 Undo the retaining bolt and disconnect the brake pad low warning light wire from the caliper **(see illustration)**. Remove the brake pads as described in Section 4, and withdraw the caliper from the vehicle.

Refitting

5 Refit the brake pads and caliper to the mounting bracket as described in Section 4.
6 Reconnect the brake hose to the caliper and where applicable fit a new sealing washer to the hose union. Ensure that the hose is correctly positioned, and not fouling any components and then tighten it to the specified torque.
7 Remove the brake hose clamp or polythene, and bleed the hydraulic system as described in Section 2. Note that, providing the precautions described were taken to minimise brake fluid loss, it should only be necessary to bleed the relevant front brake circuit.
8 Refit the roadwheel, then lower the vehicle to the ground and tighten the roadwheel nuts to the specified torque.

7 Rear brake pads – renewal

Warning: Renew BOTH sets of rear brake pads at the same time – NEVER renew the pads on only one wheel, as uneven braking may result. Note that the dust created by wear of the pads may contain asbestos, which is a health hazard. Never blow it out with compressed air, and do not inhale any of it. An approved filtering mask should be worn when working on the brakes. DO NOT use petroleum-based solvents to clean brake parts – use brake cleaner or methylated spirit only.

1 Apply the handbrake, and then jack up the rear of the vehicle and support it on axle stands (see *Jacking and vehicle support*). Remove the rear roadwheels.
2 Follow the accompanying photos **(illustrations 7.2a to 7.2g)** for the actual pad renewal procedure, bearing in mind the additional points given in the following paragraphs. Be sure to stay in order and read the caption under each illustration. Note that if the old pads are to be refitted, ensure that they are identified so that they can be returned to their original positions.
3 If the original brake pads are still serviceable, carefully clean them using a clean, fine wire brush or similar, paying particular attention to the sides and back of the metal backing

7.2a Disconnect the brake pad warning light wiring . . .

7.2b . . . and release the retaining clip (depending on model)

7.2c Remove the upper caliper guide pin bolt . . .

7.2d . . . and the lower caliper guide pin bolt

7.2e Withdraw the caliper . . .

7.2f . . . then remove the outer brake pad . . .

plate. Clean out the grooves in the friction material, and pick out any large embedded particles of dirt or debris. Carefully clean the pad locations in the caliper mounting bracket **(see illustration)**.

4 Prior to fitting the pads, check that the guide pin bolts are a snug fit in the caliper. Inspect the dust seals around the pistons for damage, and the pistons for evidence of fluid leaks, corrosion or damage.

5 If new brake pads are to be fitted, the caliper pistons must be pushed back into the cylinder to allow for the extra pad thickness **(see illustration)**. Either use a G-clamp or similar tool, or use suitable pieces of wood as levers. Clamp off the flexible brake hose leading to the caliper then connect a brake bleeding kit to the caliper bleed screw. Open the bleed screw as the pistons are retracted, the surplus brake fluid will then be collected in the bleed kit vessel. Close the bleed screw just before the caliper pistons are pushed fully into the caliper. This should ensure no air enters the hydraulic system.

Caution: The ABS unit contains hydraulic components that are very sensitive to impurities in the brake fluid. Even the smallest particles can cause the system to fail through blockage. The pad retraction method described here prevents any debris in the brake fluid expelled from the caliper from being passed back to the ABS hydraulic unit, as well as preventing any chance of damage to the master cylinder seals.

6 If new brake pads are fitted, make sure the brake pad low warning wire is fitted to the inner brake pad **(see illustration)**.

7 With the brake pads installed, depress the brake pedal repeatedly, until normal (non-assisted) pedal pressure is restored, and the pads are pressed into firm contact with the brake disc.

8 Repeat the above procedure on the remaining rear brake caliper.

9 Refit the roadwheels, then lower the vehicle to the ground and tighten the roadwheel nuts to the specified torque setting.

10 Check the hydraulic fluid level as described in *Weekly checks*.

Caution: New pads will not give full braking efficiency until they have bedded-in. Be prepared for this, and avoid hard braking as far as possible for the first hundred miles or so after pad renewal.

---

8 **Rear brake disc –**
inspection, removal and refitting

Note: Before starting work, refer to the warning at the beginning of Section 4 concerning the dangers of asbestos dust. If either disc requires renewal, both should be renewed at the same time together with new pads, to ensure even and consistent braking.

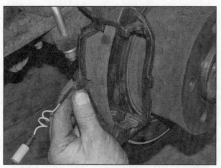

7.2g . . . and inner brake pad from the mounting bracket

7.5 Using a special tool for pushing the piston back into the caliper

Inspection

1 With the vehicle on level ground, chock the front wheels, and then jack up the rear of the vehicle and support it securely on axle stands (see *Jacking and vehicle support*). Remove the roadwheel.

2 Rotate the brake disc, and examine it for deep scoring or grooving. Light scoring is normal, but if excessive, the disc should be removed and either renewed or machined (within the specified limits) by an engineering works. The minimum thickness is given in the Specifications at the start of this Chapter.

3 Using a dial gauge **(see illustration 5.3)**, or a flat metal block and feeler blades, check that the disc run-out does not exceed the figure given in the Specifications. Measure the run-out 10.0 mm in from the outer edge of the disc.

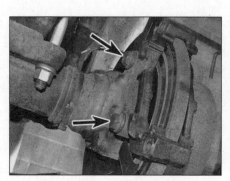

8.9a Undo the retaining bolts . . .

7.3 Apply a small amount of copper grease to the mounting bracket

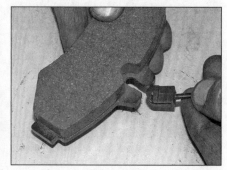

7.6 Fit the low pad warning light wire to the new pad

4 If the disc run-out is excessive, remove the disc as described later, and check that the disc-to-hub surfaces are perfectly clean. Refit the disc and check the run-out again.

5 If the run-out is still excessive, the disc should be renewed.

6 To remove a disc, proceed as follows.

Removal

7 With the vehicle on level ground, chock the front wheels, and then jack up the rear of the vehicle and support it securely on axle stands (see *Jacking and vehicle support*). Remove the roadwheel.

8 Remove the rear brake pads and caliper as described in Section 7.

9 Undo the two retaining bolts and withdraw the brake caliper mounting bracket from the brake disc **(see illustrations)**.

10 Undo the retaining screw and withdraw

8.9b . . . and withdraw the caliper mounting bracket

8.10a Undo the retaining screw . . .

8.10b . . . and remove the brake disc

8.11 Apply a small amount of copper grease to the disc flange

the brake disc from the hub assembly **(see illustrations)**. If necessary, tap the rear of the brake disc with a soft-faced mallet to free it from the hub assembly. **Note:** *Make sure the handbrake is in the full off position, if required, slacken the handbrake adjustment as described in Chapter 1.*

Refitting

11 Thoroughly clean the mating surfaces of the brake disc and hub flange ensuring that all traces of dirt and corrosion are removed **(see illustration)**.

12 Place the disc in position on the hub flange, aligning the holes in the centre part of the brake disc. Then fit the retaining screw to secure the brake disc to the hub and tighten.

13 Slide the brake caliper mounting bracket over the disc and into position on the hub assembly. Refit the two retaining bolts and tighten them to the specified torque.

9.4 Remove the brake pad warning light wire securing bolt

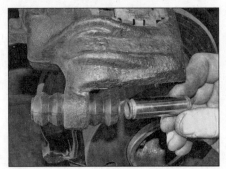

9.6b . . . and lower guide sleeves from the caliper

14 Refit the brake pads and caliper to the mounting bracket as described in Section 7.

15 Refit the roadwheel, tighten the wheel nuts to the specified torque, and then lower the vehicle to the ground.

9 Rear brake caliper – removal and refitting

Note: *Before starting work, refer to the note at the beginning of Section 2 concerning the dangers of hydraulic fluid, and to the warning at the beginning of Section 4 concerning the dangers of asbestos dust.*

Removal

1 Apply the handbrake, then jack up the rear of the vehicle and support it on axle stands (see *Jacking and vehicle support*). Remove the roadwheel.

9.6a Remove the upper . . .

9.7a Remove the upper seals from the caliper . . .

2 Minimise fluid loss by first removing the master cylinder reservoir cap and screwing it down onto a piece of polythene. Alternatively, use a brake hose clamp to clamp the flexible hose leading to the brake caliper.

3 Clean the area around the caliper brake hose union. Unscrew and remove the union, where fitted, recover the sealing washers from the hose union. Discard the washers, as new ones must be used on refitting. Plug the hose end and caliper hole, to minimise fluid loss and prevent the ingress of dust and dirt into the hydraulic system.

4 Undo the retaining bolt and disconnect the brake pad low warning light wire from the caliper **(see illustration)**. Remove the brake pads as described in Section 7, and withdraw the caliper from the vehicle.

Refitting

5 Check the rubber seals on the caliper guide pins are not split and the sleeves are free to slide in the caliper body. If required renew the sleeves and seals, before refitting the caliper.

6 Remove the guide sleeves from each side of the caliper **(see illustrations)**. Note the upper and lower guide sleeves are different.

7 Remove the seals from the caliper; making sure on the upper guide pin the inner metal ring of the seal does not stay in the caliper **(see illustrations)**.

8 Clean inside the caliper, where the guide sleeves fit, to make sure they slide easily. Then fit the new seals and sleeves, lubricating the sleeves with grease on refitting. On the upper guide pin, slide the

9.7b . . . making sure the metal sleeve is removed

9.7c Pull the lower seal/gaiter from the caliper

9.8a Fit the upper sleeve before fitting the second seal to the caliper

9.8b Slide the sleeves from side to side to make sure they move freely

sleeve into place before fitting the second seal **(see illustrations)**.

9 Refit the brake pads and caliper to the mounting bracket as described in Section 7.

10 Reconnect the brake hose to the caliper and where applicable fit a new sealing washer to the hose union. Ensure that the hose is correctly positioned, and not fouling any components and then tighten it to the specified torque.

11 Remove the brake hose clamp or polythene, and bleed the hydraulic system as described in Section 2. Note that, providing the precautions described were taken to minimise brake fluid loss, it should only be necessary to bleed the relevant front brake circuit.

12 Refit the roadwheel, then lower the vehicle to the ground and tighten the roadwheel nuts to the specified torque.

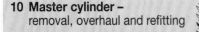

10 Master cylinder –
removal, overhaul and refitting

Note: *Before starting work, refer to the warning at the beginning of Section 2 concerning the dangers of hydraulic fluid.*

Removal

1 Remove the master cylinder reservoir cap, and siphon the hydraulic fluid from the reservoir. **Note:** *Do not siphon the fluid by mouth, as it is poisonous therefore use a syringe or an old hydrometer.* Alternatively, open the front brake caliper bleed screws,

one at a time, and gently pump the brake pedal to expel the fluid through a plastic tube connected to the screw (see Section 2).

2 Depress the securing clips and disconnect the wiring connector from the brake fluid level sensor on the reservoir **(see illustration)**.

3 Release the securing clip and disconnect the clutch hydraulic hose from the fluid reservoir **(see illustration)**. Tape over or plug the outlet.

4 Place cloth rags beneath the master cylinder to collect escaping brake fluid. Identify the brake pipes for position, then unscrew the union nuts and move the pipes to one side **(see illustration)**. Plug or tape over the pipe ends to prevent dirt entry.

5 Unscrew the two mounting nuts and withdraw the master cylinder from the vacuum servo unit **(see illustration)**. Take care not to spill fluid on the vehicle paintwork. Recover the master cylinder-to-servo unit sealing ring

and discard; a new one will be required for refitting.

6 If required, the fluid reservoir can be removed from the master cylinder by releasing the retaining tabs and pulling the reservoir up and off the mounting seals **(see illustration)**.

Overhaul

7 At the time of writing, master cylinder overhaul is not possible as no spares are available.

8 The only parts available individually are the fluid reservoir and its mounting seals, and the filler cap.

9 If the master cylinder is worn excessively, it must be renewed.

10 If new reservoir seals are to be fitted, extract the old seals from the cylinder body, lubricate the new seals with clean brake hydraulic fluid and push the seals into position.

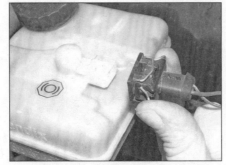

10.2 Disconnect the wiring connector

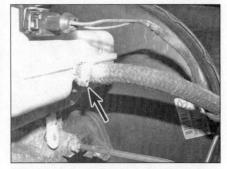

10.3 Disconnect the clutch fluid hose from the reservoir

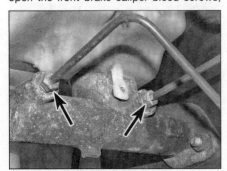

10.4 Note fitted position of metal brake pipes

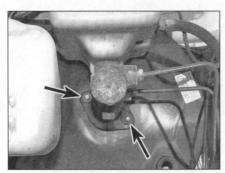

10.5 Master cylinder retaining nuts

10.6 Release the tab to remove the reservoir

11.3 Unclip the return spring from the pedal

11.4a Remove the securing clip . . .

11.4b . . . and withdraw the clevis pin

Refitting

11 Where applicable, refit the fluid reservoir to the master cylinder body, ensuring that the retaining tabs lock into position.

12 Place the master cylinder-to-servo unit sealing ring into position, and then fit the master cylinder to the servo unit. Ensure that the servo unit pushrod enters the master cylinder piston centrally. Fit the retaining nuts and tighten them to the specified torque.

13 Refit the brake pipes and tighten the union nuts securely.

14 Reconnect the clutch hydraulic hose to the fluid reservoir.

15 Reconnect the wiring connector to the brake fluid level sensor.

16 Remove the reservoir filler cap and polythene, then top-up the reservoir with fresh hydraulic fluid to the MAX mark (see Weekly checks).

17 Bleed the brake and clutch hydraulic systems as described in Section 2 and Chapter 6 then refit the filler cap. Thoroughly check the operation of the brakes and clutch before using the vehicle on the road.

11 Brake pedal – removal and refitting

Removal

1 Open the bonnet and disconnect the battery negative terminal (refer to *Disconnecting the battery* in the Reference Chapter).

2 Move the driver's seat fully rearward, and if required, remove the lower facia trim panel from under the steering column for easier access to the pedal assembly, with reference to Chapter 11.

3 Unclip and remove the brake pedal return spring from the top of the brake pedal **(see illustration)**.

4 Extract the retaining clip and clevis pin and detach the brake master cylinder pushrod from the brake pedal **(see illustrations)**.

5 Using a thin screwdriver, release the securing clip and withdraw the pivot bolt from the top of the brake pedal **(see illustrations)**.

6 The brake pedal can now be withdrawn from the pedal assembly, check the pedal bushes and renew if required **(see illustration)**.

Refitting

7 Check the clevis pin and pivot bolt for wear, renew if worn **(see illustrations)**.

8 Manoeuvre the brake pedal into position in the pedal assembly, and slide the pivot pin into position. Fit the securing clip into position, making sure the pivot pin is securely fitted. Make sure the pivot pin and bushes are lubricated with some multipurpose grease before assembly.

9 Engage the brake master cylinder pushrod with the brake pedal, and then insert the clevis pin and secure it in position with the retaining clip. Make sure the clevis pin is lubricated with some multipurpose grease before assembly.

10 Refit the return spring to the brake pedal, and make sure the pedal operates without sticking.

11 Where applicable, refit any facia trim panels, with reference to Chapter 11.

12 Reconnect the battery negative terminal on completion.

12 Vacuum servo unit – testing, removal and refitting

Testing

1 To test the operation of the servo unit, with the engine off, depress the footbrake pedal several times to exhaust the vacuum. Now start the engine, keeping the pedal firmly depressed. As the engine starts, there should be a noticeable 'give' in the brake pedal as the vacuum builds-up. Allow the engine to run for at least two minutes, and then switch it off. The brake pedal should now feel normal, but further applications should result in the pedal

11.5a Release the securing clip . . .

11.5b . . . and withdraw the pivot bolt

11.6 Check the bushes in the top of the pedal . . .

11.7 . . . and also check the pivot bolt for wear

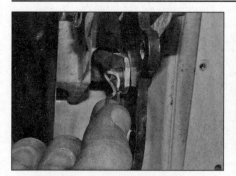

12.5a Remove the securing clip . . .

12.5b . . . and withdraw the clevis pin

12.7 Servo unit retaining nuts

feeling firmer, the pedal stroke decreasing with each application.

2 If the servo does not operate as described, first inspect the servo unit check valve as described in Section 13.

3 If the servo unit still fails to operate satisfactorily, the fault lies within the unit itself. Repairs to the unit are not possible; if faulty, the servo unit must be renewed.

Removal

4 Remove the brake master cylinder as described in Section 10.

5 Extract the retaining clip and clevis pin and detach the brake master cylinder pushrod from the brake pedal **(see illustrations)**.

6 Carefully ease the vacuum hose out of the servo unit, taking care not to displace the sealing grommet.

7 Undo the four nuts securing the servo unit to the pedal mounting bracket and bulkhead **(see illustration)**.

8 Return to the engine compartment, and lift the servo unit out of position. Where applicable, recover the servo unit-to-bulkhead gasket.

Refitting

9 Where fitted, refit the gasket, and then locate the vacuum servo unit in position on the bulkhead. Refit the four nuts and tighten them to the specified torque.

10 Engage the servo unit pushrod with the brake pedal, and then insert the clevis pin and secure it in position with the retaining clip. Make sure the clevis pin is lubricated with some multipurpose grease before assembly.

11 Refit the vacuum hose to the servo grommet, ensuring that the hose is correctly seated.

12 Refit the brake master cylinder as described in Section 10.

13 Vacuum servo unit check valve and hose – removal, testing and refitting

Removal

1 Disconnect the small vacuum pipe from the brake vacuum hose connector, near the brake servo unit **(see illustration)**.

2 Carefully ease the vacuum hose out of the servo unit, taking care not to displace the sealing grommet **(see illustration)**.

3 On 2.9 litre models unscrew the union nut, and on 2.2 litre models disconnect the quick-release fitting, and then remove the vacuum hose from the vacuum pump **(see illustration)**.

4 Unclip the vacuum hose from its supports, then remove the hose and check valve from the vehicle **(see illustration)**.

Testing

5 Examine the check valve and hose for signs of damage, and renew if necessary. The valve may be tested by blowing through it in both directions. Air should flow through the valve in one direction only, if air flows in both directions, or not at all, renew the valve and hose as an assembly.

6 Examine the check valve rubber sealing

13.1 Disconnect the vacuum pipe . . .

13.3 Disconnect the vacuum hose from the pump (2.2 litre engine)

grommet for signs of damage or deterioration, and renew as necessary.

Refitting

7 Refitting is a reversal of removal ensuring that the hose is correctly seated in the servo grommet.

8 On 2.9 litre models, tighten the hose retaining nut to the torque specified.

9 On completion, start the engine and check that there are no air leaks.

14 Vacuum pump – testing, removal and refitting

Testing

1 The operation of the braking system vacuum pump can be checked using a vacuum gauge.

13.2 . . . and withdraw the check valve from the servo

13.4 Unclip the vacuum hose from the heat shield

14.5 Disconnect the hose from the vacuum pump

14.7 Removing the vacuum pump from the cylinder head

14.10 Disconnect the vacuum pipe (arrowed) from the vacuum pump

14.11 Removing the vacuum pump (arrowed) from the front cover

14.3a Fit new O-ring seals . . .

14.3b . . . to the vacuum pump

2 Disconnect the vacuum pipe from the pump, and connect the gauge to the pump union using a suitable length of hose.

3 Start the engine and allow it to idle, and then measure the vacuum created by the pump. As a guide, a minimum of approximately 500 mm Hg should be recorded. If the vacuum registered is significantly less than this, it is likely that the pump is faulty. However, seek the advice of a Mercedes-Benz dealer before condemning the pump.

Removal

4 Disconnect the battery negative cable and position it away from the terminal.

2.2 litre models

5 Release the retaining clips and disconnect the vacuum hose from the top of the pump, which is mounted on the front of the cylinder head **(see illustration)**.

6 Unclip the wiring from across the front of

the pump and move it to one side. If required remove the oil level dipstick, to access the pump retaining bolts.

7 Undo the retaining bolts and withdraw the vacuum pump from the front of the cylinder head **(see illustration)**.

2.9 litre models

8 Remove the cooling fan as described in Chapter 3.

9 Remove the auxiliary drivebelt as described in Chapter 1.

10 Slacken the union nut and disconnect the vacuum hose from the top of the pump **(see illustration)**.

11 If necessary, remove the plastic caps, then undo the centre retaining bolts and remove the auxiliary belt pulleys, to access the pump mounting bolts **(see illustration)**.

12 Undo the retaining bolts from around the outer edge of the pump, and then withdraw it from the front of the timing case cover.

Refitting

13 Refitting is the reverse of removal, using new O-ring seals/gasket **(see illustrations)**, and making sure the pump drive flange is correctly engaged.

14 Tighten the vacuum pump mounting bolts to the specified torque.

15 Handbrake lever – removal and refitting

Removal

1 Chock the wheels, to prevent the vehicle from moving and ensure that the handbrake lever is released (off).

2 Unclip the plastic cover from the rear of the lever, and undo the two mounting bolts **(see illustrations)**.

3 Release the handbrake lever from the seat mounting, remove the retaining clip and withdraw the clevis pin to disconnect the front handbrake cable **(see illustrations)**.

4 Slide the plastic cover from the handbrake and disconnect the wiring connector from the handbrake lever warning light switch **(see illustrations)**.

Refitting

5 Refitting is the reverse of removal, bearing in mind the following points:
  a) Lubricate the end of the handbrake cable and the cable attachment on the lever with grease.

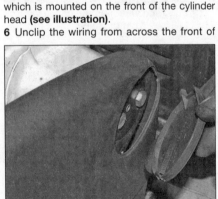

15.2a Unclip the plastic cover . . .

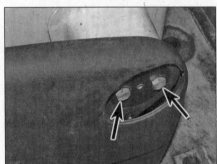

15.2b . . . and undo the two mounting bolts

b) Tighten the mounting bolts to the specified torque.

c) Adjust the handbrake as described in Chapter 1.

16 Handbrake cables and compensator – removal and refitting

Removal

1 The handbrake cable consists of three sections, a front cable, which connects the handbrake lever to the compensator unit under the centre of the vehicle cable, and two rear cables that link the compensator plate to the rear brake shoes on both sides of the vehicle. Each cable can be removed individually as follows.

2 Chock the front wheels then jack up the rear of the vehicle and securely support it on axle stands (see *Jacking and vehicle support*). Ensure that the handbrake lever is released (off).

Front cable

3 From under the vehicle, slacken the handbrake cable adjuster mechanism by slackening the securing bolt in the compensator plate **(see illustration)**.

4 Release the handbrake cable from the lever on the compensator plate **(see illustration)**.

5 Working inside the vehicle, detach the handbrake inner cable from the lever. Release the retaining clip and remove the clevis pin from the handbrake lever **(see illustrations)**.

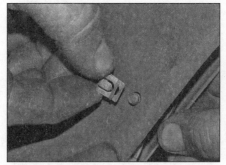

15.3a Release the retaining clip . . .

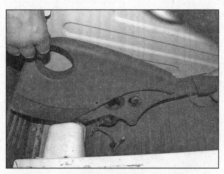

15.4a Slide the plastic cover off the handbrake . . .

6 Detach the front cable from the underbody **(see illustration)** by releasing the securing clip and then withdraw the cable from the vehicle. **Note:** *Check along the length of the cable and release it from any retaining clips/ ties.*

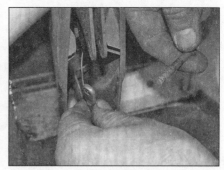

15.3b . . . and withdraw the clevis pin

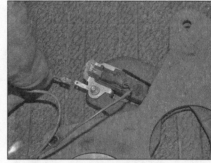

15.4b . . . and disconnect the wiring connector

Rear cables

7 Remove the handbrake shoes on the relevant side as described in Section 17.

8 Using a pair of long-nose pliers, withdraw the inner cable from the brake shoe linkage **(see illustration)**.

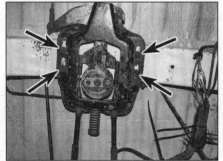

16.3 Handbrake compensator mounting bolts

16.4 Unhook the front handbrake cable from the lever

16.5a Release the retaining clip . . .

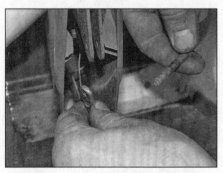

16.5b . . . and withdraw the clevis pin

16.6 Release the outer cable securing clip (arrowed)

16.8 Disconnect the inner cable from the linkage

16.9 Remove the handbrake cable securing bolt

16.10 Handbrake cable mounting bracket bolt

16.11 Remove the compensator mounting bracket

16.12 Turn the compensator over to access the cables

16.13a Unhook the inner cable from the lever . . .

16.13b . . . and pull the outer cable from the mounting bracket

9 At the rear of the brake backplate, undo the retaining bolt and withdraw the cable from the axle housing **(see illustration)**.
10 Undo the retaining bolt and release the

16.16a Twist the securing clip . . .

16.17a Remove the operating mechanism . . .

cable support bracket from the rear axle housing **(see illustration)**.
11 From under the centre of the vehicle, slacken the mounting bolts and lower the

16.16b . . . and remove the spring

16.17b . . . from the mounting bracket

compensator plate from under the vehicle body **(see illustration)**.
12 Release the front cable **(see illustration 16.4)**, and then turn the compensator unit over to access the operating lever (see illustration).
13 Release the relevant rear cable from the operating lever, and then unclip the outer cable from the mounting bracket **(see illustrations)**. Withdraw the cable from under the vehicle. **Note:** *Check along the length of the cable and release it from any retaining clips/ties.*

Compensator

14 From under the vehicle, slacken the handbrake cable adjuster mechanism by slackening the securing bolt in the compensator plate **(see illustration 16.3)**.
15 Disconnect the cables from the compensator mounting bracket as described in paragraphs 11 to 13, of this Section.
16 With the compensator removed, use a pair of pliers to remove the securing clip, and then withdraw the spring from the compensator mechanism **(see illustrations)**.
17 The compensator mechanism can now be removed from the mounting bracket **(see illustrations)**.

Refitting

18 Refitting is the reverse of removal, bearing in mind the following points:
 a) *Lubricate the handbrake cables and compensator mechanism with grease.*
 b) *Tighten the mounting bolts to the specified torque.*
 c) *Adjust the handbrake as described in Chapter 1 on completion.*

17.3 Using long-nose pliers to remove the retaining springs

17.4 Using long-nose pliers to remove the brake shoe return springs

17.5a Release the ends from the linkage . . .

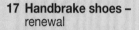

17 Handbrake shoes – renewal

⚠️ *Warning: Brake shoes must be renewed on BOTH rear wheels at the same time – NEVER renew the shoes on only one wheel, as uneven braking may result. The dust created as the shoes wear may contain asbestos, which is a health hazard. Never blow it out with compressed air, and don't inhale any of it. An approved filtering mask should be worn when working on the brakes. DO NOT use petroleum-based solvents to clean brake parts – use brake cleaner or methylated spirit only.*

Removal

1 Remove the rear brake disc as described in Section 8, making a note of the correct fitted position of all components.
2 Clean off the handbrake shoe assembly using brake cleaner, place rags below the brake assembly to catch any spillage. DO NOT use compressed air to blow out brake dust.
3 Using a pair of long-nose pliers, compress the shoe retaining springs then rotate them through 90° and remove them from the backplate. Access to the springs can be gained through the hub flange holes **(see illustration)**.
4 Carefully unhook and remove the handbrake shoe return spring, noting which way round the spring is fitted **(see illustration)**.
5 Free the ends of the shoes from the handbrake linkage plates, and remove the shoe assembly, complete with adjuctor from the vehicle **(see illustrations)**.
6 With the assembly on a bench, note each component's correct fitted location **(see illustration)**, then unhook the return springs and separate the shoes and adjuster assembly.
7 Inspect the handbrake shoes for signs of wear or contamination, and renew if necessary. It is recommended that the return springs be renewed as a matter of course. Check the shoe friction material thickness; shoes with anything less than the minimum friction material given in this Chapter's Specifications should be renewed.

17.5b . . and then remove the handbrake shoes

8 With the shoes removed, clean and inspect the condition of the shoe adjuster and expander mechanisms, and renew them if they show signs of wear or damage. If all is well, apply a fresh coat of brake grease (Mercedes-Benz recommend Molykote Paste U or G-Rapid) to the threads of the adjuster and sliding surfaces of the handbrake linkage plates. Do not allow the grease to contact the shoe friction material.

Refitting

9 Prior to installation, clean the backplate, and apply a thin smear of high-temperature brake grease (see paragraph 8) or anti-seize compound to all those surfaces of the backplate which bear on the shoes. Do not allow the lubricant to foul the friction material.
10 Assemble the shoes and the adjuster mechanism, noting the correct fitted position as noted on removal. Fully retract the adjuster and fit the return springs.

17.12a Handbrake shoes retaining springs (arrowed)

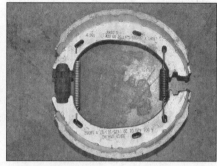

17.6 Handbrake shoe layout (N/S shown)

11 Manoeuvre the assembly into position and fit the shoe return spring, making sure it locates in the shoes securely.
12 Ensure that the shoes are correctly positioned, and secure them with the retaining springs **(see illustrations)**.
13 Check all components are correctly fitted, and centralise the handbrake shoes.
14 Refit the brake disc as described in Section 8. Prior to refitting the roadwheel, check the handbrake adjustment as described in Chapter 1.

18 Handbrake warning light switch – removal and refitting

1 Remove the handbrake lever as described in Section 15.
2 Undo the retaining bolt and remove the

17.12b Make sure they are located securely in the backplate

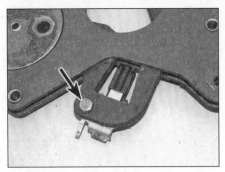

18.2 Handbrake switch securing bolt

switch from the handbrake lever bracket **(see illustration)**.

3 Refitting is a reversal of removal.

19 Stop-light switch – removal, refitting and adjustment

Removal

1 The stop-light switch is located above the brake pedal on the mounting bracket in the driver's footwell **(see illustration)**.

2 Move the driver's seat fully rearward, and if required, remove the lower facia trim panel from under the steering column for easier access to the pedal assembly, with reference to Chapter 11.

3 Turn the switch and remove it from the rear of the pedal mounting bracket **(see illustration)**.

19.1 Stop-light switch location (arrowed)

19.4 Disconnect the wiring connector

4 Disconnect the wiring connector from the stop-light switch as it is removed **(see illustration)**.

Refitting and adjustment

5 Pull the plunger of the switch out to adjust **(see illustration)**.

6 Reconnect the wiring connector to the switch.

7 Press the brake pedal down, and then insert the stop-light switch into the hole in the pedal mounting bracket, turn the switch to lock it in position.

8 The pedal can now be released, this will settle against the switch at its preset adjustment.

9 Where applicable, refit any facia trim panels, with reference to Chapter 11.

20 Anti-lock braking and traction control systems – general information

⚠️ **Warning: Diagnosis of the faults within ABS/ASR/ESP systems requires access to dedicated test equipment. For safety reasons, owners are strongly advised against attempting to investigate complex problems with these systems using standard workshop equipment.**

Note: *On models equipped with traction control, the ABS unit is a dual-function unit, and performs both the anti-lock braking system (ABS) and traction control (ASR)*

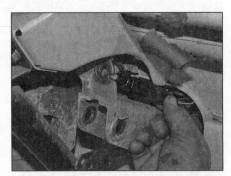

19.3 Rotate the switch to remove from mounting bracket

19.5 Pull the switch plunger out fully to reset it

system functions. On models with the Electronic Stability Program (ESP), the ABS unit is also used to modulate the brakes as required.

Models without traction control (ASR) or ESP

1 The ABS system comprises the following components:

a) *A hydraulic unit, which contains four hydraulic solenoid valves (one for each front brake, and one for each rear brake) and the electrically-driven return pump.*

b) *Four road wheel sensors (one for each front wheel, and one for each rear wheel). The sensors for each front wheel are fitted to the hubs, as are the sensors for each rear wheel.*

c) *The electronic control unit (ECU), located in the module box at the right-hand rear of the engine compartment (right as seen from the driver's seat).*

2 The purpose of the system is to prevent the wheel(s) locking during heavy braking and/or slippery road conditions. This is achieved by automatic release of the brake on the relevant wheel, followed by re-application of the brake.

3 The solenoids are controlled by the ECU, which itself receives signals from the wheel sensors, which monitor the speed of rotation of each wheel and can determine the speed at which the vehicle is travelling. It can then use this speed to determine when a wheel is decelerating at an abnormal rate compared to the speed of the vehicle, and therefore predicts when a wheel is about to lock.

4 During normal operation, the system functions in the same way as a non-ABS braking system.

5 If the ECU senses that a wheel is about to lock, it operates the relevant solenoid valve in the hydraulic unit, which then isolates from the master cylinder the relevant brake caliper(s) on the wheel(s) which is/are about to lock – effectively sealing-in the hydraulic pressure.

6 If the speed of rotation of the wheel continues to decrease at an abnormal rate, the ECU switches on the electrically-driven return pump which pumps the hydraulic fluid back into the master cylinder, releasing pressure on the brake caliper(s) so that the brake is released. Once the speed of rotation of the wheel returns to an acceptable rate, the pump stops; the solenoid valve opens, allowing the hydraulic master cylinder pressure to return to the caliper, which then re-applies the brake. This cycle can be carried out at up to 10 times a second.

7 The action of the solenoid valves and return pump creates pulses in the hydraulic circuit. When the ABS system is functioning, these pulses can be felt through the brake pedal.

8 The operation of the ABS system is entirely dependent on electrical signals. To prevent the system responding to any inaccurate signals, a built-in safety circuit monitors all signals received by the ECU. If an inaccurate signal or low battery voltage is detected, the ABS system is automatically shut down, and the warning light on the instrument panel is illuminated to inform the driver that the ABS system is not operational. Normal braking should still be available, however.

9 If a fault does develop in the ABS system, the vehicle must be taken to a Mercedes-Benz dealer for fault diagnosis and repair.

Models with traction control (ASR) and/or ESP

10 On models with traction control (ASR) and/or the stability program (ESP), the hydraulic unit performs the traction control and stability program functions as well as the anti-lock braking.

11 On models with ASR and/or ESP, a modified hydraulic unit and electronic control unit is fitted. The ABS electronic control unit (ECU) is linked to the engine management ECU, to operate the throttle valve position actuator.

12 The braking side of the system works as described above, and the rear axle speed is monitored solely by the rear wheel ABS sensor(s).

13 The traction control system prevents the rear wheels from losing traction by either gently applying the brake or by closing the throttle valve, depending on the speed of the vehicle. In extreme cases, a combination of both may be used.

14 On the braking side of the system, if a wheel is about to lose traction, the hydraulic unit uses the hydraulic pressure stored in the accumulator to gently apply the brake on the relevant wheel. Once the risk of wheel spin has passed, the hydraulic unit allows the fluid to return to the accumulator and releases the brake, allowing the wheel to rotate freely again.

15 On the throttle side of the system, if traction is about to be lost, the engine management ECM operates the throttle valve actuator and closes the throttle valve, decreasing the engine power output. Once the risk of wheel spin has passed, the actuator returns the throttle valve to its normal position and returns control of the throttle to the driver.

16 On models with the stability program (ESP), the traction control system is further refined to help retain control of the car during cornering. An accelerometer is fitted, which monitors the lateral (cornering) forces on the vehicle. If the vehicle starts to slide sideways, the system reacts by gently applying one of the brakes to help steer the vehicle – if appropriate, the throttle valve is also closed.

17 In the same way as for the ABS, the vehicle must be taken to a Mercedes-Benz dealer for testing if a fault develops in the traction control (ASR) or ESP systems.

21 Anti-lock braking and traction control components – removal and refitting

⚠ *Warning: If any of the ABS system components have been disturbed or renewed, the operation of the system must be verified before the vehicle is brought back into service. This procedure must be carried out using dedicated test equipment, and as such should be entrusted to a Mercedes-Benz dealer.*

Note: *Before starting work, refer to the note at the beginning of Section 2 concerning the dangers of hydraulic fluid.*

Hydraulic unit and ECU

Removal

1 Disconnect the battery negative terminal (refer to *Disconnecting the battery* in the Reference Chapter).

2 Remove the master cylinder reservoir cap, and siphon the hydraulic fluid from the reservoir. Alternatively, open the front brake caliper bleed screws, one at a time, and gently pump the brake pedal to expel the fluid through a plastic tube connected to the screw (see Section 2).

Caution: Do not siphon the fluid by mouth, as it is poisonous. Use a syringe or an old hydrometer.

3 The hydraulic unit and ECU are located on the left-hand side of the engine compartment, on top of the chassis leg at the front **(see illustration)**.

4 Note and record the fitted position of the brake pipes at the hydraulic unit, and then unscrew the union nuts and release the pipes. As a precaution, place absorbent rags beneath the brake pipe unions when unscrewing them. Suitably plug or cap the disconnected unions to prevent dirt entry and fluid loss.

Brake pipe locations on hydraulic unit

HL	Left rear brake
HR	Right rear brake
VL	Left front brake
VR	Right front brake
HZ1	From master cylinder (intermediate circuit)
HZ2	From master cylinder (plunger circuit)

5 Where fitted, unclip the plastic cover from the ECU and wiring connector. Release the locking lever and disconnect the wiring harness plug from the ECU on the front of the hydraulic unit.

6 Disconnect the wiring connector from the pressure sensor on the rear of the hydraulic unit.

7 Carefully pull the hydraulic unit upwards to release it from the three rubber mountings in the mounting bracket, and then manoeuvre the assembly out from its location in the engine compartment.

21.3 ABS hydraulic unit location

Refitting

8 Refitting is the reverse of the removal procedure, noting the following points:

a) Refit the brake pipes to their respective locations, and tighten the union nuts securely.

b) Ensure that the wiring is correctly routed, and that the ECU wiring harness plug is firmly pressed into position and secured locked.

c) On completion, reconnect the battery negative terminal, and then bleed the complete hydraulic system as described in Section 2.

Electronic control unit (ECU)

Removal

9 The electronic control unit (ECU) is located on the front of the ABS hydraulic unit.

10 Disconnect the battery negative terminal (refer to *Disconnecting the battery* in the Reference Chapter).

11 Where fitted, unclip the plastic cover from the ECU and wiring connector. Release the locking lever and disconnect the wiring harness plug from the ECU on the front of the hydraulic unit.

12 Thoroughly clean the area around the ECU and hydraulic modulator and exercise extreme cleanliness during the following operations.

13 Undo the six securing screws and carefully withdraw the ECU from the ABS hydraulic unit.

Refitting

14 Ensure that the mating faces of the modulator and ECU are clean and dry, do not use any sharp-edged tools for this as damage may occur.

15 Carefully position the ECU on the ABS hydraulic unit; making sure that it is sitting flat.

Note: *The seal on the rear of the ECU must not be removed, and is part of the control unit.*

16 Refit the securing screws and tighten them progressively in the sequence shown **(see illustration)**.

17 Reconnect the ECU wiring harness plug ensuring it is securely locked in position, taking great care not to damage the contact pins.

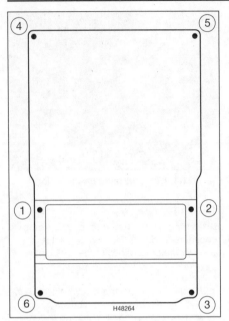

21.16 Tightening sequence of control unit

18 Refit the plastic cover to the ECU wiring connector (where applicable), and then reconnect the battery negative terminal.

Hydraulic unit pressure sensor

Removal

19 The pressure sensor is located on the rear of the ABS hydraulic unit.

20 Disconnect the battery negative terminal

21.24 Front wheel speed sensor

21.31 Fit the new clamping bush inside the hub/axle

(refer to *Disconnecting the battery* in the Reference Chapter).

21 Disconnect the wiring connector from the pressure sensor.

22 Unscrew the pressure sensor from the hydraulic unit. As a precaution, place absorbent rags beneath the brake pipe unions when unscrewing them. Suitably plug or cap the hydraulic unit to prevent dirt entry and fluid loss.

Refitting

23 Refitting is the reverse of the removal procedure, noting the following points:
 a) *Make sure all threads are clean and undamaged.*
 b) *Tighten the sensor to the specified torque setting.*
 c) *Ensure that the wiring connector is firmly pressed into position on the sensor.*
 d) *Reconnect the battery negative terminal.*
 e) *On completion, bleed the hydraulic system as described in Section 2.*

Wheel speed sensors

Note: *The speed sensor is held in position in the front hub/rear axle housing by a clamping bush, these become a tight fit in the hub over the years, so damage to the sensor and the bush will occur on removal. New speed sensor and clamping bush will be required for refitting.*

Removal

24 The front wheel speed sensor is located in the hub assembly at the front of the lower strut mounting **(see illustration)**.

21.27 Unclip the wiring from the retaining brackets

21.32a Insert the new speed sensor . . .

25 The rear wheel speed sensor is located in the halfshaft bearing cover at the top of the rear axle.

26 Apply the handbrake, then jack up the front/rear of the vehicle (depending on which sensor is to be removed) and support it on axle stands (see *Jacking and vehicle support*). Remove the relevant roadwheel.

27 Release the sensor wiring from the retaining brackets on the suspension/rear axle and unclip it from under the wheel arch **(see illustration)**.

28 The speed sensor wiring is part of the complete loom; the wiring will need to be cut through at an easily accessible point. Check the length of the wiring on the new speed sensor before cutting the wiring loom. **Note:** *The new sensor wiring will need to be soldered together and covered using heat-shrinkable sleeves.*

29 Withdraw the sensor from the front hub/axle, this will be a tight fit, so carefully tap the sensor out of position using a puller or drift – see note at beginning.

30 Once the sensor has been removed, withdraw the clamping bush from the hub. Discard, as a new sensor and clamping bush will be required for refitting.

Refitting

31 Clean the inside of the hub and check for any damage before fitting the new clamping bush to the hub/axle **(see illustration)**.

32 Apply a small amount of acid-free grease (Mercedes-Benz part No A 000 989 62 51 10) to the sides of the speed sensor, and then slide it into the new clamping bush in the hub. Press it firmly into position, until it is seated all the way in **(see illustrations)**. **Note:** *The clearance between the sensor and the target ring on the hub/halfshaft adjusts itself automatically while driving.*

33 The speed sensor wiring can now be reconnected, solder the new sensor wiring to the loom wiring on the vehicle, and cover the soldered joint using a heat-shrink sleeve.

34 Clip the sensor wiring back in position on the suspension strut/rear axle and support brackets under the wheel arch.

35 Refit the roadwheel, then lower the vehicle to the ground and tighten the roadwheel nuts to the specified torque.

21.32b . . . making sure it is fitted up to the target ring

Wheel speed sensors target rings

Note: *The speed sensor target rings are a tight fit on the front hub and rear axle halfshafts. They can be removed by using a chisel, but will need to be heated up to approx 180°c for refitting. Check on the availability of parts before removal.*

36 The front wheel speed sensor target ring is located on the rear of the hub assembly. Remove the front hub assembly, as described in Chapter 10.

37 The rear wheel speed sensor target ring is located in the rear axle halfshaft. Remove the rear axle halfshaft and wheel bearing, as described in Chapter 8.

Lateral acceleration (Yaw rate) sensor

Note: *On models with traction control (ASR) and/or the stability program (ESP), the sensor is located under the driver's front seat.*

Removal

38 Disconnect the battery negative terminal (refer to *Disconnecting the battery* in the Reference Chapter).

39 Slide the seat as far forwards as it can go and remove the cover from the seat base.

40 Working inside the rear of the seat base, undo the retaining bolts and move the relay mounting bracket and move it to one side.

41 Note the direction arrow on the sensor for refitting. Undo the two retaining bolts from the sensor, disconnect the wiring connector, and then remove it from the vehicle.

Refitting

42 Refitting is a reversal of removal. **Note:** *New bolts are recommended for refitting.*

22 Load-apportioning valve – general information

A load-apportioning valve is fitted under the rear of the vehicle **(see illustration)**; the purpose of the valve is to regulate the hydraulic pressure applied to the rear brakes according to vehicle loading. This prevents the rear brakes locking up under heavy braking when the vehicle is in a lightly-loaded condition.

The valve is mounted on the chassis in front

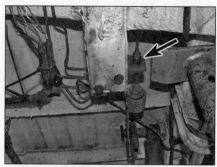

22.1 Load-apportioning valve location

of the rear axle and is operated by a lever interconnected between the valve and rear axle.

If the valve position is disturbed, it will require readjustment, which entails the use of specialised equipment (pressure gauges) and reference to several graphs depending on the vehicle body type. Any work on the load-apportioning valve should therefore be entrusted to a specialist or Mercedes-Benz dealer.

Chapter 10
Suspension and steering

Contents

Degrees of difficulty

Easy, suitable for novice with little experience	Fairly easy, suitable for beginner with some experience	Fairly difficult, suitable for competent DIY mechanic	Difficult, suitable for experienced DIY mechanic	Very difficult, suitable for expert DIY or professional

Specifications

Front suspension

Type	Transverse leaf spring inside the front subframe, telescopic shock absorbers and anti-roll bar connected to lower suspension arms by connecting links
Front spring (depending on model):	
Spring length	1300 mm
Number of leaves	1 or 2
Leaf thickness (measured at centre):	
Steel spring x 1	14.9 mm
Steel spring x 2	11.7 mm
Steel spring x 2	12.1 mm
Steel spring x 2	13.1 mm
Steel spring x 2	13.4 mm
GRP spring x 1	29.0 mm
Spring travel (per 1000N load):	
Steel spring x 1	8.88 mm
Steel spring x 2	8.88 mm
Steel spring x 2	8.1 mm
Steel spring x 2	7.22 mm
Steel spring x 2	6.68 mm
GRP spring x 1	3.6 mm
Front hub bearing endfloat.	0.02 to 0.04 mm

Rear suspension

Type	Semi-floating hypoid axle supported on semi-elliptic springs, telescopic shock absorbers and anti-roll bar connected to chassis by connecting links
Rear spring length (installed dimension – including shackle).	1470 mm

Steering

Type	Hydraulic power-assisted steering with rack-and-pinion, with adjustable tie rods
Filling capacity	1.0 litre
Fluid type	See *Lubricants and fluids*

Torque wrench settings

	Nm	lbf ft
Front suspension		
Anti-roll bar clamp bolts	30	22
Brake caliper mounting bracket bolts	170	125
Hut nut clamp bolt (for bearing adjustment)	12	9
Spring lower clamp plate to front subframe:		
M12 bolt	130	96
M10 bolt	65	48
Spring upper stop-plate to lower arm	60	44
Steering knuckle balljoint-to-lower suspension arm nut*	280	207
Subframe mounting bolts	125	92
Suspension lower arm mounting bolt/nuts	150	111
Suspension strut piston rod upper retaining nut	100	74
Suspension strut-to-steering knuckle bolts	185	137
Rear suspension		
Anti-roll bar clamp-to-rear axle bolts	25	18
Anti-roll bar link arm-to-chassis securing bolts	95	70
Leaf spring centre (M10) bolt	42	31
Leaf spring front mounting:		
M14 x 1.5 bolt	95	70
M16 x 1.5 bolt	185	137
Leaf spring rear shackle-to-body mounting:		
M12 x 1.5 bolt	90	66
M16 x 1.5 bolt	185	137
Leaf spring rear-to-spring shackle:		
M12 x 1.5 bolt	85	63
M16 x 1.5 bolt	185	137
Shock absorber lower mounting nut/bolts:		
M12 x 1.5 (8.8) nut/bolt	70	52
M12 x 1.5 (10.9) nut/bolt	110	81
Shock absorber upper mounting nut/bolts	80	59
Spring-to-axle U-bolt nuts	170	125
Steering		
Power steering fluid pipes to steering gear	42	31
Power steering pump attachments:		
High-pressure pipe union	38	28
Mounting bolts	21	15
Pulley retaining bolts	30	22
Steering column retaining bolts	25	18
Steering column universal joint-to-steering gear pinion shaft pinch-bolt*	24	18
Steering gear-to-front subframe bolts*:		
Stage 1	25	18
Stage 2	45	33
Stage 3	Angle-tighten a further 90°	
Steering wheel retaining bolt*	70	52
Track rod end balljoint nut*	130	96
Track rod end locknut on tie rod	65	48
Roadwheels		
Roadwheel nuts	190	140

* Use new nuts/bolts

1 General information

The independent front suspension is of the transverse leaf spring type, which is fitted across the inside of the front subframe. Telescopic shock absorbers are bolted to the top of the steering knuckle and are mounted under the wheel arch to the vehicle body by an upper rubber mounting point. Lower suspension arms are connected to the front subframe by rubber mounting bushes, and

to the steering knuckle by a balljoint. The front steering knuckles, which carry the hub bearings, brake calipers and disc assemblies, are bolted to the front shock absorbers, and connected to the lower arms via the balljoints. A front anti-roll bar is fitted, which has link arms at each end to connect to the lower suspension arms.

The rear axle is a live axle suspended on semi-elliptic leaf springs and utilising telescopic shock absorbers to provide the damping for the axle assembly. Further information and procedures relating to the rear axle assembly are contained in Chapter 8.

The steering column incorporates a universal joint at the lower end, which is connected to the steering gear pinion shaft. The steering gear is mounted on the front subframe, and is connected by two tie rods and track rod ends to the steering arms, which project forwards from the steering knuckles. The track rod ends are threaded to enable wheel alignment adjustment.

Power steering is fitted to all models and is driven by the auxiliary drivebelt on the front of the engine. The system has a fluid cooler, which is a loop of metal pipe that is located in front of the cooling system radiator.

2 Front hub and bearing –
removal, overhaul and refitting

⚠️ **Warning:** *Before attempting to dismantle the hub assembly, a special tool (dial test indicator) will be required to adjust the play in the wheel bearings to the specified setting on refitting.*

Removal

1 Firmly apply the handbrake, and then jack up the front of the vehicle and support it securely on axle stands (see *Jacking and vehicle support*). Remove the relevant front roadwheel.
2 Remove the front brake disc, as described in Chapter 9, Section 5.
3 Carefully tap the side of the centre grease cap to remove it from the hub **(see illustration)**.
4 Slacken the Allen bolt in the clamping nut and then unscrew the clamping nut and withdraw the thrust plate from the shaft **(see illustrations)**. Note which way around the thrust plate is fitted for reassembly.
5 Withdraw the hub assembly complete with tapered roller bearings from the steering knuckle **(see illustration)**.

Overhaul

6 Remove the outer tapered bearing from the centre of the hub **(see illustration)**.
7 Turn the hub over and then carefully lever the seal from the inside of the hub **(see**

illustration). **Note:** *Take care not to damage the speed sensor target ring, on the inside edge of the hub.*
8 Remove the inner tapered bearing from the centre of the hub **(see illustration)**.
9 Clean out the old grease from inside the

hub, and then using a drift, tap the bearing outer race from the outer part of the hub assembly **(see illustration)**.
10 Turn the hub over, and then using a drift, tap the bearing outer race from the inside of the hub assembly **(see illustration)**.

2.3 Remove the grease cap from the centre of the hub

2.4a Slacken the Allen bolt . . .

2.4b . . . remove the clamping nut . . .

2.4c . . . and remove the thrust plate

2.5 Withdraw the hub complete with bearings

2.6 Remove the outer bearing from the hub

2.7 Prise the seal out from the inside of the hub . . .

2.8 . . . and then remove the inner bearing

2.9 Using a drift to remove the outer bearing race . . .

2.10 . . . from both side of the hub

2.13 Fit the new outer bearing races . . .

2.14 . . . squarely into the hub on each side

2.15a Fit the bearing into the hub . . .

2.15b . . . and fit the new seal

2.16 Fit the outer bearing into the hub

2.17 Make sure the bearings are packed with grease before refitting

11 Thoroughly clean the hub assembly, removing all traces of dirt and grease, and polish away any burrs or raised edges, which might hinder reassembly.

12 Check for cracks or any other signs of wear or damage, and renew if necessary. Ensure that the ABS sensor ring is in good condition. Obtain new bearings and seal for reassembly.

13 Securely support the hub, and locate the inner bearing outer race in the hub **(see illustration)**. Press the race fully into position, ensuring that it enters the hub squarely, using a tubular spacer (such as a large socket), which bears only on the outer edge of the race.

14 Turn the hub over and fit the outer bearing inner race in the same way **(see illustration)**.

15 Fit the inner bearing to the inner race. Fit the oil seal into the rear of the hub, making

3.4 Shake the wheel to assess any play in the wheel bearing

sure its sealing lip is facing inwards, and press it squarely into position **(see illustrations)**.

16 Pack the hub assembly about two-thirds full of grease **(see illustration)**. The outer bearing is best fitted once the hub assembly has been fitted to the steering knuckle.

Refitting

17 On reassembly, apply a coating of grease to the bearing outer race and hub contact surfaces. Also work the grease well into the bearing tracks **(see illustration)**.

18 Apply a smear of grease to the hub rear oil seal lip, and locate the hub assembly onto the steering knuckle shaft.

19 Pack the outer bearing with grease, working it well into the bearing tracks. Fit the outer bearing into position over the steering knuckle pin, and slide it fully into the hub location.

20 Fit the thrustplate onto the steering knuckle pin and screw on the hub clamping nut. Rotate the hub assembly whilst using the hub nut to press the hub assembly onto the steering knuckle axle. Once the hub assembly is correctly seated, adjust the hub bearing endfloat as described in Section 3 and tighten the hub nut clamp bolt to the specified torque.

21 Pack the grease cap with grease, then tap it squarely into position.

22 Refit the front brake disc, as described in Chapter 9, Section 5.

23 Refit the roadwheel, tighten the wheel nuts to the specified torque, and then lower the vehicle to the ground.

3 Front hub bearing – checking and adjustment

1 Mercedes-Benz recommends the use of a dial gauge to check the hub endfloat as a means of checking the bearing adjustment. While this is certainly the method for assuring the maximum accuracy, a competent mechanic will be able to check and adjust the bearing by feel.

2 If the bearing is worn to the extent that the droning noise can be heard inside the vehicle, there is no point trying to 'adjust' the bearing to reduce the noise. Fit a new bearing as described in Section 2.

Without a dial gauge

3 Chock the rear wheels and firmly apply the handbrake. Jack up the front of the vehicle and support it on axle stands (see *Jacking and vehicle support*).

4 Grasp the wheel at the top and bottom, and shake it to assess free play **(see illustration)**. Repeat the check with the wheel held on the left and right sides. A very small amount of play may be noticed, but if the play is excessive, the bearings should be adjusted as described below.

5 If adjustment is required, the wheel must be removed. This will probably entail lowering the vehicle temporarily to loosen the wheel bolts, then raising the vehicle once more.

6 Taking care not to damage the pad friction material or the disc surface, use a large flat-bladed screwdriver to push the brake pads and pistons back into the caliper, away from the disc so that the pads do not drag.

7 Tap or prise the grease cap out from the centre of the hub **(see illustration)**. If the cap is damaged on removal, it must be renewed.

8 Using an Allen key or socket, slacken the hub nut clamp bolt so that the nut is free to turn **(see illustration)**.

9 Rotate the brake disc and at the same time lightly tighten the hub nut until the disc starts to become difficult to turn **(see illustration)**. From this point, slacken the hub nut by approximately one-third of a turn, and then tap the end of the hub spindle with a soft-faced mallet to relieve the tension on the bearing.

10 Slacken the hub nut fully, then very lightly tighten it by hand only until resistance is felt. A few attempts may be required, but there should be a clear point at which all free play is eliminated without loading the bearing. Do not tighten the hub nut using tools, or any tighter than described, as this will quickly destroy it.

11 Tighten the hub nut clamp bolt to the specified torque.

12 Pack the grease cap with fresh grease, and tap it fully back into place.

13 Refit the wheel, then lower the vehicle to the ground and tighten the wheel bolts to the specified torque. Depress the brake pedal repeatedly until normal pedal pressure returns.

14 If a new bearing has been fitted, recheck the adjustment within approximately 500 miles.

With a dial gauge

15 Chock the rear wheels, and then firmly apply the handbrake. Loosen the front wheel bolts, and then jack up the front of the vehicle and support it on axle stands (see *Jacking and vehicle support*). Remove the relevant front roadwheel.

16 Using spacers if necessary, refit two of the wheel bolts (to prevent movement of the brake disc), positioning them on opposite sides, and tightening them securely.

17 Taking care not to damage the pad friction material or the disc surface, use a large flat-bladed screwdriver to push the brake pads and pistons back into the caliper, away from the disc so that the pads do not drag.

18 Tap the grease cap out from the centre of the hub. If the cap is damaged on removal, it must be renewed.

19 Mount a dial gauge onto the front face of the hub/disc, and position the gauge probe so that it is in contact with the end of the axle shaft **(see illustration)**. Zero the gauge scale, then grasp the disc at two opposite points and pull it in and out. Note the reading obtained on the gauge, and check that the hub bearing endfloat is within the limits given in the *Specifications* at the start of this Chapter.

20 If all is well, remove the dial gauge. Pack the grease cap with grease, and tap the cap into position. Remove the wheel bolts and refit the roadwheel, then lower the vehicle to the ground and tighten the wheel bolts to the

3.7 Remove the grease cap from the centre of the hub

3.9 Using long-nose pliers to turn the clamping nut

specified torque. Depress the brake pedal several times until normal, non-assisted pedal pressure returns prior to taking the vehicle on the road.

21 If adjustment is required, use an Allen key to slacken the hub retaining nut clamp bolt until the retaining nut is free to turn.

22 Rotate the brake disc while lightly tightening the hub nut, until the disc starts to become difficult to turn. From this point, slacken the hub nut by approximately one-third of a turn, and then tap the end of the hub spindle with a soft-faced mallet to relieve the tension on the bearing.

23 Check the hub bearing endfloat as described in paragraph 19. If necessary adjust the endfloat by rotating the hub nut as required.

24 Recheck the bearing endfloat, then refit all disturbed components as described in paragraph 20.

4.3a Undo the retaining nut . . .

3.8 Slacken the Allen bolt

3.19 Using a dial gauge to check the hub bearing endfloat adjustment

25 If a new bearing has been fitted, recheck the adjustment within approximately 500 miles.

4 Steering knuckle – removal and refitting

Removal

1 Remove the front hub assembly as described in Section 2.

2 On vehicles with ABS, remove the wheel speed sensor as described in Chapter 9, Section 21.

3 Slacken the track rod end balljoint nut several turns, then use a balljoint separator tool to release the balljoint shank from the steering arm. With the balljoint released, unscrew the nut and disconnect the balljoint from the steering arm **(see illustrations)**.

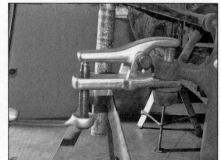

4.3b . . . then using a separator tool

4.3c . . . release the balljoint taper

4.4 Undo the lower arm balljoint nut

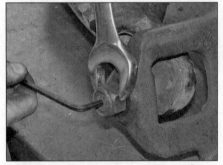

4.5 Using an Allen key to stop the balljoint from turning

4.6 Suspension strut lower mounting bolts

Discard the nut, as a new one must be used for refitting.

4 Slacken the nut securing the steering knuckle balljoint to the lower suspension arm **(see illustration)**. Attach a two-legged puller

to the lower suspension arm and tighten the puller to apply tension to the balljoint shank. Strike the end of the lower suspension arm with a hammer a few times to shock-free the balljoint shank taper.

5 Remove the puller and unscrew the balljoint retaining nut **(see illustration)**. Discard the nut, as a new one must be used for refitting.

6 Unscrew and remove the four bolts securing the steering knuckle assembly to the front suspension strut **(see illustration)**.

7 The steering knuckle can now be moved downwards, to disengage it from the lower arm balljoint. Remove the knuckle from the vehicle.

Refitting

8 Thoroughly clean the bottom end of the suspension strut and its location to the steering knuckle. Locate the knuckle onto the lower arm balljoint and fit the securing nut a couple of threads.

9 Locate the knuckle onto the strut, and then insert the mounting bolts and tighten them to the specified torque.

10 Push down on the lower suspension arm and engage the steering knuckle balljoint with the arm. The new balljoint retaining nut can now be tightened to the specified torque.

11 Locate the track rod end balljoint on the steering arm. Screw on a new nut and tighten it to the specified torque. If the balljoint shank is hollow, an Allen key can be used to prevent the balljoint from rotating as the nut is tightened. If the shank is solid, use a stout bar to lever up on the underside of the track rod end. This will lock the balljoint shank taper in the steering arm and prevent rotation as the nut is tightened.

12 On vehicles with ABS, refit the wheel speed sensor as described in Chapter 9, Section 21.

13 Refit the front hub assembly as described in Section 2.

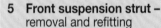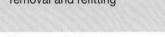

5 Front suspension strut –
   removal and refitting

Removal

1 Firmly apply the handbrake, and then jack up the front of the vehicle and support it securely on axle stands (see *Jacking and vehicle support*). Remove the roadwheel.

2 Working inside the vehicle the passenger compartment, remove the floor mat and plastic trim to access the upper mounting nut **(see illustrations)**. **Note:** *On the passenger side, remove the cover from the vehicle jack and tools to access the retaining nut. On the driver's side, it maybe necessary to undo the retaining screws and remove the accelerator pedal.*

3 Slacken the suspension strut upper mounting nut, using a Torx bit to stop the centre pushrod from turning **(see illustration)**. **Do not** take the retaining nut completely off, at this stage.

4 Unclip the wiring from the bracket on the lower part of the suspension strut **(see illustration)**.

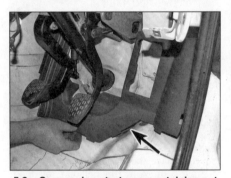

5.2a Suspension strut upper retaining nut on the right-hand side

5.2b Suspension strut upper retaining nut on the left-hand side

5.3 Using a Torx socket to prevent the strut shaft from turning

5.4 Unclip the wiring from the bottom of the strut

5.5 Remove the lower mounting bolts . . .

5 Place a jack under the lower arm, to support the weight, and then undo the suspension strut lower mounting bolts from the steering knuckle **(see illustration)**.

6 Have an assistant support the strut from under the wheel arch. The upper suspension nut can now be completely removed, and then have the assistant lower the strut to remove it from under the vehicle **(see illustration)**.

Refitting

7 Lift the suspension strut into position and insert the upper mounting through the hole in the body. Then with the aid of an assistant, screw on the upper mounting nut and tighten to the specified torque.

8 Thoroughly clean the bottom end of the suspension strut and its location to the steering knuckle. Locate the strut onto the steering knuckle and insert the retaining bolts, tighten to the specified torque.

9 Clip the wiring back into the bracket on the lower part of the suspension strut.

10 Working inside the passenger compartment, refit the plastic trims and floor mat. **Note:** *On the passenger side, refit the cover to the vehicle jack and tools. On the driver's side, refit the accelerator pedal, where removed.*

11 Refit the roadwheel, and then lower the vehicle to the ground. Tighten the roadwheel bolts to the specified torque.

---

6 Front suspension lower arm – removal and refitting

Removal

1 Firmly apply the handbrake, and then jack up the front of the vehicle and support it securely on axle stands (see *Jacking and vehicle support*). Remove the roadwheel.

2 Remove the steering knuckle as described in Section 4. If the lower balljoint is a tight fit in the steering knuckle, it can be removed with the lower arm.

3 With the jack still in position under the lower arm, undo the retaining bolts and remove the spring stop-plate from the top of the lower suspension arm **(see illustrations)**.

4 Lower the jack from under the lower arm, and then remove the front and rear mounting bolts/nuts and withdraw the lower arm from the subframe **(see illustration)**.

5 If the steering knuckle is still attached to the lower arm, slacken the nut securing the steering knuckle balljoint to the lower

5.6 . . . and withdraw the strut from under the wheel arch

suspension arm, until it is at the end of the threads. Attach a two-legged puller to the lower part of the steering knuckle, and tighten the puller to apply tension to the balljoint shank. If a puller is not available, strike the end of the balljoint with a hammer a few times to shock-free the balljoint shank taper **(see illustration)**. Fit the nut to the end of the balljoint to prevent the threads getting damaged.

6 Use an Allen key to prevent the balljoint shank from turning to release the securing nut **(see illustration)**.

Refitting

7 Locate the lower arm in position in the subframe and fit new retaining nuts/bolts **(see illustration)**. **Do not** tighten fully at this point.

8 Place a jack under the lower arm, and lift it into position under the end of the spring.

9 Refit the upper spring stop-plate to the

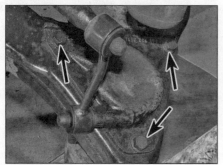

6.3a Undo the retaining bolts . . .

6.3b . . . and remove the spring stop-plate

6.4 Remove the lower suspension arm

6.5 Using a hammer to split the balljoint from the lower arm

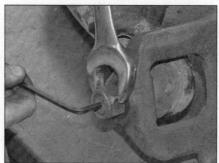

6.6 Using an Allen key to stop the balljoint from turning

6.7 Fit new lower arm securing bolts

6.9 Fit new spring stop-plate securing bolts

top of the lower suspension arm and fit new retaining bolts **(see illustration)**. Tighten to the specified torque setting.

10 Refit the steering knuckle as described in Section 4.

11 Refit the roadwheel, and then lower the vehicle to the ground and tighten the roadwheel nuts to the specified torque.

12 Finally, with the weight of the vehicle back on its wheels, tighten the lower arm-to-subframe mounting bolts to the specified torque.

7 Front suspension lower arm bushes – renewal

Note: *A Mercedes-Benz special tool (730 589 00 43 00) is necessary to carry out this work. Also the use of a press will*

be required. If these are not available, then remove the lower suspension arm and take it to your local dealer (or specialist) to have the bushes fitted to the arm.

1 Remove the front suspension lower arm, as described in Section 6.

2 If the suspension arm bushes are worn or perished, they can be withdrawn from the suspension arm using a simple puller comprising a metal tube (sockets) of suitable diameter (just less than that of the arm eye inside diameter), washers, and a long bolt and nut **(see illustration)**. Alternatively, if a press is at hand, the bushes can be pushed out using a suitable rod or a length of tube of suitable diameter.

3 To ease the fitting of the new bushes into the suspension arm, lubricate the relevant bush and the eye in the arm with multipurpose grease, and then using the special Mercedes-Benz tool, press the bush into the arm so that the bush lips are seated correctly **(see illustrations)**.

4 Wipe off any excess grease, then refit the front suspension lower arm as described in Section 6.

8 Lower suspension arm balljoint – renewal

1 Remove the lower suspension arm as described in Section 6.

2 Place the lower arm over a strong bench vice, with the sides resting on the top of the vice jaws.

3 Using a hammer, firmly tap the top of the balljoint and drift it out of the lower suspension arm **(see illustration)**.

4 Clean the balljoint locating area in the lower arm and remove any burrs that might hinder refitting.

5 Lubricate the balljoint locating area in the arm with multipurpose grease

6 Place the new balljoint in the jaws of the vice, taking care not to damage the balljoint rubber boot.

7 Fit the lower arm squarely onto the balljoint and tap the lower arm onto the balljoint. Use a large socket to fit the new balljoint back into position in the lower arm **(see illustrations)**.

8 Refit the lower suspension arm as described in Section 6.

9 Front anti-roll bar and link arms – removal, overhaul and refitting

Removal

1 Firmly apply the handbrake, and then jack up the front of the vehicle and support it securely on axle stands (see *Jacking and vehicle support*). Remove both the front roadwheels.

2 Using a lever, disconnect the anti-roll bar link from the lower suspension stop-plates on both sides of the vehicle **(see illustration)**. Apply a small amount of penetrating oil onto the bush to aid removal.

3 Undo the two bolts (one at each side)

7.2 Using a long threaded rod, washers and sockets to remove the bushes

7.3a Using a Mercedes special tool to insert the new bushes . . .

7.3b . . . into the lower arm using an hydraulic press

8.3 Using a hammer to remove the balljoint from the lower arm

8.7a Place the new balljoint onto the vice jaws . . .

8.7b . . . and use a large socket to tap the arm into place

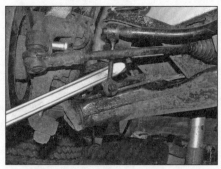

9.2 Using a long lever to disconnect the anti-roll bar link

9.3 Anti-roll bar clamp retaining bolt

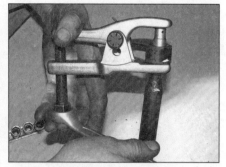

9.6 Using a balljoint separator to remove the link from the anti-roll bar

9.7 Lubricate the bushes to ease refitting

9.8a Fit the new bushes around the anti-roll bar . . .

9.8b . . . and then fit the retaining clamp

securing the anti-roll bar clamps to the subframe **(see illustration)**.

4 Unclip the upper part of the clamps from the subframe and then remove the anti-roll bar out from the front of the vehicle.

Overhaul

5 With the anti-roll bar removed, check the condition of the mounting bushes and renew as necessary.

6 To remove the link arms from the end of the anti-roll bar, use a balljoint splitter (or similar). Tighten the tool and withdraw the link arms from the end of the anti-roll bar **(see illustration)**.

7 If new bushes are required, remove the old bushes from the link arms by using a screwdriver to release them. To fit new bushes, lubricate the bushes with oil, and then press them firmly into position in the link arms **(see illustration)**.

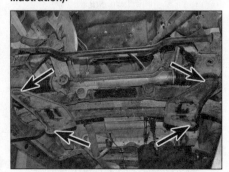

10.2 Undo the four outer mounting bolts – arrowed

8 To fit new clamp bushes to the anti-roll bar, remove the clamps from the rubber bush and then remove the bush from the anti-roll bar. Clean the rubber bush locating area on the anti-roll bar and remove any burrs. Fit the new bush in place around the anti-roll bar, and fit the clamp back in position **(see illustrations)**.

Refitting

9 Refitting is a reversal of removal, tightening all fastenings to the specified torque.

10 Front transverse leaf spring – removal and refitting

Removal

1 Firmly apply the handbrake, and then jack up the front of the vehicle and support it securely on axle stands (see *Jacking and vehicle support*). Remove both the front roadwheels.

2 Undo the front and rear retaining bolts from the two spring clamp plates under the front subframe **(see illustration)**.

3 Remove the lower suspension arms from each side of the subframe, as described in Section 6.

4 Support the front transverse leaf spring at the centre using a trolley jack, and then undo the retaining bolts (four each side) from the lower spring clamp plates **(see illustration)**.

5 With the aid of an assistant, lower the spring from under the subframe and withdraw it out from the front of the vehicle

Refitting

6 Refitting is a reversal of removal, using new nuts/bolts where applicable, and tightening all fastenings to the specified torque.

11 Rear axle leaf spring – removal, overhaul and refitting

Removal

1 Chock the front wheels then jack up the rear of the vehicle and securely support it on axle stands (see *Jacking and vehicle support*).

2 Support the rear axle with a trolley jack and remove the rear roadwheels.

3 Undo the retaining nuts, and remove the spring-to-axle U-bolts and fittings each side

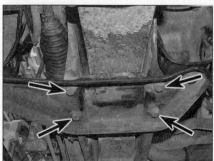

10.4 Lower spring plate mounting bolts (one side shown)

11.3a Remove the U-bolts . . .

11.3b . . . and upper mounting plate

11.4a Remove the front . . .

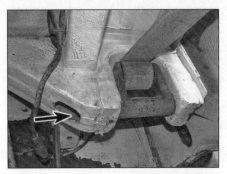

11.4b . . . and rear spring shackle bolts

11.8 Using a threaded rod and spacers to remove the bush . . .

11.9 . . . and then fitting the new bush into the spring

(see illustration). Discard the nuts, as new ones must be used for refitting.

4 Unscrew and remove the front mounting and rear mounting retaining nuts, and drive out the mounting bolts with a soft metal drift **(see illustrations)**. Discard the bolts/nuts, as new ones must be used for refitting.

5 The rear spring can now be lifted from the rear axle and withdrawn from beneath the vehicle. If necessary, lower the rear axle on the trolley jack to allow the leaf spring to be removed, making sure that the brake hoses and handbrake cables are not damaged.

6 Examine the front and rear mounting bushes/shackle, and check the condition of the U-bolts and spring leaves; renew any faulty components.

Overhaul

7 With the leaf spring removed, check the condition of the mounting bushes and shackle bushes, renew as necessary.

8 If new bushes are required, remove the old bushes from the leaf spring, by using a threaded rod, washers and a length of tube to fit over the end of the eye on the leaf spring. Tighten the nuts on the threaded rod to push the bush out from the leaf spring **(see illustration)**.

9 To fit new bushes, lubricate the bushes with oil, and then press them firmly into position using the threaded rod, nuts and washers, as used on removal **(see illustration)**.

10 To fit new bushes to the shackle, on the rear of the leaf spring again use a threaded rod, washers and a length of tube to fit over the end of the eye on the shackle. Tighten the nuts on the threaded rod to push the bush out from the leaf spring **(see illustration)**.

11 To fit new bushes, lubricate the bushes with oil, and then press them firmly into position using the threaded rod, nuts and washers, as used on removal **(see illustration)**.

Refitting

12 Refitting is a reversal of removal, but note the following additional points:

a) *Before refitting the leaf spring, check the dimension of the rear spring including shackle as specified in the specifications* **(see illustration)**.

b) *Make sure the locating peg on the underside of the leaf spring is located in the axle when fitting* **(see illustration)**.

11.10 Using a threaded rod and spacers to remove the bush . . .

11.11 . . . and then fitting the new bush into the spring hanger

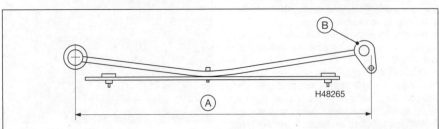

11.12a Before fitting the rear spring, set shackle (B) to installed dimension of spring (A)

11.12b Make sure locating peg (arrowed) aligns with the rear axle

c) Use new retaining nuts on the spring-to-axle U-bolts and the spring mounting bolts.

d) Tighten all nuts and bolts to the specified torque, noting that the mounting bolt nuts must not be fully tightened until after the vehicle is lowered to the ground.

12 Rear shock absorber – removal and refitting

Note: *The upper mounting bolts can become seized in the chassis and may break, it is recommended that new bolts/nuts be used on refitting.*

Removal

1 Chock the front wheels then jack up the rear of the vehicle and securely support it on axle stands (see *Jacking and vehicle support*).

12.4 ... and upper mounting bolt

12.5c ... slide off the lever ...

2 Support the rear axle with a trolley jack.
3 Undo the retaining nut, and withdraw the shock absorber lower mounting bolt **(see illustration)**.
4 On the right-hand rear shock absorber, unscrew the upper mounting bolt and remove the shock absorber **(see illustration)**.
5 On the left-hand rear shock absorber, release the securing clip, unhook the return spring and remove the load sensing lever from the shock absorber upper mounting bolt **(see illustrations)**. Then unscrew the upper mounting bolt and remove the shock absorber.
6 To test the shock absorber for efficiency, grip the upper or lower mounting eye in a vice, and then pump the piston repeatedly through its full stroke. If the resistance is weak or is felt to be uneven, the shock absorber is defective and must be renewed. It must also be renewed if it is leaking fluid. It is advisable to renew both rear shock absorbers at the same time, or the handling characteristics of the vehicle could be adversely affected.

Refitting

7 Refitting is a reversal of removal. Ensure that the mounting bolts are tightened to the specified torque.

13 Rear anti-roll bar and link arms – removal, overhaul and refitting

Note: *A Mercedes-Benz special tool (601 589 04 43 00) is required, or a tapered sleeve manufactured to aid refitting.*

12.5a Release the securing clip ...

12.5d ... and remove the upper mounting bolt

12.3 Undo the lower mounting bolt ...

Removal

1 Firmly apply the handbrake, and then jack up the rear of the vehicle and support it securely on axle stands (see *Jacking and vehicle support*). Remove both the rear roadwheels.
2 Unscrew the nut and bolt from each side and detach the anti-roll bar connecting links from the vehicle chassis **(see illustration)**.
3 Undo the mounting bolts (two bolts each side) and release the anti-roll bar clamps from the rear axle **(see illustration)**. Note the fitted position of the handbrake cable support brackets on the lower bolts for refitting.
4 Manoeuvre the anti-roll bar out from under the rear of the vehicle, releasing it from the handbrake cables. Take care not to stretch or damage the cables as the anti-roll bar is withdrawn.

12.5b ... unhook the return spring ...

13.2 Disconnect the anti-roll bar connecting links from the chassis

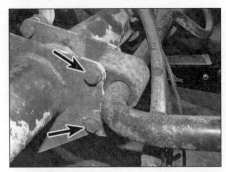

13.3 Rear anti-roll bar clamp retaining bolts

13.6 Disconnect the connecting links from the anti-roll bar

13.7 Using a threaded rod, washers and a socket to remove the bush

13.8 Fitting the new bush using a tapered sleeve to guide the bush into place

13.9a Undo the retaining bolts . . .

Overhaul

5 With the anti-roll bar removed, check the condition of the mounting bushes and renew as necessary.

6 To remove the link arms from the end of the anti-roll bar, undo the nut and bolt at each end of the anti-roll bar **(see illustration)**.

7 If new bushes are required, remove the old bushes by using a threaded rod, washers and a length of tube (large socket) to fit over the end of the eye. Tighten the nuts on the threaded rod to push the bush out from the anti-roll bar/link arms **(see illustration)**.

8 To fit new bushes, lubricate the bushes with oil, and then pull them into position using threaded rod, nuts and washers **(see illustration)**. To make this easier, a tapered sleeve can be used to allow the bush to be drawn into the eye on the end of the bar. A Mercedes-Benz special tool (601 589 04 43 00) is available, if required.

9 To fit new clamp bushes to the anti-roll bar, undo the two retaining bolts/nuts and remove the flat plate, then remove the clamp from around the rubber bush. The rubber bush can then be removed from the anti-roll bar **(see illustrations)**. Clean the rubber bush locating area on the anti-roll bar and remove any burrs. Fit the new bush in place around the anti-roll bar, and fit the clamp back in position.

Refitting

10 Refitting is a reversal of removal, tightening all fastenings to the specified torque.

13.9b . . . remove the flat plate . . .

13.9c . . . and clamping plate . . .

13.9d . . . then the rubber bush

14.3 Unscrew the retaining bolt securing the steering wheel to the column

14 Steering wheel – removal and refitting

> **Warning: Make sure that the airbag safety recommendations given in Chapter 12 are followed, to prevent personal injury.**

Removal

1 Working at the back of the steering wheel, undo the two retaining screws holding the airbag/cover in position on the steering wheel centre. Turn the steering from side to side to access the retaining screws at the rear of the steering wheel. On models with airbags, refer to procedures in Chapter 12.

2 Set the front wheels in the straight-ahead position, and then remove the ignition key to lock the column in position.

3 Unscrew the Allen bolt securing the steering wheel to the column **(see illustration)**.

4 Check that there are alignment marks between the steering column shaft and steering wheel. If no marks are visible, suitably mark the wheel and column shaft with quick-drying paint to ensure correct alignment when refitting **(see illustration)**.

14.4 If no alignment marks are visible, mark wheel and column shaft with quick-drying paint

14.7 Fit new bolt to the steering wheel

5 Refit the Allen bolt a couple of threads and then grip the steering wheel with both hands and carefully rock it from side-to-side to release it from the splines on the steering column. When released from the splines, remove the Allen bolt fully. As the steering wheel is being removed, guide any wiring (where applicable) through the aperture in the wheel, taking care not to damage the wiring connectors.

Refitting

6 Refit the steering wheel, aligning the marks made prior to removal. Where applicable, route the wiring connectors through the steering wheel aperture. **Note:** *Make sure the airbag/horn wiring is routed correctly. If necessary, refer to the procedures contained in Chapter 12.*

7 Clean the threads in the steering column, then fit the new Allen bolt **(see illustration)**, and tighten to the specified torque.
8 Release the steering lock, and refit the airbag as described in Chapter 12.

15 Ignition switch/ steering column lock – removal and refitting

Removal

1 Disconnect the battery negative terminal (refer to *Disconnecting the battery* in the Reference Chapter).
2 Remove the steering column shrouds as described in Chapter 11.

3 Remove the ignition key and unclip the plastic transponder coil from the top of the ignition barrel. If required, trace the wiring and disconnect the wiring connector to completely remove.
4 Insert the ignition key into the ignition switch/lock, and turn it to the first detent position **(see illustration)**.
5 Turn the ignition barrel cap a quarter of a turn anti-clockwise and then withdraw the ignition switch from the lock cylinder housing **(see illustrations)**. Note the fitted position of the barrel to the housing for refitting.
6 If required, using two thin screwdrivers, release the retaining clips and remove the ignition switch wiring connector from the rear of the ignition switch housing **(see illustrations)**.

15.4 Turn key to the first position

15.5a Turn the ignition barrel cap anti-clockwise . . .

15.5b . . . and remove the switch

15.6a Release the two retaining clips (arrowed) . . .

15.6b . . . using thin screwdrivers . . .

15.6c . . . and withdraw the wiring connector

15.9a Locate the locking plunger (arrowed) . . .

15.9b . . . into the recess in the ignition switch cap

16.4 Unclip the return spring from the mounting bracket

16.5 Undo the steering column lower joint securing bolt

7 To remove the lock housing from the steering column, first remove the combination switch from the top of the steering column as described in Chapter 12, Section 4.

8 Use a hammer and chisel to release the

'shear' bolts from the lock housing. Discard the bolts, as new ones will be required for refitting.

Refitting

9 Refitting is a reversal of removal. Making sure the locking plunger on the side of the housing locates correctly with the recess inside the ignition barrel cap (see illustrations).

10 Fit new special 'shear' bolts to the steering lock housing on refitting.

---

16 Steering column – removal and refitting

Removal

1 Remove the steering wheel, as described in Section 14.

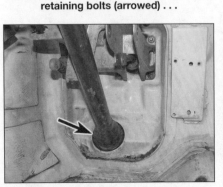

16.6a Remove the steering column upper retaining bolts (arrowed) . . .

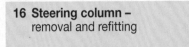

17.4 Anti-roll bar clamp retaining bolt

2 Remove the steering column shrouds and trim panels, as described in Chapter 11.

3 Remove the central fuse box from under the steering column, clock spring/angle sensor and combination switches, as described in Chapter 12.

4 Unclip the brake pedal return spring from the steering column mounting bracket (see illustration).

5 Working inside the engine compartment, undo the pinch-bolt securing the steering column to the steering rack (see illustration). Note the fitted position, by marking the universal joint and steering rack pinion, and then slide the universal joint from the steering rack pinion. Note that a new pinch-bolt will be required for refitting.

6 Working inside the vehicle, undo the two steering column mounting bolts and remove the column from vehicle, withdrawing the rubber gaiter from the floor panel (see illustrations).

Refitting

7 Refitting is a reversal of removal, but note the following additional points:

 a) Ensure that both the steering column and roadwheels are centralised when refitting the universal joint to the rack pinion in the position noted on removal secure with a new pinch-bolt.

 b) Tighten all fastenings to the specified torque.

 c) Refit the steering wheel as described in Section 15.

 d) Refit the steering column shrouds and trim panels as described in Chapter 11.

 e) Refit the fusebox, clock spring/angle sensor and switches as described in Chapter 12.

 f) Ensure that all wiring is securely connected and correctly routed.

---

17 Steering gear – removal and refitting

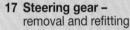

Removal

1 Disconnect the battery negative terminal (refer to Disconnecting the battery in the Reference Chapter).

2 Set the front wheels in the straight-ahead position, and then remove the ignition key to lock the column in position.

3 Firmly apply the handbrake, and then jack up the front of the vehicle and support it securely on axle stands (see Jacking and vehicle support). Remove both front roadwheels.

4 Undo the two bolts (one at each side) securing the anti-roll bar clamps to the subframe (see illustration). Move the anti-roll bar down to allow easier removal of the steering gear.

5 Slacken the track rod end balljoint nut several turns, then use a balljoint separator

16.6b . . . and withdraw the column from the lower rubber mounting (arrowed)

17.5 Using the separator tool to release the balljoint taper

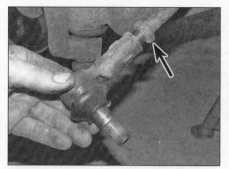

17.6 Slacken the locknut (arrowed), and then count the number of turns

17.8 Disconnect the fluid pipes from the steering rack

tool to release the balljoint shank from the steering arm. With the balljoint released, unscrew the nut and disconnect the balljoint from the steering arm on both sides **(see illustration)**. Discard the nut, as a new one must be used for refitting.

6 On the driver's side, slacken the locknut and remove the track rod end from the tie rod **(see illustration)**.

7 Using a trolley jack, support the engine and remove the right-hand engine mounting.

8 Thoroughly clean the area around the fluid pipe connections on the steering gear **(see illustration)**. Place a suitable container beneath the steering gear, then unscrew the retaining nuts and withdraw the pipes from the pinion housing. Allow the fluid to drain into the container as the pipes are released. Cover the pipe ends and steering gear orifices after disconnection, to prevent the ingress of foreign matter.

9 Undo the lower pinch-bolt securing the steering column universal joint to the steering gear pinion shaft **(see illustration)**. Note the fitted position by marking the universal joint and steering rack pinion, and then slide the universal joint from the steering rack pinion. Note that a new pinch-bolt will be required for refitting.

10 Undo the four bolts securing the steering gear to the front subframe **(see illustration)**, noting the position of the hose retaining bracket on the upper left-hand mounting bolt. Discard the mounting bolts, as a new ones must be used for refitting.

11 Move the steering gear to the right and

17.9 Undo the steering column lower joint securing bolt

swivel the steering housing forwards, then manoeuvre the steering gear out through the front of the vehicle.

Refitting

12 Refitting is a reversal of removal, but note the following additional points:
a) *Ensure that both the steering wheel and steering gear are centralised when refitting the intermediate shaft flexible coupling to the steering gear pinion.*
b) *If a new steering gear unit is being fitted, the straight-ahead position can be ascertained by halving the number of turns necessary to move the rack from lock-to-lock.*
c) *Use new bolts for the steering gear, universal joint pinch-bolt and track rod end balljoints.*
d) *Tighten all fastenings to the specified torque.*

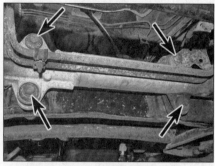

17.10 Undo the power steering rack mounting bolts

e) *Fill and bleed the power steering hydraulic system as described in Section 22.*
f) *Have the front wheel alignment checked and adjusted at the earliest opportunity.*

18 Steering gear rubber gaiters – renewal

1 Remove the track rod end as described in Section 19.

2 Note the position of the track rod end locknut by counting the number of threads from the nut face to the end of the track rod. Record this figure, then unscrew and remove the locknut **(see illustration)**.

3 Remove the clips, and slide the gaiter from the track rod and steering gear housing **(see illustrations)**.

4 Slide the new gaiter over the track rod,

18.2 Remove the locking nut from the track rod

18.3a Remove the inner . . .

18.3b . . . and outer securing clip . . .

18.3c . . . and withdraw the gaiter from the steering rack

18.4 Slide the new gaiter into place . . .

18.5 . . . and secure in place with new retaining clips

and onto the steering gear. Where applicable, make sure that the gaiter locates in the cut-outs provided in the track rod and steering gear housing **(see illustration)**.

5 Fit and tighten the clips, ensuring that the gaiter is not twisted **(see illustration)**.

6 Screw the track rod end locknut onto the track rod, and position it with the exact number of threads exposed as noted during removal.

7 Refit the track rod end as described in Section 19.

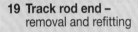

19 Track rod end – removal and refitting

Removal

1 Firmly apply the handbrake, and then jack up the front of the vehicle and support

it securely on axle stands (see *Jacking and vehicle support*). Remove the relevant front roadwheel.

2 Loosen the track rod end securing locknut on the track rod a quarter turn, while holding the track rod stationary with a second spanner on the flats provided **(see illustration)**. If necessary, use a wire brush to remove rust from the nut and threads and lubricate the threads with penetrating oil before unscrewing the nut. As an additional check, measure the visible amount of threads on the track rod using vernier calipers. This will ensure the track rod end is refitted in the same position.

3 Slacken the track rod end balljoint nut several turns, then use a balljoint separator tool to release the balljoint shank from the steering arm **(see illustration)**. With the balljoint released, unscrew the nut and disconnect the balljoint from the steering arm.

Discard the nut, as a new one must be used for refitting.

4 Unscrew the track rod end from the track rod, counting the number of turns necessary to remove it and taking care not to disturb the locknut **(see illustration)**.

Refitting

5 Screw the new track rod end onto the track rod the exact number of turns as noted during removal.

6 Engage the track rod end balljoint shank in the steering arm, and screw on the new retaining nut. Tighten the nut to the specified torque. If the shank of the balljoint turns, use an Allen key to hold it still while tightening the securing nut **(see illustration)**.

7 Tighten the track rod end locknut.

8 Refit the roadwheel, then lower the vehicle to the ground, and tighten the roadwheel nuts to the specified torque.

9 Have the front wheel alignment checked and adjusted at the earliest opportunity.

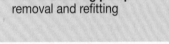

20 Power steering pump – removal and refitting

Removal

1 Open the bonnet and siphon off as much of the power steering fluid from the reservoir as possible, taking care not to introduce dirt into the system.

2 Working as described in Chapter 1, release the drivebelt tension and unhook the drivebelt

19.2 Track rod end securing locknut (arrowed)

19.3a Using the separator tool . . .

19.3b . . . to release the balljoint taper

19.4 Unscrew the track rod end, noting the number of turns

19.6 Using an Allen key to prevent the balljoint shaft from turning

from the pump pulley. If the power steering pump pulley requires removal, slacken the retaining bolts prior to releasing the tension on the belt **(see illustration)**.

3 Be prepared for fluid spillage, and position a suitable container beneath the fluid pipes and hoses before removing. When removed, plug the pipe/hose ends and steering pump/reservoir orifices, to prevent fluid leakage and to keep dirt out of the hydraulic system.

4 Wipe clean the area around the pump union, undo the securing nut and disconnect the high-pressure pipe from the pump (see illustration). Discard the sealing ring from the high-pressure pipe, as new one will be required for refitting.

5 On 2.2 litre models slacken the retaining clip and disconnect the return hose from the bottom of the fluid **reservoir.**

6 On 2.9 litre models, undo the securing nut and disconnect the fluid return pipe from the fluid reservoir.

7 Slacken and remove the power steering pump mounting bolts, and remove the pump assembly from the engine compartment **(see illustrations)**.

Refitting

8 If the power steering pump is faulty, seek the advice of your Mercedes-Benz dealer as to the availability of spare parts. If spares are available, it may be possible to have the pump overhauled by a suitable specialist or alternately obtain an exchange unit. If not, the pump must be renewed.

9 Refit the pump and tighten the mounting bolts to the specified torque.

10 Reconnect the high-pressure pipe and return hose/pipe, tightening the union nuts to the specified torque. Use new sealing rings, where applicable.

11 If removed, refit the pulley to the power steering pump, making sure it is fitted the correct way round and tighten the retaining bolts to the specified torque.

12 Fit the drivebelt and tension as described in Chapter 1.

13 On completion, refill the reservoir and bleed the hydraulic system as described in Section 22.

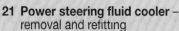

21 Power steering fluid cooler – removal and refitting

Removal

1 The power steering fluid cooler is a loop of metal pipe that is located above the intercooler, in front of the radiator **(see illustration)**.

2 Undo the retaining screws and remove the front grille, with reference to Chapter 11.

3 On models from Feb. 2000, undo the retaining bolts and remove the front cross-member from above the radiator **(see illustration)**.

20.2 Remove the auxiliary drivebelt from the pulley

20.7a Undo the power steering pump . . .

4 Position a suitable container beneath the fluid cooler, and then clamp the two fluid hoses on the left-hand side of the cooler. Use brake hose clamps or similar tools to clamp the hoses, taking care not to damage them.

5 Release the retaining clips and disconnect the fluid hoses from the cooler pipe **(see**

21.1 Power steering fluid cooler, in front of radiator

21.5 Disconnect the power steering fluid pipes

20.4 Disconnect the high-pressure pipe (arrowed) from the pump

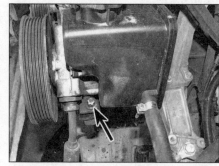

20.7b . . . mounting bolts (arrowed)

illustration). Allow the surplus fluid to drain into the container. Cover the hose ends and fluid cooler orifices after disconnection to prevent the ingress of foreign matter.

6 Undo the fluid cooler pipe retaining clamp screws and manoeuvre the cooler pipes out from its location **(see illustrations)**.

21.3 Remove the front crossmember

21.6a Undo the fluid cooler . . .

21.6b . . . securing clip screws

Refitting

7 Refitting is a reversal of removal. On completion, fill and bleed the power steering hydraulic system as described in Section 22.

22 Power steering hydraulic system – bleeding

1 This will normally only be required if any part of the hydraulic system has been disconnected.

2 Referring to *Weekly checks*, remove the fluid reservoir filler cap, and top-up with the specified fluid to the maximum level mark.

3 Firmly apply the handbrake, and then jack up the front of the vehicle and support it securely on axle stands (see *Jacking and vehicle support*).

4 With the engine switched off, slowly turn the steering wheel from lock-to-lock several times, adding fluid to the reservoir as necessary. Continue turning the steering wheel from lock-to-lock until the fluid level in the reservoir stops dropping. Do not hold the wheel on either lock, as this imposes strain on the hydraulic system.

5 Start the engine and allow it to idle, then slowly turn the steering wheel from lock-to-lock several times, adding fluid to the reservoir as necessary. Continue turning the steering wheel from lock-to-lock until the fluid level in the reservoir stops dropping. Do not hold the wheel on either lock, as this imposes strain on the hydraulic system.

6 Stop the engine, lower the vehicle to the ground and recheck the fluid level. Top-up the fluid if necessary.

23 Wheel alignment and steering angles – general information

Definitions

1 A vehicle's steering and suspension geometry is defined in four basic settings **(see illustration)** – all angles are expressed in degrees (toe settings are also expressed as a measurement); the steering axis is defined as an imaginary line drawn through the axis of the suspension strut, extended where necessary to contact the ground.

2 Camber is the angle between each roadwheel and a vertical line drawn through its centre and tyre contact patch, when viewed from the front or rear of the vehicle. Positive camber is when the roadwheels are tilted outwards from the vertical at the top; negative camber is when they are tilted inwards. The camber angle is not adjustable.

3 Castor is the angle between the steering axis and a vertical line drawn through each roadwheel's centre and tyre contact patch, when viewed from the side of the vehicle. Positive castor is when the steering axis is tilted so that it contacts the ground ahead of the vertical; negative castor is when it contacts the ground behind the vertical. The castor angle is not adjustable.

4 Toe is the difference, viewed from above, between lines drawn through the roadwheel centres and the vehicle's centre-line. 'Toe-in' is when the roadwheels point inwards, towards each other at the front, while 'toe-out' is when they splay outwards from each other at the front.

5 The front wheel toe setting is adjusted by screwing the track rod in or out of its track rod ends, to alter the effective length of the track rod assembly.

6 Rear wheel toe setting is not adjustable.

Checking and adjustment

7 Due to the special measuring equipment necessary to check the wheel alignment and steering angles, and the skill required to use it properly, the checking and adjustment of these settings is best left to a Mercedes-Benz dealer or similar expert. Note that most tyre-fitting shops now possess sophisticated checking equipment.

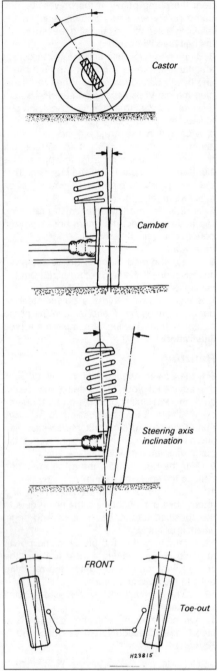

23.1 Wheel alignment and steering angles

Chapter 11
Bodywork and fittings

Contents

Degrees of difficulty

Easy, suitable for novice with little experience	**Fairly easy,** suitable for beginner with some experience	**Fairly difficult,** suitable for competent DIY mechanic	**Difficult,** suitable for experienced DIY mechanic	**Very difficult,** suitable for expert DIY or professional

Specifications

Torque wrench settings	Nm	lbf ft
Bonnet hinge retaining nuts	23	17
Door check strap to A-pillar:		
M6 bolts	10	7
M8 bolts	35	26
Door check strap to door	10	7
Door lock securing Torx screws*	10	7
Seat belt height adjuster:		
Upper bolt.	35	26
Lower bolt.	23	17
Seat belt/inertia reel mounting bolts	35	26
Seat retaining bolts	25	18

* Use new fasteners

1 General information

The body and chassis on all versions of the Sprinter is of all-steel construction. Three basic chassis types are available: short-wheelbase, medium-wheelbase and long-wheelbase models.

The three main body types are Van, Bus and Chassis Cab. Twin opening rear doors and side opening door(s) are available. The bodyshell is as aerodynamic in shape as possible, to promote economy and reduce wind noise levels.

Extensive use is made of plastic materials, mainly on the interior, but also in exterior components. The front and rear bumpers are injection-moulded from a synthetic material, which is very strong and yet light. Plastic components such as wheel arch liners are fitted to the underside of the vehicle, to improve the body's resistance to corrosion.

Due to the large number of specialist applications of this vehicle range, information contained in this Chapter is given on parts found to be common on the popular factory-produced versions. No information is provided on special body versions.

2 Maintenance –
bodywork and underframe

The general condition of a vehicle's bodywork is the one thing that significantly affects its value. Maintenance is easy, but needs to be regular. Neglect, particularly after minor damage, can lead quickly to further deterioration and costly repair bills. It is important also to keep watch on those parts of the vehicle not immediately visible, for instance the underside, inside all the wheel arches, and the lower part of the engine compartment.

The basic maintenance routine for the bodywork is washing – preferably with a lot of water, from a hose. This will remove all the loose solids, which may have stuck to the vehicle. It is important to flush these off in such a way as to prevent grit from scratching the finish. The wheel arches and underframe need washing in the same way, to remove any accumulated mud, which will retain moisture and tend to encourage rust. Paradoxically enough, the best time to clean the underframe and wheel arches is in wet weather, when the mud is thoroughly wet and soft. In very wet weather, the underframe is usually cleaned of large accumulations automatically, and this is a good time for inspection.

Periodically, except on vehicles with a wax-based underbody protective coating, it is a good idea to have the whole of the underframe of the vehicle steam-cleaned, engine compartment included, so that a thorough inspection can be carried out to see what minor repairs and renovations are necessary. Steam cleaning is available at many garages, and is necessary for the removal of the accumulation of oily grime, which sometimes is allowed to become thick in certain areas. If steam-cleaning facilities are not available, there are some excellent grease solvents available which can be brush-applied; the dirt can then be simply hosed off. Note that these methods should not be used on vehicles with wax-based underbody protective coating, or the coating will be removed. Such vehicles should be inspected annually, preferably just prior to winter, when the underbody should be washed down, and any damage to the wax coating repaired. Ideally, a completely fresh coat should be applied. It would also be worth considering the use of such wax-based protection for injection into door panels, sills, box sections, etc, as an additional safeguard against rust damage, where such protection is not provided by the vehicle manufacturer.

After washing paintwork, wipe off with a chamois leather to give an unspotted clear finish. A coat of clear protective wax polish will give added protection against chemical pollutants in the air. If the paintwork sheen has dulled or oxidised, use a cleaner/polisher combination to restore the brilliance of the shine. This requires a little effort, but such dulling is usually caused because regular washing has been neglected. Care needs to be taken with metallic paintwork, as special non-abrasive cleaner/polisher is required to avoid damage to the finish. Always check that the door and ventilator opening drain holes and pipes are completely clear, so that water can be drained out. Brightwork should be treated in the same way as paintwork. Windscreens and windows can be kept clear of the smeary film, which often appears, by the use of proprietary glass cleaner. Never use any form of wax or other body or chromium polish on glass.

3 Maintenance –
upholstery and carpets

Mats and carpets should be brushed or vacuum-cleaned regularly, to keep them free of grit. If they are badly stained, remove them from the vehicle for scrubbing or sponging, and make quite sure they are dry before refitting. Seats and interior trim panels can be kept clean by wiping with a damp cloth. If they do become stained (which can be more apparent on light-coloured upholstery), use a little liquid detergent and a soft nail brush to scour the grime out of the grain of the material. Do not forget to keep the headlining clean in the same way as the upholstery. When using liquid cleaners inside the vehicle, do not over-wet the surfaces being cleaned. Excessive damp could get into the seams and padded interior, causing stains, offensive odours or even rot.

4 Minor body damage –
repair

Minor scratches

If the scratch is very superficial, and does not penetrate to the metal of the bodywork, repair is very simple. Lightly rub the area of the scratch with a paintwork renovator, or a very fine cutting paste, to remove loose paint from the scratch, and to clear the surrounding bodywork of wax polish. Rinse the area with clean water.

Apply touch-up paint to the scratch using a fine paintbrush; continue to apply fine layers of paint until the surface of the paint in the scratch is level with the surrounding paintwork. Allow the new paint at least two weeks to harden, and then blend it into the surrounding paintwork by rubbing the scratch area with a paintwork renovator or a very fine cutting paste. Finally, apply wax polish.

Where the scratch has penetrated right through to the metal of the bodywork, causing the metal to rust, a different repair technique is required. Remove any loose rust from the bottom of the scratch with a penknife, and then apply rust-inhibiting paint to prevent the formation of rust in the future. Using a rubber or nylon applicator, fill the scratch with bodystopper paste. If required, this paste can be mixed with cellulose thinners to provide a very thin paste that is ideal for filling narrow scratches. Before the stopper-paste in the scratch hardens, wrap a piece of smooth cotton rag around the top of a finger. Dip the finger in cellulose thinners, and quickly sweep it across the surface of the stopper-paste in the scratch; this will ensure that the surface of the stopper-paste is slightly hollowed. The scratch can now be painted over as described earlier in this Section.

Dents

When deep denting of the vehicle's bodywork has taken place, the first task is to pull the dent out, until the affected bodywork almost attains its original shape. There is little point in trying to restore the original shape completely, as the metal in the damaged area will have stretched on impact, and cannot be reshaped fully to its original contour. It is better to bring the level of the dent up to a point, which is about 3 mm below the level of the surrounding bodywork. In cases where the dent is very shallow anyway, it is not worth trying to pull it out at all. If the underside of the dent is accessible, it can be hammered out gently from behind, using a mallet with a wooden or plastic head. Whilst doing this, hold a suitable block of wood firmly against the outside of the panel, to absorb the impact from the hammer blows and thus prevent a large area of the bodywork from being 'belled-out'.

Should the dent be in a section of the

bodywork that has a double skin, or some other factor making it inaccessible from behind, a different technique is called for. Drill several small holes through the metal inside the area – particularly in the deeper section. Then screw long self-tapping screws into the holes, just sufficiently for them to gain a good purchase in the metal. Now the dent can be pulled out by pulling on the protruding heads of the screws with a pair of pliers.

The next stage of the repair is the removal of the paint from the damaged area, and from an inch or so of the surrounding 'sound' bodywork. This is accomplished most easily by using a wire brush or abrasive pad on a power drill, although it can be done just as effectively by hand, using sheets of abrasive paper. To complete the preparation for filling, score the surface of the bare metal with a screwdriver or the tang of a file, or alternatively, drill small holes in the affected area. This will provide a really good 'key' for the filler paste.

To complete the repair, see the Section on filling and respraying.

Rust holes or gashes

Remove all paint from the affected area, and from an inch or so of the surrounding 'sound' bodywork, using an abrasive pad or a wire brush on a power drill. If these are not available, a few sheets of abrasive paper will do the job most effectively. With the paint removed, you will be able to judge the severity of the corrosion, and therefore decide whether to renew the whole panel (if this is possible) or to repair the affected area. New body panels are not as expensive as most people think, and it is often quicker and more satisfactory to fit a new panel than to attempt to repair large areas of corrosion.

Remove all fittings from the affected area, except those, which will act as a guide to the original shape of the damaged bodywork (e.g. headlight shells etc). Then, using tin snips or a hacksaw blade, remove all loose metal and any other metal badly affected by corrosion. Hammer the edges of the hole inwards, in order to create a slight depression for the filler paste.

Wire-brush the affected area to remove the powdery rust from the surface of the remaining metal. Paint the affected area with rust-inhibiting paint, if the back of the rusted area is accessible, treat this also.

Before filling can take place, it will be necessary to block the hole in some way. This can be achieved by the use of aluminium or plastic mesh, or aluminium tape.

Aluminium or plastic mesh, or glass-fibre matting, is probably the best material to use for a large hole. Cut a piece to the approximate size and shape of the hole to be filled, then position it in the hole so that its edges are below the level of the surrounding bodywork. It can be retained in position by several blobs of filler paste around its periphery.

Aluminium tape should be used for small or very narrow holes. Pull a piece off the roll, trim it to the approximate size and shape required, then pull off the backing paper (if used) and stick the tape over the hole; it can be overlapped if the thickness of one piece is insufficient. Burnish down the edges of the tape with the handle of a screwdriver or similar, to ensure that the tape is securely attached to the metal underneath.

Filling and respraying

Before using this Section, see the Sections on dent, deep scratch, rust holes and gash repairs.

Many types of bodyfiller are available, but generally speaking, those proprietary kits, which contain a tin of filler paste and a tube of resin hardener, are best for this type of repair. A wide, flexible plastic or nylon applicator will be found invaluable for imparting a smooth and well-contoured finish to the surface of the filler.

Mix up a little filler on a clean piece of card or board – measure the hardener carefully (follow the maker's instructions on the pack), otherwise the filler will set too rapidly or too slowly. Using the applicator, apply the filler paste to the prepared area; draw the applicator across the surface of the filler to achieve the correct contour and to level the surface. As soon as a contour that approximates to the correct one is achieved, stop working the paste – if you carry on too long, the paste will become sticky and begin to 'pick-up' on the applicator. Continue to add thin layers of filler paste at 20-minute intervals, until the level of the filler is just proud of the surrounding bodywork.

Once the filler has hardened, the excess can be removed using a metal plane or file. From then on, progressively finer grades of abrasive paper should be used, starting with a 40-grade production paper, and finishing with a 400-grade wet-and-dry paper. Always wrap the abrasive paper around a flat rubber, cork, or wooden block – otherwise the surface of the filler will not be completely flat. During the smoothing of the filler surface, the wet-and-dry paper should be periodically rinsed in water. This will ensure that a very smooth finish is imparted to the filler at the final stage.

At this stage, the 'dent' should be surrounded by a ring of bare metal, which in turn should be encircled by the finely 'feathered' edge of the good paintwork. Rinse the repair area with clean water, until all of the dust produced by the rubbing-down operation has gone.

Spray the whole area with a light coat of primer – this will show up any imperfections in the surface of the filler. Repair these imperfections with fresh filler paste or bodystopper, and once more smooth the surface with abrasive paper. Repeat this spray-and-repair procedure until you are satisfied that the surface of the filler, and the feathered edge of the paintwork, are perfect. Clean the repair area with clean water, and allow to dry fully.

The repair area is now ready for final spraying. Paint spraying must be carried out in a warm, dry, windless and dust-free atmosphere. This condition can be created artificially if you have access to a large indoor working area, but if you are forced to work in the open, you will have to pick your day very carefully. If you are working indoors, dousing the floor in the work area with water will help to settle the dust that would otherwise be in the atmosphere. If the repair area is confined to one body panel, mask off the surrounding panels; this will help to minimise the effects of a slight mis-match in paint colours. Bodywork fittings (e.g. chrome strips, door handles etc) will also need to be masked off. Use genuine masking tape, and several thicknesses of newspaper, for the masking operations.

Before commencing to spray, agitate the aerosol can thoroughly, and then spray a test area (an old tin, or similar) until the technique is mastered. Cover the repair area with a thick coat of primer; the thickness should be built up using several thin layers of paint, rather than one thick one. Using 400-grade wet-and-dry paper, rub down the surface of the primer until it is really smooth. While doing this, the work area should be thoroughly doused with water, and the wet-and-dry paper periodically rinsed in water. Allow to dry before spraying on more paint.

Spray on the topcoat, again building up the thickness by using several thin layers of paint. Start spraying at one edge of the repair area, and then, using a side-to-side motion, work until the whole repair area and about 2 inches of the surrounding original paintwork is covered. Remove all masking material 10 to 15 minutes after spraying on the final coat of paint.

Allow the new paint at least two weeks to harden, then, using a paintwork renovator, or a very fine cutting paste, blend the edges of the paint into the existing paintwork. Finally, apply wax polish.

Plastic components

With the use of more and more plastic body components by the vehicle manufacturers (e.g. bumpers. spoilers, and in some cases major body panels), rectification of more serious damage to such items has become a matter of either entrusting repair work to a specialist in this field, or renewing complete components. Repair of such damage by the DIY owner is not really feasible, owing to the cost of the equipment and materials required for effecting such repairs. The basic technique involves making a groove along the line of the crack in the plastic, using a rotary burr in a power drill. The damaged part is then welded back together, using a hot-air gun to heat up and fuse a plastic filler rod into the groove. Any excess plastic is then removed, and the area rubbed down to a smooth finish. It is important that a filler rod of the correct plastic is used, as body components can be made of a variety of different types (e.g. polycarbonate, ABS, polypropylene).

Damage of a less serious nature (abrasions, minor cracks etc) can be repaired by the DIY

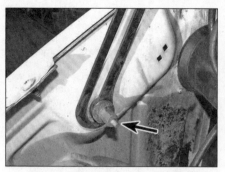

6.2 Bonnet stay securing nut/bolt

7.2 Bonnet lock retaining bolts (arrowed)

7.3 Disconnect the bonnet release cable

owner using a two-part epoxy filler repair material. Once mixed in equal proportions, this is used in similar fashion to the bodywork filler used on metal panels. The filler is usually cured in twenty to thirty minutes, ready for sanding and painting.

If the owner is renewing a complete component himself, or if he has repaired it with epoxy filler, he will be left with the problem of finding a suitable paint for finishing which is compatible with the type of plastic used. At one time, the use of a universal paint was not possible, owing to the complex range of plastics encountered in body component applications. Standard paints, generally speaking, will not bond to plastic or rubber satisfactorily. However, it is now possible to obtain a plastic body parts finishing kit, which consists of a pre-primer treatment, a primer and coloured topcoat. Full instructions are normally supplied with a kit, but basically, the method of use is to first apply the pre-primer to the component concerned, and allow it to dry for up to 30 minutes. Then the primer is applied, and left to dry for about an hour before finally applying the special-coloured topcoat. The result is a correctly coloured component, where the paint will flex with the plastic or rubber, a property that standard paint does not normally possess.

5 Major body damage – repair

With the exception of Chassis Cab versions, the chassis members are spot-welded to the underbody, and in this respect can be termed of being monocoque or unit construction. Major damage repairs to this type of body combination must of necessity be carried out by body shops with welding and hydraulic straightening facilities.

Extensive damage to the body may distort the chassis, and result in unstable and dangerous handling, as well as excessive wear to tyres and suspension or steering components. It is recommended that checking of the chassis alignment be entrusted to a Mercedes-Benz agent or accident repair specialist with special checking jigs.

6 Bonnet – removal, refitting and adjustment

Removal

1 Open the bonnet, and have an assistant support the bonnet.
2 Undo the securing nut and disconnect the bonnet stay bracket from the inner wing panel **(see illustration)**.
3 Mark around the bonnet hinges, to show the outline of their fitted positions for correct realignment on assembly.
4 With the assistant still supporting the bonnet, unscrew and remove the hinge retaining nuts, and then lift the bonnet clear of the vehicle.

Refitting

5 Refitting is a reversal of removal. Tighten the hinge nuts fully when bonnet alignment is satisfactory. Apply a small amount of grease to the hinges.

Adjustment

6 Adjustment of the bonnet fit is available by loosening the hinges and moving it to the correct position required. Further adjustment can be made by slackening the locknut on the bonnet upper catch, and then realigning it. Also there are rubber bump stops on the bonnet, which can be adjusted. The bonnet requires adjustment to give an even clearance between its outer edges and the surrounding panels. Adjust the front bump stops to align the edges of the bonnet with the front wing panels and grille. When aligned, retighten all the relevant retaining nuts securely.

7 Bonnet lock – removal and refitting

Removal

1 Open the bonnet.
2 Undo the two bolts and withdraw the bonnet lock from the front crossmember **(see illustration)**.
3 Turn the bonnet lock over and disconnect the bonnet release cable from the lock assembly **(see illustration)**.

Refitting

4 Refitting is a reversal of removal.

8 Door trim panels – removal and refitting

Front doors

Removal

1 Release the two locking clips and remove the lower door pocket from the door **(see illustrations)**.
2 On models with manual window regulators, release the securing ring at the rear of the

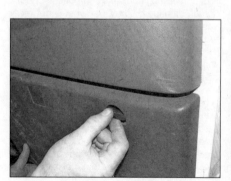

8.1a Rotate the locking clips . . .

8.1b . . . and remove the lower trim panel

handle by pushing it to one side, and then release the handle from the regulator shaft splines **(see illustrations)**.

3 Carefully unclip the plastic cover from the inner panel grab handle **(see illustrations)**.

4 On models with electric windows, unclip the switch trim cover from the top of the grab handle and disconnect the wiring connectors from the switches.

5 Undo the two screws securing the trim panel to the door **(see illustrations)**.

6 Lift the door trim panel upwards and then carefully withdraw the trim panel from the door. If required, use a suitable tool and prise the panel around its outer and lower edges to release it from the door **(see illustrations)**.

7 On later models, unclip the outer cable from the release lever housing and then unhook the inner cable from the release lever **(see illustration)**. The panel can now be completely withdrawn from the door.

8 On early models, undo the three retaining screws and remove the door release lever housing from inside the door trim panel **(see illustration)**. The panel can now be completely withdrawn from the door.

Refitting

9 Refitting is a reversal of removal. On models with manual window regulators, refit the locking ring to the regulator handle, and then push the handle onto the regulator shaft in the position noted on removal.

Rear and sliding doors

Removal

10 Remove the interior handle (where

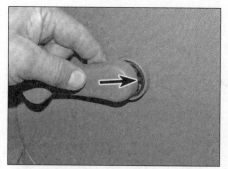
8.2a Slide the securing ring in the direction of the arrow . . .

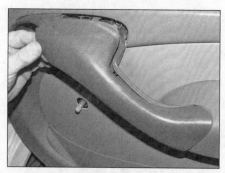
8.3a Unclip the trim cover (models from 2000)

applicable) by lifting up the trim covers and undoing the retaining screws.

11 Where fitted, the trim panels are secured by plastic retaining clips, the removal of which requires the use of a suitable forked tool. These clips are easily broken, so take

8.2b . . . and remove the window winder handle

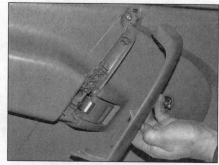
8.3b Unclip the trim cover (models up to 2000)

care when prising them free. Remove the trim panel.

Refitting

12 Refitting is a reversal of removal. Align the panel, and press the clips into position.

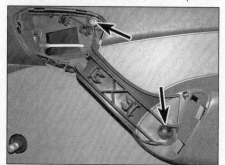
8.5a Undo the retaining screws (models from 2000)

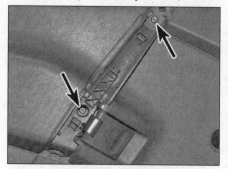
8.5b Undo the retaining screws (models up to 2000)

8.6a Remove the door trim panel . . .

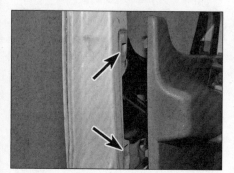
8.6b . . . by lifting it out from the door frame

8.7 Unclip the door operating cable

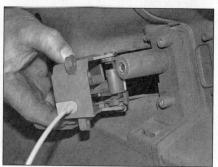
8.8 Remove the release lever housing from the trim panel

9.1 Undo the retaining screw . . .

9.2a . . . pull the handle outwards . . .

9.2b . . . and unclip it from the door panel

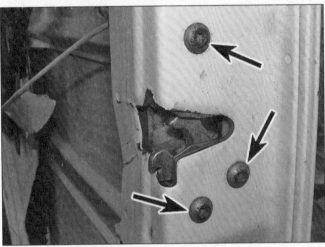

9.10a Undo the retaining screws . . .

9.10b . . . and remove the door lock unit

9 Front door fittings –
removal and refitting

Exterior handle

Removal

1 Open the door and undo the securing screw from the end of the door panel (see illustration).
2 Pull the rear of the handle out from the door and then unhook the front edge of the handle (see illustrations).

Refitting

3 Refitting is a reversal of removal.

Door lock cylinder

Removal

4 Remove the exterior handle as described in paragraphs 1 to 3.
5 Insert the key into the lock cylinder and turn it to the right until it stops.
6 Working through the spring in the back of the lock barrel, push the retaining peg through the slot in the housing and withdraw the lock cylinder and key out from the door handle.

Refitting

7 Refitting is a reversal of removal. Note the lock cylinder will only fit in one position.

Door lock unit

Removal

8 Remove the front door trim panel as described in Section 8.
9 On models with central locking, pull back the rubber grommet between the door and the A-pillar and unplug the wiring connectors. Note the routing of the wiring and the connections for refitting.
10 Undo the three Torx screws and remove the door lock unit, complete with inner door handle release cable from the door (see illustrations). Discard the self-locking screws, as new ones will be required for refitting.
11 Where applicable, extract the retaining

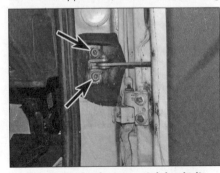

10.3 Door check strap retaining bolts

clips and cut off the cable-ties securing the release cable/wiring harness to the doorframe.

Refitting

12 Refitting is a reversal of removal. When refitting the lock, make sure the lever on the top of the lock unit is positioned behind the outer door handle lever. Fit new self-locking screws to the door lock and tighten to the specified torque setting.

10 Front door –
removal, refitting and adjustment

Removal

1 On models with central locking/electric windows, disconnect the battery negative terminal (refer to Disconnecting the battery in the Reference Chapter).
2 Open the door, and position a suitable padded jack or support blocks underneath the lower part of the door; don't lift the door, just take its weight.
3 Undo the two screws and remove the door check strap bracket from the body pillar (see illustration).
4 On models with central locking/electric windows, pull back the rubber grommet

between the door and the A-pillar and disconnect the wiring connectors. Note the routing of the wiring and the connections for refitting.

5 Unscrew the retaining screws from the upper and lower door hinge pins (see illustrations).

6 With the aid of an assistant, lift the door to release the hinge pins from the hinge bracket, and then remove the door.

Refitting and adjustment

7 Refitting is a reversal of removal. Use thread-lock on the check strap securing bolts. Open and shut the door to ensure that it does not bind with the body aperture at any point. Adjust the door striker plate if necessary (see illustration).

11 Sliding side door fittings – removal and refitting

Exterior handle

Removal

1 Slide the door open, remove the rubber grommet and undo the securing screw from the end of the door panel (see illustration).

2 Pull the front of the handle out from the door and then unhook the rear edge of the handle (see illustrations).

Refitting

3 Refitting is a reversal of removal.

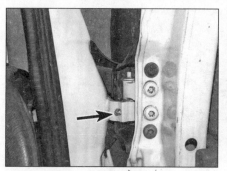
10.5a Undo the upper . . .

Door lock cylinder

Removal

4 Remove the exterior handle as described in paragraphs 1 and 2, and then withdraw the lock housing with the handle (see illustration).

5 Insert the key into the lock cylinder and turn it to the right until it stops.

6 Working through the spring in the back of the lock barrel, push the retaining peg through the slot in the housing and withdraw the lock cylinder and key out from the door handle.

Refitting

7 Refitting is a reversal of removal. Note the lock cylinder will only fit in one position.

Interior release handle and mechanism

Removal

8 Where fitted release the retaining clips and

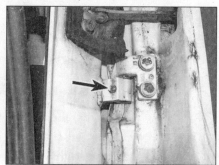
10.5b . . . and lower hinge securing bolts

10.7 Door striker plate securing bolts

remove the door trim panel from the inside of the door.

9 Remove the plastic plug from the handle and undo the securing screw (see illustrations).

10 Pull the release lever back and undo

11.1 Undo the door handle retaining screw

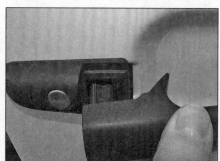
11.2a Pull the handle outwards . . .

11.2b . . . and unclip it from the door panel

11.4 Withdraw the lock housing with the handle

11.9a Remove the plastic cover . . .

11.9b . . . and remove the retaining screw

11.10 Pull handle back and remove retaining screw

11.11 Note the location of the operating lever when removing

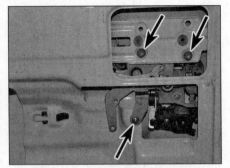

11.12a Undo the retaining screws . . .

11.12b . . . and remove the release mechanism from the door

11.15 Door lock retaining screws

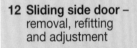

12 Sliding side door – removal, refitting and adjustment

Note: *Before slackening any retaining bolts, make alignment marks on the guide supports to aid alignment when refitting. An assistant will be required to support the weight of the door when removing the sliding brackets, and also to help with removal.*

Removal

1 Undo the retaining screw, and remove the end stop from the centre rail **(see illustration)**. Discard the self-locking screws, as new ones will be required for refitting.
2 Slide the door open, and then mark the position of the lower mounting bracket on the door. Unscrew the bolts securing the door lower guide support **(see illustration)**.
3 Mark the position of the upper mounting bracket on the door. With the aid of an assistant to support the weight of the door on the centre rail, remove the bolts securing the upper guide support **(see illustration)**.
4 Support the door at each end, slide it to the rear of the centre rail **(see illustration)**, and then carefully remove it from the vehicle.
5 To remove the upper carriage from the rail, slide it to the rear of the track and withdraw it from the vehicle **(see illustration)**.
6 To remove the lower carriage from the rail, withdraw the plastic covers from the side step and undo the retaining screws. Unclip the plastic cover from the step and

the retaining screw behind the lever **(see illustration)**.
11 Withdraw the interior handle from the door, noting the fitted position of the operating lever **(see illustration)**.
12 Undo the three retaining screws and withdraw the release mechanism out from the door panel **(see illustrations)**. If required unclip the release cable from the release mechanism.

Refitting

13 Refitting is a reversal of removal.

Door lock unit

Removal

14 Where fitted release the retaining clips and remove the door trim panel from the inside of the door.
15 Slide the door open and undo the three Torx screws from the rear end of the door **(see illustration)**.

16 Working from inside the rear of the vehicle, slide the door forwards, so that it is possible to remove the door lock unit, complete with release cable from the interior release handle, from inside the door aperture. Discard the self-locking screws, as new ones will be required for refitting.
17 On models with central locking, trace the wiring from the lock and then disconnect the wiring block connector. Note the routing of the wiring and the connections for refitting.
18 Where applicable, extract the retaining clips and cut off the cable-ties securing the release cable/wiring harness to the door frame.

Refitting

19 Refitting is a reversal of removal. Fit new self-locking screws to the door lock and tighten to the specified torque setting.

12.1 Remove the centre rail end cap

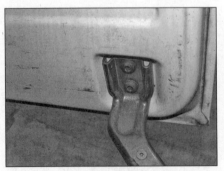

12.2 Lower mounting bracket retaining bolts

12.3 Upper mounting bracket retaining bolts

12.4 Slide the door from the centre rail

12.5 Slide the upper carriage from the top rail

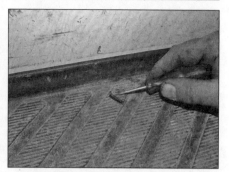

12.6a Remove the plastic covers . . .

12.6b . . . remove the retaining screws . . .

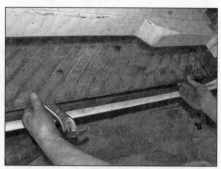

12.6c . . . lift up the plastic step cover . . .

12.6d . . . and slide the lower carriage from the bottom rail

unhook the carriage from the lower track **(see illustrations)**.

Refitting

7 Refitting is a reversal of removal. Align the door and engage it onto the centre track, then reconnect the fittings. Fit new self-locking screw to the end stop on the centre rail. Clean the rails and sliding carriages, and then apply grease to lubricate the rails.

Adjustment

8 To adjust the height, slacken the lower and upper support bolts to reposition the door as required, then tighten them and recheck the fitting.
9 Check the door for satisfactory flush-fitting adjustment. To adjust slacken the screws on the guide wedge on the front edge of the sliding door, adjuster the guide as required, then retighten to secure **(see illustration)**.

10 When fitted, and in the closed position, the door should be aligned flush to the surrounding body, and should close securely. If required, adjust the striker plate position to suit **(see illustration)**.

13 Rear door fittings – removal and refitting

Exterior handle (right-hand door)
Removal
1 Open the door and undo the securing screw from the end of the door panel **(see illustration)**.
2 Pull the rear of the handle out from the door and then unhook the front edge of the handle **(see illustrations 9.2a and 9.2b)**.
Refitting
3 Refitting is a reversal of removal.

Door lock cylinder
Removal
4 Remove the exterior handle as described in paragraphs 1 and 2, and then withdraw the lock housing with the handle **(see illustration 11.4)**.
5 Insert the key into the lock cylinder and turn it to the right until it stops.
6 Working through the spring in the back of the lock barrel, push the retaining peg through the slot in the housing and withdraw the lock cylinder and key out from the door handle.
Refitting
7 Refitting is a reversal of removal. Note the lock cylinder will only fit in one position.

Door lock unit
Removal
8 Where fitted, release the retaining clips and remove the door inner trim panel.

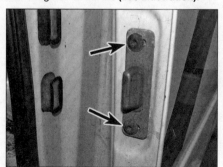

12.9 Door guide wedge securing bolts

12.10 Door striker plate securing bolts

13.1 Exterior handle retaining screw

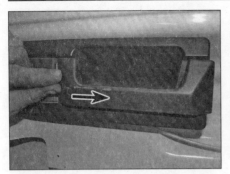

13.12a Slide the trim in the direction of the arrow . . .

13.12b . . . to remove it from the inner handle

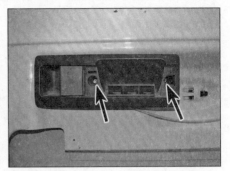

13.13a Undo the two retaining screws . . .

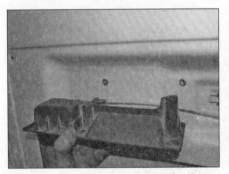

13.13b . . . and remove it from the door

13.16 Clamp a pair of vice grips onto the upper locking rod

9 On models with central locking, trace the wiring from the lock and then disconnect the wiring block connector. Note the routing of the wiring and the connections for refitting.
10 Undo the three Torx screws and remove the door lock unit from inside the door aperture. Disconnect the inner door handle release cable from the lever on the lock unit. Discard the self-locking screws, as new ones will be required for refitting.

Refitting

11 Refitting is a reversal of removal. Fit new self-locking screws to the door lock and tighten to the specified torque setting.

Interior release handle (right-hand door)

Removal

12 Push the handle cover to the side and unclip it from the handle housing (see illustrations).
13 Undo the two securing screws and remove the release handle housing from the door (see illustrations).
14 If required unclip the release cable from the rear of the handle assembly.

Refitting

15 Refitting is a reversal of removal.

Locking rod mechanism (left-hand door)

Removal

16 Open both rear doors and clamp a pair of grips on the upper locking rod on the left-hand door (see illustration).
17 Undo the four retaining screws from the locking rod handle mounting plate and remove it from the end of the door (see illustrations).
18 The upper locking rod can now be withdrawn through the top of the door (see illustration).
19 The lower locking rod can now be withdrawn through the inside of the door aperture (see illustration).

Refitting

20 Refitting is a reversal of removal, making

13.17a Undo the retaining screws . . .

13.17b . . . from the locking rod handle mounting plate

13.18 Withdraw the upper rod through the top of the door

13.19 Withdraw the lower rod through the inside of the door

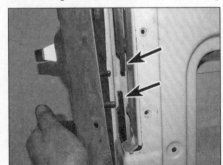

13.20a Locate the two locking rods (arrowed) onto the handle levers

13.20b Make sure the plastic guides are located securely

14.1 Detach the safety check strap from the body

14.3 Hinge-to-door retaining bolts

14.6a Slacken the hinge mounting bolts ...

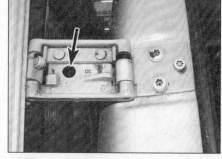

14.6b ... and then adjust through the hole (arrowed) in the hinge

14.7 Door striker plate adjusting nut

sure the two pegs on the rear of the handle mounting plate locate in the holes in the end of the locking rods **(see illustrations)**. When inserting the rods, make sure the plastic guides are correctly seated inside the door panel.

14 Rear doors – removal, refitting and adjustment

Removal

1 Open the rear doors, and then detach the safety check strap from the body on the side which the door is being removed **(see illustration)**.
2 Mark around the periphery of each door hinge with a suitable marker pen to show the fitted position of the hinges when refitting the door.

3 Have an assistant support the door, undo the retaining bolts from each hinge, and withdraw the door **(see illustration)**.

Refitting and adjustment

4 Refitting is a reversal of removal. Align the hinges with the previously-made marks, and then tighten the bolts. Ensure that the check strap is central with the door when reconnected.
5 Open and shut the doors, and ensure that they don't bind with the body aperture at any point.
6 Adjust the door hinges by slackening the hinge mounting bolts and then with the door closed, adjust the Allen screw from outside of the rear hinge through the access hole **(see illustrations)**. When adjusted to the correct position, open the door and tighten the hinge mounting bolts.
7 To align the rear doors so that they are flush,

slacken the securing nut and adjust the striker plate on the locking rod mounting plate **(see illustration)**.

15 Front door window regulator – removal and refitting

Removal

1 Position the window so that it is at the top of the doorframe, and then secure it in place using strong tape **(see illustration)**.
2 Remove the door inner trim panel as described in Section 8.
3 On vehicles with electric windows, disconnect the wiring connector from the window regulator motor.
4 Undo the four retaining screws and slide the window regulator and mounting bracket forwards to release the crank lever from the

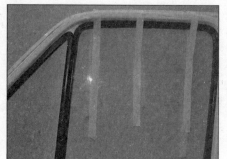

15.1 Using masking tape to hold the window glass in position

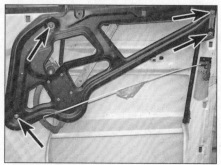

15.4a Undo the retaining bolts (arrowed) ...

15.4b ... and remove the window regulator assembly

15.4c Slide the operating lever from the window glass lower rail

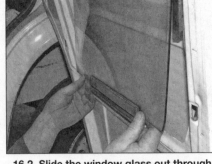

16.2 Slide the window glass out through the bottom of the door

17.2a Indentation in the guide rail surround . . .

rail at the bottom of the window glass **(see illustrations)**.
5 Depending on model, either drill out the rivets or undo the retaining bolts to remove the window regulator from the mounting bracket.

Refitting

6 Refitting is a reversal of removal. Before refitting the door trim panel, raise and lower the window to ensure that it operates in a satisfactory manner.

16 Front door window glass – removal and refitting

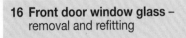

Removal

1 Remove the window regulator as described in Section 15.
2 Support the window glass and then remove

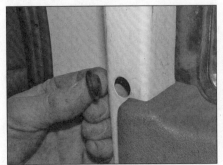

19.1a Remove the rubber grommet . . .

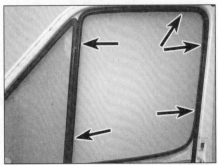

17.2b . . . to identify where the retaining clips are positioned

the masking tape. Carefully lower the window glass out through the lower part of the door **(see illustration)**.

Refitting

3 Refitting is a reversal of removal. Before refitting the door trim panel, raise and lower the window to ensure that it operates in a satisfactory manner.

17 Front door quarter glass – removal and refitting

Removal

1 Remove the front door window glass as described in Section 16.
2 Carefully unclip the sliding window guide rail from the doorframe. Note the small indentations around the guide rail to show

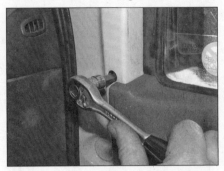

19.1b . . . and undo the retaining screw

where the securing clips are located **(see illustrations)**.
3 Remove the window sealing frame from the outside of the sliding window glass aperture.
4 Press the quarter glass outwards using firm hand pressure, whilst simultaneously pulling free the rubber weatherstrip from the top corner. Apply a small amount of lubricant spray to moisten the rubber seal to aid removal.

Refitting

5 Refitting is a reversal of removal, using a small amount of lubricant spray on the rubber seals to aid refitting. Before refitting the door trim panel, raise and lower the window to ensure that it operates in a satisfactory manner.

18 Windscreen and fixed/sliding windows – removal and refitting

The windscreen and fixed/sliding side window assemblies are direct-glazed to the body, using special adhesive. Purpose-made tools are required to remove the old glass and fit the new, and therefore this work is best entrusted to a specialist.

19 Exterior mirrors – removal and refitting

Complete mirror

Removal

1 Carefully prise out the rubber grommet and remove the retaining screw from the doorframe **(see illustrations)**. Take care not to drop the retaining screw into the inside of the door.
2 On models with electric mirrors, remove the door trim panel as described in Section 8, and then disconnect the wiring connector, noting the routing of the wiring for refitting.
3 Support the mirror and then undo the two Torx screws securing the front of the mirror base to the door **(see illustration)**.
4 Remove the mirror assembly from the

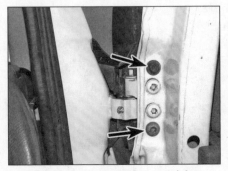

19.3 Undo the two mirror retaining screws . . .

outside of the door and where applicable withdraw the wiring connector out through the door frame (see illustration).

Refitting

5 Refitting is a reversal of removal. On electric mirrors, make sure the wiring is routed and connected correctly before refitting the door trim panel.

Mirror glass

Removal

6 Carefully press the lower part of the mirror glass inwards (see illustration).
7 Pull the mirror glass upwards to release it from the guides in the mirror housing (see illustrations).
8 On models with heated mirrors, disconnect the wiring connectors from the rear of the mirror glass.

Refitting

9 Refitting is a reversal of removal. On heated mirrors, make sure the wiring is connected securely before refitting the glass.

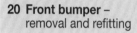

20 Front bumper – removal and refitting

Removal

1 Remove the number plate from the bumper (see illustration).
2 Undo the two retaining screws from behind the number plate (see illustration).
3 Undo the two bolts (one each side), securing the ends of the bumper just above the footsteps (see illustration).
4 With the aid of an assistant, pull the bumper cover forwards, releasing it at each end from the guides on the lower part of the wing panels (see illustration).
5 Check the rear of the bumper cover for wiring connections (eg, outside air temperature sensor), disconnect any connections and remove the bumper cover from the vehicle.
6 If required, undo the two bolts and remove the footsteps from the front crossmember (see illustration).

19.4 . . . and remove the mirror from the door frame

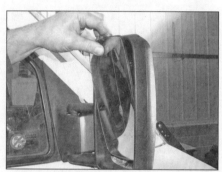

19.7a Slide the mirror glass upwards . . .

19.6 Push the lower part of the mirror glass inwards

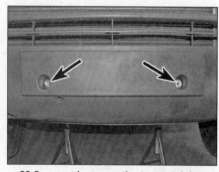

19.7b . . . to release it from the guide in the housing

Refitting

7 Refitting is a reversal of removal. Align the bumper correctly before fully-tightening

the retaining bolts. Make sure any wiring connectors have been refitted, where applicable.

20.1 Remove the front number plate . . .

20.3 Undo the outer retaining screws (one side shown)

20.4 Slide the bumper cover forwards to remove

20.2 . . . and remove the two retaining screws

20.6 Front step retaining bolts

21.1a Remove the reflector . . .

21.1b . . . and remove the retaining bolt

21.3 Release the plastic cover securing clips

21.4a Release the side locating clips . . .

21.4b . . . and rear locating clips

21.6 Rear bumper plastic guides

21 Rear bumper – removal and refitting

Removal

1 Unscrew the reflectors from the rear bumper cover and remove the securing bolts **(see illustrations)**.
2 Release the securing clips from the underside of the bumper, along the lower edge.
3 On models with rear-end door step, remove the retaining clips by pressing the centre pin inwards and then releasing the clip from the step **(see illustration)**. New clips will be required for refitting.
4 With the aid of an assistant, pull the bumper cover rearwards, releasing it at each end from the guides on the lower part of the wing panels and from the lower rear valance **(see illustrations)**.
5 Check the rear of the bumper cover for wiring connections (eg, reversing sensors), disconnect any connections and remove the bumper/step cover from the vehicle.
6 If required, undo the retaining screws at each side and remove the bumper guides from the rear panel **(see illustration)**.

Refitting

7 Refitting is a reversal of removal, using new retaining clips on the rear step cover. Align the bumper correctly before fully-tightening the retaining bolts. Make sure any wiring connectors have been refitted, where applicable.

22 Radiator grille – removal and refitting

Removal

1 Open the bonnet.

Models up to 2000

2 Remove the two retaining clips from the top of the grille panel by slackening them with a screwdriver and then releasing the clip from the grille **(see illustrations)**.
3 Release the upper part of the grille panel from the locating hooks at each end of the grille panel **(see illustration)**.
4 Lift the grille panel upwards and withdraw

22.2a Undo the two plastic retaining screws . . .

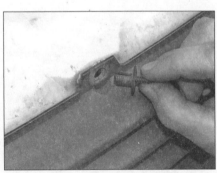

22.2b . . . and release the securing clips

22.3 Unclip the upper part of the grille

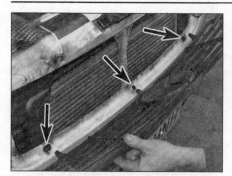

22.4 Lift the grille out from the lower locating holes (arrowed)

22.5a Press out the centre pins . . .

22.5b . . . and release the securing clips

it from the lower crossmember locating points **(see illustration)**.

Models from 2000

5 Remove the three retaining screws/clips from the top of the grille panel. If securing clips are used, remove them by pressing the centre pin inwards, and then releasing the clip from the grille **(see illustrations)**.

6 Undo the two retaining screws securing the lower edges of the grille panel in position **(see illustration)**.

7 Withdraw the grille panel from the front of the vehicle **(see illustration)**.

Refitting

8 Refitting is a reversal of removal. Check the alignment of the grille with the surrounding panels.

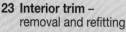

23 Interior trim – removal and refitting

Door trim panels

1 Refer to the procedures contained in Section 8.

A-pillar trim

Removal

2 Pull the door seal away from the side of the A-pillar trim **(see illustration)**.

3 Unclip the upper edge of the trim away from the pillar to disengage the retaining clips, then lift the trim up to disengage the lower lugs from the facia **(see illustration)**.

Refitting

4 Refitting is a reversal of removal.

B-pillar trim

Removal

5 Unclip the plastic cover off the seat belt lower mounting, then unscrew the mounting bolt and disconnect it from the seat frame **(see illustrations)**. Ensure that the spacer and washer remain in place on the mounting bolt when it is removed.

6 Pull the door seal away from the side of the B-pillar trim.

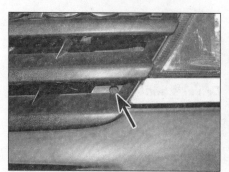

22.6 Undo the retaining screws from the lower corners of the grille

7 Unclip the upper edge of the trim away from the pillar to disengage the retaining clips, working carefully down to the trim to release the securing clips **(see illustration)**.

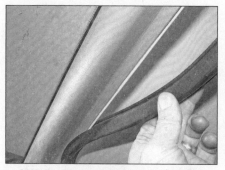

23.2 Peel back the seal from the door aperture

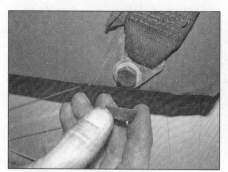

23.5a Unclip the plastic cover . . .

22.7 Withdraw the grille from the front of the vehicle

8 Feed the end of the seat belt through the opening in the trim panel, and then remove the B-pillar trim from the vehicle **(see illustration)**.

23.3 Unclip the A-pillar trim panel

23.5b . . . and undo the mounting bolt

23.7 Unclip the B-pillar trim panel

23.8 Withdraw the seat belt through the trim panel

(where applicable), then remove the seat from the vehicle.

Refitting

5 Refitting is a reversal of removal. Tighten the mountings to the specified torque.

Refitting

9 Refitting is a reversal of removal, ensuring that the seat belt height adjuster is aligned with the trim panel correctly. Tighten the mountings to the specified torque.

Load space trim

Removal

10 The load space trim panels are secured by a combination of screws and plastic retaining clips, the removal of which requires the use of a suitable forked tool. These clips are easily broken, so take care when prising them free.
11 Remove the rear seats, where applicable, for access to the panel attachments.
12 Release the panel retaining clips and screws, and withdraw the panel.

Refitting

13 Refitting is a reversal of removal.

24 Seats –
removal and refitting

Driver's seat

Removal

1 Unclip the plastic cover off the seat belt lower mounting, then unscrew the mounting bolt and disconnect it from the seat frame **(see illustrations 23.5a and 23.5b)**. Ensure that the spacer and washer remain in place on the mounting bolt when it is removed.
2 Move the seat fully to the rear, and then undo the two front seat rail retaining bolts.
3 Then move the seat fully to the front and undo the two rear seat rail retaining bolts.
4 Check for any wiring to the underside of the seat and disconnect any wiring connectors

Front passenger's seat (single)

Removal

6 Unclip the plastic cover off the seat belt lower mounting, then unscrew the mounting bolt and disconnect it from the seat frame **(see illustrations 23.5a and 23.5b)**. Ensure that the spacer and washer remain in place on the mounting bolt when it is removed.
7 Undo the four seat base mounting bolts (two at each side).
8 Check for any wiring to the underside of the seat and disconnect any wiring connectors (where applicable), then remove the seat from the vehicle.

Refitting

9 Refitting is a reversal of removal. Tighten the mountings to the specified torque.

Front passenger's seat (bench)

10 Where fitted, remove the headrests from the back of the bench seat.
11 Unclip the plastic cover off the seat belt lower mounting, then unscrew the mounting bolt and disconnect it from the side of the seat frame **(see illustrations 23.5a and 23.5b)**. Ensure that the spacer and washer remain in place on the mounting bolt when it is removed.
12 Unclip the cover (where fitted) from the centre anchorage point, and then undo the mounting bolt **(see illustration)**.
13 Undo the two seat mounting bolts (one at each side) from the base of the seat **(see illustrations)**.
14 Lift the rear of the bench seat upwards and tilt it forwards to access the centre seat belt anchorage bolt **(see illustration)**.
15 Undo the seat belt anchorage bolt and remove the bench seat from the vehicle **(see illustration)**.

Refitting

16 Refitting is a reversal of removal. Tighten the mountings to the specified torque.

24.12 Remove the centre seat belt mounting bolt

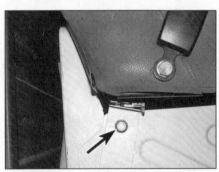

24.13a Undo the seat frame mounting bolts . . .

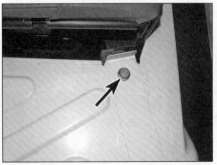

24.13b . . . from each side of the seat base

24.14 Tilt the seat forwards

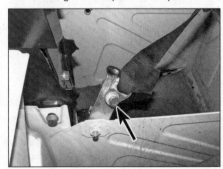

24.15 Undo the seat belt anchorage bolt

25.2 Seat belt height adjuster retaining bolts

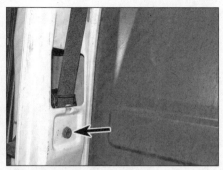

25.3 Seat belt inertia reel mounting bolt

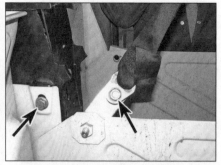

25.8 Undo the mounting bolts . . .

25.9 . . . and withdraw the mounting post out from the seat base

25.10 Unclip the plastic cover . . .

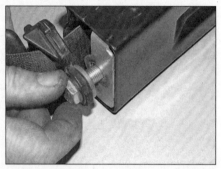

25.11 . . . and remove the upper mounting

Rear seats

17 Depending on model, various combinations of rear seats may be fitted, according to vehicle type and specification. The removal and refitting procedures are essentially the same as those described previously for the front seats.

25 Seat belt components – removal and refitting

Front seat belt

Removal

1 Remove the B-pillar trim as described in Section 23.

2 Undo the two retaining bolts and remove the height adjuster from the B-pillar **(see illustration)**.

3 Undo the retaining bolt and remove the inertia reel from the B-pillar **(see illustration)**.

4 On models with airbags, disconnect the wiring connector from the inertia reel as it is removed.

Refitting

5 Refitting is a reversal of removal, ensuring that the height adjuster engages correctly in the B-pillar. Tighten the retaining bolts to the specified torque.

Front centre seat belt

Removal

6 On vehicles equipped with a double front

passenger's bench seat, the seat belt inertia reel is fitted internally within a mounting post.

7 To access the seat belt mounting post, undo the mounting bolts on the rear of the bench seat and tilt it forwards, with reference to Section 24.

8 With the seat tilted forwards, undo the seat belt lower mounting bolt and the inertia reel mounting post lower retaining bolt **(see illustration)**.

9 Lift the mounting post out from the rear of the seat base and remove it from the vehicle **(see illustration)**.

10 Slacken the retaining screws (one at each side), but do not remove these completely at this point. The plastic cover can then be removed from the top of the mounting post **(see illustration)**.

11 Undo the mounting bolt and disconnect

the seat belt anchorage plate from the top of the mounting post **(see illustration)**.

12 Remove the two screws from the side of the mounting post (the ones that were slackened in paragraph 10) and withdraw the upper mounting bracket **(see illustrations)**. Note the fitted position of the mounting plate for refitting.

13 Undo the inertia reel mounting bolt at the lower end of the mounting post and withdraw the inertia reel from inside the mounting post **(see illustrations)**.

Refitting

14 Refitting is a reversal of removal, unwind the seat belt from the inertia reel and feed it down through the mounting post before fitting the mounting bolts. Tighten the retaining bolts to the specified torque.

25.12a Remove the side retaining screws . . .

25.12b . . . and remove the upper mounting bracket

25.13a Undo the mounting bolt . . .

25.13b . . . and slide the inertia reel out from the mounting post

17 On the passenger side with a bench seat, the front seat belt stalk is mounted at the centre of the seat base. To access the seat belt stalk mounting point, undo the mounting bolts on the rear of the bench seat and tilt it forwards, with reference to Section 24. With the seat tilted forwards, undo the seat belt stalk mounting bolt and then remove the seat belt stalk from the seat frame **(see illustration)**.

18 For the centre belt with a bench seat, follow the procedures as described in paragraph 15.

Refitting

19 Refitting is a reversal of removal. Tighten the mounting bolts to the specified torque.

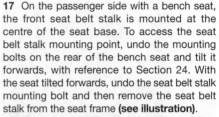

26 Facia panel components –
removal and refitting

Note: *Disconnect the battery negative terminal (refer to Disconnecting the battery in the Reference Chapter), before working on any components on the facia panel.*

Steering column shrouds

Removal

1 Turn the locking peg and remove the cover from the fusebox **(see illustration)**.

2 Undo the retaining nut from the lower part of the shroud **(see illustration)**.

3 Undo the two retaining screws from the upper part of the lower shroud and remove it from under the steering column **(see illustrations)**.

4 Undo the two retaining screws and remove the upper shroud from the top of the steering column **(see illustrations)**.

25.15 Seat belt stalk mounted to seat base

25.17 Centre seat belt stalk mounted to lower seat frame

the mounting bolt and remove the stalk from the side of the seat frame **(see illustration)**. Ensure that any spacers or washers remain with mounting bolt when it is removed.

16 On the passenger side with a single seat, follow the procedures as described in paragraph 15.

Seat belt stalks

Removal

15 On the driver's side, the front seat belt stalk is mounted on the side of the seat base. Unclip the plastic cover (where fitted) off the seat stalk mounting bolt, and then unscrew

26.1 Unclip the fusebox cover

26.2 Undo the lower retaining nut

26.3a Undo the upper retaining screws . . .

26.3b . . . and remove the lower steering column shroud

26.4a Undo the retaining screws . . .

26.4b . . . and remove the upper steering column shroud

26.6 Undo the two retaining screws . . .

26.7 . . . and remove the front trim panel

26.9a Undo the two retaining screws . . .

26.9b . . . and remove the upper trim cover

26.11 Unclip the switch panel from the facia

26.12a Pull the heater control knobs off . . .

Refitting

5 Refitting is a reversal of removal.

Instrument panel surround (models from 2000)

Removal

6 Undo the two screws from inside the top edge of the instrument panel **(see illustration)**.
7 Pull the front trim panel away from the facia to release the retaining clips, and then remove it from the facia **(see illustration)**.
8 As the panel is removed from the facia, disconnect the wiring connectors from the switches, noting their fitted positions.
9 Undo the two retaining screws and unclip the upper trim cover from the top of the instrument panel **(see illustrations)**.

Refitting

10 Refitting is a reversal of removal.

Instrument panel surround (models up to 2000)

Removal

11 Unclip the switch panel from the right-hand side of the steering column and disconnect the two vacuum hoses **(see illustration)**. Note their fitted position for refitting.
12 Pull the three heater control knobs from the heater control switches and remove the securing nuts **(see illustrations)**.
13 Remove the radio/CD player, as described in Chapter 12.
14 Unclip the cover from below the radio

aperture and undo the retaining screw **(see illustration)**.
15 Remove the passenger side trim and undo the retaining screws on the left-hand side of the trim panel **(see illustration)**.

16 Unclip the right-hand speaker cover from the top of the facia panel and undo the retaining screw **(see illustrations)**.
17 Undo the retaining screw from the right-hand lower side of the trim panel, and

26.12b . . . and undo the retaining nuts

26.14 Unclip the trim and undo the retaining screw

26.15 Undo the two side retaining screws

26.16a Unclip the speaker cover grille . . .

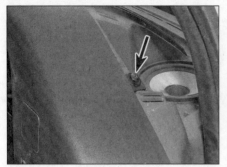

26.16b ... and undo the retaining screw

26.17 Remove the instrument trim panel

26.20 Unclip the upper tray panel ...

26.21 ... and remove the mounting bracket

26.22a Use a piece of wire to release the retaining clips ...

26.22b ... and remove the trim panel from the facia

then pull the trim panel away from the facia to release the retaining clips **(see illustration)**.

18 As the panel is withdrawn, disconnect the wiring connectors from the switches, noting their fitted positions.

Refitting

19 Refitting is a reversal of removal.

Passenger storage compartment (models from 2000)

Removal

20 Lift the tray panel up at the front and then unclip it from the top of the glove compartment **(see illustration)**.
21 Undo the two retaining screws and remove the cross bracket from the top of the compartment **(see illustration)**.
22 Unclip the storage compartment from the facia by inserting a bent piece of wire through the heater vents to release the securing clips **(see illustrations)**.

Refitting

23 Refitting is a reversal of removal.

Facia centre panel (models from 2000)

Removal

24 Unclip the note holder from the facia and undo the retaining screw **(see illustrations)**.
25 Release the securing clips and withdraw the storage compartment from the facia panel **(see illustration)**. On models with a tachograph, withdraw it from the facia and also unclip the metal cage from the facia.
26 Unclip the gear lever gaiter from the centre panel and undo the retaining screw **(see illustrations)**.
27 Undo the two retaining screws from the lower part of the trim panel, and then pull the

26.24a Unclip the note holder ...

26.24b ... and undo the retaining screw

26.25 Withdraw the storage compartment

26.26a Unclip the gear lever gaiter ...

26.26b ... and undo the retraining screw

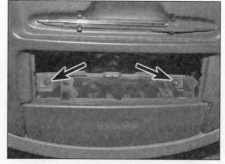

26.27a Undo the two lower retaining screws ...

26.27b ... and unclip the centre trim panel from the facia

trim panel away from the facia to release the retaining clips **(see illustrations)**.
28 As the panel is withdrawn, disconnect the wiring connectors from the switches, noting their fitted positions.
29 If required, undo the three retaining screws to remove the lower storage drawer **(see illustrations)**.

Refitting

30 Refitting is a reversal of removal.

Glove compartment (models from 2000)

Removal

31 Open the glove compartment lid and undo the three retaining screws from inside the glove compartment **(see illustration)**.
32 Withdraw the glove compartment from the facia panel and disconnect the wiring connector from the light unit as it is removed **(see illustrations)**.

Refitting

33 Refitting is a reversal of removal.

Upper facia panel (models from 2000)

Removal

34 Remove the instrument panel surround, passenger storage compartment and facia centre panel as described previously in this section.
35 Remove the radio/CD player, as described in Chapter 12.

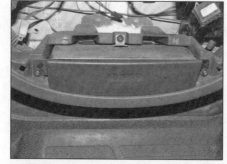

26.29a Undo the three retaining screws ...

36 Remove the A-pillar trim panels on both sides as described in Section 23.
37 Unclip the speaker grille panels from each end of the facia panel **(see illustration)**.

26.31 Undo the three retaining screws ...

26.32b ... and disconnect the wiring connector

26.29b ... and remove the storage compartment from the facia

38 Unclip the vent grille panel from the top of the facia panel **(see illustration)**.
39 Undo the retaining screws from the instrument aperture **(see illustration)**.

26.32a ... slide the glove compartment from the facia ...

26.37 Unclip the speaker grille from the end of the facia

26.38 Unclip the speaker/vent grille from the top of the facia

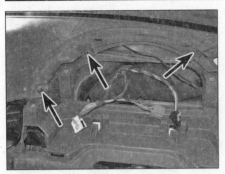

26.39 Undo the retaining screws on the right-hand side of the facia

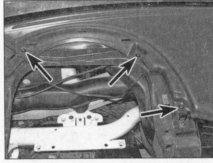

26.40 Undo the retaining screws on the left-hand side of the facia

26.41a Undo the two retaining screws . . .

26.41b . . . and remove the upper part of the facia

40 Undo the retaining screws from the passenger side storage compartment aperture (see illustration).

41 Undo the two retaining screws from the front of the upper facia, and then lift it upwards

to remove it from the lower facia panel (see illustrations).

Refitting

42 Refitting is a reversal of removal.

Lower facia panel (models from 2000)

Removal

43 Remove the following facia panels as described previously in this Section:

a) Steering column shrouds.

b) Instrument panel surround.

c) Upper facia panel.

44 Remove the heater control panel as described in Chapter 3.

45 Undo the retaining screws and remove the trim covers from each end of the facia panel (see illustration).

46 Unclip the speakers from each end of the facia panel (see illustration).

47 Undo the retaining screws from inside the speaker apertures at each end of the facia panel (see illustration).

48 Undo the retaining screws and remove the three air vents from the front of the facia panel (see illustration).

49 Undo the retaining screws from the lower part of the facia panel at each end of the facia (see illustration).

50 Undo the two retaining screws from inside the centre section of the facia panel (see illustration).

51 Undo the retaining bolt and lower the fusebox from the steering column, with reference to Chapter 12 (see illustration).

52 Move the wiring to one side and undo the two retaining screws from each side of the steering column (see illustration).

53 Detach the ventilation ducts from the

26.45 Undo the two end cover securing screws

26.46 Remove the speakers . . .

26.47 . . . and undo the retaining screws

26.48 Remove the air vents

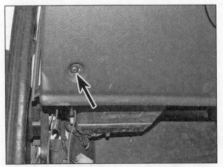

26.49 Undo the retaining screws from the lower ends of the facia

26.50 Undo the facia centre panel lower retaining screws

heater housing, and then check that all wiring has been disconnected **(see illustration)**.

54 Working along the top of the lower facia panel, undo the retaining screws and then manoeuvre the lower facia panel out from inside of the vehicle **(see illustration)**.

Refitting

55 Refitting is a reversal of removal ensuring that all wiring is correctly reconnected and all mountings securely tightened.

Complete facia panel (models up to 2000)

Removal

56 Remove the A-pillar trim panels on both sides as described in Section 23.

57 Remove the following facia panels as described previously in this Section:
 a) *Steering column shrouds.*
 b) *Instrument panel surround.*
 c) *Facia centre panel.*
 d) *Driver's side switch/vent panel.*

58 Remove the following components as described in Chapter 12:
 a) *Instrument panel.*
 b) *Tachograph (where fitted).*
 c) *Radio/cassette/CD player.*
 d) *Facia speakers*

59 Remove the heater control panel as described in Chapter 3.

60 Undo the retaining screws from under the speaker grille at each end of the facia panel.

61 Remove the ashtray, and disconnect the wiring connector from the cigarette lighter.

62 Undo the four retaining screws and remove the centre console from the lower part of the facia panel.

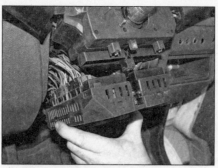

26.51 Remove the fusebox from under the steering column

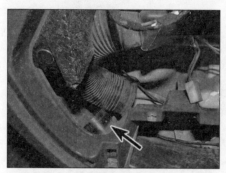

26.53 Disconnect the ventilation ducts from the heater

63 Undo the four retaining screws from the lower part of the knee bolster trim panel on the passenger side, and then undo the two upper retaining screws and remove the trim panel from the facia panel.

64 Detach the ventilation ducts from the heater housing, and then check that all wiring has been disconnected.

26.52 Undo the retaining screws each side of the steering column

26.54 Remove the facia panel out from the vehicle

65 Working along the facia panel, undo the retaining screws and then maneuver the facia panel out from inside of the vehicle.

Refitting

66 Refitting is a reversal of removal ensuring that all wiring is correctly reconnected and all mountings securely tightened.

Chapter 12
Body electrical systems

Contents

Degrees of difficulty

| Easy, suitable for novice with little experience | 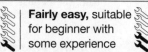 | Fairly easy, suitable for beginner with some experience | Fairly difficult, suitable for competent DIY mechanic | Difficult, suitable for experienced DIY mechanic | Very difficult, suitable for expert DIY or professional | |

Specifications

Fuses and relays
Refer to the wiring diagrams commencing on page 12•16.

Bulbs   Wattage

Direction indicator lights:
  Front... 21 (PY21W amber glass)
  Rear 21 (P21W)
Direction indicator side repeater lights..................... 5 (W5W)
Foglights:
  Front... 55 (H1 type)
  Rear (driver's side only) 21 (P21W)
Headlights:
  Dipped beam .... 55 (H1 type)
  Main beam .... 55 (H1 type)
Interior lights in passenger and load compartments .... 18 (K type)
Interior lights with reading light .... 10 (K type)
Number plate light:
  Pick-up models 5 (R5W)
  All other models 5 (C5W)
Perimeter lights (Pick-up models) 5 (R5W)
Reversing lights 21 (P21W)
Sidelights 5 (W5W)
Side marker lights/outline lights 5 (W5W)
Stop-light (additional)................................. 21 (P21W)
Stop/tail lights 21/5 (P21/5W)
Tail lights (Pick-up models)............................. 5 (R5W)

Torque wrench settings

	Nm	lbf ft
Passenger airbag retaining bolts*...........................	10	7
Windscreen wiper arm-to-spindle nuts	20	15
Windscreen wiper motor crank arm nut	20	15
Windscreen wiper motor bracket-to-body bolts	10	7
Windscreen wiper spindle nuts	10	7

* Use new bolts.

1 General information and precautions

⚠️ *Warning: Before carrying out any work on the electrical system, read through the precautions given in 'Safety first!' at the beginning of this manual, and in Chapter 5.*

1 The electrical system is of the 12 volt negative earth type. Power for the lights and all electrical accessories is supplied by a lead-calcium type battery, which is charged by the engine-driven alternator.

2 This Chapter covers repair and service procedures for the various electrical components not associated with the engine. Information on the battery, alternator and starter motor can be found in Chapter 5.

3 It should be noted that, prior to working on any component in the electrical system, the battery negative terminal should first be disconnected, to prevent the possibility of electrical short-circuits and/or fires.

Caution: Before proceeding, refer to 'Disconnecting the battery' in the Reference Chapter for further information.

2 Electrical fault finding – general information

Note: *Refer to the precautions given in 'Safety first!' and in Section 1 of this Chapter before starting work. The following tests relate to testing of the main electrical circuits, and should not be used to test delicate electronic circuits, particularly where an electronic control module is used.*

General

1 A typical electrical circuit consists of an electrical component; any switches, relays, motors, fuses, fusible links or circuit breakers related to that component, and the wiring and connectors which link the component to both the battery and the chassis. To help to pinpoint a problem in an electrical circuit, wiring diagrams are included at the end of this Chapter.

2 Before attempting to diagnose an electrical fault, first study the appropriate wiring diagram, to obtain a complete understanding of the components included in the particular circuit concerned. The possible sources of a fault can be narrowed down by noting if other components related to the circuit are operating properly. If several components or circuits fail at one time, the problem is likely to be related to a shared fuse or earth connection.

3 Electrical problems usually stem from simple causes, such as loose or corroded connections, a faulty earth connection, a blown fuse, a melted fusible link, or a faulty relay (refer to Section 3 for details of testing relays). Visually inspect the condition of all

fuses, wires and connections in a problem circuit before testing the components. Use the wiring diagrams to determine which terminal connections will need to be checked in order to pinpoint the trouble spot.

4 The basic tools required for electrical fault-finding include a circuit tester or voltmeter (a 12 volt bulb with a set of test leads can also be used for certain tests); an ohmmeter (to measure resistance and check for continuity); a battery and set of test leads; and a jumper wire, preferably with a circuit breaker or fuse incorporated, which can be used to bypass suspect wires or electrical components. Before attempting to locate a problem with test instruments, use the wiring diagram to determine where to make the connections.

5 To find the source of an intermittent wiring fault (usually due to a poor or dirty connection, or damaged wiring insulation), a 'wiggle' test can be performed on the wiring. This involves wiggling the wiring by hand to see if the fault occurs as the wiring is moved. It should be possible to narrow down the source of the fault to a particular section of wiring. This method of testing can be used in conjunction with any of the tests described in the following sub-Sections.

6 Apart from problems due to poor connections, two basic types of fault can occur in an electrical circuit – open-circuit, or short-circuit.

7 Open-circuit faults are caused by a break somewhere in the circuit, which prevents current from flowing. An open-circuit fault will prevent a component from working.

8 Short-circuit faults are caused by a 'short' somewhere in the circuit, which allows the current flowing in the circuit to 'escape' along an alternative route, usually to earth. Short-circuit faults are normally caused by a breakdown in wiring insulation, which allows a feed wire to touch either another wire, or an earthed component such as the bodyshell. A short-circuit fault will normally cause the relevant circuit fuse to blow.

Finding an open-circuit

9 To check for an open-circuit, connect one lead of a circuit tester or the negative lead of a voltmeter either to the battery negative terminal or to a known good earth.

10 Connect the other lead to a connector in the circuit being tested, preferably nearest to the battery or fuse. At this point, battery voltage should be present, unless the lead from the battery or the fuse itself is faulty (bearing in mind that some circuits are live only when the ignition switch is moved to a particular position).

11 Switch on the circuit, then connect the tester lead to the connector nearest the circuit switch on the component side.

12 If voltage is present (indicated either by the tester bulb lighting or a voltmeter reading, as applicable), this means that the section of the circuit between the relevant connector and the switch is problem-free.

13 Continue to check the remainder of the circuit in the same fashion.

14 When a point is reached at which no voltage is present, the problem must lie between that point and the previous test point with voltage. Most problems can be traced to a broken, corroded or loose connection.

Finding a short-circuit

15 To check for a short-circuit; first disconnect the load(s) from the circuit (loads are the components which draw current from a circuit, such as bulbs, motors, heating elements, etc).

16 Remove the relevant fuse from the circuit, and connect a circuit tester or voltmeter to the fuse connections.

17 Switch on the circuit, bearing in mind that some circuits are live only when the ignition switch is moved to a particular position.

18 If voltage is present (indicated either by the tester bulb lighting or a voltmeter reading, as applicable), this means that there is a short-circuit.

19 If no voltage is present during this test, but the fuse still blows with the load(s) reconnected, this indicates an internal fault in the load(s).

Finding an earth fault

20 The battery negative terminal is connected to 'earth' – the metal of the engine/transmission and the vehicle body – and many systems are wired so that they only receive a positive feed, the current returning via the metal of the vehicle body. This means that the component mounting and the body form part of that circuit. Loose or corroded mountings can therefore cause a range of electrical faults, ranging from total failure of a circuit, to a puzzling partial failure. In particular, lights may shine dimly (especially when another circuit sharing the same earth point is in operation), motors (eg, wiper motors or the heater blower motor) may run slowly, and the operation of one circuit may have an apparently unrelated effect on another. Note that on many vehicles, earth straps are used between certain components, such as the engine/transmission and the body, usually where there is no metal-to-metal contact between components, due to flexible rubber mountings, etc.

21 To check whether a component is properly earthed, disconnect the battery and connect one lead of an ohmmeter to a known good earth point. Connect the other lead to the wire or earth connection being tested. The resistance reading should be zero; if not, check the connection as follows.

22 If an earth connection is thought to be faulty, dismantle the connection, and clean both the bodyshell and the wire terminal (or the component earth connection mating surface) back to bare metal. Be careful to remove all traces of dirt and corrosion, and then use a knife to trim away any paint, so that a clean metal-to-metal joint is made. On reassembly, tighten the joint fasteners securely; if a wire terminal is being refitted, use serrated washers between the terminal and the bodyshell, to ensure a clean and secure connection. When the connection is remade, prevent the onset of corrosion in the future by applying a coat of petroleum jelly or silicone-based grease, or by spraying on (at regular intervals) a proprietary water-dispersant lubricant.

3 Fuses and relays –
general information

Fuses

1 The main fuses and relays are located in the fuse/relay box situated below the steering column. To gain access, turn the locking screw anti-clockwise a quarter of a turn and hinge the cover downwards **(see illustration)**.

2 Additional fuses and relays are located in the fuse/relay box under the driver's seat. To gain access, release the catches at the top of the cover and then unclip the cover from the bottom **(see illustration)**.

3 The fuses and relays are identified on the diagram on the inside surface of the fuse/relay box cover or lid. Each fuse is also marked with its rating. Plastic tweezers are attached to the inside face of the lid to remove and fit the fuses.

4 To remove a fuse, pull it out of the holder, preferably using the tweezers, then slide the fuse sideways from the tweezers. The wire within the fuse is clearly visible, and it will be broken if the fuse is blown.

5 Always renew a fuse with one of an identical rating. Never renew a fuse more than once without tracing the source of the trouble. The fuse rating is stamped on top of the fuse.

6 Fusible links are incorporated in the positive feed from the battery, their function being to protect the main wiring loom in the event of a short-circuit. When the links blow, all of the wiring circuits are disconnected, and will remain so until the cause of the malfunction is repaired and the link renewed.

Relays

7 A relay is an electrically-operated switch, which is used for the following reasons:

a) *A relay can switch a heavy current remotely from the circuit in which the current is flowing, allowing the use of lighter-gauge wiring and switch contacts.*

b) *A relay can receive more than one control input, unlike a mechanical switch.*

c) *A relay can have a timer function – for example an intermittent wiper delay.*

8 The relays and timers are located in the two fuse/relay boxes. The various relays can be removed from their locations by carefully pulling them from the sockets.

9 If a system controlled by a relay becomes inoperative and the relay is suspect, listen to the relay as the circuit is operated. If the relay is functioning, it should be possible to hear

3.1 Fusebox located under steering column

it click as it is energised. If the relay proves satisfactory, the fault lies with the components or wiring of the system. If the relay is not being energised, then it is not receiving a main supply voltage or a switching voltage, or the relay is faulty.

4 Switches –
removal and refitting

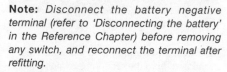

Note: *Disconnect the battery negative terminal (refer to 'Disconnecting the battery' in the Reference Chapter) before removing any switch, and reconnect the terminal after refitting.*

Ignition switch/ steering column lock

1 Refer to Chapter 10.

4.5a Undo the retaining bolt . . .

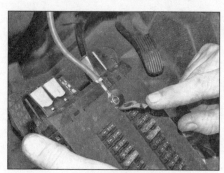

4.5c . . . unclip the plastic cover . . .

3.2 Fusebox located under driver's seat

Steering column combination switch and fusebox

2 The steering column combination switch consists of left-hand and right-hand assemblies. The left-hand switch assembly comprises the headlight dip/flasher switch and the direction indicator switch; the right-hand switch assembly comprises the wiper/washer switch.

3 Remove the steering wheel as described in Chapter 10, Section 14.

4 Remove the steering column shrouds as described in Chapter 11, Section 26.

5 Undo the securing bolt at the top of the fusebox under the steering column. Hinge the fusebox down and disconnect the wiring connectors from the rear of the fusebox. Unclip the plastic cover and undo the nut securing the main feed cable **(see illustrations)** The fusebox can then be removed from under the steering column.

4.5b . . . disconnect the wiring connectors . . .

4.5d . . . and undo the cable retaining nut

4.8 Undo the two retaining screws

4.10a Using a small screwdriver . . .

4.10b . . . unclip the switch trim panel

4.12 Release the switch securing clips

4.15 Remove the switch from the panel

6 On models with airbags fitted, slacken the two securing screws in the rotary 'clock spring' contact unit. These do not need to be removed completely. Disconnect the wiring connectors to the rotary unit, and then withdraw it from the top of the steering column. Note the fitted position of the rotary connector unit for refitting.
7 On models with electronic stability program (ESP) fitted, disconnect the wiring connector from the steering angle sensor, and then withdraw it from the top of the steering column. Note the fitted position of the angle sensor for refitting; the locking lug of the angle sensor must locate in the groove in the steering column.
8 Remove the two retaining screws from under the combination switch, then lift the switch upwards and off the top of the steering column **(see illustration)**.
9 Refitting is a reversal of removal.

Facia side switches (models up to 2000)

10 Using a small screwdriver unclip the switch panel from the facia **(see illustrations)**.
11 To remove the light control switch from the panel, first disconnect the vacuum pipes from the switch noting their fitted position. Disconnect the wiring connector from the rear of the switch and then unclip the switch from the switch panel.
12 Depending on vehicle specification and equipment fitted, the remaining switches in the panel can be removed by releasing the securing clips at the rear of the panel and then withdrawing the switch from the switch

panel **(see illustration)**. Disconnect the wiring connectors from the rear of the switch.
13 Refitting is a reversal of removal.

Facia centre panel switches

14 Remove the facia centre panel as described in Chapter 11, Section 26.
15 Depress the retaining tabs at the rear of the relevant switch, and withdraw the switch from the panel **(see illustration)**.
16 Refitting is a reversal of removal.

Instrument surround panel switches

17 Remove the facia centre panel as described in Chapter 11, Section 26.
18 Depress the retaining tabs at the rear of the relevant switch, and withdraw the switch from the panel **(see illustration 4.15)**.
19 Refitting is a reversal of removal.

5.3a Remove the retaining screws . . .

Stop-light switch

20 Refer to Chapter 9, Section 19.

Handbrake warning light switch

21 Refer to Chapter 9, Section 18.

Electric window switch

22 Carefully unclip the cover from the grab handle on the inside of the door trim panel.
23 Unclip the small switch panel from the top of the inner grab handle and disconnect the wiring connectors from the rear of the switches.
24 Depress the retaining tabs at the rear of the switch, and withdraw the switch from the panel.
25 Refitting is a reversal of removal.

Heating/ventilation/ air conditioning system switches

26 The switches are all an integral part of the heating/ventilation control unit. Refer to Chapter 3, Section 8, to remove the heater control panel.

---

5 **Instrument panel** – removal and refitting

Note: *At the time of writing there was no information on the stripdown of the instrument panel to renew any components. See your local Mercedes-Benz dealer for availability of any spares to repair the instrument panel.*

Removal

1 Disconnect the battery negative terminal (refer to *Disconnecting the battery* in the Reference Chapter).
2 Remove the instrument panel surround as described in Chapter 11, Section 26.
3 On models up to 2000, undo the two screws securing the top of the instrument panel to the facia, then tilt the instrument panel down and unclip the locating pegs at the bottom of the instrument panel **(see illustrations)**.
4 On models from 2000, undo the two screws securing the top of the instrument panel to the facia, and then lift the instrument panel upwards to release the locating pegs at the bottom of the instrument panel **(see illustrations)**.

5.3b . . . from the instrument panel . . .

5.3c . . . and then unclip the locating pegs from the facia

5.4a Undo the two retaining screws . . .

5.4b . . . and then lift the instrument panel out from the facia

5.5 Disconnect the wiring connectors

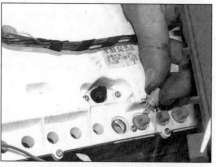

5.6 Remove the bulb and holder

5 Withdraw the instrument panel from the facia, release the securing clips and disconnect the wiring connector(s) at the rear of the panel **(see illustration)**.
6 On models up to 2000, if required, untwist the bulbholder, and withdraw it from the rear face of the panel **(see illustration)**. Remove the bulb from its holder, where applicable.

Refitting

7 Refitting is a reversal of removal.

6 Tachograph – removal and refitting

Note 1: *Where fitted, there are a number of different types of tachograph available for these vehicles. Some are fitted with anti-tamper seals, check with your local dealer or specialist to obtain new seals before removal.*
Note 2: *Mercedes-Benz use a special tool (part No 000 545 0744) to remove the tachograph from the facia. Alternatively, a suitable tool can be fabricated from 3 mm diameter wire, such as welding rod.*

Removal

1 Turn the ignition key to position 0.
2 Insert the special tools into the holes on the front of the unit at each end, and then push them until they snap into place. The tachograph can then be slid out of the facia.
3 Remove the anti-tamper seal from the wiring connection cover, and then the cover

can be removed. Discard the anti-tamper seal, as a new one will be required for refitting.
4 Disconnect the wiring connections at the rear of the unit, and remove the unit from the vehicle.
5 Remove the special tools.

Refitting

6 To refit the tachograph, reconnect the wiring connector and secure the cover in place by using a new anti-tamper seal. Push the unit firmly into the facia until the retaining lugs snap into place.

7 Headlight beam alignment – general information

1 Accurate adjustment of the headlight beam is only possible using optical beam-setting equipment, and this work should therefore

7.2 Disconnecting vacuum pipe

be carried out by a Mercedes-Benz dealer or suitably-equipped workshop.
2 Early models (up to 2000) have a pneumatic headlight beam adjustment system **(see illustration)**, controlled via a switch in the facia. There are two vacuum hoses fitted to the rear of the switch (connector A has a black hose and connector B has a black/green hose). With the vehicle unladen, the switch should be set in position 0. With the vehicle partially- or fully-loaded, set the switch position to provide adequate illumination without dazzling oncoming drivers.
3 Later models (from 2000) have an electric headlight beam adjustment system **(see illustration)**, controlled via a switch in the facia. With the vehicle unladen, the switch should be set in position 0. With the vehicle partially- or fully-loaded, set the switch position to provide adequate illumination without dazzling oncoming drivers.

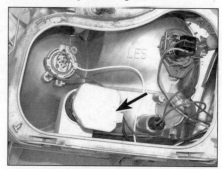

7.3 Electric headlight adjuster (arrowed)

7.4 Manual adjusters on the rear of the headlights

4 All models have manual adjusters on the rear of the headlight unit for initial setting. This should be set when the vehicle is unladen and the switch on the facia is set to 0. The outer adjuster on the rear of the light unit is for the horizontal adjustment and the inner one for vertical adjustment **(see illustration)**.

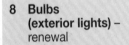

8 Bulbs (exterior lights) – renewal

General

1 Whenever a bulb is renewed, note the following points:

a) *Make sure the switch is in the OFF position for the bulb you are working on.*

b) *Remember that if the light has just been in use, the bulb may be extremely hot.*

c) *Always check the bulb contacts and*

8.4a Release the retaining clip arrowed . . .

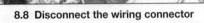

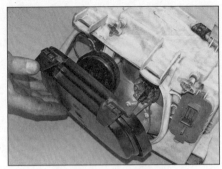

8.2 Unclip the rear cover

holder, ensuring that there is clean metal-to-metal contact between the bulb and its live(s) and earth. Clean off any corrosion or dirt before fitting a new bulb.

d) *Wherever bayonet-type bulbs are fitted, ensure that the live contact(s) bear firmly against the bulb contact.*

e) *Always ensure that the new bulb is of the correct rating, and that it is completely clean before fitting it; this applies particularly to headlight/foglight bulbs.*

Headlight

Models up to 2000

2 Depress the two tabs at the top of the headlight unit and remove the cover at the rear of the headlight unit **(see illustration)**.

3 Disconnect the wiring connector from the rear of the bulb **(see illustration)**.

4 Compress the leg of the retaining spring clip and pivot the clip off the bulb. Lift the bulb out of the light unit **(see illustrations)**. When

8.4b . . . and remove the headlight bulb

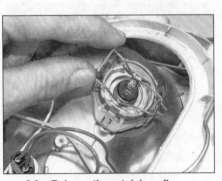

8.9a Release the retaining clip . . .

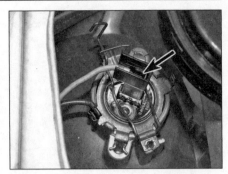

8.3 Disconnect the wiring connector

handling the new bulb, use a tissue or clean cloth to avoid touching the glass with the fingers; moisture and grease from the skin can cause blackening and rapid failure of this type of bulb. If the glass is accidentally touched, wipe it clean using methylated spirit.

5 Fit the new bulb to the headlight unit and secure with the spring clip. Reconnect the wiring connector.

6 Refit the plastic cover to the rear of the headlight unit. Check for satisfactory operation on completion.

Models from 2000

7 Release the two wire clips at each side of the headlight unit and remove the cover at the rear of the headlight unit **(see illustration)**.

8 Disconnect the wiring connector from the rear of the bulb **(see illustration)**.

9 Release the retaining spring clip and pivot the clip off the bulb. Lift the bulb out of the light unit **(see illustrations)**. When handling

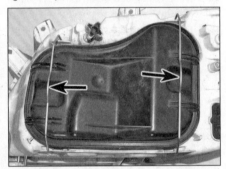

8.7 Release the clip on the rear cover

8.9b . . . and remove the headlight bulb

8.8 Disconnect the wiring connector

8.13 Remove the bulbholder . . .

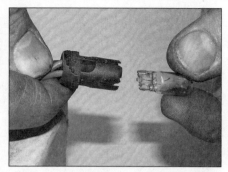

8.14 . . . and pull the capless type bulb to remove

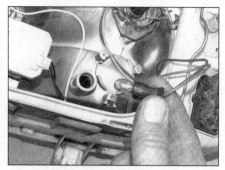

8.17 Remove the bulbholder . . .

8.18 . . . and pull the capless type bulb to remove

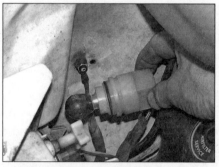

8.20a Twist the bulbholder to remove (models up to 2000)

8.20b Twist the bulbholder to remove (models from 2000)

the new bulb, use a tissue or clean cloth to avoid touching the glass with the fingers; moisture and grease from the skin can cause blackening and rapid failure of this type of bulb. If the glass is accidentally touched, wipe it clean using methylated spirit.

10 Fit the new bulb to the headlight unit and secure with the spring clip. Reconnect the wiring connector.

11 Refit the plastic cover to the rear of the headlight unit. Check for satisfactory operation on completion.

Front sidelight

Models up to 2000

12 Depress the two tabs at the top of the headlight unit and remove the cover at the rear of the headlight unit **(see illustration 8.2)**.

13 Pull the sidelight bulbholder from the rear of the headlight, and withdraw the bulb and holder **(see illustration)**.

14 Remove the bulb from the bulbholder **(see illustration)**.

15 Fit the new bulb using a reversal of the removal procedure. Check for satisfactory operation on completion.

Models from 2000

16 Release the two wire clips at each side of the headlight unit and remove the cover at the rear of the headlight unit **(see illustration 8.7)**.

17 Pull the sidelight bulbholder from the rear of the headlight, and withdraw the bulb and holder **(see illustration)**.

18 Remove the bulb from the bulbholder **(see illustration)**.

19 Fit the new bulb using a reversal of the removal procedure. Check for satisfactory operation on completion.

Direction indicator

20 Twist the indicator bulbholder anti-

clockwise, and remove it from the rear of the headlight unit **(see illustrations)**.

21 The bulb is a bayonet-fit in the holder, and can be removed by pressing it and twisting in an anti-clockwise direction **(see illustrations)**.

22 Fit the new bulb using a reversal of the removal procedure. Check for satisfactory operation on completion.

Direction indicator side repeater

23 Carefully remove the direction indicator side repeater from the front wing panel, by sliding it forwards and unclipping the rear of the light unit from the wing **(see illustration)**.

24 Untwist the bulbholder from the rear of the side repeater, and withdraw the bulb **(see illustrations)**.

25 Fit the new bulb using a reversal of the removal procedure. Check for satisfactory operation on completion.

8.21 Push the bulb in and twist to remove

8.23 Unclip the side repeater

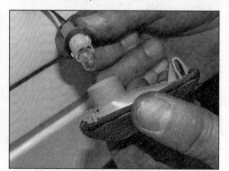

8.24a Twist the bulbholder to remove . . .

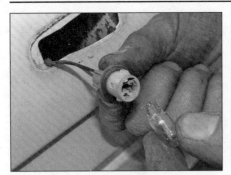

8.24b . . . and pull the capless type bulb to remove

8.29a Unclip the bulbholder . . .

8.29b . . . and disconnect the wiring connector

Additional side marker/ direction indicator

26 Undo the retaining screws and remove the light lens/cover.

27 The bulb is a bayonet-fit in the holder, and can be removed by pressing it and twisting in an anti-clockwise direction.

28 Fit the new bulb using a reversal of the removal procedure. Check for satisfactory operation on completion.

Rear light cluster

Van and Crew cab models

29 Unclip the plastic bulbholder from the rear of the light unit, withdraw the light cluster and release the locking clip to disconnect the wiring connector (see illustrations).

30 The bulbs are a bayonet-fit in the holder, and can be removed by pressing the relevant bulb in and twisting it in an anti-clockwise direction (see illustration).

31 Fit the new bulb(s) using a reversal of the removal procedure. Check for satisfactory operation on completion.

Luton/box van models

32 Unclip and release the outer trim from around the rear light lens, and then remove the rear lens from the light unit base (see illustrations).

33 The bulbs are a bayonet-fit in the holder, and can be removed by pressing the relevant bulb in and twisting it in an anti-clockwise direction (see illustration).

34 Fit the new bulb(s) using a reversal of the removal procedure. Check for satisfactory operation on completion.

Pick-up truck models

35 Undo the retaining screws and remove the rear lens from the light unit base.

36 The bulbs are a bayonet-fit in the holder, and can be removed by pressing the relevant bulb in and twisting it in an anti-clockwise direction.

37 Fit the new bulb(s) using a reversal of the removal procedure. Check for satisfactory operation on completion.

Number plate light

38 Prise free the light unit using a small screwdriver, and then remove the festoon type bulb from its holder by pulling it free (see illustrations).

39 Fit the new bulb using a reversal of the removal procedure. Check for satisfactory operation on completion.

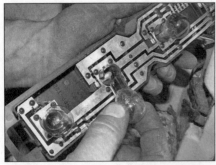

8.30 Push the bulb in and twist to remove

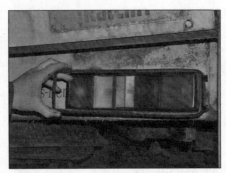

8.32a Unclip the outer trim surround . . .

8.32b . . . and then remove the rear lens

8.33 Push the bulb in and twist to remove

8.38a Unclip the number plate light unit . . .

8.38b . . . and remove the festoon type bulb

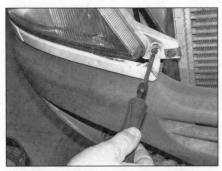

10.2a Undo the retaining screw . . .

10.2b . . . and unclip the lower trim from the headlight

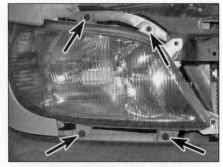

10.3 Headlight retaining screws

10.4a Remove the headlight unit . . .

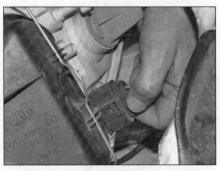

10.4b . . . and disconnect the wiring connector

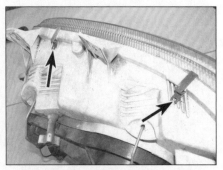

10.5 Headlight glass securing clips (two upper clips shown)

9 Bulbs (interior lights) – renewal

General

1 Refer to Section 10, paragraph 1.

Courtesy lights

2 Insert a small screwdriver blade into the indent in the light unit, and carefully prise it free.
3 The courtesy lights have festoon-type bulbs, and this type is simply prised free from its holder.
4 Fit the new bulb using a reversal of the removal procedure. Check for satisfactory operation on completion.

Instrument panel illumination and warning lights

5 Procedures for the removal and refitting of the instrument panel and warning light bulbs are contained in Section 5. **Note:** *On vehicles manufactured from February 2000 onward, the instrument panel is a sealed assembly and cannot be dismantled.*

Stepwell light

6 Carefully prise the light unit from its location and twist the bulbholder to remove it from the light unit. Pull the bulb from the bulbholder.
7 Fit the new bulb using a reversal of the removal procedure. Check for satisfactory operation on completion.

Heater control illumination

8 Remove the heater/air conditioning control panel as described in Chapter 3. At the time of writing there was no information on the stripdown of the heater control panel to renew any bulbs. See your local Mercedes-Benz dealer for availability of any spares for the illumination of the heater control panel.

10 Exterior light units – removal and refitting

Note: *Disconnect the battery negative terminal (refer to Disconnecting the battery in the Reference Chapter) before removing any light unit. Reconnect the terminal after refitting.*

Headlight/direction indicator (models from 2000)

1 Remove the front grille as described in Chapter 11, Section 22.
2 Undo the retaining screw and remove the cover from below the headlight unit **(see illustrations)**.
3 Undo the four screws securing the headlight unit to the vehicle **(see illustration)**.
4 Withdraw the headlight unit from its location, disconnect the wiring connector, and then remove the unit from the vehicle **(see illustrations)**.
5 If required, release the retaining clips from around the edge of the headlight unit, and remove the headlight glass **(see illustration)**.

6 Refit in the reverse order of removal. Refer to Section 7 for details on headlight beam alignment. Check the headlights and indicators for satisfactory operation on completion.

Headlight (models up to 2000)

7 Remove the front grille as described in Chapter 11, Section 22.
8 Remove the front indicator as described in paragraphs 13 and 14 in this Section.
9 Undo the four screws securing the headlight unit to the vehicle **(see illustrations)**.
10 Withdraw the headlight unit from its location, disconnect the wiring connector and vacuum pipe, and then remove the unit from the vehicle **(see illustrations)**.
11 If required, release the retaining clips from around the edge of the headlight unit, and remove the headlight glass **(see illustration 10.5)**.

10.9a Headlight retaining screws . . .

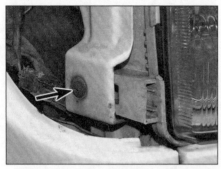

10.9b . . . and one retaining screw on the outside

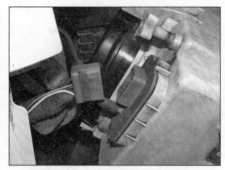

10.10a Disconnect the wiring connector . . .

10.10b . . . and the vacuum pipe

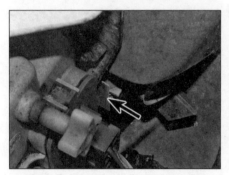

10.13 Release the indicator securing clip . . .

10.14 . . . and remove the indicator

10.18 Rear light unit securing nuts

12 Refit in the reverse order of removal. Refer to Section 7 for details on headlight beam alignment. Check the headlights for satisfactory operation on completion.

Direction indicator (models up to 2000)

13 Working in the front corner of the engine compartment release the retaining clip at the rear of the headlight unit **(see illustration)**.
14 Release the retaining clip by prising it away from the headlight unit, and then withdrawing the indicator light unit out from the front of the vehicle **(see illustration)**.
15 Refit in the reverse order of removal. Check the indicators for satisfactory operation on completion.

Direction indicator side repeater

16 Removal and refitting of the light unit is part of the bulb renewal procedure. Refer to the procedures contained in Section 8.

11.3 Disconnect the vacuum pipe . . .

Rear light cluster

Van and Crew cab models

17 Unclip the plastic bulbholder from the rear of the light unit, withdraw the light cluster and disconnect the wiring connector **(see illustrations 8.29a and 8.29b)**.
18 Undo the four nuts from the studs at the rear of the light cluster assembly **(see illustration)**.
19 Withdraw the light cluster assembly outwards from the rear of the vehicle.
20 Refit in the reverse order of removal. Check the lights for satisfactory operation on completion.

Luton/box van models

21 Unclip and release the outer trim from around the rear light lens, and then remove the rear lens from the light unit base **(see illustrations 8.32a and 8.32b)**.
22 Working under the rear of the vehicle, undo the retaining nuts from the rear of the light unit.
23 Withdraw the light cluster assembly outwards from the rear of the vehicle and disconnect the wiring connector.
24 Refit in the reverse order of removal. Check the lights for satisfactory operation on completion.

Pick-up truck models

25 Undo the retaining screws and remove the rear lens from the light unit base.
26 Working under the rear of the vehicle, undo the retaining nuts from the rear of the light unit.

27 Withdraw the light cluster assembly outwards from the rear of the vehicle and disconnect the wiring connector.
28 Refit in the reverse order of removal. Check the lights for satisfactory operation on completion.

Number plate light

29 Removal and refitting of the light unit is part of the bulb renewal procedure. Refer to the procedures contained in Section 8.

11 Headlight levelling actuator/motor – removal and refitting

Note: *Read the information on headlight beam alignment in Section 7 before removing the levelling actuator/motor.*
1 Remove the headlight unit as described in Section 10.

Models up to 2000

2 Depress the two tabs at the top of the headlight unit and remove the cover at the rear of the headlight unit **(see illustration 8.2)**.
3 Disconnect the vacuum pipe from the actuator **(see illustration)**.
4 Rotate the levelling actuator and withdraw it from the rear of headlight, while disconnecting the pullrod balljoint from the rear of the headlight reflector **(see illustration)**.
5 Refit in the reverse order of removal. Make sure the balljoint is connected securely in the socket on the back of the headlight reflector.

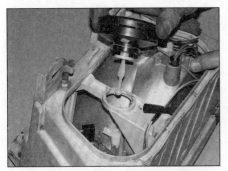

11.4 . . . and remove the actuator

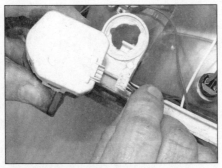

11.7 Disconnect the wiring connector . . .

11.8 . . . and remove the actuator

Check for satisfactory operation of the levelling actuator on completion.

Models from 2000

6 Release the two wire clips at each side of the headlight unit and remove the cover at the rear of the headlight unit **(see illustration 8.7)**.
7 Disconnect the wiring connector from the levelling motor **(see illustration)**.
8 Rotate the levelling motor and withdraw it from the rear of headlight, while disconnecting the pullrod balljoint from the rear of the headlight reflector **(see illustration)**.
9 Refit in the reverse order of removal. Make sure the balljoint is connected securely in the socket on the back of the headlight reflector. Check for satisfactory operation of the levelling motor on completion.

12 Horn – removal and refitting

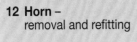

Removal

1 The horn is located behind the right-hand headlight unit inside the engine compartment **(see illustration)**.
2 To make access easier remove the air cleaner housing as described in Chapter 4A, Section 2.
3 Detach the wiring connectors from the horn **(see illustration)**, then unscrew the horn mounting bracket bolt and withdraw the horn.
4 If required, the horn can be separated from the mounting bracket by undoing the retaining nut.

Refitting

5 Refit in the reverse order of removal. Check for satisfactory operation on completion.

13 Wiper arms – removal and refitting

Removal

1 With the wipers 'parked' (ie, in the normal at-rest position), mark the position of the blades on the windscreen, using a wax crayon or strips of masking tape.

12.1 Horn location – behind the O/S headlight unit

2 Disconnect the washer pipe from the connection on the front panel below the windscreen **(see illustration)**.
3 Lift up the plastic cap from the bottom of the wiper arm, and loosen the nut one or two turns **(see illustrations)**.

13.2 Disconnect the washer pipe

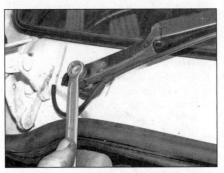

13.3b . . . and undo the securing nut

12.3 Disconnect the wiring connector

4 Lift the wiper arm and release it from the taper on the spindle by easing it from side to side. If necessary, use a puller to release it.
5 Completely remove the nut and withdraw the wiper arm from the spindle **(see illustration)**.

13.3a Unclip the plastic cover . . .

13.5 Release the wiper arm from the spindle

14.4 Remove the spindle securing nut and washer

14.5 Disconnect the wiring connector

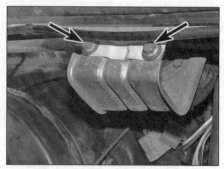

14.6a Undo the mounting bolts . . .

14.6b . . . and remove the wiper motor and linkage

14.8 Undo the crank arm securing nut

14.9 Wiper motor mounting bolts

If necessary, remove the blade from the arm as described in *Weekly checks*.

Refitting

6 Refitting is a reversal of removal. Make sure the arm is fitted in its previously-noted position before tightening the nut to the specified torque.

14 Windscreen wiper motor and linkage – removal and refitting

Removal

1 Disconnect the battery negative terminal (refer to *Disconnecting the battery* in the Reference Chapter).
2 Remove the wiper arms as described in Section 13.
3 Remove the heater ventilation box from

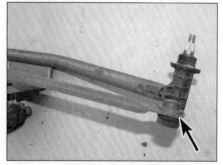

14.10 Wiper linkage balljoint

inside the engine compartment, as described in Chapter 3, Section 8.
4 Slacken and remove the securing nuts and washers from the wiper arm spindles **(see illustration)**.
5 Disconnect the wiper motor wiring connector **(see illustration)**.
6 Undo the two bolts securing the wiper motor bracket to the bulkhead, and remove the complete motor and linkage assembly from the vehicle **(see illustrations)**.
7 Mark the position of the motor crank arm in relation to the motor mounting bracket to aid installation.
8 Undo the crank arm retaining nut and withdraw the crank arm from the motor shaft **(see illustration)**.
9 Undo the three retaining bolts **(see illustration)**, and then remove the motor from the mounting bracket.
10 To remove the linkage arms, prise the linkage balljoints off the pivot housing shaft **(see illustration)** and crank arm ballpins, using an open-ended spanner as a lever. Recover the felt washers, noting their fitted positions.

Refitting

11 Refitting is a reversal of removal, noting the following points:
 a) *Ensure that the motor crank arm is correctly realigned, as noted during removal, as it is refitted to the motor shaft.*
 b) *Refit the heater ventilation box with reference to Chapter 3.*
 c) *Refit the wiper arms with reference to Section 13.*

 d) *On completion, reconnect the battery and check the wipers for satisfactory operation.*

15 Windscreen washer reservoir – removal and refitting

Removal

1 Open the bonnet and undo the two retaining screws from the reservoir **(see illustrations)**.
2 Lift the reservoir up to disengage the locating lug with the grommet in the inner wing panel **(see illustration)**.
3 Disconnect the wiring connector and washer hose from the reservoir pump. Fit blanking plug over the end of the outlet pipe on the pump to prevent washer fluid loss.
4 Remove the windscreen washer reservoir out from the engine bay, taking care not to spill any fluid **(see illustration)**.

15.1a Undo the upper securing nut . . .

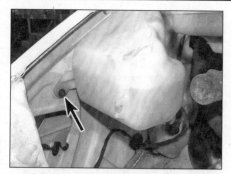

15.1b ... and the lower securing nut

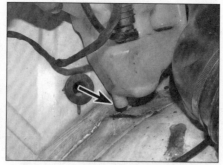

15.2 Lift the reservoir to withdraw the locating peg

15.4 Remove the reservoir from out of the engine compartment

16.2a Using the special tools to withdraw the radio ...

5 If required, the pump can be removed from the reservoir by prising it from its location. Recover the seal after removal of the pump. **Note:** *If the pump is to be removed from the reservoir, make sure the reservoir is empty or a container is available to catch the washer fluid.*

Refitting

6 Refitting is a reversal of removal. Lubricate the pump seal (if removed) with a little washing-up liquid, to ease fitting.
7 On completion, top-up the reservoir with the required water/washer solution mix, and check for leaks and satisfactory operation.

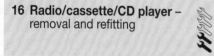

16 Radio/cassette/CD player –
removal and refitting

Note: *Two special tools, obtainable from most vehicle accessory shops, are required for removal.*

17.1a Unclip the speaker grille from the facia (models up to 2000)

16.2b ... or use a couple of Allen keys to release the clips

Alternatively, suitable tools can be fabricated from 3 mm diameter wire, such as welding rod.

Removal

1 Disconnect the battery negative terminal (refer to *Disconnecting the battery* in the Reference Chapter).
2 Insert the special tools into the holes on the front of the unit, and push them until they snap into place. The radio/cassette/CD player can then be slid out of the facia **(see illustrations)**.
3 Disconnect the aerial and wiring connections at the rear of the unit, and remove the unit from the vehicle **(see illustration)**.
4 Remove the special tools.

Refitting

5 Refitting is a reversal of removal bearing in mind the following points:
 a) When the leads are reconnected to the

17.1b Unclip the speaker grille from the facia (models from 2000)

16.3 Disconnect the wiring connectors and aerial lead

  rear of the unit, press it into position to the point where the retaining clips are felt to engage.
 b) On units with a security code, reactivate the unit in accordance with the code and the instructions given in the Mercedes-Benz Audio Operating Manual, usually supplied with the vehicle.

17 Loudspeakers –
removal and refitting

Removal

1 Unclip the speaker grille cover from the end of the facia panel **(see illustrations)**.
2 Withdraw the speaker from the end of the facia panel and disconnect the wiring connectors **(see illustration)**.

17.2 Remove the speaker from the end of the facia

Refitting

3 Refitting is a reversal of removal.

18 Anti-theft alarm system – general information

1 Most models in the range are fitted with an anti-theft alarm system, incorporating an engine immobiliser, as standard equipment. The system is activated when the vehicle is locked, and has both active and passive capabilities. The active section includes the front, side and rear door lock actuators, bonnet lock, audio unit security and the alarm horn. The passive section includes the ignition key transponder, passive anti-theft system (PATS) transceiver and LED, starter relay, and fuel injection pump.

2 When activating the anti-theft alarm system, there is a 20 second delay during which time it is still possible to open the vehicle without triggering the alarm. After the 20 second delay, the system monitors all doors and bonnet, provided they are closed. If one of these items is closed later, the system will monitor it after the 20-second delay.

3 If the alarm is triggered, the alarm horn will sound for a period of 30 seconds, and the hazard lights will flash for a period of 5 minutes. An attempt to start the engine or remove the audio unit automatically triggers the alarm horn.

4 To deactivate the system, one of the front doors must be unlocked with the ignition key or remote control. The rear doors may be unlocked with the ignition key or remote control with the alarm still activated, however the alarm is again reactivated when the rear doors are locked.

5 The PATS includes a starter inhibitor circuit, which makes it impossible to start the engine with the system armed. The immobiliser is deactivated by a transponder chip built into the ignition key.

6 The PATS transceiver unit is fitted around the ignition switch, and it 'reads' the code from a microchip in the ignition key. This means that any keys must be obtained through a Mercedes-Benz dealer – any keys cut locally will not contain the microchip, and will therefore not disarm the immobiliser.

7 If any attempt is made to remove the audio unit while the alarm is active the alarm will sound.

19 Airbag system – general information and precautions

General information

Depending on model, a driver's airbag is fitted as standard equipment. The airbag is fitted in the steering wheel centre pad.

Additionally, a passenger's airbag located in the facia is optionally available.

The system is armed only when the ignition is switched on, however, a reserve power source maintains a power supply to the system in the event of a break in the main electrical supply. The steering wheel and facia airbags are activated by a 'g' sensor (deceleration sensor), and controlled by an electronic control unit located under the facia.

The airbags are inflated by a gas generator, which forces the bag out from its location in the steering wheel or facia.

Precautions

⚠️ **Warning: The following precautions must be observed when working on vehicles equipped with an airbag system, to prevent the possibility of personal injury.**

General precautions

a) Do not disconnect the battery with the engine running.

b) Before carrying out any work in the vicinity of the airbag, removal of any of the airbag components, or any welding work on the vehicle, de-activate the system as described in the following sub-Section.

c) Do not attempt to test any of the airbag system circuits using test meters or any other test equipment.

d) If the airbag warning light comes on, or any fault in the system is suspected, consult a Mercedes-Benz dealer without delay. **Do not** attempt to carry out fault diagnosis, or any dismantling of the components.

Precautions when handling an airbag

a) Transport the airbag by itself, bag upward.

b) Do not put your arms around the airbag.

c) Carry the airbag close to the body, bag outward.

d) Do not drop the airbag or expose it to impacts.

e) Do not attempt to dismantle the airbag unit.

f) Do not connect any form of electrical equipment to any part of the airbag circuit.

Precautions when storing an airbag

a) Store the unit in a cupboard with the airbag upward.

b) Do not expose the airbag to temperatures above 80ºC.

c) Do not expose the airbag to flames.

d) Do not attempt to dispose of the airbag – consult a Mercedes-Benz dealer.

e) Never refit an airbag, which is known to be faulty or damaged.

De-activation of airbag system

The system must be de-activated before carrying out any work on the airbag components or surrounding area:

a) Switch on the ignition and check the

operation of the airbag warning light on the instrument panel. The light should illuminate when the ignition is switched on, then extinguish.

b) Switch off the ignition.

c) Remove the ignition key.

d) Switch off all electrical equipment.

e) Disconnect the battery negative terminal (refer to 'Disconnecting the battery' in the Reference Chapter).

f) Insulate the battery negative terminal and the end of the battery negative lead to prevent any possibility of contact.

g) Wait for at least two minutes before carrying out any further work. Wait at least ten minutes if the airbag warning light did not operate correctly.

Activation of airbag system

To activate the system on completion of any work, proceed as follows:

a) Ensure that there are no occupants in the vehicle, and that there are no loose objects around the vicinity of the steering wheel.

b) Ensure that the ignition is switched off then reconnect the battery negative terminal.

c) Open the driver's door and switch on the ignition, without reaching in front of the steering wheel. Check that the airbag warning light illuminates briefly then extinguishes.

d) Switch off the ignition.

e) If the airbag warning light does not operate as described in paragraph c), consult a Mercedes-Benz dealer before driving the vehicle.

20 Airbag system components – removal and refitting

⚠️ **Warning: Refer to the precautions given in Section 19 before attempting to carry out work on any of the airbag components.**

1 De-activate the airbag system as described in the previous Section, then proceed as described under the relevant heading.

Driver's airbag

2 Turn the steering wheel as necessary, so that one of the airbag unit retaining bolts becomes accessible from the rear of the steering wheel and undo the retaining bolt. Turn the steering wheel again until the second bolt is accessible, and then undo this bolt also.

3 Withdraw the airbag unit from the steering wheel, far enough to access the wiring connectors.

4 Disconnect the airbag wiring connector, and the horn wiring connectors, from the rear of the unit, and remove it from the vehicle.

5 Refitting is a reversal of the removal procedure, with reference to Section 19.

Passenger's airbag

Models from 2000

6 Unclip the upper tray trim panel from the top of the facia panel **(see illustration)**.

7 Undo the two retaining screws and remove the retaining brackets, noting their fitted position for refitting.

8 Undo the three retaining bolts along the rear of the airbag unit and discard, as new ones will be required for refitting.

9 Carefully withdraw the airbag forward until the wiring connector is in view on the side of the unit.

10 Release the locking clip and disconnect the airbag wiring connector from the right-hand side of the airbag unit.

11 Refitting is a reversal of the removal procedure, with reference to Section 19.

Models up to 2000

12 Unclip the speaker grille from the top of the facia panel on the passenger side.

13 Working in the passenger footwell, disconnect the wiring connector (black/grey cable) for the airbag unit.

14 Undo the retaining screws and unclip the upper tray panel from the top of the facia panel on the passenger side.

15 Undo the retaining bolts along the rear of the airbag unit and discard, as new ones will be required for refitting.

16 Carefully withdraw the airbag forward until the wiring connector is in view on the side of the unit.

17 Release the locking clip and disconnect the airbag wiring connector from the left-hand side of the airbag unit.

18 Refitting is a reversal of the removal procedure, with reference to Section 19.

Airbag control unit

19 The airbag control unit is located under the driver's seat, inside the metal base.

20 To make access easier, remove the driver's seat as described in Chapter 11, Section 24.

21 Where fitted remove the plastic trim cover from the top of the seat base.

22 Undo the retaining bolts and remove the relay mounting bracket from the front of the seat base and move it to one side.

23 Remove the plastic cover from the top of the control unit.

24 Undo the two securing bolts from the control unit, noting the earth cable to one of the mounting bolts.

25 Remove the control unit from inside the seat base and disconnect the wiring connectors. Note the fitted position of the control unit, check for a direction arrow, which must face forwards.

26 Refitting is a reversal of the removal procedure, with reference to Section 19.

Airbag rotary connector

27 Remove the steering wheel as described in Chapter 10, Section 14.

28 Slacken the two securing screws in the rotary 'clock spring' connector unit. **Note:** *The screws do not need to be removed completely.*

20.6 Unclip the upper tray panel from the facia

29 Disconnect the wiring connectors to the rotary unit, and then withdraw it from the top of the steering column. Note the fitted position of the rotary connector unit for refitting.

30 Refitting is a reversal of the removal procedure, with reference to Section 19.

Angle sensor (electronic stability program)

31 Remove the airbag rotary connector as described in paragraphs 27 to 29.

32 Disconnect the wiring connector from the steering angle sensor, and then withdraw it from the top of the steering column. Note the fitted position of the angle sensor for refitting; the locking lug of the angle sensor must locate in the groove in the steering column.

33 Refitting is a reversal of the removal procedure, with reference to Section 19.

Mercedes-Benz Sprinter wiring diagrams

Diagram 1

WARNING: *This vehicle is fitted with a supplemental restraint system (SRS) consisting of a combination of driver (and passenger) airbag(s), side impact protection airbags and seatbelt pre-tensioners. The use of electrical test equipment on any SRS wiring systems may cause the seatbelt pre-tensioners to abruptly retract and airbags to explosively deploy, resulting in potentially severe personal injury. Extreme care should be taken to correctly identify any circuits to be tested to avoid choosing any of the SRS wiring in error.*

For further information see airbag system precautions in body electrical systems chapter.

Note: The SRS wiring harness can normally be identified by yellow and/or orange harness or harness connectors.

Key to symbols

Dashed outline denotes part of a larger item, containing in this case an electronic or solid state device. 5/17 denotes connector 5, pin 17.

Solenoid actuator

Heating element

Earth point & location

Wire colour (red with yellow tracer) — Rt/Ge —

Bulb

Switch

Fuse/fusible link — **F26**

Resistor

Variable resistor

Variable resistor

Wire splice, soldered joint, or unspecified connector

Connecting wires

Diode

Light-emitting diode

Item number **12**

Motor/pump

Typical steering column fusebox ④

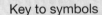

Fuse	Rating	Circuit protected
F1	15A	RH sidelight, RH tail light, level control circuit
F2	15A	RH main beam
F3	15A	LH main beam, main beam warning light
F4	15A	Reversing lights, instrument cluster warning lights
F5	15A	Stop lights, heated washer jets
F6	20A	Wundscreen washer motor
F7	15A	Horn, heated rear window, immobiliser
F8	20A	Interior lights, diagnostic connector
F9	15A	Hazard warning lights
F10	15A	Instrument illumination
F11	15A	LH sidelight, LH tail light
F12	15A	RH dip beam
F13	15A	LH dip beam, rear foglight
F14	15A	Front and rear foglight
F15	15A	Audio system, air bag
F16	-	Spare
F17	-	Spare
F18	-	Spare

Relays

A Direction indicator relay
B Wiper relay

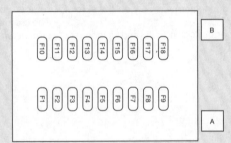

Earth locations

E1	On roof, behind rear view mirror
E2	Behind RH headlight
E3	Behind RH headlight
E4	On LH side engine bulkhead
E5	On driver's seat frame
E6	Behind LH tail light
E7	Below LH headlight
E8	Below RH A pillar
E9	On engine
E10	Near driver's side airbag
E11	Below LH headlight
E12	On steering column

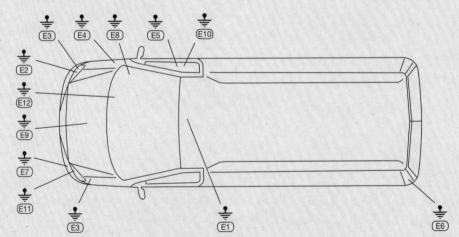

H47194

Wire colours

Sw	Black	Rs	Pink
Br	Brown	Rt	Red
Bl	Blue	Vi	Violet
Gn	Green	Ws	White
Gr	Grey	Ge	Yellow
Nf	Neutral		

Key to items

1 Battery
2 Alternator
3 Starter motor
4 Steering column fusebox
5 Ignition switch
6 Starter lock-out switch
7 Engine management control unit
8 Horn
9 Horn switch
10 Horn relay
11 Steering wheel clock springs
12 Engine management main relay
13 Glow plug control unit
14 Glow plugs
15 Additional battery isolation relay
16 Additional battery
17 Additional battery fuse
18 Body manufacturer's fuses
19 Body manufacturer's connector
20 Body manufacturer's terminal 15 relay
21 Body manufacturer's terminal D+ relay

Diagram 2

H47195

Typical starting & charging

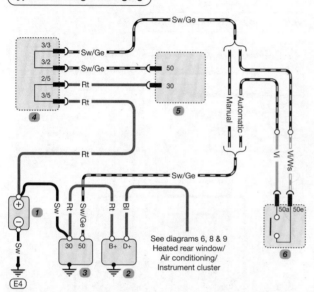

Typical horn

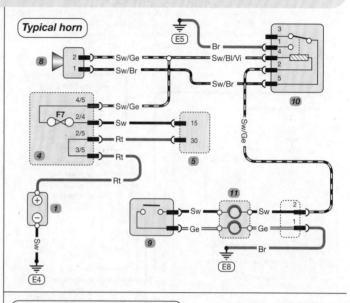

Typical pre-heating system

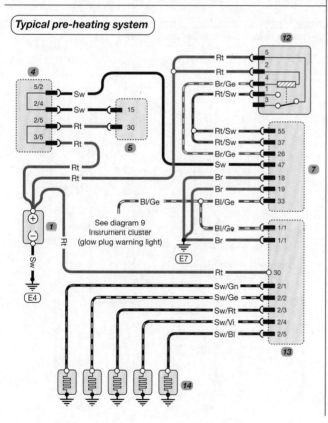

Typical additional battery system

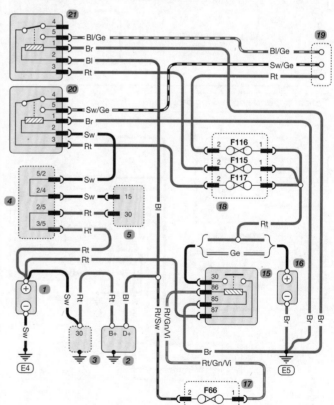

Wire colours

Sw	Black	**Rs**	Pink
Br	Brown	**Rt**	Red
Bl	Blue	**Vi**	Violet
Gn	Green	**Ws**	White
Gr	Grey	**Ge**	Yellow
Nf	Neutral		

Key to items

1 Battery
4 Steering column fusebox
5 Ignition switch
25 Ignition relay
26 Centre sliding roof switch
27 Centre sliding roof motor
28 Rear sliding roof switch
29 Rear sliding roof motor
30 Under seat fusebox
31 Tipper control switch

32 Tipper control cable connector
33 Stop light switch
34 Reversing light switch
35 High level stop light
36 LH rear light unit
   a = stop light
   b = reversing light
   c = tail light
37 RH rear stop light
   (as above)

38 LH headlight unit
   a = sidelight
39 RH headlight unit
   (as above)
40 LH number plate light
41 RH number plate light
42 Light switch
43 Direction indicator switch

Diagram 3

H47196

Typical sunroof

Typical stop and reversing lights

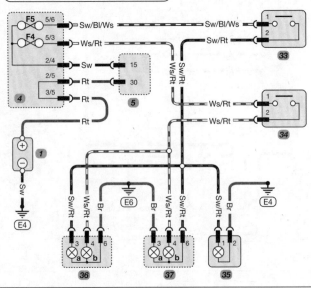

Typical side, tail & number plate lights

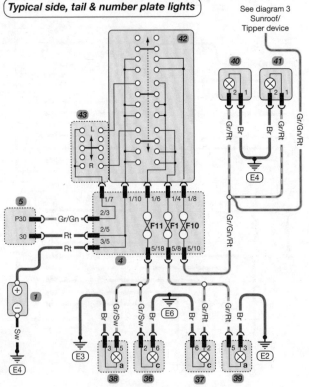

See diagram 3
Sunroof/
Tipper device

Typical tipper device wiring provision

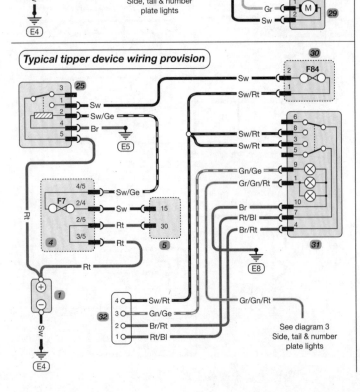

See diagram 3
Side, tail & number
plate lights

Wire colours

Sw	Black	**Rs**	Pink
Br	Brown	**Rt**	Red
Bl	Blue	**Vi**	Violet
Gn	Green	**Ws**	White
Gr	Grey	**Ge**	Yellow
Nf	Neutral		

Key to items

1 Battery
4 Steering column fusebox
  a = control unit
  b = direction indicator relay
5 Ignition switch
30 Under seat fusebox
36 LH rear light unit
  d = direction indicator
  e = foglight
37 RH rear stop light
  (as above)

38 LH headlight unit
  b = dip beam
  c = main beam
  d = foglight
39 RH headlight unit
  (as above)
42 Light switch
43 Direction indicator switch
47 Headlight dip switch
48 Hazard warning switch
49 LH front direction indicator

50 LH indicator side repeater
51 RH front direction indicator
52 RH indicator side repeater
53 Foglight switch
  a = rear foglight indicator
  b = switch illumination
54 Cigar lighter
55 Accessory socket

Diagram 4

H47197

Typical headlights

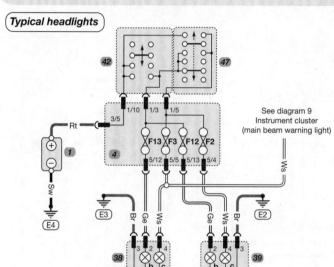

See diagram 9
Instrument cluster
(main beam warning light)

Typical foglights

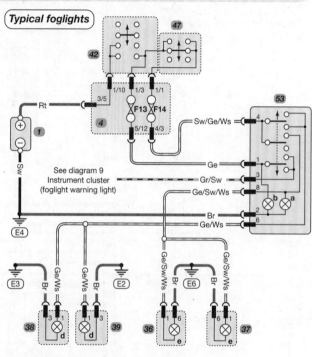

See diagram 9
Instrument cluster
(foglight warning light)

Typical direction indicators & hazard warning lights

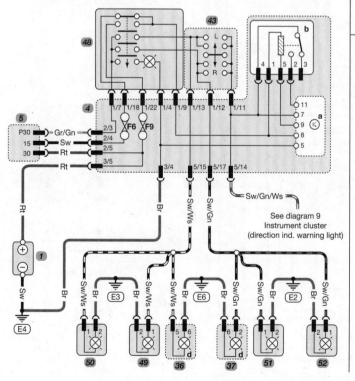

See diagram 9
Instrument cluster
(direction ind. warning light)

Typical cigar lighter & accessory socket

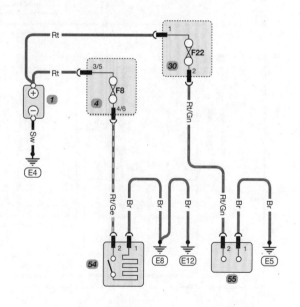

Wire colours

Sw	Black	**Rs**	Pink
Br	Brown	**Rt**	Red
Bl	Blue	**Vi**	Violet
Gn	Green	**Ws**	White
Gr	Grey	**Ge**	Yellow
Nf	Neutral		

Key to items

1 Battery
4 Steering column fusebox
30 Under seat fusebox
42 Light switch
60 Driver's lighting push button switch
61 Rear lighting push button switch
62 Reading light switch
63 Interior lighting relay
64 Driver's reading light
65 Interior light 1
66 Interior light 2

67 Interior light 3
68 LH front entrance light
69 LH rear entrance light
70 RH front entrance light
71 RH rear entrance light
72 Driver's door contact switch
73 Passenger's door contact switch
74 LH rear door contact switch
75 RH rear door contact switch
76 LH sliding door entry light
77 RH sliding door entry light

78 LH sliding door switch
79 RH sliding door switch
80 Load area rear door switch
81 Centre interior light
82 Rear interior light
83 LH side interior light
84 RH side interior light
85 Rear interior light
86 Centre rear interior light
87 Centre front interior light

Diagram 5

H47198

Typical interior lighting

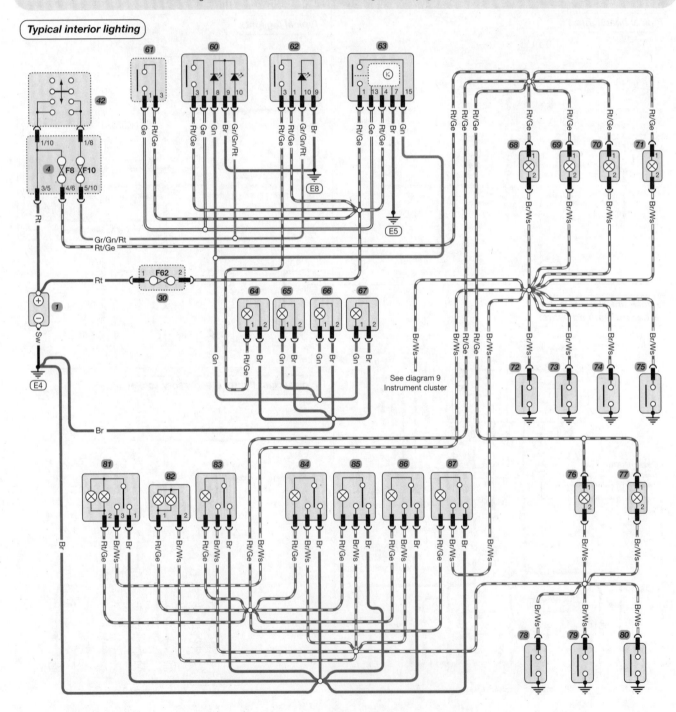

See diagram 9
Instrument cluster

Wire colours

Sw	Black	**Rs**	Pink
Br	Brown	**Rt**	Red
Bl	Blue	**Vi**	Violet
Gn	Green	**Ws**	White
Gr	Grey	**Ge**	Yellow
Nf	Neutral		

Key to items

1 Battery
4 Steering column fusebox
5 Ignition switch
30 Under seat fusebox
42 Light switch
90 D+ circuit relay
91 Heated rear window switch
92 Heated rear window relay
93 LH heated rear window
94 RH heated rear window
95 Heater blower switch
96 Heater blower resistors
97 Heater blower motor
98 Heater blower relay 1
99 Heater blower relay 2
100 Recirculation solenoid
101 Antenna unit
102 Audio unit
103 LH front speaker
104 RH front speaker
105 LH rear speaker
106 RH rear speaker
107 Body manufacturer's connector

Diagram 6

H47199

Typical heated rear window

Typical heater blower – models without air conditioning

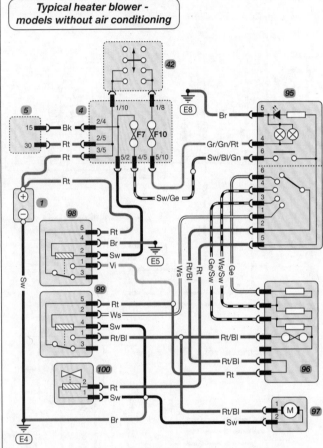

Typical audio system

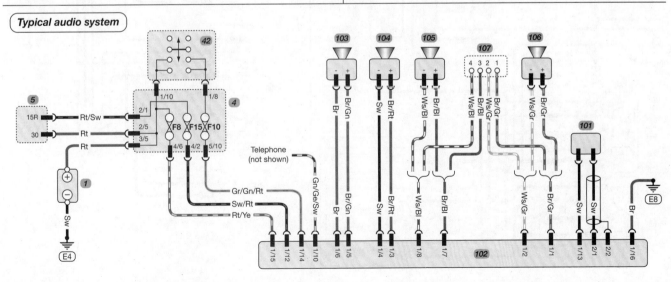

Wire colours

Sw	Black	Rs	Pink
Br	Brown	Rt	Red
Bl	Blue	Vi	Violet
Gn	Green	Ws	White
Gr	Grey	Ge	Yellow
Nf	Neutral		

Key to items

1 Battery
4 Steering column fusebox
  a = control unit
  c = wiper relay
5 Ignition switch
25 Ignition relay
30 Under seat fusebox
42 Light switch
110 Wash/wipe switch
111 Wiper motor
112 Washer pump
113 Driver's door window switch
114 Passenger's door window switch
115 Driver's window motor
116 Passenger's window motor
117 Electric mirror switch
118 LH mirror assembly
119 RH mirror assembly

Diagram 7

H47200

Typical wash/wipe

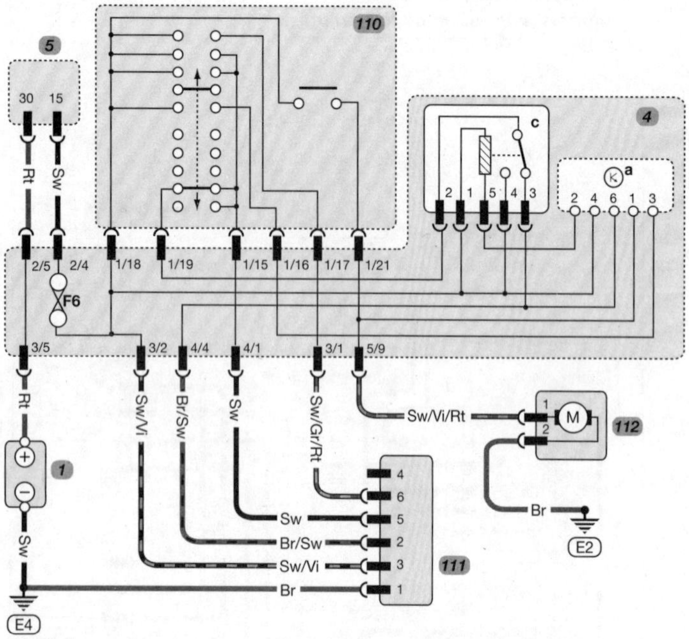

Typical electric windows

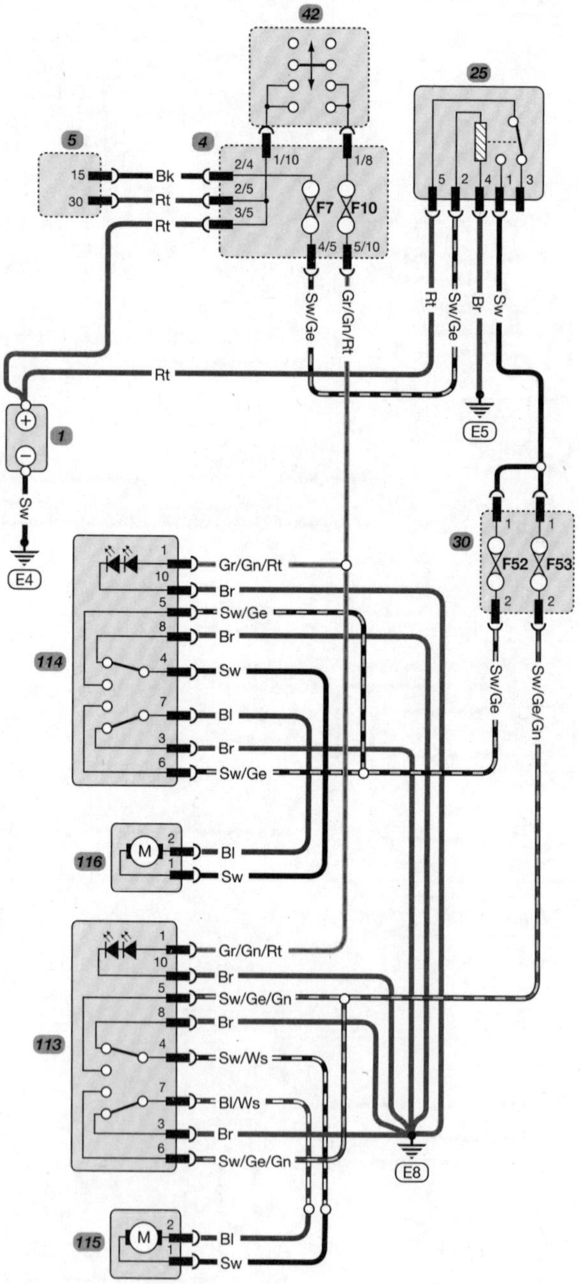

Typical electric mirrors

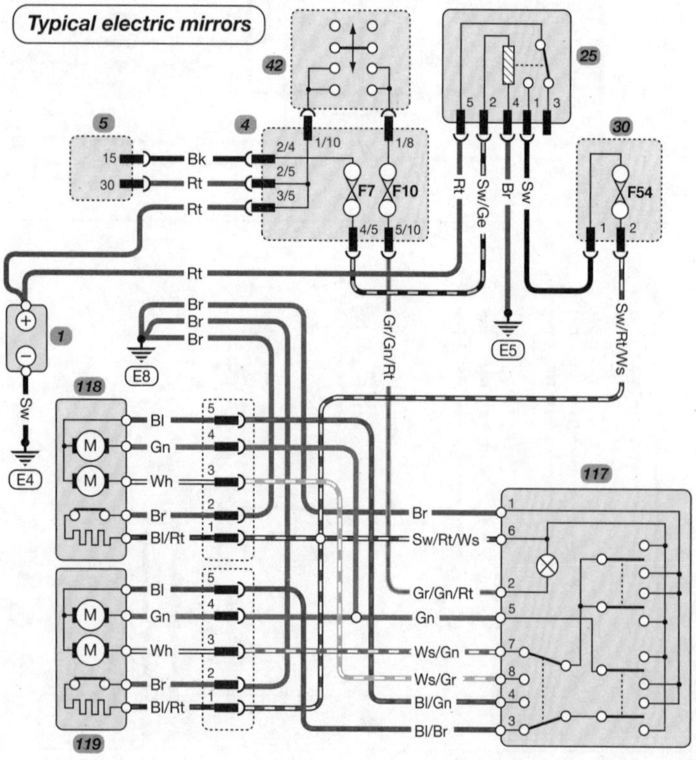

Wire colours

Sw	Black	Rs	Pink
Br	Brown	Rt	Red
Bl	Blue	Vi	Violet
Gn	Green	Ws	White
Gr	Grey	Ge	Yellow
Nf	Neutral		

Key to items

1   Battery
4   Steering column fusebox
5   Ignition switch
25 Ignition relay
30 Under seat fusebox
42 Light switch
90 D+ circuit relay
95 Heater blower switch
97 Heater blower motor
98 Heater blower relay 1
99 Heater blower relay 2
100 Recirculation solenoid
125 Central locking control unit
126 LH door lock motor
127 RH door lock motor
128 LH sliding door lock motor
129 RH sliding door/LH door (crewcab) lock motor
130 Load area rear door lock motor
131 Air conditioning switch
132 Evaporator temperature switch
133 Compressor diode
134 Air conditioning cut-off relay
135 Compressor clutch
136 Air conditioning dual pressure switch

Diagram 8

H47201

Typical central locking

Typical air conditioning

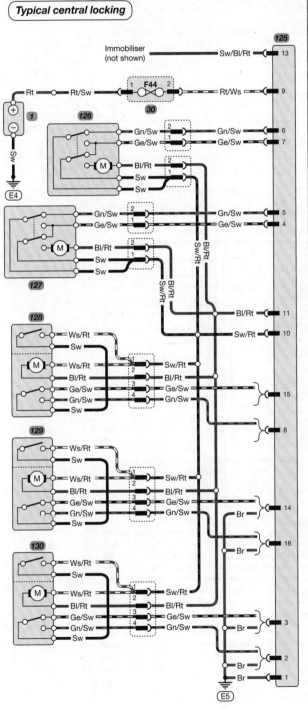

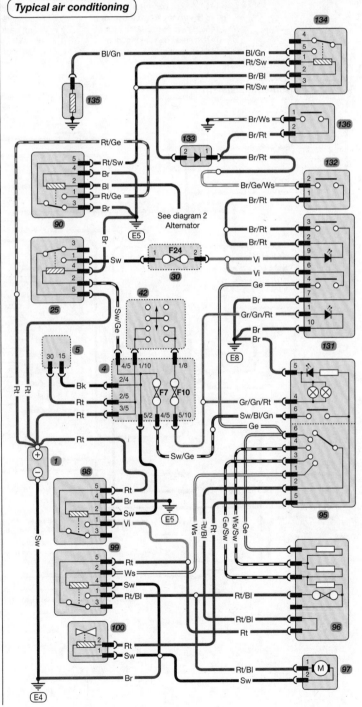

Wire colours

Sw	Black	Rs	Pink
Br	Brown	Rt	Red
Bl	Blue	Vi	Violet
Gn	Green	Ws	White
Gr	Grey	Ge	Yellow
Nf	Neutral		

Key to items

1 Battery
4 Steering column fusebox
5 Ignition switch
25 Ignition relay
30 Under seat fusebox
42 Light switch
90 D+ circuit relay
140 Coolant level switch
141 Oil pressure switch
142 Handbrake switch
143 Low brake fluid switch
144 LH front pad wear sensor
145 RH front pad wear sensor
146 LH rear pad wear sensor
147 RH rear pad wear sensor
148 Differential lock switch

149 Oil level control unit
150 Oil level switch
151 Coolant temperature sensor
152 Fuel level gauge
153 Air temperature sensor
154 Tachometer sensor
155 Instrument cluster
a = main beam warning light
b = glow plug/immobiliser warning light
c = low coolant level warning light
d = direction indicator warning light
e = oil pressure switch
f = handbrake warning light
g = brake pad/fluid level warning light
h = alternator warning light
i = differential lock warning light

Diagram 9

j = oil level warning light
k = airbag warning light
l = trans. power take off warning light
m = ABS warning light
n = TCS warning light
o = engine fault warning light
p = cruise control warning light
q = coolant temperature gauge
r = fuel gauge
s = speedometer
t = information display
u = clock
v = tachometer
w = illumination
x = control unit

H47202

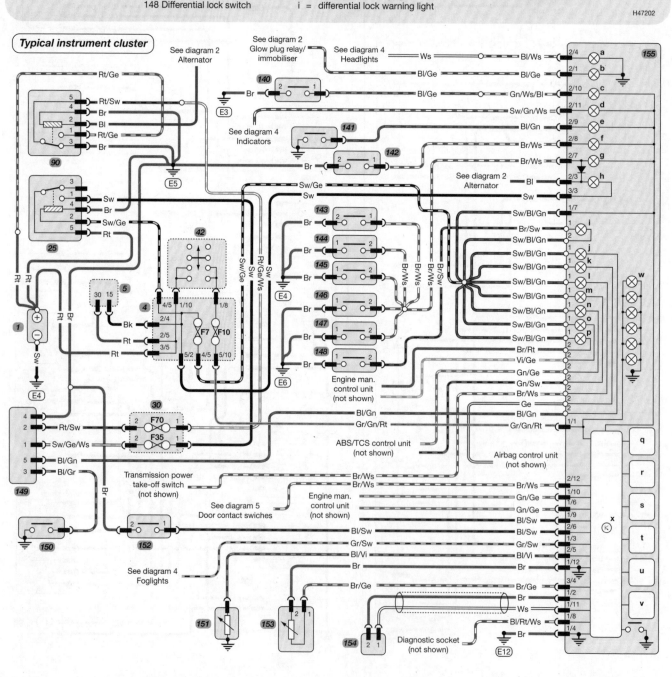

Dimensions and weights

Note: *All figures are approximate and may vary according to model. Refer to manufacturer's data for exact figures.*

Dimensions

Wheelbase:
  Short wheelbase. . . . . .2997 mm
  Medium wheelbase . . . . .3556 mm
  Long wheelbase . . . . .4013 mm
Overall length:
  Short wheelbase . . . . .4978 mm
  Medium wheelbase . . . . .5740 mm
  Long wheelbase . . . . .6680 mm
Turning circle:
  Short wheelbase. . . . . .12.3 metres
  Medium wheelbase . . . . .13.6 metres
  Long wheelbase . . . . .15.6 metres
Max loading length:
  Van:
    Short wheelbase. . . . . .2600 mm
    Medium wheelbase . . . . .3265 mm
    Long wheelbase . . . . .4300 mm
  Dropside:
    Short wheelbase. . . . . .2850 mm
    Medium wheelbase . . . . 3400/3600 mm
    Long wheelbase . . . . .4300 mm
  Crew cab:
    Short wheelbase. . . . . .2120 mm
    Medium wheelbase. . . . . .2700 mm
    Long wheelbase . . . . 3400/3600 mm
Cargo area:
  Van:
    Short wheelbase. . . . . 4.4 m²
    Medium wheelbase. . . . . 5.2/5.5 m²
    Long wheelbase . . . . 7.1/7.4 m²
  Dropside:
    Short wheelbase. . . . . 5.8 m²
    Medium wheelbase. . . . . 6.9/7.6 m²
    Long wheelbase . . . . 8.7/9.2 m²
  Crew cab:
    Short wheelbase. . . . . 4.3 m²
    Medium wheelbase. . . . . 5.5/5.8 m²
    Long wheelbase . . . . 6.9/7.7 m²

Weights

Van kerb weight:
  Short wheelbase:
    3.0t:
      Standard roof . . . . 2120 to 2180 kg
      High roof . . . . 2155 to 2215 kg
    3.5t:
      Standard roof . . . . 2145 to 2205 kg
      High roof . . . . 2180 to 2240 kg
  Medium wheelbase:
    3.0t:
      Standard roof . . . . 2205 to 2270 kg
      High roof . . . . 2235 to 2300 kg
    3.5t:
      Standard roof . . . . 2230 to 2295 kg
      High roof . . . . 2260 to 2325 kg
    5.0t:
      Standard roof . . . . 2470 to 2530 kg
      High roof . . . . 2520 to 2560 kg
  Long wheelbase:
    3.5t:
      High roof . . . . 2415 to 2480 kg
    5.0t:
      High roof . . . . 2710 to 2750 kg
Dropside kerb weight:
  Short wheelbase:
    3.0t . . . . 1915 to 1985 kg
    3.5t . . . . 1930 to 2000 kg
  Medium wheelbase:
    3.0t . . . . 1950 to 2035 kg
    3.5t . . . . 1955 to 2040 kg
    4.6t . . . . 2295 to 2325 kg
    5.0t . . . . 2270 to 2325 kg
  Long wheelbase:
    3.5t . . . . 2035 to 2120 kg
    4.6t . . . . 2385 to 2415 kg
    5.0t . . . . 2360 to 2415 kg
Crew cab kerb weight:
  Short wheelbase:
    3.0t . . . . .2075 kg
    3.5t . . . . 2085 to 2150 kg
  Medium wheelbase:
    3.0t . . . . 2115 to 2135 kg
    3.5t . . . . 2120 to 2205 kg
    4.6t . . . . 2425 to 2455 kg
    5.0t . . . . 2400 to 2455 kg
  Long wheelbase:
    3.5t . . . . 2190 to 2275 kg
    4.6t . . . . 2535 to 2565 kg
    5.0t . . . . 2510 to 2565 kg

Fuel economy

Although depreciation is still the biggest part of the cost of motoring for most car owners, the cost of fuel is more immediately noticeable. These pages give some tips on how to get the best fuel economy.

Working it out

Manufacturer's figures

Car manufacturers are required by law to provide fuel consumption information on all new vehicles sold. These 'official' figures are obtained by simulating various driving conditions on a rolling road or a test track. Real life conditions are different, so the fuel consumption actually achieved may not bear much resemblance to the quoted figures.

How to calculate it

Many cars now have trip computers which will

display fuel consumption, both instantaneous and average. Refer to the owner's handbook for details of how to use these.

To calculate consumption yourself (and maybe to check that the trip computer is accurate), proceed as follows.

1. Fill up with fuel and note the mileage, or zero the trip recorder.
2. Drive as usual until you need to fill up again.
3. Note the amount of fuel required to refill the tank, and the mileage covered since the previous fill-up.
4. Divide the mileage by the amount of fuel used to obtain the consumption figure.

For example:

    Mileage at first fill-up (a) = 27,903
    Mileage at second fill-up (b) = 28,346
    Mileage covered (b - a) = 443
    Fuel required at second fill-up = 48.6 litres

The half-completed changeover to metric units in the UK means that we buy our fuel

in litres, measure distances in miles and talk about fuel consumption in miles per gallon. There are two ways round this: the first is to convert the litres to gallons before doing the calculation (by dividing by 4.546, or see Table 1). So in the example:

    48.6 litres ÷ 4.546 = 10.69 gallons
    443 miles ÷ 10.69 gallons = 41.4 mpg

The second way is to calculate the consumption in miles per litre, then multiply that figure by 4.546 (or see Table 2).

So in the example, fuel consumption is:

    443 miles ÷ 48.6 litres = 9.1 mpl
    9.1 mpl x 4.546 = 41.4 mpg

The rest of Europe expresses fuel consumption in litres of fuel required to travel 100 km (l/100 km). For interest, the conversions are given in Table 3. In practice it doesn't matter what units you use, provided you know what your normal consumption is and can spot if it's getting better or worse.

Table 1: conversion of litres to Imperial gallons

litres	1	2	3	4	5	10	20	30	40	50	60	70
gallons	0.22	0.44	0.66	0.88	1.10	2.24	4.49	6.73	8.98	11.22	13.47	15.71

Table 2: conversion of miles per litre to miles per gallon

miles per litre	5	6	7	8	9	10	11	12	13	14
miles per gallon	23	27	32	36	41	46	50	55	59	64

Table 3: conversion of litres per 100 km to miles per gallon

litres per 100 km	4	4.5	5	5.5	6	6.5	7	8	9	10
miles per gallon	71	63	56	51	47	43	40	35	31	28

Maintenance

A well-maintained car uses less fuel and creates less pollution. In particular:

Filters

Change air and fuel filters at the specified intervals.

Oil

Use a good quality oil of the lowest viscosity specified by the vehicle manufacturer (see *Lubricants and fluids*). Check the level often and be careful not to overfill.

Spark plugs

When applicable, renew at the specified intervals.

Tyres

Check tyre pressures regularly. Under-inflated tyres have an increased rolling resistance. It is generally safe to use the higher pressures specified for full load conditions even when not fully laden, but keep an eye on the centre band of tread for signs of wear due to over-inflation.

When buying new tyres, consider the 'fuel saving' models which most manufacturers include in their ranges.

Driving style

Acceleration

Acceleration uses more fuel than driving at a steady speed. The best technique with modern cars is to accelerate reasonably briskly to the desired speed, changing up through the gears as soon as possible without making the engine labour.

Air conditioning

Air conditioning absorbs quite a bit of energy from the engine – typically 3 kW (4 hp) or so. The effect on fuel consumption is at its worst in slow traffic. Switch it off when not required.

Anticipation

Drive smoothly and try to read the traffic flow so as to avoid unnecessary acceleration and braking.

Automatic transmission

When accelerating in an automatic, avoid depressing the throttle so far as to make the transmission hold onto lower gears at higher speeds. Don't use the 'Sport' setting, if applicable.

When stationary with the engine running, select 'N' or 'P'. When moving, keep your left foot away from the brake.

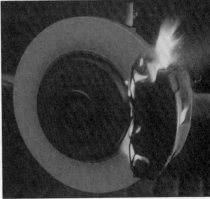

Braking

Braking converts the car's energy of motion into heat – essentially, it is wasted. Obviously some braking is always going to be necessary, but with good anticipation it is surprising how much can be avoided, especially on routes that you know well.

Carshare

Consider sharing lifts to work or to the shops. Even once a week will make a difference.

Electrical loads

Electricity is 'fuel' too; the alternator which charges the battery does so by converting some of the engine's energy of motion into electrical energy. The more electrical accessories are in use, the greater the load on the alternator. Switch off big consumers like the heated rear window when not required.

Freewheeling

Freewheeling (coasting) in neutral with the engine switched off is dangerous. The effort required to operate power-assisted brakes and steering increases when the engine is not running, with a potential lack of control in emergency situations.

In any case, modern fuel injection systems automatically cut off the engine's fuel supply on the overrun (moving and in gear, but with the accelerator pedal released).

Gadgets

Bolt-on devices claiming to save fuel have been around for nearly as long as the motor car itself. Those which worked were rapidly adopted as standard equipment by the vehicle manufacturers. Others worked only in certain situations, or saved fuel only at the expense of unacceptable effects on performance, driveability or the life of engine components.

The most effective fuel saving gadget is the driver's right foot.

Journey planning

Combine (eg) a trip to the supermarket with a visit to the recycling centre and the DIY store, rather than making separate journeys.

When possible choose a travelling time outside rush hours.

Load

The more heavily a car is laden, the greater the energy required to accelerate it to a given speed. Remove heavy items which you don't need to carry.

One load which is often overlooked is the contents of the fuel tank. A tankful of fuel (55 litres / 12 gallons) weighs 45 kg (100 lb) or so. Just half filling it may be worthwhile.

Lost?

At the risk of stating the obvious, if you're going somewhere new, have details of the route to hand. There's not much point in achieving record mpg if you also go miles out of your way.

Parking

If possible, carry out any reversing or turning manoeuvres when you arrive at a parking space so that you can drive straight out when you leave. Manoeuvering when the engine is cold uses a lot more fuel.

Driving around looking for free on-street parking may cost more in fuel than buying a car park ticket.

Premium fuel

Most major oil companies (and some supermarkets) have premium grades of fuel which are several pence a litre dearer than the standard grades. Reports vary, but the consensus seems to be that if these fuels improve economy at all, they do not do so by enough to justify their extra cost.

Roof rack

When loading a roof rack, try to produce a wedge shape with the narrow end at the front. Any cover should be securely fastened – if it flaps it's creating turbulence and absorbing energy.

Remove roof racks and boxes when not in use – they increase air resistance and can create a surprising amount of noise.

Short journeys

The engine is at its least efficient, and wear is highest, during the first few miles after a cold start. Consider walking, cycling or using public transport.

Speed

The engine is at its most efficient when running at a steady speed and load at the rpm where it develops maximum torque. (You can find this figure in the car's handbook.) For most cars this corresponds to between 55 and 65 mph in top gear.

Above the optimum cruising speed, fuel consumption starts to rise quite sharply. A car travelling at 80 mph will typically be using 30% more fuel than at 60 mph.

Supermarket fuel

It may be cheap but is it any good? In the UK all supermarket fuel must meet the relevant British Standard. The major oil companies will say that their branded fuels have better additive packages which may stop carbon and other deposits building up. A reasonable compromise might be to use one tank of branded fuel to three or four from the supermarket.

Switch off when stationary

Switch off the engine if you look like being stationary for more than 30 seconds or so. This is good for the environment as well as for your pocket. Be aware though that frequent restarts are hard on the battery and the starter motor.

Windows

Driving with the windows open increases air turbulence around the vehicle. Closing the windows promotes smooth airflow and

reduced resistance. The faster you go, the more significant this is.

And finally . . .

Driving techniques associated with good fuel economy tend to involve moderate acceleration and low top speeds. Be considerate to the needs of other road users who may need to make brisker progress; even if you do not agree with them this is not an excuse to be obstructive.

Safety must always take precedence over economy, whether it is a question of accelerating hard to complete an overtaking manoeuvre, killing your speed when confronted with a potential hazard or switching the lights on when it starts to get dark.

Conversion factors

Length (distance)

Inches (in)	x 25.4	= Millimetres (mm)	x 0.0394	= Inches (in)
Feet (ft)	x 0.305	= Metres (m)	x 3.281	= Feet (ft)
Miles	x 1.609	= Kilometres (km)	x 0.621	= Miles

Volume (capacity)

Cubic inches (cu in; in³)	x 16.387	= Cubic centimetres (cc; cm³)	x 0.061	= Cubic inches (cu in; in³)
Imperial pints (Imp pt)	x 0.568	= Litres (l)	x 1.76	= Imperial pints (Imp pt)
Imperial quarts (Imp qt)	x 1.137	= Litres (l)	x 0.88	= Imperial quarts (Imp qt)
Imperial quarts (Imp qt)	x 1.201	= US quarts (US qt)	x 0.833	= Imperial quarts (Imp qt)
US quarts (US qt)	x 0.946	= Litres (l)	x 1.057	= US quarts (US qt)
Imperial gallons (Imp gal)	x 4.546	= Litres (l)	x 0.22	= Imperial gallons (Imp gal)
Imperial gallons (Imp gal)	x 1.201	= US gallons (US gal)	x 0.833	= Imperial gallons (Imp gal)
US gallons (US gal)	x 3.785	= Litres (l)	x 0.264	= US gallons (US gal)

Mass (weight)

Ounces (oz)	x 28.35	= Grams (g)	x 0.035	= Ounces (oz)
Pounds (lb)	x 0.454	= Kilograms (kg)	x 2.205	= Pounds (lb)

Force

Ounces-force (ozf; oz)	x 0.278	= Newtons (N)	x 3.6	= Ounces-force (ozf; oz)
Pounds-force (lbf; lb)	x 4.448	= Newtons (N)	x 0.225	= Pounds-force (lbf; lb)
Newtons (N)	x 0.1	= Kilograms-force (kgf; kg)	x 9.81	= Newtons (N)

Pressure

Pounds-force per square inch (psi; lbf/in²; lb/in²)	x 0.070	= Kilograms-force per square centimetre (kgf/cm²; kg/cm²)	x 14.223	= Pounds-force per square inch (psi; lbf/in²; lb/in²)
Pounds-force per square inch (psi; lbf/in²; lb/in²)	x 0.068	= Atmospheres (atm)	x 14.696	= Pounds-force per square inch (psi; lbf/in²; lb/in²)
Pounds-force per square inch (psi; lbf/in²; lb/in²)	x 0.069	= Bars	x 14.5	= Pounds-force per square inch (psi; lbf/in²; lb/in²)
Pounds-force per square inch (psi; lbf/in²; lb/in²)	x 6.895	= Kilopascals (kPa)	x 0.145	= Pounds-force per square inch (psi; lbf/in²; lb/in²)
Kilopascals (kPa)	x 0.01	= Kilograms-force per square centimetre (kgf/cm²; kg/cm²)	x 98.1	= Kilopascals (kPa)
Millibar (mbar)	x 100	= Pascals (Pa)	x 0.01	= Millibar (mbar)
Millibar (mbar)	x 0.0145	= Pounds-force per square inch (psi; lbf/in²; lb/in²)	x 68.947	= Millibar (mbar)
Millibar (mbar)	x 0.75	= Millimetres of mercury (mmHg)	x 1.333	= Millibar (mbar)
Millibar (mbar)	x 0.401	= Inches of water (inH₂O)	x 2.491	= Millibar (mbar)
Millimetres of mercury (mmHg)	x 0.535	= Inches of water (inH₂O)	x 1.868	= Millimetres of mercury (mmHg)
Inches of water (inH₂O)	x 0.036	= Pounds-force per square inch (psi; lbf/in²; lb/in²)	x 27.68	= Inches of water (inH₂O)

Torque (moment of force)

Pounds-force inches (lbf in; lb in)	x 1.152	= Kilograms-force centimetre (kgf cm; kg cm)	x 0.868	= Pounds-force inches (lbf in; lb in)
Pounds-force inches (lbf in; lb in)	x 0.113	= Newton metres (Nm)	x 8.85	= Pounds-force inches (lbf in; lb in)
Pounds-force inches (lbf in; lb in)	x 0.083	= Pounds-force feet (lbf ft; lb ft)	x 12	= Pounds-force inches (lbf in; lb in)
Pounds-force feet (lbf ft; lb ft)	x 0.138	= Kilograms-force metres (kgf m; kg m)	x 7.233	= Pounds-force feet (lbf ft; lb ft)
Pounds-force feet (lbf ft; lb ft)	x 1.356	= Newton metres (Nm)	x 0.738	= Pounds-force feet (lbf ft; lb ft)
Newton metres (Nm)	x 0.102	= Kilograms-force metres (kgf m; kg m)	x 9.804	= Newton metres (Nm)

Power

Horsepower (hp)	x 745.7	= Watts (W)	x 0.0013	= Horsepower (hp)

Velocity (speed)

Miles per hour (miles/hr; mph)	x 1.609	= Kilometres per hour (km/hr; kph)	x 0.621	= Miles per hour (miles/hr; mph)

Fuel consumption*

Miles per gallon, Imperial (mpg)	x 0.354	= Kilometres per litre (km/l)	x 2.825	= Miles per gallon, Imperial (mpg)
Miles per gallon, US (mpg)	x 0.425	= Kilometres per litre (km/l)	x 2.352	= Miles per gallon, US (mpg)

Temperature

Degrees Fahrenheit = (°C x 1.8) + 32   Degrees Celsius (Degrees Centigrade; °C) = (°F - 32) x 0.56

It is common practice to convert from miles per gallon (mpg) to litres/100 kilometres (l/100km), where mpg x l/100 km = 282

Spare parts are available from many sources, including maker's appointed garages, accessory shops, and motor factors. To be sure of obtaining the correct parts, it will sometimes be necessary to quote the vehicle identification number. If possible, it can also be useful to take the old parts along for positive identification. Items such as starter motors and alternators may be available under a service exchange scheme – any parts returned should be clean.

Our advice regarding spare parts is as follows.

Officially appointed garages

This is the best source of parts which are peculiar to your vehicle, and which are not otherwise generally available (eg, badges, interior trim, certain body panels, etc). It is also the only place at which you should buy parts if the vehicle is still under warranty.

Accessory shops

These are very good places to buy materials and components needed for the maintenance of your vehicle (oil, air and fuel filters, light bulbs, drivebelts, greases, brake pads, touch-up paint, etc). Components of this nature sold by a reputable shop are usually of the same standard as those used by the vehicle manufacturer.

Besides components, these shops also sell tools and general accessories, usually have convenient opening hours, charge lower prices, and can often be found close to home. Some accessory shops have parts counters where components needed for almost any repair job can be purchased or ordered.

Motor factors

Good factors will stock all the more important components which wear out comparatively quickly, and can sometimes supply individual components needed for the overhaul of a larger assembly (eg, brake seals and hydraulic parts, bearing shells, pistons, valves). They may also handle work such as cylinder block reboring, crankshaft regrinding, etc.

Engine reconditioners

These specialise in engine overhaul and can also supply components. It is recommended that the establishment is a member of the Federation of Engine Re-Manufacturers, or a similar society.

Tyre and exhaust specialists

These outlets may be independent, or members of a local or national chain. They frequently offer competitive prices when compared with a main dealer or local garage, but it will pay to obtain several quotes before making a decision. When researching prices, also ask what extras may be added – for instance fitting a new valve, balancing the wheel and tyre disposal all both commonly charged on top of the price of a new tyre.

Other sources

Beware of parts or materials obtained from market stalls, car boot sales, on-line auctions or similar outlets. Such items are not invariably sub-standard, but there is little chance of compensation if they do prove unsatisfactory. In the case of safety-critical components such as brake pads, there is the risk not only of financial loss, but also of an accident causing injury or death.

Second-hand components or assemblies obtained from a vehicle breaker can be a good buy in some circumstances, but this sort of purchase is best made by the experienced DIY mechanic.

Vehicle identification

Modifications are a continuing and unpublished process in vehicle manufacture, quite apart from major model changes. Spare parts manuals and lists are compiled upon a numerical basis, the individual vehicle numbers being essential to correct identification of the component required.

When ordering spare parts, always give as much information as possible. Quote the vehicle type, year of manufacture and vehicle identification and/or engine numbers as appropriate.

The *vehicle identification plate* is attached to the driver's seat base **(see illustration)** and includes the Vehicle Identification Number (VIN), vehicle weight information and paint and trim colour codes. On some models it may also be on a sticker attached to the front crossmember, under the bonnet.

More information is given on a sticker, which is behind the lower trim panel on the driver's door **(see illustration)**.

The *transmission number* is given on a plate, which is attached to the left-hand side of the transmission housing **(see illustration)**.

The *engine number* is either stamped on to the rear of the cylinder block, near the transmission mounting face, or on to the front left-hand face of the cylinder block, depending on engine type. The engine number can also be found on the vehicle's registration document (V5C or log book). The engine code is the first part of the engine number.

Engine codes are as follows:

2.2 litre (2148cc) engines

80 bhp – fitted to 208, 308 & 408 models 611.987
107 bhp – fitted to 211, 311 & 411 models 611.981
127 bhp – fitted to 213, 313 & 413 models . . . . 611.981 & 611.983

2.9 litre (2874cc) engines

101 bhp – fitted to 210, 310 & 410 models 602.980
114 bhp – fitted to 212, 312 & 412 models 602.980
127 bhp – fitted to 212, 312 & 412 models 602.980

Vehicle identification plate attached to the driver's seat base

Vehicle information, behind the trim panel on the driver's door

Transmission identification plate

Whenever servicing, repair or overhaul work is carried out on the car or its components, observe the following procedures and instructions. This will assist in carrying out the operation efficiently and to a professional standard of workmanship.

Joint mating faces and gaskets

When separating components at their mating faces, never insert screwdrivers or similar implements into the joint between the faces in order to prise them apart. This can cause severe damage which results in oil leaks, coolant leaks, etc upon reassembly. Separation is usually achieved by tapping along the joint with a soft-faced hammer in order to break the seal. However, note that this method may not be suitable where dowels are used for component location.

Where a gasket is used between the mating faces of two components, a new one must be fitted on reassembly; fit it dry unless otherwise stated in the repair procedure. Make sure that the mating faces are clean and dry, with all traces of old gasket removed. When cleaning a joint face, use a tool which is unlikely to score or damage the face, and remove any burrs or nicks with an oilstone or fine file.

Make sure that tapped holes are cleaned with a pipe cleaner, and keep them free of jointing compound, if this is being used, unless specifically instructed otherwise.

Ensure that all orifices, channels or pipes are clear, and blow through them, preferably using compressed air.

Oil seals

Oil seals can be removed by levering them out with a wide flat-bladed screwdriver or similar implement. Alternatively, a number of self-tapping screws may be screwed into the seal, and these used as a purchase for pliers or some similar device in order to pull the seal free.

Whenever an oil seal is removed from its working location, either individually or as part of an assembly, it should be renewed.

The very fine sealing lip of the seal is easily damaged, and will not seal if the surface it contacts is not completely clean and free from scratches, nicks or grooves. If the original sealing surface of the component cannot be restored, and the manufacturer has not made provision for slight relocation of the seal relative to the sealing surface, the component should be renewed.

Protect the lips of the seal from any surface which may damage them in the course of fitting. Use tape or a conical sleeve where possible. Where indicated, lubricate the seal lips with oil before fitting and, on dual-lipped seals, fill the space between the lips with grease.

Unless otherwise stated, oil seals must be fitted with their sealing lips toward the lubricant to be sealed.

Use a tubular drift or block of wood of the appropriate size to install the seal and, if the seal housing is shouldered, drive the seal down to the shoulder. If the seal housing is unshouldered, the seal should be fitted with its face flush with the housing top face (unless otherwise instructed).

Screw threads and fastenings

Seized nuts, bolts and screws are quite a common occurrence where corrosion has set in, and the use of penetrating oil or releasing fluid will often overcome this problem if the offending item is soaked for a while before attempting to release it. The use of an impact driver may also provide a means of releasing such stubborn fastening devices, when used in conjunction with the appropriate screwdriver bit or socket. If none of these methods works, it may be necessary to resort to the careful application of heat, or the use of a hacksaw or nut splitter device. Before resorting to extreme methods, check that you are not dealing with a left-hand thread!

Studs are usually removed by locking two nuts together on the threaded part, and then using a spanner on the lower nut to unscrew the stud. Studs or bolts which have broken off below the surface of the component in which they are mounted can sometimes be removed using a stud extractor.

Always ensure that a blind tapped hole is completely free from oil, grease, water or other fluid before installing the bolt or stud. Failure to do this could cause the housing to crack due to the hydraulic action of the bolt or stud as it is screwed in.

For some screw fastenings, notably cylinder head bolts or nuts, torque wrench settings are no longer specified for the latter stages of tightening, "angle-tightening" being called up instead. Typically, a fairly low torque wrench setting will be applied to the bolts/nuts in the correct sequence, followed by one or more stages of tightening through specified angles.

When checking or retightening a nut or bolt to a specified torque setting, slacken the nut or bolt by a quarter of a turn, and then retighten to the specified setting. However, this should not be attempted where angular tightening has been used.

Locknuts, locktabs and washers

Any fastening which will rotate against a component or housing during tightening should always have a washer between it and the relevant component or housing.

Spring or split washers should always be renewed when they are used to lock a critical component such as a big-end bearing retaining bolt or nut. Locktabs which are folded over to retain a nut or bolt should always be renewed.

Self-locking nuts can be re-used in non-critical areas, providing resistance can be felt when the locking portion passes over the bolt or stud thread. However, it should be noted that self-locking stiffnuts tend to lose their effectiveness after long periods of use, and should then be renewed as a matter of course.

Split pins must always be replaced with new ones of the correct size for the hole.

When thread-locking compound is found on the threads of a fastener which is to be re-used, it should be cleaned off with a wire brush and solvent, and fresh compound applied on reassembly.

Special tools

Some repair procedures in this manual entail the use of special tools such as a press, two or three-legged pullers, spring compressors, etc. Wherever possible, suitable readily-available alternatives to the manufacturer's special tools are described, and are shown in use. In some instances, where no alternative is possible, it has been necessary to resort to the use of a manufacturer's tool, and this has been done for reasons of safety as well as the efficient completion of the repair operation. Unless you are highly-skilled and have a thorough understanding of the procedures described, never attempt to bypass the use of any special tool when the procedure described specifies its use. Not only is there a very great risk of personal injury, but expensive damage could be caused to the components involved.

Environmental considerations

When disposing of used engine oil, brake fluid, antifreeze, etc, give due consideration to any detrimental environmental effects. Do not, for instance, pour any of the above liquids down drains into the general sewage system, or onto the ground to soak away. Many local council refuse tips provide a facility for waste oil disposal, as do some garages. You can find your nearest disposal point by calling the Environment Agency on 08708 506 506 or by visiting www.oilbankline.org.uk.

Note: It is illegal and anti-social to dump oil down the drain. To find the location of your local oil recycling bank, call 08708 506 506 or visit www.oilbankline.org.uk.

The jack supplied with the vehicle tool kit should only be used for changing roadwheels – see *Wheel changing* at the front of this manual. Ensure the jack head is correctly engaged before attempting to raise the vehicle **(see illustration)**. When carrying out any other kind of work, raise the vehicle using a hydraulic jack, and always supplement the jack with axle stands positioned under the vehicle jacking points.

When jacking up the vehicle with a trolley jack, position the jack head under one of the relevant jacking points. **Do not** jack the vehicle under the sump or any of the steering or suspension components. Supplement the jack using axle stands.

 Warning: Never work under, around, or near a raised vehicle, unless it is adequately supported in at least two places.

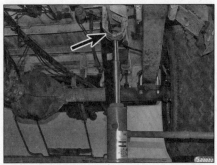

Jacking and supporting points

Disconnecting the battery

Numerous systems fitted to the vehicle require battery power to be available at all times, either to ensure their continued operation (such as the clock) or to maintain control unit memories which would be erased if the battery were to be disconnected. Whenever the battery is to be disconnected therefore, first note the following, to ensure that there are no unforeseen consequences of this action:

a) First, on any vehicle with central locking, it is a wise precaution to remove the key from the ignition, and to keep it with you, so that it does not get locked in if the central locking should engage accidentally when the battery is reconnected.

b) Depending on vehicle and specification, the Mercedes-Benz anti-theft alarm system may be of the type which is automatically activated when the vehicle battery is disconnected and/ or reconnected. To prevent the alarm sounding on models so equipped, switch the ignition on, then off, and disconnect the battery within 15 seconds. If the alarm is activated when the battery is reconnected, deactivate the alarm by locking and unlocking one of the front doors.

c) If a security-coded audio unit is fitted, and the unit and/or the battery is disconnected, the unit will not function again on reconnection until the correct security code is entered. Details of this procedure, which varies according to the unit fitted, are given in the vehicle audio system operating instructions. Ensure you have the correct code before you disconnect the battery. If you do not have the code or details of the correct procedure, but can supply proof of ownership and a legitimate reason for wanting this information, a Mercedes-Benz dealer may be able to help.

d) The engine management ECU is of the 'self-learning' type, meaning that as it operates, it also monitors and stores the settings which give optimum engine performance under all operating conditions. When the battery is disconnected, these settings are lost and the ECU reverts to the base settings programmed into its memory at the factory. On restarting, this may lead to the engine running/idling roughly for a short while, until the ECU has relearned the optimum settings. This process is best accomplished by taking the vehicle on a road test (for approximately 15 minutes), covering all engine speeds and loads, concentrating mainly in the 2500 to 3500 rpm region.

e) On all models, when reconnecting the battery after disconnection, switch on the ignition and wait 10 seconds to allow the electronic vehicle systems to stabilise and re-initialise.

Introduction

A selection of good tools is a fundamental requirement for anyone contemplating the maintenance and repair of a motor vehicle. For the owner who does not possess any, their purchase will prove a considerable expense, offsetting some of the savings made by doing-it-yourself. However, provided that the tools purchased meet the relevant national safety standards and are of good quality, they will last for many years and prove an extremely worthwhile investment.

To help the average owner to decide which tools are needed to carry out the various tasks detailed in this manual, we have compiled three lists of tools under the following headings: *Maintenance and minor repair, Repair and overhaul*, and *Special*. Newcomers to practical mechanics should start off with the *Maintenance and minor repair* tool kit, and confine themselves to the simpler jobs around the vehicle. Then, as confidence and experience grow, more difficult tasks can be undertaken, with extra tools being purchased as, and when, they are needed. In this way, a *Maintenance and minor repair* tool kit can be built up into a *Repair and overhaul* tool kit over a considerable period of time, without any major cash outlays. The experienced do-it-yourselfer will have a tool kit good enough for most repair and overhaul procedures, and will add tools from the *Special* category when it is felt that the expense is justified by the amount of use to which these tools will be put.

Maintenance and minor repair tool kit

The tools given in this list should be considered as a minimum requirement if routine maintenance, servicing and minor repair operations are to be undertaken. We recommend the purchase of combination spanners (ring one end, open-ended the other); although more expensive than open-ended ones, they do give the advantages of both types of spanner.

- [ ] *Combination spanners:*
  Metric - 8 to 19 mm inclusive
- [ ] *Adjustable spanner - 35 mm jaw (approx.)*
- [ ] *Spark plug spanner (with rubber insert) - petrol models*
- [ ] *Spark plug gap adjustment tool - petrol models*
- [ ] *Set of feeler gauges*
- [ ] *Brake bleed nipple spanner*
- [ ] *Screwdrivers:*
  Flat blade - 100 mm long x 6 mm dia
  Cross blade - 100 mm long x 6 mm dia
  Torx - various sizes (not all vehicles)
- [ ] *Combination pliers*
- [ ] *Hacksaw (junior)*
- [ ] *Tyre pump*
- [ ] *Tyre pressure gauge*
- [ ] *Oil can*
- [ ] *Oil filter removal tool (if applicable)*
- [ ] *Fine emery cloth*
- [ ] *Wire brush (small)*
- [ ] *Funnel (medium size)*
- [ ] *Sump drain plug key (not all vehicles)*

Repair and overhaul tool kit

These tools are virtually essential for anyone undertaking any major repairs to a motor vehicle, and are additional to those given in the *Maintenance and minor repair* list. Included in this list is a comprehensive set of sockets. Although these are expensive, they will be found invaluable as they are so versatile - particularly if various drives are included in the set. We recommend the half-inch square-drive type, as this can be used with most proprietary torque wrenches.

The tools in this list will sometimes need to be supplemented by tools from the *Special* list:

- [ ] *Sockets to cover range in previous list (including Torx sockets)*
- [ ] *Reversible ratchet drive (for use with sockets)*
- [ ] *Extension piece, 250 mm (for use with sockets)*
- [ ] *Universal joint (for use with sockets)*
- [ ] *Flexible handle or sliding T "breaker bar" (for use with sockets)*
- [ ] *Torque wrench (for use with sockets)*
- [ ] *Self-locking grips*
- [ ] *Ball pein hammer*
- [ ] *Soft-faced mallet (plastic or rubber)*
- [ ] *Screwdrivers:*
  Flat blade - long & sturdy, short (chubby), and narrow (electrician's) types
  Cross blade – long & sturdy, and short (chubby) types
- [ ] *Pliers:*
  Long-nosed
  Side cutters (electrician's)
  Circlip (internal and external)
- [ ] *Cold chisel - 25 mm*
- [ ] *Scriber*
- [ ] *Scraper*
- [ ] *Centre-punch*
- [ ] *Pin punch*
- [ ] *Hacksaw*
- [ ] *Brake hose clamp*
- [ ] *Brake/clutch bleeding kit*
- [ ] *Selection of twist drills*
- [ ] *Steel rule/straight-edge*
- [ ] *Allen keys (inc. splined/Torx type)*
- [ ] *Selection of files*
- [ ] *Wire brush*
- [ ] *Axle stands*
- [ ] *Jack (strong trolley or hydraulic type)*
- [ ] *Light with extension lead*
- [ ] *Universal electrical multi-meter*

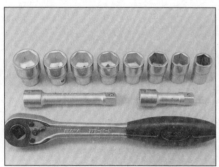

Sockets and reversible ratchet drive

Brake bleeding kit

Torx key, socket and bit

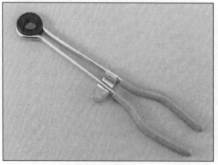

Hose clamp

Angular-tightening gauge

Special tools

The tools in this list are those which are not used regularly, are expensive to buy, or which need to be used in accordance with their manufacturers' instructions. Unless relatively difficult mechanical jobs are undertaken frequently, it will not be economic to buy many of these tools. Where this is the case, you could consider clubbing together with friends (or joining a motorists' club) to make a joint purchase, or borrowing the tools against a deposit from a local garage or tool hire specialist.

The following list contains only those tools and instruments freely available to the public, and not those special tools produced by the vehicle manufacturer specifically for its dealer network. You will find occasional references to these manufacturers' special tools in the text of this manual. Generally, an alternative method of doing the job without the vehicle manufacturers' special tool is given. However, sometimes there is no alternative to using them. Where this is the case and the relevant tool cannot be bought or borrowed, you will have to entrust the work to a dealer.

- ☐ Angular-tightening gauge
- ☐ Valve spring compressor
- ☐ Valve grinding tool
- ☐ Piston ring compressor
- ☐ Piston ring removal/installation tool
- ☐ Cylinder bore hone
- ☐ Balljoint separator
- ☐ Coil spring compressors (where applicable)
- ☐ Two/three-legged hub and bearing puller
- ☐ Impact screwdriver
- ☐ Micrometer and/or vernier calipers
- ☐ Dial gauge
- ☐ Tachometer
- ☐ Fault code reader
- ☐ Cylinder compression gauge
- ☐ Hand-operated vacuum pump and gauge
- ☐ Clutch plate alignment set
- ☐ Brake shoe steady spring cup removal tool
- ☐ Bush and bearing removal/installation set
- ☐ Stud extractors
- ☐ Tap and die set
- ☐ Lifting tackle

Buying tools

Reputable motor accessory shops and superstores often offer excellent quality tools at discount prices, so it pays to shop around.

Remember, you don't have to buy the most expensive items on the shelf, but it is always advisable to steer clear of the very cheap tools. Beware of 'bargains' offered on market stalls, on-line or at car boot sales. There are plenty of good tools around at reasonable prices, but always aim to purchase items which meet the relevant national safety standards. If in doubt, ask the proprietor or manager of the shop for advice before making a purchase.

Care and maintenance of tools

Having purchased a reasonable tool kit, it is necessary to keep the tools in a clean and serviceable condition. After use, always wipe off any dirt, grease and metal particles using a clean, dry cloth, before putting the tools away. Never leave them lying around after they have been used. A simple tool rack on the garage or workshop wall for items such as screwdrivers and pliers is a good idea. Store all normal spanners and sockets in a metal box. Any measuring instruments, gauges, meters, etc, must be carefully stored where they cannot be damaged or become rusty.

Take a little care when tools are used. Hammer heads inevitably become marked, and screwdrivers lose the keen edge on their blades from time to time. A little timely attention with emery cloth or a file will soon restore items like this to a good finish.

Working facilities

Not to be forgotten when discussing tools is the workshop itself. If anything more than routine maintenance is to be carried out, a suitable working area becomes essential.

It is appreciated that many an owner-mechanic is forced by circumstances to remove an engine or similar item without the benefit of a garage or workshop. Having done this, any repairs should always be done under the cover of a roof.

Wherever possible, any dismantling should be done on a clean, flat workbench or table at a suitable working height.

Any workbench needs a vice; one with a jaw opening of 100 mm is suitable for most jobs. As mentioned previously, some clean dry storage space is also required for tools, as well as for any lubricants, cleaning fluids, touch-up paints etc, which become necessary.

Another item which may be required, and which has a much more general usage, is an electric drill with a chuck capacity of at least 8 mm. This, together with a good range of twist drills, is virtually essential for fitting accessories.

Last, but not least, always keep a supply of old newspapers and clean, lint-free rags available, and try to keep any working area as clean as possible.

Micrometers

Dial test indicator ("dial gauge")

Oil filter removal tool (strap wrench type)

Compression tester

Fault code reader

This is a guide to getting your vehicle through the MOT test. Obviously it will not be possible to examine the vehicle to the same standard as the professional MOT tester. However, working through the following checks will enable you to identify any problem areas before submitting the vehicle for the test.

It has only been possible to summarise the test requirements here, based on the regulations in force at the time of printing. Test standards are becoming increasingly stringent, although there are some exemptions for older vehicles.

An assistant will be needed to help carry out some of these checks.

The checks have been sub-divided into four categories, as follows:

1 Checks carried out **FROM THE DRIVER'S SEAT**

2 Checks carried out **WITH THE VEHICLE ON THE GROUND**

3 Checks carried out **WITH THE VEHICLE RAISED AND THE WHEELS FREE TO TURN**

4 Checks carried out on **YOUR VEHICLE'S EXHAUST EMISSION SYSTEM**

---

1 Checks carried out **FROM THE DRIVER'S SEAT**

Handbrake

☐ Test the operation of the handbrake. Excessive travel (too many clicks) indicates incorrect brake or cable adjustment.
☐ Check that the handbrake cannot be released by tapping the lever sideways. Check the security of the lever mountings.

Footbrake

☐ Depress the brake pedal and check that it does not creep down to the floor, indicating a master cylinder fault. Release the pedal, wait a few seconds, then depress it again. If the pedal travels nearly to the floor before firm resistance is felt, brake adjustment or repair is necessary. If the pedal feels spongy, there is air in the hydraulic system which must be removed by bleeding.

☐ Check that the brake pedal is secure and in good condition. Check also for signs of fluid leaks on the pedal, floor or carpets, which would indicate failed seals in the brake master cylinder.
☐ Check the servo unit (when applicable) by operating the brake pedal several times, then keeping the pedal depressed and starting the engine. As the engine starts, the pedal will move down slightly. If not, the vacuum hose or the servo itself may be faulty.

Steering wheel and column

☐ Examine the steering wheel for fractures or looseness of the hub, spokes or rim.
☐ Move the steering wheel from side to side and then up and down. Check that the steering wheel is not loose on the column, indicating wear or a loose retaining nut. Continue moving the steering wheel as before, but also turn it slightly from left to right.
☐ Check that the steering wheel is not loose on the column, and that there is no abnormal movement of the steering wheel, indicating

wear in the column support bearings or couplings.

Windscreen, mirrors and sunvisor

☐ The windscreen must be free of cracks or other significant damage within the driver's field of view. (Small stone chips are acceptable.) Rear view mirrors must be secure, intact, and capable of being adjusted.

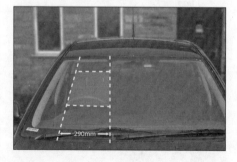

☐ The driver's sunvisor must be capable of being stored in the "up" position.

Seat belts and seats

Note: *The following checks are applicable to all seat belts, front and rear.*

☐ Examine the webbing of all the belts (including rear belts if fitted) for cuts, serious fraying or deterioration. Fasten and unfasten each belt to check the buckles. If applicable, check the retracting mechanism. Check the security of all seat belt mountings accessible from inside the vehicle.

☐ Seat belts with pre-tensioners, once activated, have a "flag" or similar showing on the seat belt stalk. This, in itself, is not a reason for test failure.

☐ The front seats themselves must be securely attached and the backrests must lock in the upright position.

Doors

☐ Both front doors must be able to be opened and closed from outside and inside, and must latch securely when closed.

2 Checks carried out WITH THE VEHICLE ON THE GROUND

Vehicle identification

☐ Number plates must be in good condition, secure and legible, with letters and numbers correctly spaced – spacing at (A) should be 33 mm and at (B) 11 mm.

☐ The VIN plate and/or homologation plate must be legible.

Electrical equipment

☐ Switch on the ignition and check the operation of the horn.

☐ Check the windscreen washers and wipers, examining the wiper blades; renew damaged or perished blades. Also check the operation of the stop-lights.

☐ Check the operation of the sidelights and number plate lights. The lenses and reflectors must be secure, clean and undamaged.

☐ Check the operation and alignment of the headlights. The headlight reflectors must not be tarnished and the lenses must be undamaged.

☐ Switch on the ignition and check the operation of the direction indicators (including the instrument panel tell-tale) and the hazard warning lights. Operation of the sidelights and stop-lights must not affect the indicators - if it does, the cause is usually a bad earth at the rear light cluster.

☐ Check the operation of the rear foglight(s), including the warning light on the instrument panel or in the switch.

☐ The ABS warning light must illuminate in accordance with the manufacturers' design. For most vehicles, the ABS warning light should illuminate when the ignition is switched on, and (if the system is operating properly) extinguish after a few seconds. Refer to the owner's handbook.

Footbrake

☐ Examine the master cylinder, brake pipes and servo unit for leaks, loose mountings, corrosion or other damage.

☐ The fluid reservoir must be secure and the fluid level must be between the upper (**A**) and lower (**B**) markings.

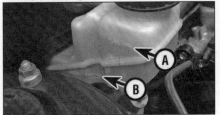

☐ Inspect both front brake flexible hoses for cracks or deterioration of the rubber. Turn the steering from lock to lock, and ensure that the hoses do not contact the wheel, tyre, or any part of the steering or suspension mechanism. With the brake pedal firmly depressed, check the hoses for bulges or leaks under pressure.

Steering and suspension

☐ Have your assistant turn the steering wheel from side to side slightly, up to the point where the steering gear just begins to transmit this movement to the roadwheels. Check for excessive free play between the steering wheel and the steering gear, indicating wear or insecurity of the steering column joints, the column-to-steering gear coupling, or the steering gear itself.

☐ Have your assistant turn the steering wheel more vigorously in each direction, so that the roadwheels just begin to turn. As this is done, examine all the steering joints, linkages, fittings and attachments. Renew any component that shows signs of wear or damage. On vehicles with power steering, check the security and condition of the steering pump, drivebelt and hoses.

☐ Check that the vehicle is standing level, and at approximately the correct ride height.

Shock absorbers

☐ Depress each corner of the vehicle in turn, then release it. The vehicle should rise and then settle in its normal position. If the vehicle continues to rise and fall, the shock absorber is defective. A shock absorber which has seized will also cause the vehicle to fail.

Exhaust system

☐ Start the engine. With your assistant holding a rag over the tailpipe, check the entire system for leaks. Repair or renew leaking sections.

3 Checks carried out
WITH THE VEHICLE RAISED AND THE WHEELS FREE TO TURN

Jack up the front and rear of the vehicle, and securely support it on axle stands. Position the stands clear of the suspension assemblies. Ensure that the wheels are clear of the ground and that the steering can be turned from lock to lock.

Steering mechanism

☐ Have your assistant turn the steering from lock to lock. Check that the steering turns smoothly, and that no part of the steering mechanism, including a wheel or tyre, fouls any brake hose or pipe or any part of the body structure.
☐ Examine the steering rack rubber gaiters for damage or insecurity of the retaining clips. If power steering is fitted, check for signs of damage or leakage of the fluid hoses, pipes or connections. Also check for excessive stiffness or binding of the steering, a missing split pin or locking device, or severe corrosion of the body structure within 30 cm of any steering component attachment point.

Front and rear suspension and wheel bearings

☐ Starting at the front right-hand side, grasp the roadwheel at the 3 o'clock and 9 o'clock positions and rock gently but firmly. Check for free play or insecurity at the wheel bearings, suspension balljoints, or suspension mount-ings, pivots and attachments.
☐ Now grasp the wheel at the 12 o'clock and 6 o'clock positions and repeat the previous inspection. Spin the wheel, and check for roughness or tightness of the front wheel bearing.

☐ If excess free play is suspected at a component pivot point, this can be confirmed by using a large screwdriver or similar tool and levering between the mounting and the component attachment. This will confirm whether the wear is in the pivot bush, its retaining bolt, or in the mounting itself (the bolt holes can often become elongated).

☐ Carry out all the above checks at the other front wheel, and then at both rear wheels.

Springs and shock absorbers

☐ Examine the suspension struts (when applicable) for serious fluid leakage, corrosion, or damage to the casing. Also check the security of the mounting points.
☐ If coil springs are fitted, check that the spring ends locate in their seats, and that the spring is not corroded, cracked or broken.
☐ If leaf springs are fitted, check that all leaves are intact, that the axle is securely attached to each spring, and that there is no deterioration of the spring eye mountings, bushes, and shackles.

☐ The same general checks apply to vehicles fitted with other suspension types, such as torsion bars, hydraulic displacer units, etc. Ensure that all mountings and attachments are secure, that there are no signs of excessive wear, corrosion or damage, and (on hydraulic types) that there are no fluid leaks or damaged pipes.
☐ Inspect the shock absorbers for signs of serious fluid leakage. Check for wear of the mounting bushes or attachments, or damage to the body of the unit.

Driveshafts (fwd vehicles only)

☐ Rotate each front wheel in turn and inspect the constant velocity joint gaiters for splits or damage. Also check that each driveshaft is straight and undamaged.

Braking system

☐ If possible without dismantling, check brake pad wear and disc condition. Ensure that the friction lining material has not worn excessively, (A) and that the discs are not fractured, pitted, scored or badly worn (B).

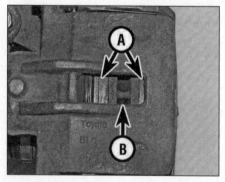

☐ Examine all the rigid brake pipes underneath the vehicle, and the flexible hose(s) at the rear. Look for corrosion, chafing or insecurity of the pipes, and for signs of bulging under pressure, chafing, splits or deterioration of the flexible hoses.
☐ Look for signs of fluid leaks at the brake calipers or on the brake backplates. Repair or renew leaking components.
☐ Slowly spin each wheel, while your assistant depresses and releases the footbrake. Ensure that each brake is operating and does not bind when the pedal is released.

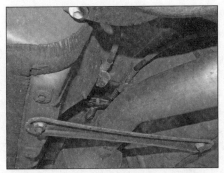

□ Examine the handbrake mechanism, checking for frayed or broken cables, excessive corrosion, or wear or insecurity of the linkage. Check that the mechanism works on each relevant wheel, and releases fully, without binding.

□ It is not possible to test brake efficiency without special equipment, but a road test can be carried out later to check that the vehicle pulls up in a straight line.

Fuel and exhaust systems

□ Inspect the fuel tank (including the filler cap), fuel pipes, hoses and unions. All components must be secure and free from leaks.

□ Examine the exhaust system over its entire length, checking for any damaged, broken or missing mountings, security of the retaining clamps and rust or corrosion.

Wheels and tyres

□ Examine the sidewalls and tread area of each tyre in turn. Check for cuts, tears, lumps, bulges, separation of the tread, and exposure of the ply or cord due to wear or damage. Check that the tyre bead is correctly seated on the wheel rim, that the valve is sound and properly seated, and that the wheel is not distorted or damaged.

□ Check that the tyres are of the correct size for the vehicle, that they are of the same size

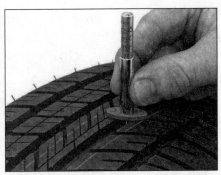

and type on each axle, and that the pressures are correct.

□ Check the tyre tread depth. The legal minimum at the time of writing is 1.6 mm over at least three-quarters of the tread width. Abnormal tread wear may indicate incorrect front wheel alignment.

Body corrosion

□ Check the condition of the entire vehicle structure for signs of corrosion in load-bearing areas. (These include chassis box sections, side sills, cross-members, pillars, and all suspension, steering, braking system and seat belt mountings and anchorages.) Any corrosion which has seriously reduced the thickness of a load-bearing area is likely to cause the vehicle to fail. In this case professional repairs are likely to be needed.

□ Damage or corrosion which causes sharp or otherwise dangerous edges to be exposed will also cause the vehicle to fail.

4 Checks carried out on YOUR VEHICLE'S EXHAUST EMISSION SYSTEM

Petrol models

□ The engine should be warmed up, and running well (ignition system in good order, air filter element clean, etc).

□ Before testing, run the engine at around 2500 rpm for 20 seconds. Let the engine drop to idle, and watch for smoke from the exhaust. If the idle speed is too high, or if dense blue or black smoke emerges for more than 5 seconds, the vehicle will fail. Typically, blue smoke signifies oil burning (engine wear); black smoke means unburnt fuel (dirty air cleaner element, or other fuel system fault).

□ An exhaust gas analyser for measuring carbon monoxide (CO) and hydrocarbons (HC) is now needed. If one cannot be hired or borrowed, have a local garage perform the check.

CO emissions (mixture)

□ The MOT tester has access to the CO limits for all vehicles. The CO level is measured at idle speed, and at 'fast idle' (2500 to 3000 rpm). The following limits are given as a general guide:

At idle speed – Less than 0.5% CO
At 'fast idle' – Less than 0.3% CO
Lambda reading – 0.97 to 1.03

□ If the CO level is too high, this may point to poor maintenance, a fuel injection system problem, faulty lambda (oxygen) sensor or catalytic converter. Try an injector cleaning treatment, and check the vehicle's ECU for fault codes.

HC emissions

□ The MOT tester has access to HC limits for all vehicles. The HC level is measured at 'fast idle' (2500 to 3000 rpm). The following limits are given as a general guide:

At 'fast idle' – Less then 200 ppm

□ Excessive HC emissions are typically caused by oil being burnt (worn engine), or by a blocked crankcase ventilation system ('breather'). If the engine oil is old and thin, an oil change may help. If the engine is running badly, check the vehicle's ECU for fault codes.

Diesel models

□ The only emission test for diesel engines is measuring exhaust smoke density, using a calibrated smoke meter. The test involves accelerating the engine at least 3 times to its maximum unloaded speed.

Note: *On engines with a timing belt, it is VITAL that the belt is in good condition before the test is carried out.*

□ With the engine warmed up, it is first purged by running at around 2500 rpm for 20 seconds. A governor check is then carried out, by slowly accelerating the engine to its maximum speed. After this, the smoke meter is connected, and the engine is accelerated quickly to maximum speed three times. If the smoke density is less than the limits given below, the vehicle will pass:

Non-turbo vehicles: 2.5m-1
Turbocharged vehicles: 3.0m-1

□ If excess smoke is produced, try fitting a new air cleaner element, or using an injector cleaning treatment. If the engine is running badly, where applicable, check the vehicle's ECU for fault codes. Also check the vehicle's EGR system, where applicable. At high mileages, the injectors may require professional attention.

Engine

- ☐ Engine fails to rotate when attempting to start
- ☐ Engine rotates, but will not start
- ☐ Engine difficult to start when cold
- ☐ Engine difficult to start when hot
- ☐ Starter motor noisy or excessively-rough in engagement
- ☐ Engine starts, but stops immediately
- ☐ Engine idles erratically
- ☐ Engine misfires at idle speed
- ☐ Engine misfires throughout the driving speed range
- ☐ Engine hesitates on acceleration
- ☐ Engine stalls
- ☐ Engine lacks power
- ☐ Engine backfires
- ☐ Oil pressure warning light illuminated with engine running
- ☐ Engine runs-on after switching off
- ☐ Engine noises

Cooling system

- ☐ Overheating
- ☐ Overcooling
- ☐ External coolant leakage
- ☐ Internal coolant leakage
- ☐ Corrosion

Fuel and exhaust systems

- ☐ Excessive fuel consumption
- ☐ Fuel leakage and/or fuel odour
- ☐ Excessive noise or fumes from exhaust system

Clutch

- ☐ Pedal travels to floor – no pressure or very little resistance
- ☐ Clutch fails to disengage (unable to select gears)
- ☐ Clutch slips (engine speed increases, with no increase in vehicle speed)
- ☐ Judder as clutch is engaged
- ☐ Noise when depressing or releasing clutch pedal

Transmission

- ☐ Noisy in neutral with engine running
- ☐ Noisy in one particular gear
- ☐ Difficulty engaging gears
- ☐ Jumps out of gear
- ☐ Vibration
- ☐ Lubricant leaks

Propeller shaft

- ☐ Vibration when accelerating or decelerating
- ☐ Noise (grinding or high-pitched squeak) when moving slowly
- ☐ Noise (knocking or clicking) when accelerating or decelerating

Rear axle

- ☐ Roughness or rumble from the rear of the vehicle (perhaps less with the handbrake slightly applied)
- ☐ Noise (high-pitched whine) increasing with road speed
- ☐ Noise (knocking or clicking) when accelerating or decelerating
- ☐ Lubricant leaks

Braking system

- ☐ Vehicle pulls to one side under braking
- ☐ Noise (grinding or high-pitched squeal) when brakes applied
- ☐ Excessive brake pedal travel
- ☐ Brake pedal feels spongy when depressed
- ☐ Excessive brake pedal effort required to stop vehicle
- ☐ Judder felt through brake pedal or steering wheel when braking
- ☐ Brakes binding
- ☐ Rear wheels locking under normal braking

Suspension and steering

- ☐ Vehicle pulls to one side
- ☐ Wheel wobble and vibration
- ☐ Excessive pitching and/or rolling around corners, or during braking
- ☐ Wandering or general instability
- ☐ Excessively-stiff steering
- ☐ Excessive play in steering
- ☐ Lack of power assistance
- ☐ Tyre wear excessive

Electrical system

- ☐ Battery will not hold a charge for more than a few days
- ☐ Ignition/no-charge warning light remains illuminated with engine running
- ☐ Ignition/no-charge warning light fails to come on
- ☐ Lights inoperative
- ☐ Instrument readings inaccurate or erratic
- ☐ Horn inoperative, or unsatisfactory in operation
- ☐ Windscreen wipers inoperative, or unsatisfactory in operation
- ☐ Windscreen washers inoperative, or unsatisfactory in operation
- ☐ Electric windows inoperative, or unsatisfactory in operation
- ☐ Central locking system inoperative, or unsatisfactory in operation

Introduction

The vehicle owner who does his or her own maintenance according to the recommended service schedules should not have to use this section of the manual very often. Modern component reliability is such that, provided those items subject to wear or deterioration are inspected or renewed at the specified intervals, sudden failure is comparatively rare. Faults do not usually just happen as a result of sudden failure, but develop over a period of time. Major mechanical failures in particular are usually preceded by characteristic symptoms over hundreds or even thousands of miles. Those components that do occasionally fail without warning are often small and easily carried in the vehicle.

With any fault-finding, the first step is to decide where to begin investigations. Sometimes this is obvious, but on other occasions, a little detective work will be necessary. The owner who makes half a dozen haphazard adjustments or replacements may be successful in curing a fault (or its symptoms), but will be none the wiser if the fault recurs, and ultimately may have spent more time and money than was necessary. A calm and logical approach will be found to be more satisfactory in the long run. Always take into account any warning signs or abnormalities that may have been noticed in the period preceding the fault – power loss, high or low gauge readings, unusual smells,

etc – and remember that failure of components such as fuses may only be pointers to some underlying fault.

The pages that follow provide an easy-reference guide to the more common problems, which may occur during the operation of the vehicle. These problems and their possible causes are grouped under headings denoting various components or systems, such as Engine, Cooling system, etc. The general Chapter, which deals with the problem, is also shown in brackets; refer to the relevant part of that Chapter for system-specific information. Whatever the fault, certain basic principles apply. These are as follows:

Verify the fault. This is simply a matter of

being sure that you know what the symptoms are before starting work. This is particularly important if you are investigating a fault for someone else, who may not have described it very accurately.

Don't overlook the obvious. For example, if the vehicle won't start, is there fuel in the tank? (Don't take anyone else's word on this particular point, and don't trust the fuel gauge either!) If an electrical fault is indicated, look for loose or broken wires before digging out the test gear.

Cure the disease, not the symptom. Substituting a flat battery with a fully charged one will get you off the hard shoulder, but if the underlying cause is not attended to, the new battery will go the same way.

Don't take anything for granted. Particularly, don't forget that a 'new' component may itself be defective (especially if it's been rattling around in the boot for months), and don't leave components out of a fault diagnosis sequence just because they are new or recently fitted.

When you do finally diagnose a difficult fault, you'll probably realise that all the evidence was there from the start.

Consider what work, if any, has recently been carried out. Many faults arise through careless or hurried work. For instance, if any work has been performed under the bonnet, could some of the wiring have been dislodged or incorrectly routed, or a hose trapped? Have all the fasteners been properly tightened? Were new, genuine parts and new gaskets used? There is often a certain amount of detective work to be done in this case, as an apparently unrelated task can have far-reaching consequences.

Diesel fault diagnosis

The majority of starting problems on small diesel engines are electrical in origin. The mechanic who is familiar with petrol engines but less so with diesel may be inclined to view the diesel's injectors and pump in the same light as the spark plugs and distributor, but this is generally a mistake.

When investigating complaints of difficult starting for someone else, make sure that the correct starting procedure is understood and is being followed. Some drivers are unaware of the significance of the preheating warning light – many modern engines are sufficiently forgiving for this not to matter in mild weather, but with the onset of winter, problems begin.

As a rule of thumb, if the engine is difficult to start but runs well when it has finally got going, the problem is electrical (battery, starter motor or preheating system). If poor performance is combined with difficult starting, the problem is likely to be in the fuel system. The low-pressure (supply) side of the fuel system should be checked before suspecting the injectors and high-pressure pump. The most common fuel supply problem is air getting into the system, and any pipe from the fuel tank forwards must be scrutinised if air leakage is suspected. Normally the pump is the last item to suspect, since unless it has been tampered with, there is no reason for it to be at fault.

Engine

Engine fails to rotate when attempting to start

- [ ] Battery terminal connections loose or corroded *(see Weekly checks)*
- [ ] Battery discharged or faulty (Chapter 5)
- [ ] Broken, loose or disconnected wiring in the starting circuit (Chapter 5)
- [ ] Defective starter solenoid or ignition switch (Chapter 5 or 12)
- [ ] Defective starter motor (Chapter 5)
- [ ] Starter pinion or flywheel ring gear teeth loose or broken (Chapter 2A, 2B or 5)
- [ ] Engine earth strap broken or disconnected (Chapter 5)
- [ ] Engine suffering 'hydraulic lock' (eg, from water drawn into the engine after traversing flooded roads, or from a serious internal coolant leak) – consult a main dealer for advice

Engine rotates, but will not start

- [ ] Fuel tank empty
- [ ] Battery discharged (engine rotates slowly) (Chapter 5)
- [ ] Battery terminal connections loose or corroded *(see Weekly checks)*
- [ ] Immobiliser fault, or 'uncoded' ignition key being used (Chapter 12 or *Roadside repairs*)
- [ ] Preheating system faulty (Chapter 5)
- [ ] Fuel injection/engine management system fault (Chapter 4A)
- [ ] Air in fuel system (Chapter 4A)
- [ ] Major mechanical failure (Chapter 2A, 2B, or 2C)

Engine difficult to start when cold

- [ ] Battery discharged (Chapter 5)
- [ ] Battery terminal connections loose or corroded *(see Weekly checks)*
- [ ] Preheating system faulty (Chapter 5)
- [ ] Fuel injection/engine management system fault (Chapter 4A)
- [ ] Wrong grade of engine oil used (*Weekly checks*, Chapter 1)
- [ ] Low cylinder compression (Chapter 2A or 2B)
- [ ] Air in fuel system (Chapter 4A)

Engine difficult to start when hot

- [ ] Air filter element dirty or clogged (Chapter 1)
- [ ] Fuel injection/engine management system fault (Chapter 4A)

- [ ] Low cylinder compression (Chapter 2A or 2B)
- [ ] Air in fuel system (Chapter 4A)

Starter motor noisy or excessively-rough in engagement

- [ ] Starter pinion or flywheel ring gear teeth loose or broken (Chapter 2A, 2B or 5)
- [ ] Starter motor mounting bolts loose or missing (Chapter 5)
- [ ] Starter motor internal components worn or damaged (Chapter 5)

Engine starts, but stops immediately

- [ ] Fuel injection/engine management system fault (Chapter 4A)

Engine idles erratically

- [ ] Air filter element clogged (Chapter 1)
- [ ] Uneven or low cylinder compression (Chapter 2A or 2B)
- [ ] Camshaft lobes worn (Chapter 2A or 2B)
- [ ] Fuel injection/engine management system fault (Chapter 4A)
- [ ] Air in fuel system (Chapter 4A)

Engine misfires at idle speed

- [ ] Faulty injector(s) (Chapter 4A)
- [ ] Uneven or low cylinder compression (Chapter 2A or 2B)
- [ ] Disconnected, leaking, or perished crankcase ventilation hoses (Chapter 4B)
- [ ] Fuel injection/engine management system fault (Chapter 4A)

Engine misfires throughout the driving speed range

- [ ] Fuel filter choked (Chapter 1)
- [ ] Fuel tank vent blocked, or fuel pipes restricted (Chapter 4A)
- [ ] Faulty injector(s) (Chapter 4A)
- [ ] Uneven or low cylinder compression (Chapter 2A or 2B)
- [ ] Blocked catalytic converter (Chapter 4B)
- [ ] Fuel injection/engine management system fault (Chapter 4A)
- [ ] Engine overheating (Chapter 3)

Engine hesitates on acceleration

- [ ] Faulty injector(s) (Chapter 4A)
- [ ] Fuel injection/engine management system fault (Chapter 4A)

Engine (continued)

Engine stalls

- [ ] Fuel filter choked (Chapter 1)
- [ ] Fuel tank vent blocked, or fuel pipes restricted (Chapter 4A)
- [ ] Faulty injector(s) (Chapter 4A)
- [ ] Fuel injection/engine management system fault (Chapter 4A)

Engine lacks power

- [ ] Air filter element blocked (Chapter 1)
- [ ] Fuel filter choked (Chapter 1)
- [ ] Fuel pipes blocked or restricted (Chapter 4A)
- [ ] Engine overheating (Chapter 3)
- [ ] Accelerator pedal position sensor faulty (Chapter 4A)
- [ ] Faulty injector(s) (Chapter 4A)
- [ ] Uneven or low cylinder compression (Chapter 2A or 2B)
- [ ] Fuel injection/engine management system fault (Chapter 4A)
- [ ] Blocked catalytic converter (Chapter 4B)
- [ ] Brakes binding (Chapter 1 or 9)
- [ ] Clutch slipping (Chapter 6)

Engine backfires

- [ ] Fuel injection/engine management system fault (Chapter 4A)
- [ ] Blocked catalytic converter (Chapter 4B)

Oil pressure warning light illuminated with engine running

- [ ] Low oil level, or incorrect oil grade (see Weekly checks)
- [ ] Faulty oil pressure warning light switch, or wiring damaged (Chapter 2A or 2B)
- [ ] Worn engine bearings and/or oil pump (Chapter 2A, 2B or 2C)
- [ ] High engine operating temperature (Chapter 3)
- [ ] Oil pump pressure relief valve defective (Chapter 2A or 2B)
- [ ] Oil pump pick-up strainer clogged (Chapter 2A or 2B)

Engine runs-on after switching off

- [ ] Excessive carbon build-up in engine (Chapter 2A, 2B or 2C)
- [ ] High engine operating temperature (Chapter 3)
- [ ] Fuel injection/engine management system fault (Chapter 4A)

Engine noises

Pre-ignition (pinking) or knocking during acceleration or under load

- [ ] Excessive carbon build-up in engine (Chapter 2A, 2B or 2C)
- [ ] Fuel injection/engine management system fault (Chapter 4A)
- [ ] Faulty injector(s) (Chapter 4A)

Whistling or wheezing noises

- [ ] Leaking exhaust manifold gasket or pipe-to-manifold joint (Chapter 4A)
- [ ] Leaking vacuum hose (Chapter 4A, 4B or 9)
- [ ] Blowing cylinder head gasket (Chapter 2A or 2B)
- [ ] Partially blocked or leaking crankcase ventilation system (Chapter 4B)

Tapping or rattling noises

- [ ] Worn valve gear or camshaft(s) (Chapter 2A, 2B or 2C)
- [ ] Ancillary component fault (coolant pump, alternator, etc) (Chapter 3, 5, etc)

Knocking or thumping noises

- [ ] Worn big-end bearings (regular heavy knocking, perhaps less under load) (Chapter 2C)
- [ ] Worn main bearings (rumbling and knocking, perhaps worsening under load) (Chapter 2C)
- [ ] Piston slap – most noticeable when cold, caused by piston/bore wear (Chapter 2C)
- [ ] Ancillary component fault (coolant pump, alternator, etc) (Chapter 3, 5, etc)
- [ ] Engine mountings worn or defective (Chapter 2A or 2B)
- [ ] Front suspension or steering components worn (Chapter 10)

Cooling system

Overheating

- [ ] Insufficient coolant in system (see Weekly checks)
- [ ] Thermostat faulty (Chapter 3)
- [ ] Radiator core blocked, or grille restricted (Chapter 3)
- [ ] Cooling fan faulty (Chapter 3)
- [ ] Inaccurate cylinder head temperature sensor (Chapter 3 or 4A)
- [ ] Airlock in cooling system (Chapter 1 or 3)
- [ ] Expansion tank pressure cap faulty (Chapter 1 or 3)
- [ ] Engine management system fault (Chapter 4A)

Overcooling

- [ ] Thermostat faulty (Chapter 3)
- [ ] Inaccurate cylinder head temperature sensor (Chapter 3 or 4A)
- [ ] Cooling fan faulty (Chapter 3)
- [ ] Engine management system fault (Chapter 4A)

External coolant leakage

- [ ] Deteriorated or damaged hoses or hose clips (Chapter 1)
- [ ] Radiator core or heater matrix leaking (Chapter 3)
- [ ] Expansion tank pressure cap faulty (Chapter 1 or 3)
- [ ] Coolant pump internal seal leaking (Chapter 3)
- [ ] Coolant pump gasket leaking (Chapter 3)
- [ ] Boiling due to overheating (Chapter 3)
- [ ] Cylinder block core plug leaking (Chapter 2C)

Internal coolant leakage

- [ ] Leaking cylinder head gasket (Chapter 2A or 2B)
- [ ] Cracked cylinder head or cylinder block (Chapter 2A, 2B or 2C)

Corrosion

- [ ] Infrequent draining and flushing (Chapter 1)
- [ ] Incorrect coolant mixture or inappropriate coolant type (Chapter 1)

Fuel and exhaust systems

Excessive fuel consumption

☐ Air filter element dirty or clogged (Chapter 1)
☐ Fuel injection system fault (Chapter 4A)
☐ Engine management system fault (Chapter 4A)
☐ Crankcase ventilation system blocked (Chapter 4B)
☐ Tyres underinflated (see Weekly checks)
☐ Brakes binding (Chapter 1 or 9)
☐ Fuel leak, causing apparent high consumption (Chapter 1 or 4A)

Fuel leakage and/or fuel odour

☐ Damaged or corroded fuel tank, pipes or connections (Chapter 4A)

Excessive noise or fumes from exhaust system

☐ Leaking exhaust system or manifold joints (Chapter 1 or 4A)
☐ Leaking, corroded or damaged silencers or pipe (Chapter 1 or 4A)
☐ Broken mountings causing body or suspension contact (Chapter 1 or 4A)

Clutch

Pedal travels to floor – no pressure or very little resistance

☐ Air in hydraulic system/faulty master or slave cylinder (Chapter 6)
☐ Faulty hydraulic release system (Chapter 6)
☐ Faulty clutch release/slave cylinder (Chapter 6)
☐ Broken diaphragm spring in clutch pressure plate (Chapter 6)

Clutch fails to disengage (unable to select gears)

☐ Air in hydraulic system/faulty master or release/slave cylinder (Chapter 6)
☐ Faulty hydraulic release system (Chapter 6)
☐ Clutch disc sticking on transmission input shaft splines (Chapter 6)
☐ Clutch disc sticking to flywheel or pressure plate (Chapter 6)
☐ Faulty pressure plate assembly (Chapter 6)
☐ Clutch release mechanism worn or incorrectly assembled (Chapter 6)

Clutch slips (engine speed increases, with no increase in vehicle speed)

☐ Faulty hydraulic release system (Chapter 6)

☐ Clutch disc linings excessively worn (Chapter 6)
☐ Clutch disc linings contaminated with oil or grease (Chapter 6)
☐ Faulty pressure plate or weak diaphragm spring (Chapter 6)

Judder as clutch is engaged

☐ Clutch disc linings contaminated with oil or grease (Chapter 6)
☐ Clutch disc linings excessively worn (Chapter 6)
☐ Faulty or distorted pressure plate or diaphragm spring (Chapter 6).
☐ Worn or loose engine or transmission mountings (Chapter 2A or 2B)
☐ Clutch disc hub or transmission input shaft splines worn (Chapter 6)

Noise when depressing or releasing clutch pedal

☐ Faulty clutch release/slave cylinder (Chapter 6)
☐ Worn or dry clutch pedal bushes (Chapter 6)
☐ Faulty pressure plate assembly (Chapter 6)
☐ Pressure plate diaphragm spring broken (Chapter 6)
☐ Broken clutch disc cushioning springs (Chapter 6)

Transmission

Noisy in neutral with engine running

☐ Lack of oil (Chapter 7)
☐ Input shaft bearings worn (noise apparent with clutch pedal released, but not when depressed) (Chapter 7)*
☐ Clutch release/slave cylinder faulty (noise apparent with clutch pedal depressed, possibly less when released) (Chapter 6)

Noisy in one particular gear

☐ Worn, damaged or chipped gear teeth (Chapter 7)*

Difficulty engaging gears

☐ Clutch fault (Chapter 6)
☐ Worn, damaged, or poorly-adjusted gearchange (Chapter 7)
☐ Lack of oil (Chapter 7)
☐ Worn synchroniser units (Chapter 7)*

Jumps out of gear

☐ Worn, damaged, or poorly-adjusted gearchange (Chapter 7)
☐ Worn synchroniser units (Chapter 7)*
☐ Worn selector forks (Chapter 7)*

Vibration

☐ Lack of oil (Chapter 7)
☐ Worn bearings (Chapter 7)*

Lubricant leaks

☐ Leaking driveshaft or selector shaft oil seal (Chapter 7)
☐ Leaking housing joint (Chapter 7)*
☐ Leaking input shaft oil seal (Chapter 7)*

* Although the corrective action necessary to remedy the symptoms described is beyond the scope of the home mechanic, the above information should be helpful in isolating the cause of the condition, so that the owner can communicate clearly with a professional mechanic.

Propeller shaft

Vibration when accelerating or decelerating
☐ Propeller shaft out of balance or incorrectly fitted (Chapter 8)
☐ Propeller shaft flange bolts loose (Chapter 8)
☐ Excessive wear in universal joints (Chapter 8)
☐ Excessive wear in centre bearings (Chapter 8)

Noise (grinding or high-pitched squeak) when moving slowly
☐ Excessive wear in universal joints (Chapter 8)
☐ Excessive wear in centre bearings (Chapter 8)

Noise (knocking or clicking) when accelerating or decelerating
☐ Propeller shaft flange bolts loose (Chapter 8)
☐ Excessive wear in universal joints (Chapter 8)
☐ Excessive wear in centre bearings (Chapter 8)

Rear axle

Roughness or rumble from the rear of the vehicle (perhaps less with the handbrake slightly applied)
☐ Rear hub bearings worn (Chapter 8)
☐ Differential pinion flange bolts loose (Chapter 8)
☐ Loose rear spring U-bolts (Chapter 8)
☐ Roadwheel nuts loose (Chapter 1 and 10)

Lubricant leaks
☐ Leaking oil seal (Chapter 8)
☐ Leaking differential housing cover joint (Chapter 8)

Braking system

Note: *Before assuming that a brake problem exists, make sure that the tyres are in good condition and correctly inflated, that the front wheel alignment is correct, and that the vehicle is not loaded with weight in an unequal manner. Apart from checking the condition of all pipe and hose connections, any faults occurring on the anti-lock braking system should be referred to a Mercedes-Benz dealer for diagnosis.*

Vehicle pulls to one side under braking
☐ Worn, defective, damaged or contaminated brake pads/shoes on one side (Chapter 1 or 9)
☐ Seized or partially-seized brake caliper/wheel cylinder piston (Chapter 1 or 9)
☐ A mixture of brake pad/shoe lining materials fitted between sides (Chapter 1 or 9)
☐ Brake caliper mounting bolts loose (Chapter 9)
☐ Worn or damaged steering or suspension components (Chapter 1 or 10)

Noise (grinding or high-pitched squeal) when brakes applied
☐ Brake pad/shoe friction lining material worn down to wear sensor or metal backing (Chapter 1 or 9)
☐ Excessive corrosion of brake disc/drum (may be apparent after the vehicle has been standing for some time (Chapter 1 or 9)
☐ Foreign object (stone chipping, etc) trapped between brake disc and shield (Chapter 1 or 9)

Excessive brake pedal travel
☐ Faulty master cylinder (Chapter 9)
☐ Air in hydraulic system (Chapter 1 or 9)
☐ Faulty vacuum servo unit (Chapter 9)
☐ Faulty vacuum pump (Chapter 9)
☐ Disconnected, damaged or insecure brake servo vacuum hose (Chapter 9)

Brake pedal feels spongy when depressed
☐ Air in hydraulic system (Chapter 1 or 9)
☐ Deteriorated flexible rubber brake hoses (Chapter 1 or 9)
☐ Master cylinder mounting nuts loose (Chapter 9)
☐ Faulty master cylinder (Chapter 9)

Excessive brake pedal effort required stopping vehicle
☐ Faulty vacuum servo unit (Chapter 9)
☐ Faulty vacuum pump (Chapter 9)
☐ Disconnected, damaged or insecure brake servo vacuum hose (Chapter 9)
☐ Primary or secondary hydraulic circuit failure (Chapter 9)
☐ Seized brake caliper/wheel cylinder piston (Chapter 9)
☐ Brake pads/shoes incorrectly fitted (Chapter 9)
☐ Incorrect grade of brake pads/shoes fitted (Chapter 9)
☐ Brake pad/shoe linings contaminated (Chapter 1 or 9)

Judder felt through brake pedal or steering wheel when braking
Note: *Under heavy braking on models equipped with ABS, vibration may be felt through the brake pedal. This is a normal feature of ABS operation, and does not constitute a fault.*
☐ Excessive run-out or distortion of discs/drums (Chapter 1 or 9)
☐ Brake pad/shoe linings worn (Chapter 1 or 9)
☐ Brake caliper mounting bolts loose (Chapter 9)
☐ Wear in suspension or steering components or mountings (Chapter 1 or 10)
☐ Front wheels out of balance (see *Weekly checks*)

Brakes binding
☐ Seized brake caliper/wheel cylinder piston (Chapter 9)
☐ Faulty master cylinder (Chapter 9)

Rear wheels locking under normal braking
☐ Rear brake shoe linings contaminated or damaged (Chapter 1 or 9)
☐ Rear brake drum warped (Chapter 1 or 9)

Suspension and steering

Note: *Before diagnosing suspension or steering faults, be sure that the trouble is not due to incorrect tyre pressures, mixtures of tyre types, or binding brakes.*

Vehicle pulls to one side

- ☐ Defective tyre *(see Weekly checks)*
- ☐ Excessive wear in suspension or steering components (Chapter 1 or 10)
- ☐ Incorrect front wheel alignment (Chapter 10)
- ☐ Accident damage to steering or suspension components (Chapter 1 or 10)

Wheel wobble and vibration

- ☐ Front wheels out of balance (vibration felt mainly through the steering wheel) *(see Weekly checks)*
- ☐ Rear wheels out of balance (vibration felt throughout the vehicle) *(see Weekly checks)*
- ☐ Roadwheels damaged or distorted *(see Weekly checks)*
- ☐ Faulty or damaged tyre *(see Weekly checks)*
- ☐ Worn steering or suspension joints, bushes or components (Chapter 1 or 10)
- ☐ Wheel nuts loose (Chapter 1)

Excessive pitching and/or rolling around corners, or during braking

- ☐ Defective shock absorbers (Chapter 1 or 10)
- ☐ Broken or weak spring and/or suspension component (Chapter 1 or 10)
- ☐ Worn or damaged anti-roll bar or mountings (Chapter 1 or 10)

Wandering or general instability

- ☐ Incorrect front wheel alignment (Chapter 10)
- ☐ Worn steering or suspension joints, bushes or components (Chapter 1 or 10)
- ☐ Roadwheels out of balance *(see Weekly checks)*
- ☐ Faulty or damaged tyre *(see Weekly checks)*
- ☐ Wheel nuts loose (Chapter 1)
- ☐ Defective shock absorbers (Chapter 1 or 10)
- ☐ Power steering system fault (Chapter 10)

Excessively-stiff steering

- ☐ Seized steering linkage balljoint or suspension balljoint (Chapter 1 or 10)
- ☐ Incorrect front wheel alignment (Chapter 10)
- ☐ Steering rack damaged (Chapter 10)
- ☐ Power steering system fault (Chapter 10)

Excessive play in steering

- ☐ Worn steering column/intermediate shaft joints (Chapter 10)
- ☐ Worn track rod balljoints (Chapter 1 or 10)
- ☐ Worn steering rack (Chapter 10)
- ☐ Worn steering or suspension joints, bushes or components (Chapter 1 or 10)

Lack of power assistance

- ☐ Power steering system fault (Chapter 10)
- ☐ Faulty steering rack (Chapter 10)

Tyre wear excessive

Tyres worn on inside or outside edges

- ☐ Tyres underinflated (wear on both edges) *(see Weekly checks)*
- ☐ Incorrect camber or castor angles (wear on one edge only) (Chapter 10)
- ☐ Worn steering or suspension joints, bushes or components (Chapter 1 or 10)
- ☐ Excessively-hard cornering or braking
- ☐ Accident damage

Tyre treads exhibit feathered edges

- ☐ Incorrect toe-setting (Chapter 10)

Tyres worn in centre of tread

- ☐ Tyres overinflated *(see Weekly checks)*

Tyres worn on inside and outside edges

- ☐ Tyres underinflated *(see Weekly checks)*

Tyres worn unevenly

- ☐ Tyres/wheels out of balance *(see Weekly checks)*
- ☐ Excessive wheel or tyre run-out
- ☐ Worn shock absorbers (Chapter 1 or 10)
- ☐ Faulty tyre *(see Weekly checks)*

Electrical system

Note: *For problems associated with the starting system, refer to the faults listed under 'Engine' earlier in this Section.*

Battery will not hold a charge for more than a few days

- ☐ Battery defective internally (Chapter 5)
- ☐ Battery terminal connections loose or corroded *(see Weekly checks)*
- ☐ Auxiliary drivebelt worn or faulty automatic adjuster (Chapter 1)
- ☐ Alternator not charging at correct output (Chapter 5)
- ☐ Alternator or voltage regulator faulty (Chapter 5)
- ☐ Short-circuit causing continual battery drain (Chapter 5 or 12)

Ignition/no-charge warning light remains illuminated with engine running

- ☐ Auxiliary drivebelt broken, worn, or faulty automatic adjuster (Chapter 1)

- ☐ Internal fault in alternator or voltage regulator (Chapter 5)
- ☐ Broken, disconnected, or loose wiring in charging circuit (Chapter 5 or 12)

Ignition/no-charge warning light fails to come on

- ☐ Warning light bulb blown (Chapter 12)
- ☐ Broken, disconnected, or loose wiring in warning light circuit (Chapter 5 or 12)
- ☐ Alternator faulty (Chapter 5)

Lights inoperative

- ☐ Bulb blown (Chapter 12)
- ☐ Corrosion of bulb or bulbholder contacts (Chapter 12)
- ☐ Blown fuse (Chapter 12)
- ☐ Faulty relay (Chapter 12)
- ☐ Broken, loose, or disconnected wiring (Chapter 12)
- ☐ Faulty switch (Chapter 12)

Electrical system (continued)

Instrument readings inaccurate or erratic

Fuel or temperature gauges give no reading

- [ ] Faulty gauge sender unit (Chapter 3 or 4A)
- [ ] Wiring open-circuit (Chapter 12)
- [ ] Faulty gauge (Chapter 12)

Fuel or temperature gauges give continuous maximum reading

- [ ] Faulty gauge sender unit (Chapter 3 or 4A)
- [ ] Wiring short-circuit (Chapter 12)
- [ ] Faulty gauge (Chapter 12)

Horn inoperative, or unsatisfactory in operation

Horn operates all the time

- [ ] Horn push either earthed or stuck down (Chapter 12)
- [ ] Horn cable-to-horn push earthed (Chapter 12)

Horn fails to operate

- [ ] Blown fuse (Chapter 12)
- [ ] Cable or connections loose, broken or disconnected (Chapter 12)
- [ ] Faulty horn (Chapter 12)

Horn emits intermittent or unsatisfactory sound

- [ ] Cable connections loose (Chapter 12)
- [ ] Horn mountings loose (Chapter 12)
- [ ] Faulty horn (Chapter 12)

Windscreen wipers inoperative, or unsatisfactory in operation

Wipers fail to operate, or operate very slowly

- [ ] Wiper blades stuck to screen, or linkage seized or binding (Chapter 12)
- [ ] Blown fuse (Chapter 12)
- [ ] Battery discharged (Chapter 5)
- [ ] Cable or connections loose, broken or disconnected (Chapter 12)
- [ ] Faulty relay (Chapter 12)
- [ ] Faulty wiper motor (Chapter 12)

Wiper blades sweep over too large or too small an area of the glass

- [ ] Wiper blades incorrectly fitted, or wrong size used (see Weekly checks)
- [ ] Wiper arms incorrectly positioned on spindles (Chapter 12)
- [ ] Excessive wear of wiper linkage (Chapter 12)
- [ ] Wiper motor or linkage mountings loose or insecure (Chapter 12)

Wiper blades fail to clean the glass effectively

- [ ] Wiper blade rubbers dirty, worn or perished (see Weekly checks)
- [ ] Wiper blades incorrectly fitted, or wrong size used (see Weekly checks)
- [ ] Wiper arm tension springs broken, or arm pivots seized (Chapter 12)
- [ ] Insufficient windscreen washer additive to adequately remove road film (see Weekly checks)

Windscreen washers inoperative, or unsatisfactory in operation

One or more washer jets inoperative

- [ ] Blocked washer jet
- [ ] Disconnected, kinked or restricted fluid hose (Chapter 12)
- [ ] Insufficient fluid in washer reservoir (see Weekly checks)

Washer pump fails to operate

- [ ] Broken or disconnected wiring or connections (Chapter 12)
- [ ] Blown fuse (Chapter 12)
- [ ] Faulty washer switch (Chapter 12)
- [ ] Faulty washer pump (Chapter 12)

Washer pump runs for some time before fluid is emitted from jets

- [ ] Faulty one-way valve in fluid supply hose (Chapter 12)

Electric windows inoperative, or unsatisfactory in operation

Window glass will only move in one direction

- [ ] Faulty switch (Chapter 12)

Window glass slow to move

- [ ] Battery discharged (Chapter 5)
- [ ] Regulator seized or damaged, or in need of lubrication (Chapter 11)
- [ ] Door internal components or trim fouling regulator (Chapter 11)
- [ ] Faulty motor (Chapter 11)

Window glass fails to move

- [ ] Blown fuse (Chapter 12)
- [ ] Faulty relay (Chapter 12)
- [ ] Broken or disconnected wiring or connections (Chapter 12)
- [ ] Faulty motor (Chapter 11)

Central locking system inoperative, or unsatisfactory in operation

Complete system failure

- [ ] Remote handset battery discharged, where applicable
- [ ] Blown fuse (Chapter 12)
- [ ] Faulty relay (Chapter 12)
- [ ] Broken or disconnected wiring or connections (Chapter 12)
- [ ] Faulty motor (Chapter 11)

Latch locks but will not unlock, or unlocks but will not lock

- [ ] Remote handset battery discharged, where applicable
- [ ] Faulty master switch (Chapter 12)
- [ ] Broken or disconnected latch operating rods or levers (Chapter 11)
- [ ] Faulty relay (Chapter 12)
- [ ] Faulty motor (Chapter 11)

One solenoid/motor fails to operate

- [ ] Broken or disconnected wiring or connections (Chapter 12)
- [ ] Faulty operating assembly (Chapter 11)
- [ ] Broken, binding or disconnected latch operating rods or levers (Chapter 11)
- [ ] Fault in door latch (Chapter 11)

Note: *References throughout this index are in the form* "Chapter number" • "Page number". *So, for example, 2C•15 refers to page 15 of Chapter 2C.*

*Note: References throughout this index are in the form "**Chapter number**" • "**Page number**". So, for example, 2C•15 refers to page 15 of Chapter 2C.*

Preserving Our Motoring Heritage

< *The Model J Duesenberg Derham Tourster. Only eight of these magnificent cars were ever built – this is the only example to be found outside the United States of America*

Almost every car you've ever loved, loathed or desired is gathered under one roof at the Haynes Motor Museum. Over 300 immaculately presented cars and motorbikes represent every aspect of our motoring heritage, from elegant reminders of bygone days, such as the superb Model J Duesenberg to curiosities like the bug-eyed BMW Isetta. There are also many old friends and flames. Perhaps you remember the 1959 Ford Popular that you did your courting in? The magnificent 'Red Collection' is a spectacle of classic sports cars including AC, Alfa Romeo, Austin Healey, Ferrari, Lamborghini, Maserati, MG, Riley, Porsche and Triumph.

A Perfect Day Out

Each and every vehicle at the Haynes Motor Museum has played its part in the history and culture of Motoring. Today, they make a wonderful spectacle and a great day out for all the family. Bring the kids, bring Mum and Dad, but above all bring your camera to capture those golden memories for ever. You will also find an impressive array of motoring memorabilia, a comfortable 70 seat video cinema and one of the most extensive transport book shops in Britain. The Pit Stop Cafe serves everything from a cup of tea to wholesome, home-made meals or, if you prefer, you can enjoy the large picnic area nestled in the beautiful rural surroundings of Somerset.

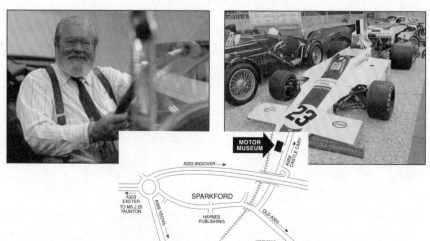

> *John Haynes O.B.E., Founder and Chairman of the museum at the wheel of a Haynes Light 12.*

< *Graham Hill's Lola Cosworth Formula 1 car next to a 1934 Riley Sports.*

The Museum is situated on the A359 Yeovil to Frome road at Sparkford, just off the A303 in Somerset. It is about 40 miles south of Bristol, and 25 minutes drive from the M5 intersection at Taunton.
Open 9.30am - 5.30pm (10.00am - 4.00pm Winter) 7 days a week, *except Christmas Day, Boxing Day and New Years Day*
Special rates available for schools, coach parties and outings Charitable Trust No. 292048